Northwestern University Studies in History
NUMBER I

Louis Blanc

HIS LIFE AND HIS CONTRIBUTION TO THE RISE
OF FRENCH JACOBIN-SOCIALISM

Leo A. Loubère

University of Buffalo

Northwestern University Press

1961

The publication of this book has been aided by contributions from friends of James Alton James and by the Warshauer Trust Fund.

TO EVELYN

The Clio of my household

Acknowledgments

I am greatly indebted to the Department of History of Northwestern University for the guidance and encouragement bestowed upon me in my research and writing. Indeed, it is doubtful if this book would have been completed had it not been for the suggestions of Professors Richard Brace, George Romani, and Richard Leopold. But naturally, if there are imperfections, they are mine.

To my wife I express immense gratitude for her advice and, above all, for her patient toleration of a husband more often before his desk than at her side.

I am also grateful to the editors of the *Journal of Modern History,* the *Journal of the History of Ideas,* the *Revue d'histoire moderne et contemporaine,* and the *International Review of Social History,* for their kind permission to use material from articles I published in their periodicals. A good deal of the research for this book was carried on in France during 1951–52, thanks to the French Government which granted me a fellowship at that time.

Table of Contents

Introduction

This book is a presentation of the life and the thoughts of Louis Blanc. Both are important, and as far as possible I have striven to avoid the weaknesses of his earlier biographers who tended to emphasize his ideas while ignoring his daily activities. An exception to this generalization was Edouard Renard. His work marked a considerable improvement over that of his predecessors; however, his study is limited by its purely descriptive rather than analytical approach.

Attempting to combine description and interpretation, I have felt it necessary to keep in mind two major considerations. Blanc was the first socialist to enter a French government—or any government—in the nineteenth century. This precipitate rise to power was the major action of his public career. A study of his life, therefore, must determine to what extent he prepared for power and how his exercise of it influenced his activity after 1848. As for his thought, he was the true exponent of Jacobin-socialism. A biography, therefore, must explain his combination of Jacobin politics and socialist economics, and assess the extent to which it influenced French history.

My description of Blanc's life will deal chiefly with his public activities. Very little is known about his private affairs. Many of his papers were destroyed during the Commune of 1871, and a great deal of his preserved correspondence has been sold and scattered. But even if we possessed more of his letters it is doubtful that they would throw much new light on his private existence. The documents that remain suggest that he rarely included personal information in them and his letters were short and limited in interest.

Perhaps it will seem to some readers that I devote an excessive amount of space to Blanc's ideas. The modern romantic biography dwells on a man's career, or his love affairs, or his intrigues and diversions. This approach would violate a certain *mystique* of my subject. Blanc refused to see a distinction between an idea and a deed, contending that an idea was an act in itself. As for the importance of the man he wrote, "Eh! what did it matter that the man was overthrown, that he was trodden underfoot, if his work survived, if the furrow was ploughed?" Now his major contribution was intellectual: he was a far more skillful thinker than a politician, and a dismal failure as an organizer. Consequently, his biography naturally turns about his philosophy. His inner workings, as well as his psychic conflicts, are often revealed in his thought.

However, to complement this emphasis upon ideas, I try steadily to indicate the influence of Blanc's public experiences upon his thought. His philosophy underwent change, and these changes were always the outcome of the events in which he participated or which affected him strongly. His action and his thought, then, were as much intertwined as his Jacobin politics and his socialist economics. The one makes little sense without the other.

Buffalo, 1959

Louis Blanc

CHAPTER ONE

The Making of a Journalist

I

🥀 LOUIS BLANC was born into a turbulent world and into a family suffering from this turbulence. His grandfather, a prosperous merchant from the Midi, had been guillotined in 1793 for political opposition. His father had managed to escape the same fate by fleeing from prison, but had not succeeded in improving his financial position until he took a post in the Bonapartist government of Spain. There, in the city of Madrid, on October 29, 1811, Louis Blanc was born. When the French were forced to retreat and the fortunes of the family declined once more, the father began to reveal signs of a persecution complex; he finally abandoned his wife after the birth of his second son, Charles. Louis was then sent to live with his maternal grandmother in Corsica where he was reared in the traditions of the Old Regime. He was therefore well prepared for the Bourbon restoration in 1815, after which the condition of the Blancs improved. Not only did the father return, but he obtained a royal pension for himself and two scholarships for his sons.

Louis and Charles, already inseparable, attended the royal Collège de Rodez in 1821. Following the typical routine of boarding students, they lived and studied in a prescribed milieu, shut away from external life. The teachers were clergymen and sought to inspire in their students a deep attachment to Catholic and legitimist ideals; in fact, the entire curriculum was subordinated to this highly practical goal. Courses in history ignored the Enlightenment, and if the Revolution was mentioned, it was treated as a sinful affair. Louis Blanc later asserted that what he learned in school was to hate the Revolution and the makers of revolution.[1] Considering his instruction, it is quite astonishing that he came not only to like history but even to write it. The younger students learned texts by heart, reciting them verbatim as they recited the catechism. When they entered the upper grades, they generally no longer studied history, for they had, in the eyes of the good fathers, learned all that they needed to know.[2]

Philosophy was hardly more advanced. Since most modern rationalists were taboo, philosophy remained largely scholastic in content and methods. The teacher dictated from erudite notes. Then the students disputed on certain points, reducing their arguments to syllogistic formulae. Here

3

Louis excelled, and his disputations in clear, precise diction gained for him each year prizes in both rhetoric and philosophy.[3] Biblical study also formed part of the program, and the Bible, far more than the classical or scholastic writings, far more than the catechism, made a profound impression upon him. From the philosophers he learned to reason, but from the Bible he learned to feel. From it he first derived his sense of fraternity and he would later transform the Christ of the Evangelists into a sentimental socialist.

II

The Revolution of 1830 opened a new phase in the life of Louis Blanc. He and Charles had completed their studies shortly before its outbreak; by mid-July they were undecided about their future. Their mother was dead and their father, half insane, lived on a meager pension. Having no desire to remain in Rodez, they turned their eyes eagerly toward Paris, the pole star of hope and ambition. Equipped with more youthful optimism than hard cash, they quit the school on July 26. They were on the road when they learned of the king's abdication, news which perhaps caused them some consternation, since they were probably thinking of obtaining posts in the government. Their dismay, however, did not endure; indeed, they were prepared for all eventualities, and with the same insight that caused fancy shopkeepers in the Rue de Richelieu to erase "Purveyor to the King" from their windows, the brothers cut the *fleur-de-lys* buttons from their school uniforms. This act, opportunistic and indicative that the Blancs were not die-hard legitimists, was symbolic. Their quitting of Rodez, with its tranquil and fairly comfortable way of life, marked a definite break with the past. Not only the new climate of opinion but even more the conditions of life in Paris, led them to alter radically their ideas.

They arrived in the capital in early August. Remnants of barricades remained, and the air, hot and heavy, still smelled of smoldering debris. The two witnessed mass demonstrations of democrats demanding popular elections. They read numerous placards calling for a new revolution. This was a novel and exciting world for the young Southerners, aged nineteen and seventeen. But the excitement of city life did not fill their stomachs nor provide lodgings. They had no hope of employment in the new regime; it classified the Blanc family among its enemies and at once cut off the father's pension. The sons could therefore expect no aid from him, nor did their education fit them for earning a living. It was during these desperate days that Charles often wished he had been trained as a simple artisan; but, as was customary, he and Louis had been trained to be gentlemen and were too proud to accept unskilled manual labor.

The high cost of Parisian living soon began to eat up their little store of money. Shortly after their arrival they rented a cramped attic room.

The mansard ceiling was so low that merely to change shirts became a difficult feat. Despite their economy the brothers, after a month, were almost penniless and still without work. Louis finally overcame his pride and sought aid. He went first to the Corsican-born ambassador of Russia, Count Pozzo di Borgo, a genial old man whose influence, unfortunately, had declined. The Count offered him money rather than an acceptable post. Louis, more Corsican than his compatriot, placed the money on a table and retired in silence.[4] As he hurried down the street, relating the incident to Charles who had waited outside, his pride was inflated by his disdainful renunciation. Charles, however, found the gesture a bit too heroic, even for Louis whom he worshipped. Louis, far more than his brother, was humiliated by the very thought of penury and by all the petty acts it forced upon him. House cleaning he consented to, provided he dusted and swept behind closed doors. Marketing and the haggling over prices that it involved he absolutely refused. So Charles, who concluded that a genius must never perform such a *corvée*, bought the food while his brother waited outside.[5]

All this was dismal enough, but the failure to find suitable work was the greatest blow to the pride of the elder Blanc. Employers smiled, thinking him a mere child, for he was small, and at nineteen, as at forty, he had the appearance of a boy. His roundish face was beardless and framed by abundant black hair. His nose was not large, but somewhat broad with small nostrils, of a piece with his full lips and large eyes filled with earnestness and vigor. In desperation he tried tutoring. Few pupils came to him. Soon he and Charles were on the brink of destitution, reduced to a diet of dry bread which Louis, hungry as he often was, refused, insisting that he had eaten out and that Charles must finish the loaf. Possibly urged by Charles, possibly by his own pride which revolted against his state, Louis sought the help of an uncle who brusquely but good-naturedly pressed 300 francs into his hands and promised to renew the sum every six months.[6] This allowance brought amelioration but not solution to the problem of livelihood. To supplement it, Louis worked as a clerk, then again as a tutor; but always detesting his existence as an intellectual flunky, he did not remain long in either job. Perhaps his impatience was whetted by the vision of wealth and good food and warm rooms that he and Charles glimpsed when they visited well-to-do relatives. Afterward, dejection settled back upon them as they returned to their cold room.

Paris by day called forth different moods. The brothers, usually quitting their room in the morning, passed many happy days visiting museums, or strolling like true provincials among the massive palaces and public monuments. If toward the end of the day Charles became fatigued and discouraged, Louis comforted him with visions of better times to come.[7] Their mutual affection, which later inspired Alexandre Dumas to write his *Corsican Brothers*, tempered somewhat the sharper pain of poverty.

The bond between them, forged by blood, common feeling, and shared hardship, was in no way weakened by divergent interests. Charles was attracted by art, whereas Louis was interested in history, politics, and journalism. He sought the aid of a family friend, who led him to see Eric Decazes, then *grand référendaire* of the Chamber of Peers. The old duke, seeing before him a little fellow, stroked Blanc's cheek protectively, "Very well," he said, "we'll see what can be done for this little boy." Louis withdrew, humiliated. Little boy, indeed! He was to avenge himself, however, for in March, 1848, as head of the Luxembourg Commission, he slept in the duke's bed, which had been hastily vacated after the July Monarchy fell.[8] Finally Louis obtained a tutorial post in the Hallette family residing at Arras. He left for that city in 1832. When he later returned to Paris he had accomplished another stage in his intellectual development.

III

Little is known about Blanc's life in Arras. There is reason to believe that there he came under new influences which expanded his knowledge of social conditions and turned him further away from the legitimism of his youth. Probably the first of these new stimuli was his employer, Alexis Hallette, a self-educated entrepreneur who invented several mechanical devices and who became an active proponent of the benefits of machine production.[9] Louis Blanc also came to place full faith in the power of science and mechanization to create an economy of plenty for everyone.[10]

Moreover, it was during his sojourn in Arras that Louis entered into more intimate contact with the workers. It is highly probable that his sympathy for them was quickened at this time. His own severe poverty had already led him to question the justice in existing social conditions.[11] The workers in Arras were not well off, the median daily wage being about 2½ francs for the skilled.[12] Louis spoke with them, observed at first hand their living conditions and outlook, and was delighted to find that they were eager to learn.[13] Certainly his later socialism was based on his love of the working-class and his deep conviction of its capacity for improvement. However, when he left the northern provincial town he lost intimate contact with workers and did not recover it until 1848. In this interval his concept of the people became more abstract and idealized, akin to the *peuple* of Jean-Jacques Rousseau.[14]

The workers, however idealized, never contributed directly to the elaboration of those ideas which came to form his socio-political philosophy. The workers in the Pas-de-Calais were either indifferent to or ignorant of politics.[15] And in this respect they hardly differed from the majority of their compatriots in town and countryside. During the Restoration and July Monarchy there was almost a conspiracy of silence against the democratic tradition.[16] Few indeed were the children reared in republican ideals; most, like Louis Blanc, had been taught that the Republic and the Reign of Terror were twin evils. His gravitation toward the left, therefore, was the result of circumstance and was guided as much by the action of fiery intellectuals as by the example of the workers.

Blanc's first significant mentor was the editor of the *Propagateur du Pas-de-Calais*. Frédéric Degeorge had welcomed the July Revolution, but soon decided that Orleanism was merely tri-colored Bourbonism. When Louis came under his influence, he was a vigorous champion of Jacobin republicanism.[17] The young tutor had earlier read Jean-Jacques Rousseau when in Paris.[18] Now, under the benevolent guidance of Degeorge, he expanded his knowledge of democratic ideas. It was also in the offices of the *Propagateur* that he was introduced to the literary style of political journalism.[19] And here he began his career as a writer, a modest beginning limited chiefly to book reviews. However, reviews often served as a medium for subtle opposition to the government as well as for the defense of democracy. In fact, it was in these reviews that Blanc first joined that small group of writers essaying to defend the First Republic by washing from it the blood of the Terror.[20] His reviews indicate that he had found the leisure to read Rousseau, Morelly, Gabriel Bonnot de Mably, Charles Secondat, baron de Montesquieu, and Voltaire. Already he preferred the first three, particularly Rousseau.

It was also at this time that he revealed his admiration for Maximilian Robespierre. After having won a literary prize from the Academy of Arras for a poem, "Hôtel des Invalides," he entered a second contest in 1834 with a work entitled, "Éloge de Manuel, député." The judges decided that two lines were too laudatory of both Maximilian Robespierre and Georges-Jacques Danton. Before they would grant another prize, they demanded their suppression. Not yet intransigent on such points, Louis Blanc acceded. Shortly after he sent his poems to Pierre Béranger, the popular *chansonnier* who, having read them, made him swear never to write another.[21]

Louis accepted this wise decision. But he could not follow the old man's advice to enter politics, the rights to vote and stand for office being preserved for the rich. There was, nonetheless, a road to power that had opened not long before—journalism. His gaze now turned eagerly again to Paris; he missed the city and he longed for his brother. And, of course, the important journals were in the capital. His ambition was to join the *National*, the most famous of republican dailies. Armed with a letter of introduction to one of its editors, Blanc bade his farewells and followed his ambition once more to the great city.

IV

Louis Blanc found himself again in a revolutionary atmosphere; indeed, his coming and going coincided remarkably with the Parisian predilection for barricades. In 1830 when he arrived, in 1832 when he departed, and again in 1834 when he returned, the capital was the scene

of uprising. The last two upheavals had been bloodily repressed, and it is
possible that their failure impressed the young journalist with the ad-
vantages of peaceful reform. Oppression, however, could not turn him
away from the reform movement, nor stamp out the movement itself.

The social and intellectual milieu which Blanc now entered was markedly oppositional, at times openly rebellious. In the generation of the
1830's and 1840's there were small but articulate groups of writers whose
spirit was irreconcilable with the regime. Among them, disquietude and
discontent were more common than was satisfaction. There was, on the
one hand, a humanitarian fervor which, swelled by romantic sentiment,
openly condemned the harsh living conditions of the workers. A vast
literature appeared, keenly critical and replete with solutions for the burn-
ing issue of the times, the social issue. Increasingly, political discussions
acquired marked social overtones. On the other hand, there was the frustration of many ambitions. A large number of young men refused to believe that society was a static hierarchy with each person assigned a place
by divine arrangement. The Revolution of 1789 and Napoleon had
opened careers to talent and had cleared away many of the obstacles to
social mobility.[22]

For the generation of Louis Blanc, warfare was largely replaced by
reading, and love of fighting by love of knowledge. Young men had much
to learn, because official education during the Empire and Restoration
had left vast gaps in their intellectual training. Of course, the traditional
love of glory did not disappear, but the king's policy of peace offered it no
brilliant opportunities. Therefore many young men turned to politics.
The government, however, was not prepared to encourage young men to
enter politics or to open the parliament to aspirants not in accord with
its conservative principles. By the mid-1830's the king had promulgated a
severe press law, had encouraged cabinet instability as a means of fur-
thering his ambition for personal rule, and had perfected the art of
political corruption in order to control the assembly.[23]

At first men of republican tendencies had favored Louis Philippe, but
they soon formed an opposition group, never very large, but as determined and as outspoken as the press laws permitted. Frustrated in their
political ambitions by the narrow electoral laws, many of them turned,
like Louis Blanc, to journalism. Soon after his return to Paris he went to
to the offices of the *National,* where he found no opening. His discouragement was short-lived; he subsequently became a writer for the *Bon Sens.*

When the *Bon Sens* was founded, soon after the June uprising of 1832,
it was intended to serve as the organ of the liberal and dynastic opposition which included Odilon Barrot; Jacques Lafitte, the famous banker;
and François Arago, the scientist. These men, firm constitutionalists,
did not attack kingship as an office; rather, they feared the growing
personal power of Louis Philippe. Their program called for the reconciliation of monarch with the principles of 1789.[24] One of the directors,

Louis Cauchois-Lemaire, leaned heavily toward monarchy; the other, Victor Rodde, helped to popularize the paper by appealing to the masses. Its changing motto (on one occasion, "The voice of the people is the voice of God," and on another, "All for and by the people") attracted readers among the working class. But the secret societies soon began to complain that it was too moderate, even anti-democratic. By mid-1833 the *Populaire* of Etienne Cabet began to eclipse it.[25] Shortly after Blanc joined it a change of policy occurred when Cauchois-Lemaire, whom Blanc later stamped as a "bourgeois," quit the staff.[26] The more radical Rodde was in command, and his young collaborator soon fell under his influence as he had earlier fallen under that of Degeorge.[27] The dynamism of both men awakened Blanc's romantic admiration. He found in them his ideal of the true Gallic type, the new chivalry of democracy, armed with pen to defend a free press.

This was the heroic era of republican journalism which was struggling not only for its integrity but also for its right to exist as an agency of legal opposition. The police, seeking to destroy it, prosecuted it at every opportunity. Fear of acquittal did not cause the public prosecutor to hesitate; the costs of defense were heavy, and there was the possibility of conviction and fine. Fines were heavy; by 1841 the three law courts of Paris alone had collected the enormous sum of 427,672 francs from the opposition journals of the city.[28] Louis Blanc was all too correct when he wrote that the road taken by the champions of freedom and justice was a long, hard one. But inspired by men like Rodde, he consistently refused to compromise at the expense of free expression and denounced those "who dare not state without fatigue and without fear everything which appears to them true, and everything which appears to them just. To halt before error that one can combat," he declared "is a crime against reason, and to retreat before injustice that one can destroy, a crime against humanity." [29] Intoxicated with his cause, he came to look upon the press as the agency best equipped to destroy injustice and to propagate truth. Journalism became for him what poetry was for Victor Hugo: "a magistracy, and almost a priesthood."

Rodde greatly admired Blanc and groomed him as his eventual successor. It was, however, against the wishes of the owner that in 1836 Blanc became the head of this fairly well-known Parisian daily. He was only twenty-four years old and his youthfulness raised a problem for the staff. In order not to shock the public the editorship was divided between Blanc and another journalist, with the latter serving as the public representative. In case of discord between them, the entire editorial staff was to decide the issue.

The responsibilities of an editor were particularly delicate at this time. The government resorted to new legislation, the September Laws, which raised the *caution* or bond and forbade criticism of both king and Charter. It was in part the financial hardships created by the government

and in part changing social conditions which slowly brought about a
revolution in the press. As the standard of living was rising and the body
of subscribers growing, journalism became an increasingly potent influence. A class of men was formed which managed to live by writing.
Louis Blanc became part of this group, and yet its standards caused him
much anxiety. Journalism as a sole means of livelihood, he feared, would
lead to venality and loss of freedom; professional columnists would not
readily sacrifice their income to enter the lists against constituted authority. On the contrary, they would become a vested interest. To prevent this compromise of principle he urged them to imitate Rousseau,
who had copied music for a livelihood and written books to instruct
the public. Of course no one, least of all Blanc, heeded this advice. He
became a professional journalist, won both success and money, but also
preserved his independence.

By independence Blanc did not mean that a writer must never take
sides; he meant rather that a writer must never become committed, because of purely economic considerations, to the defense of wealth. He
was not yet a socialist, but he already displayed a Jacobin distrust of high
finance,[30] and he had no illusions about the venality of many journalists.
Therefore he looked to the best journalists as high priests of a new industrial age to chase the merchants from the sacred temple, the editorial
office. He also wanted to banish what was to him the very symbol of
capitalism, commercial advertising, from the pages of the journals, where
it occupied space needed for philosophy, history, art, everything that
elevated the minds of men. Advertising, he insisted, was by nature crass,
banal, cynical, and false. When a maker of a patent medicine tried to
insert an ad in his paper, Blanc insisted on proof that the product was
effective!

The opposite view was held by Émile de Girardin, director of the
Presse. He abandoned long political discussions and wooed subscribers
with fashion articles, with his wife's witty chronicles of Paris, and with
serial stories. He also pushed the sale of advertising space in order to
lower the subscription price from eighty to forty francs, or twenty francs
less than the price of the Bon Sens. Before long, intense rivalry grew up
between the new commercial press and the old political press, with the
latter often at a disadvantage because of insufficient capital. Editors
like Blanc always had financial worries, opposing as they did not only
advertising but also the selling of stock to persons with no real political
interest in the paper. Eager for profits, these investors, Blanc warned,
would transform journalism into a business venture by subordinating
edification to profit. Lower prices would hardly benefit readers if the
press became the "mouthpiece of speculation."[31] In consequence of these
views Blanc was highly critical of Girardin whom he publicly labelled a
spéculateur. It was nevertheless against his opposition that the editorial
staff of his journal published an extravagantly critical attack upon

Girardin. The *spéculateur* hereupon sued for defamation, and when Armand Carrel, editor of the *National*, sided with Blanc's paper, Girardin replied in an article that provoked a duel. Carrel was mortally wounded.

This catastrophe weighed heavily on Blanc. Two years earlier he had written: "Dueling is a sacrifice made by ignorant people to the fanaticism of vanity. It is a sanguinary equality established between injustice and law, insolence and reason. Dueling is a violent and absurd negation of the superiority of the virtuous man over the clever man. . . . Dueling is a diminutive of assassination." [32] Yet he did not favor its immediate prohibition. "Dueling does not punish the provocation," he reasoned, "but discourages provocative acts. It does not avenge the outraged and sensitive man, but it shelters him against outrage. Abolish dueling and you create the dictatorship of insult." Blanc despised those writers who profited from calumny. His ideal of style was one which "imposed truth, by showing proof of a calm, thoughtful yet energetic and decided conviction."

An aversion for extremism formed one of the main traits of his personality. Blanc held firm convictions but the first of these was moderation. Consequently, he opposed regicide and violent revolution, he refused to join those secret societies which abetted violence, and he warned the workers against demagogues, *agents provocateurs,* even against trade unions, seeing in strikes the futility of unprepared, isolated action. He had no faith in the notion of "spontaneous action" so dear to Louis Auguste Blanqui and the syndicalists of a later date. He criticized the revolts of the 1830's because they were not prepared by ideas; they were the work of men who put more faith in force than in intelligence, who made of progress "the matter of a mere *coup d'état.*" To win the young men away from these activists he distinguished between two types of opposition: the kind initiated by individuals and the kind inspired by ideas. "The first is useful," he wrote, "where revolution is alive in all men's minds and awaits only a signal to get under way, where the people's hatreds need only a watchword in order to meet, comprehend and march together to combat." But where the people are not ready, as in France, individual conspiracies are dangerous and uncertain: "They demand from the present what only the future can grant." Not so with a conspiracy of ideas which "recruits not men but people." [33] Blanc's program envisaged the rise of the masses, change by the will of the majority enlightened by the teaching of a progressive minority. He did not want a *coup de main* but a revolution: rapid change by peaceful means under the pressure of public opinion, a renunciation of privileges by the wealthy and the unity of classes cemented by the bonds of fraternal patriotism. There should be another great August Fourth.

Blanc never imagined that he could win the favor of the government and its apologists to his program. He sought recruits preferably among the enlightened bourgeoisie, artisans, and some of the legitimists of the far right—that is, all those antagonistic to Orleanism. Even then, he did not expect from most of the legitimists any positive assistance. He was not in sympathy with them, having abandoned his monarchist heritage; he characterized them as effete, cynical, and timid. It was the underprivileged on whom he counted for positive action and whom he hoped to infuse with republican ideals.

He favored the Republican party largely because he found among its leaders those generous sentiments seeking to elevate the masses. Although the Republicans looked toward the future rather than toward the past they were, he reasoned, the true representatives of that traditional French type which had brought glory and hegemony to the country. It was not the decadent nobility, resembling in no way their great ancestors, but the republicans who were France's modern heroes, astir with life and energy, and eager to sacrifice themselves for a great cause. Admiring their courage, he hoped to moderate their proclivity for violent action inspired more by vague sentiment than precise goals. If the party, he wrote, was to become an effective agency of reform, it must elaborate a clear program based on well-studied decisions. With this long preparation in mind he counseled, "Patience is also a republican virtue. . . . It is the nature and glory of élite minds to precede their epoch; but violence is not permissible." [34]

Hoping to restrain the party by impartial counsel, Blanc tried not to become immersed in it. He even had a deep suspicion of political organizations. "Nothing equals the egoism of parties," he reasoned, "unless it is their ingratitude. Those whom their passions choose for leaders, they want for slaves." [35] To keep his independence he sought to inspire the party rather than to become an integral part of it; therefore, he never actively tried to improve its organization. Unfortunately, his decision to stand aloof contributed to his weakness in 1848, when he formed part of the Provisional Government. He failed at this critical period to win the backing of a well-organized group, and his independence before 1848 became isolation during and after that year.

Instead of a disciplined party, what Blanc wanted in the late 1830's was a rallying of men of good will around a definite program. Doctrinal unity rather than hierarchical control promised to safeguard individual freedom and also to provide the means for winning governmental power. From his activity during 1837, Blanc reasoned that a loose-knit progressive group would be in a better position to win allies from among all men opposed to the narrow electorate of the monarchy. Such a group would also find it easier to spread its doctrines among the amorphous opposition and to assume leadership.

When the chamber was dismissed toward the close of 1837, followed by a call for new elections, Blanc felt the time opportune for putting his plan into action. He and his good friend Jacques-François Dupont (of Bussac) took the initiative in forming an electoral committee whose purpose was to get all qualified voters to the polls, and to present them with a large slate of reform candidates. This goal required that the entire opposition rally around a moderate program. The groups Blanc invited were the dynastic Left headed by Odilon Barrot, and the so-called "radicals" headed by François Arago, Jacques Dupont de l'Eure, and Jacques Lafitte. The latter were radical in name only, forming rather the right wing of the republican party. Blanc considered their presence indispensable, while he desired that of Barrot for prestige. What he planned was a committee of illustrious men, renowned for moderation, whom "calumny would not dare attack." However, the liberal monarchists revealed their fear of men like Blanc and withdrew, leaving a rump dominated by the moderate republicans (François Arago, Étienne Garnier-Pagès, and Alexandre Marie) and the Jacobins (Blanc and Alexandre Ledru-Rollin).[36] This reform committee was a prefiguration of the Provisional Government of 1848, save that the younger Garnier-Pagès, Louis-Antoine, would replace his deceased brother. But in 1837 these men had practically no influence in the elections which returned the government's usual majority. General indifference among the people and aggressive corruption among the prefects had the expected result.

Blanc's participation in the electoral campaign had the effect of bringing the *Bon Sens* ostensibly into the republican camp. When he had joined its staff it was not definitely part of the opposition. However, under the influence of Rodde it had brought up social issues and workers were invited to contribute to a special column, the *Tribune des prolétaires*. It was partly on the basis of their writings that Blanc convinced himself of their willingness and ability to learn. To appeal to those "who judge with their natural intelligence," the editors used simple language and kept the price down. The result was that in 1836, shortly after Blanc became editor, its circulation attained 1,647, chiefly in Paris. His honorarium soon rose to 2,000 francs a year, a large sum in a profession with its own proletariat.

Although materially well-off, he yet felt himself restrained by his employer, especially after June, 1835 when the *Revue républicaine,* in which appeared his more radical articles, ceased to exist. He found no other adequate outlets. This situation reached a crisis in 1838 when the railroad question came up for debate in the chamber. On February 15 the government presented a bill providing for a large network of railroads which it intended to construct. Financiers and businessmen, scenting here a source of immense profit, rose up in arms against the administration, pronouncing it incompetent in economic matters and quite incapable of realizing grandiose schemes like railways. The state must not become "industrial." At once loud clamor arose. How, it was asked, could private capital be found for the vast national lines proposed? And what would

be the political role of the railroad companies? In the chamber, Alphonse
de Lamartine and several others, in the press, the *National, Bon Sens,*
and *Journal du peuple* demanded construction by the state.

Blanc considered the problem from a triple point of view, which shows
how far he had come to regard the state as an instrument of progress and
private investment as an evil. From the moral point of view, he argued, the
sale of stock in the new companies, leading as it must to a baccanale of
speculation, would undermine public as well as administrative honesty.
From the industrial view private companies were incompetent to build
railroads. They desired to realize profits as quickly as possible and therefore would keep rates high, placing an extra burden on industry and the
poor traveller. The state, however, being "immortal" and in no hurry to
recoup expenses, need not levy high rates since its source of revenue
came from taxation. Unlike the new companies it had a vast competent
personnel already trained in public service to take over the management.
The state would serve the public while the corporations would serve only
themselves. From the political point of view these large corporations
would become too powerful; they would corrupt and control politicians
and civil servants and constitute a veritable private state within the
national state. Suppose, he warned, that foreign or anti-nationalistic
men obtained control of the railroads, how would France defend herself
against treason in wartime? If the roads had been in the hands of those
whose privileges the Revolution of 1789 destroyed, this revolution would
have been impossible.[37]

The *étatisme* of Louis Blanc, who went much farther in this direction than Lamartine, was not to the liking of his employer. Blanc, insisting that an "honest man ought to prefer his conviction to his position,"
quit the journal in August, 1838. The entire editorial staff accompanied
him, so popular had he become. Soon afterward, the paper ceased publication.

CHAPTER TWO

The Origins of French Jacobin-Socialism

I

ℰ LOUIS BLANC, twenty-nine years of age, and ostensibly without position, was now prepared to do his best work. The ten years following his resignation from the *Bon Sens* made up his golden decade. In this space of time, so brief in the life of a man who lived to be seventy-one, he produced the great doctrinal works in which he laid out his blueprints for a better society. With these books he stepped into the front ranks of the social movement, and in 1848 became the cynosure of the Parisian working class.

The reasons for his fame must now be examined. What precisely did he represent? Herman Pechan has presented him as the forerunner of Karl Marx and Ferdinand Lassale, and therefore as the innovator of "modern socialism." [1] Pechan was apparently of the opinion that German socialism was the only form of modern social theory. More generally, Blanc has been called a state socialist. [2] The term, however, is quite vague. He has also been called "the forerunner of modern democratic Socialism." [3] But today the terms "democratic socialism" and "social democracy" have lost much of their former meaning: they might describe either a civil libertarian government or a form of totalitarianism. Indeed, the word "democracy" itself made for confusion in the nineteenth century. [4] There is need, then, for further definition. Certain socialist ideologies, and the forces which brought them into politics, require a more accurate interpretation. For France, only one author, Marcel Prélot, made this latter topic the subject of a special study. [5] Unfortunately, he fell somewhat short of his goal, especially on the pre-1848 period. The purpose of this chapter, therefore, is to offer a precise explanation of one of the currents of early French socialist philosophy, here called Jacobin-socialism, and of Blanc's relation to it. This task calls for an investigation of the efforts made by certain left-wing thinkers to unite two distinct ideologies: Jacobin democracy and co-operative socialism.

The seminal ideas of the Jacobin-socialist philosophy appeared during

15

the eighteenth century and were largely drawn from two contrasting theories of property: the radicalist theory, which sought to make property accessible to all men by parceling it among them as individual proprietors; and the socialist theory which intended to make it available to all men by transferring it to them as collective owners, thus necessitating the equitable division of produce rather than of land. Here was, and still is, the basic difference between pure radicalism and pure socialism; but in general, these two tendencies—the term "schools" would be misleading here—have not been so sharply separated in the past as to preclude a vague rapprochement. It is true that Rousseau, the father of French radicalism, had practically no relations with Morelly and Gabriel Bonnot de Mably, the precursors of French socialism. Yet, he was not at one with the nascent liberals who had come to look upon private property as a natural right. Regulation and even dispossession were not, Rousseau held, violations of natural law.[6] However, he defended property, on condition that no person possessed an excess of it, that is, no greater amount than a person could cultivate himself. Thus grew up the radicalist distinction between a property right as a natural absolute, and possession as a social contingency. In contrast, Morelly and Mably took the position that private ownership of land, whether as property or possession, was the cause of social evil.

The two tendencies held several points in common. Like the radicals, Morelly and Mably viewed social evil as the loss of virtue. And again like the radicals, they defined virtue as obedience to the state and as an absence of luxury and laziness. In addition, both schools were essentially agrarian in outlook and tended to share an equal distrust of the very rich as well as the very poor of the cities.[7] But, on the whole, the two methods of thought were kept distinct, for political ideals as well as views on property, during the eighteenth century. Radicalism was a democratic movement emphasizing popular sovereignty, whereas the real socialists gave little attention to politics and did not view the idea of popular government with special favor.[8] Moreover, the socialists were quite pessimistic and could not share the romantic enthusiasm of Rousseau, the belief in the goodness of man, or the belief in progress.

During the Convention of 1792–95 the Jacobins, claiming to be faithful disciples of Rousseau, were in control, and their Republic of Virtue assumed a decidedly anti-socialist stand. However, Maximilian Robespierre went farther than Rousseau when he gave a marked social orientation to the Rights of Man. He proclaimed that society owed to the individual the right to work or to assistance when incapacitated.[9] Not all the Jacobins shared his views. Yet, the dominance of liberal individualism and of laissez faire was challenged and Robespierre's proposed Declaration of the Rights of Man took its place beside *Le contrat social* as another chapter in the democratic bible. Louis Blanc later wrote that certain

Jacobins, with Robespierre, "the Incorruptible," as their head, had recognized the need of fraternal aid among men and of the intervention of an active power to protect the weak.[10] On the other hand, he realized that Jacobin radicalism and socialism were distinct.

The first significant effort to bring the two movements together occurred only in the mid-1790's with the Conspiracy of Equals. This affair was a desperate reaction against the Directory and, as such, attracted both Jacobin radicals and Babouvian socialists. These men, not always happy in one another's company, were able to smooth over their differences in May, 1796. François-Noel Babeuf, better known as Gracchus Babeuf, with Philippe Buonarroti and others of the conspiracy were deeply influenced by Rousseau. For Babeuf, therefore, the political ideals of Robespierre became synonymous with democracy.[11] The conspirators put forward the Constitution of 1793 as a minimum program. However, the Babouvians were not overly concerned with political theories and Jacobinism did not assume a large place in their proclamations.

The influence of Mably showed more clearly in their key documents: the *Manifeste, Acte d'insurrection,* and *Analyse de la doctrine.* Like the philosophical cleric but with more than his enthusiasm, they proclaimed that real equality could not exist without the "community of goods," that "the land belongs to no one, its fruits belong to everyone." Unlike Mably, they looked to a Jacobin state to bring about a collectivist society. In reality, the conspirators did not look forward to an immediate promulgation of the still-born 1793 Constitution. They planned to set up a *comité insurrecteur* to carry out the plot, and to reactivate the Terror.[12]

The conspiracy failed. It was primarily a bourgeois movement, with little cohesion and hardly any working-class following. Vague in its ideological content, it left to succeeding generations an inspirational legend rather than a real program. This legend was preserved by Philippe Buonarroti in his *Conspiration pour l'égalité dite de Babeuf,* published in Brussels in 1828 and in Paris two years later. These two volumes of memoirs had a marked influence on a new generation of Jacobins.[13] Blanc later wrote a representative encomium of the author: "As for his opinions, they are of celestial origin, since they tended to bring back among men the cult of evangelical fraternity."[14] The old conspirator's importance lay in the fact that he quickened the social orientation of Jacobin politics as it renewed its vigor.

The revolution of July, 1830, witnessed the rebirth of political radicalism. As yet, its followers were no more than a handful of devotees assembled in a society called Friends of the People whose program reaffirmed the democratic principles of 1793.[15] Like their Jacobin predecessors, they were petty bourgeois who had little to do with urban labor. Nonetheless, the society gave some attention to labor problems, and suggested that the skilled workers form voluntary co-operatives or associations.[16] It also set up an "industrial commission" to study a project favoring "exchange banks for industrial products." [17]

Dissolved in 1833 the Friends of the People was replaced by the Society of the Rights of Man, in which there was a more determined effort to modify orthodox radicalism along the lines of neo-socialist principles. Latter-day Jacobins like Godfrey Cavaignac, and Babouvians like Charles Teste and René Voyer d'Argenson, thrown together once more by common opposition to the government, rediscovered the old formula of the Conspiracy of Equals: "Bread and the Constitution of 1793." [18] A noticeable evolution, however, was the emergence of a new type of revolutionary, one less concerned with rural problems than with those of urban workers. This change was an inevitable result of a growing economy and a rising laboring class more conscious of its plight and more determined to bring about reform. Workers, however, only influenced the society; they never dominated it. The leaders were petty bourgeois Jacobins who also laid plans for a new committee of public safety composed of a virtuous élite to guide the people toward "universal association."

During the July Monarchy the word *association* acquired the effect of a messianic formula, attracting all groups of the left, whether radical or socialist. Almost cabalistically vague, it lent itself to a variety of meanings. Most of the members of the Rights of Man conceived principally of a political association, such as the one to which they belonged. At first only a few, such as François Raspail and Cavaignac, represented a kind of social radicalism which emphasized extensive popular control and some popular ownership in economic production and distribution. Thinking in terms of petty industry and commerce, they envisaged political clubs for the present and producers' associations of employers and workers for the future.

Before long there appeared in the Rights of Man a small group of thinkers primarily interested in labor problems and anxious to win labor support. Influenced more by the nascent co-operative movement than by Babouvian socialism, they broadened the concept of political association, adding to it the ideals of economic and social reform. They went beyond even the pure co-operators who tended to ignore politics, and found in the radicalist state the source of credit necessary for financing workers' associations. This plan, a conscious effort to give a social aim to the radical movement, was elaborated most cogently by Marc Dufraisse in his pamphlet, *Association des travailleurs*, published by the Rights of Man in 1833. In this same year appeared another official pamphlet, *De l'égalité,* by Jean-Jacques Vignerte, who wrote, "The day when France will be free and the nation sovereign, the essence of the duties of the republic will be to furnish the proletarians with the means of forming co-operative associations and of exploiting themselves their industry." [19] He went beyond Cavaignac in that he looked forward to the abolition of wages and he was considerably in advance of most radicals in his glorification of machines. He, along with Voyer d'Argenson, rejected the idea of property, whether large or small, as a natural right, and d'Argenson attributed almost unlimited power to society, which might dispose of both the life and property of each person for the benefit and justice of all.[20] The extreme left of the Rights of Man, however, was only a small minority, for while most members attributed considerable power to the Jacobin state, they hardly conceived of it as an agency to socialize the economy.

The disappearance of the society in 1834 brought to an end the plaiting together of the two threads making up the French Jacobin-socialist tradition. There occurred, so to speak, the great dispersal. Branching off to the left were those who continued the Babouvian thread with its *mystique* of "creative revolution." The moderates, on the other hand, grew steadily weaker from 1834 to 1839, almost ceasing to exist as a group. Without political effect as individuals, many of them fled into exile, while others languished in state prisons.

This setback was partly counterbalanced by the significant activity of a number of intellectuals from whose minds would emerge the essential credo of the Jacobin-socialist philosophy. They were inspired men and needed every bit of their fervor to attain an objective rendered doubly difficult, first, by the fact that many radicals, fearful of the latter-day Babouvians, grew increasingly distrustful of all collectivist ideas, and second, by the absence from the socialist tradition of any real democratic political basis on which to build. Neither Charles Fourier, who was apolitical, nor Henri Saint-Simon, who was autocratic, had provided for such a basis.

Charles Fourier and Robert Owen were the real founders of the modern co-operative movement. Both of them laid plans for associations of several hundred persons, which Fourier called the Phalange and Owen the Village of Co-operation.[21] Both of these thinkers imagined it possible to set up independent, more or less isolated communes, under the auspices of benevolent capitalists. Owen emphasized the importance of environment in the formation of character; Fourier the importance of a variety of jobs in making men happy. Fourier was more influential in the rise of Jacobin-socialism as a critic of capitalist competition, which he thought the basic evil. Here he influenced Blanc who reached the same conclusion. But neither he nor his disciples saw any intimate relation between politics and social change.

Saint-Simon looked to the wealthy businessmen to head an authoritarian administration and to control the economy.[22] His great hope for the future derived from his belief in the usefulness of credit as an economic stimulant and his desire for uncontrolled rulership by an economic and scientific élite. In both respects he influenced young thinkers such as

Louis Blanc. He accepted the workers as part of the useful industrial class and would allow those with talent to rise in the administrative hierarchy. But his appeal was chiefly to the wealthy bourgeois. Interestingly enough, the more definite democratization of socialism began largely as a reaction against the autocratic and theocratic implications of Saint-Simonism. This work was inaugurated by two of the disciples who broke away from the school, P.-J.-B. Buchez and Pierre Leroux.[23]

By 1830 Buchez began to reveal an admiration for Jacobinism. At the same time he laid out his program for a workers' association, making a significant contribution to the co-operative movement. However, his effort was directed toward reconciling rather than fusing what he considered two distinct entities, popular representative government and producers' associations. The hand of the politician, he concluded, revealed a tendency to pick the pocket of individual freedom and therefore must be kept from two most precious treasures: economics and religion.[24]

Pierre Leroux also defended popular sovereignty and representative government. He later explained his mission during the 1830's: "I served in explaining by the formula of the Republic, what Saint-Simon, Jean-Jacques Rousseau, and Owen wanted to say. . . . This was the synthesis that I elaborated more than any other." [25] But Leroux was not a full-fledged Jacobin radical, repudiating as he did the politically fundamentalist idea of a unicameral legislature. Enchanted with the number three, he desired the juxtaposition of three councils, which would have created that bogey of the radicals, a "mixed government." In spite of this trinitarian heresy, he called for an interventionist state based on popular sovereignty and manhood suffrage, a government filled with the spirit of Rousseau. "The legislator," he wrote, "must be made to intervene, because it has been demonstrated that not to recognize in politics any other principle but individualism and laissez faire, is to surrender the lower classes to brutal exploitation." [26] He was convinced of the permanent utility of representative government. It "harmonizes the struggle and expresses unity," and brings into accord "the sentiments which move toward the future . . . [and] the interests and sentiments which are attached to the present." Here, as we shall see, was the source of Blanc's concept of "social virtue," and the author of the *Organisation du travail* also learned from Leroux that the "true Republic is socialism. To wish the triumph of the Republic in France without socialism is absurd." [27]

Looking forward to the eventual disappearance of the proletariat, he coined the word *socialisme* and applied it to his rather vague scheme for industrial co-operation and to his concept of industrial property. The whole process of industrial production, he reasoned, was collective in nature, the work of all society including the dead as well as the living; consequently, manufactured articles formed a common stock from which each person was to draw according to need, capacity, and work. The term *socialiste*, however, cannot be applied to his plan for agriculture inasmuch as he called for the generalization, not the collectivization, of land.

Despite the limitations of Leroux and Buchez, both of these seminal thinkers kept alive during the 1830's the ideals of social unity and popular sovereignty. In 1839 a new, more clearly defined Jacobin-socialism appeared with the writings of Louis Blanc.

CHAPTER THREE

The Philosopher of Democracy

I

𝕎 WHEN LOUIS BLANC quit the *Bon Sens* he had in mind exciting plans for the basic transformation of society. The mission he assigned himself went far beyond the limited scope of a daily newspaper. Rather he felt the need for a review dealing in ideas to continue the work of the *Revue républicaine*. It was therefore logical for Jacques Dupont (of Bussac), editor of the defunct journal, to assist him in launching a new one and to form part of its editorial staff. Like Blanc he was a disciple of Rousseau; hence their organ was politically radical, but with a pronounced socialistic tendency. In fact, it was the first periodical which might be classified as Jacobin-socialist. However, since its editor-in-chief intended to make it a rallying point for all shades of progressive opinion, it was entitled *Revue de progrès politique, social et littéraire*. Its first number appeared in January, 1839.

The immediate goal was to find a new principle of authority which would serve to unify society. The opening issue, in which Blanc explained this goal, dwelled upon three unities: political, economic, and moral. Political unity had existed before 1789 in the person of the king, but royalty led fatally to *lettres de cachet*, that is, to arbitrary, unjust tyranny. Economic unity had existed before the Revolution in the guilds, but they oppressed the poor. Moral unity had existed in the Catholic church, but it led to the Inquisition. The bourgeois, in the name of reform, destroyed these outmoded instruments of integration and authority by successfully championing their new principle of individualism. Since this principle was unacceptable to Blanc, he set out to find new unities. In politics this goal would be achieved through democracy. In industry, there was need for a "reorganization of work." In the realm of the spirit, solidarity would be found in a new social religion. This, however vague, was for Blanc the progressive middle way between despotism and anarchy. To explain in detail this middle way was the ultimate purpose of the review.[1]

II

Louis Blanc's philosophy grew out of two complementary premises: first, man is basically good, and second, his goodness will emerge only in a Jacobin-socialist environment.

Belief in human benevolence was certainly not new, having been popularized by Rousseau during the eighteenth century. In the early 1830's Blanc came under the spell of the almost deified Jean-Jacques, and found in human emotions a great force. He accepted man as a passionate creature, and discerning in the heart the origins of man's sense of justice, contended that hope for the future lay in this trait. However, while human nature is innately emotive, there exists at birth no precise idea of justice, which is the product of education and environment. The instinct is like amorphous clay in need of shaping. This is what Blanc understood by the proclamation of man's goodness: that man is born with capacity for justice.

Evil exists, but is not part of man save as an extraneous element introduced by a bad milieu. Therefore not human nature but institutions have to be reformed. Man is a creation of God and it would be blasphemy to assert that God would mix perversity in his handiwork. All men, rich and poor alike, are victims of the "tyranny of things: ignorance, indigence, abandonment, bad example, and the suffering of soul and body." These evils are unwittingly fostered by competitive capitalism and monarchical government, the two institutions that have awakened jealousy, defiance, and hatred in each "soul" and have stifled bit by bit all those generous inspirations of faith, devotion, and poetry.

It is apparent that Blanc was much closer to the school of innate ideas than to that of empiric sensationalism. He roundly condemned Voltaire for introducing Locke into France and for decrying Descartes' metaphysics. He argued:

> By his thought man spreads himself outward and is prodigal of himself, by sensation on the contrary he draws everything to himself. . . . He becomes a point of convergence in the middle of the universe. What importance attributed to the individual! But also what encouragement to egoism! In the logic of such a system, do not expect from man that sublime devotion to abstract misfortune, to remote suffering: the sensualist has only relative notions; he is interested only in what he touches; he pities only visible suffering, only perceptible misfortune; . . . He will not have, unless his heart contradicts his theory, those noble impulses which, on the wings of thought, with the disinterest that they give and the suddenness of their flight, transport us beyond the sensible world and elevate us from surrounding sensation up to the peaks where we embrace humanity.[2]

By the logic of his system Blanc was led to deny that an idea is the outcome of sensation, because in his political and social philosophies he was generally dealing with abstractions, with conditions that ought to exist, rather than with those that already existed and which might be studied empirically through sensation. He failed to observe that Lockian sensationalism had not hindered the highly abstract thought of the Enlightenment, and that in decrying it he weakened the psychological basis of environmentalism. Moreover, his own social ideas were based on the need to improve the milieu in order to facilitate the full development of man's capacities, an eighteenth-century belief derived largely from Locke. But the sensationalists posited that the individual is the point of concentration to which environmental forces flow, while Blanc insisted that the right milieu will draw man out of himself and spread him, so to speak, over the community. Man becomes social and society unified as a result.

Society, Blanc taught, had become divided into two classes, the bourgeois and the people, with the bourgeois the dominant class. By bourgeois he meant "all those citizens who, possessing the instruments of work or capital, work with their own resources and depend on others only in a certain measure. They are more or less free." [3] He never really clarified his attitude toward these citizens. In one paragraph he could write that they have contributed much to modern civilization and possess real virtues: love of work, absence of fanatacism, domesticity, and frugality. On the other hand he pointed out that they have "neither *bon ton,* nor good taste, nor the sober elegance of plebeian habitudes, nor the delicacy of aristocratic usages." Their leaders are stock brokers, speculators, and sharpers, who have no "vast belief." What they need, he asserted, is inspiration from the people. [4]

By people he meant all those "citizens who, possessing no capital, depend completely on others, even for the prime necessities of life. They are free only in name." This class, we suppose, was made up not exclusively of manual laborers but of all persons receiving salaries. Blanc's egregious error was to imagine that this class was compact, homogeneous in outlook, without any real sociological difference between the lawyer's clerk, the factory worker, and the skilled artisan. The term *peuple* was most ambiguous, as was the term *prolétaire,* both of which gained currency during the July Monarchy. Both included not only the petty bourgeois and workers of the towns, but sometimes the agricultural workers and small farmers as well. Blanc never clarified the position of the agrarian mass and lent them little attention. What he desired was the unification of the liberal bourgeois and the people, because the well-to-do, if guided by the people, possessed both technical skill and generous sentiment. However, he was convinced that the first propulsion toward socialism would come from below, from the urban lower classes, who were endowed with a divine mission. He genuinely believed in the motto of the *Bon Sens,* "The voice of the people is the voice of God," and discerned a spark of divinity beneath the coarse exterior of the mass. Hence he insisted: "It is not for the virtues that one can love the people: One ought to love them vicious and gross, one ought to love them for the virtues they do not have, and which they would have, had they not been robbed of their share of education and had their right to joy not been measured in an iniquitous manner." [5]

The people, he assured himself, would respond more readily to new ideals than the comfortable bourgeois, for these ideals lay unshapen in the mass, and the people's heroic rise would itself become a great force enveloping all classes. The people's grossness would disappear almost magically as they were educated and surrounded by better institutions. Therefore he set about, like a builder of new worlds, to draw the ground plans, the proper governmental and social institutions on which future felicity would solidly rest.

III

When elaborating his political philosophy Louis Blanc, unlike most liberals, was not chiefly concerned with politics as an end in itself. Government must serve a useful purpose, must have a lofty goal: an equalitarian society. Therefore he sought, on the one hand, to infuse radicalism with socialist ideals, and warned his colleagues in the Republican party that unless they adopted a broad reform program the lower classes would continue to ignore them.[6] On the other hand, he endeavored to give the socialist movement a political aim; this endeavor was more successful.[7] Since the 1840's French socialism has never lost sight for any long period of the close relation between governmental action and social conditions.

In this relation, he concluded, lay the key to success, since without political force all movements looking toward progressive changes are doomed to frustration. Competition has brought to society such devastating chaos that the only remedy is a new principle of authority.[8] Although emphasizing political authority, he denied that his proposals would lead, as the liberals insisted, to the enslavement of the individual by a master state. He affirmed, rather, that only through political action could the great majority of individuals become liberated from economic oppression. Naturally his definition of freedom was not that of the liberals, a difference clearly revealed when he explained that "liberty consists not only of the accorded *right*, but also of the *power* given to a man to exercise, to develop his faculties under the rule of justice and under the safeguard of law."[9] Unregulated liberty did not seem to him compatible with justice. Therefore he never glorified the state of nature in which, he held, the strong oppressed the weak. He was rather closer to Hobbes who believed that life in a state of nature was nasty, brutish, and short, and with a deferential respect he corrected Jean-Jacques by asserting that men formed governments, not to preserve their natural independence, but to acquire social liberty. He therefore condemned laissez faire, discerning in it the sanctioning of a sort of bourgeois state of nature where the rich were free to oppress the poor. Of course he was aware that certain governments acted to preserve this class tyranny, yet, unlike the anarchists, he was not inclined to feel that government by its inherent nature must be oppressive. Like Marx—indeed before Marx—he maintained that the state must be captured by popular forces and used for liberating men from the horrors of poverty. Not to capture the state would leave it as a potent weapon in the hands of the enemies of reform.[10] The humane duty of the state, then, is to offer the lower class the means, that is, the credit necessary to purchase the implements of work. This will lead to economic enfranchisement, an important step toward the full liberation of each individual, for economic security leads to physical well-being which in turn leads to moral improvement. But, Blanc went on with a note of sternness, the individual cannot progress for and by himself. The welfare of each person is so intimately bound to the welfare of his fellow men that only by mutual aid rather than individual competition will each improve himself. Like Rousseau, he conceived of social freedom, distinct from natural independence, as a possession man enjoys only while part of a group which shelters him, and only while under the beneficent control of a state that uplifts him. Society provides protection; the state grants liberty which is growth, elevation of the spirit, repose of the mind. The state and freedom, then, are not contradictory but correlative terms.[11]

Such a social role presupposes a democratic state. "In a true democracy," Blanc explained, "the State is society itself, acting in this capacity in all matters which have an evidently social character." [12] Here the state is thought of as political power emanating from the people, neither different from nor independent of their volition, but at one with it. The state is controlled power, a government whose ideas cannot deviate from nor repudiate its mandate inasmuch as its very existence grows out of that mandate. Beneath a mystical terminology, designed to strike the romantic reader's imagination, lay Blanc's real concept: a popularly elected government consisting of energetic deputies willing and able to serve the mass of voters. His ideas fell really in a sort of middle ground between Hegelian *étatisme* and classical liberalism, and indeed, with deeper sincerity than many liberals, he repudiated the notion of *raison d'état*. This repudiation explains why he voted against the laws exiling the Bonapartist pretender, Louis Napoleon, in 1848, and the Orleanist pretender, the Count of Paris, in the 1870's. On both occasions he braved the hostile criticism of frightened liberals and the wild rage of fellow radicals because he would not prolong, for the sake of political security, the exile of compatriots willing to obey the law. He also went farther than many liberals in emphasizing that the state was competent chiefly in matters of national interest. To handle local affairs he recognized the validity of certain bodies such as the communes and the social workshops.

Blanc was particularly favorable to the creation of communal autonomy. It is true that he advocated political centralization by which the power to direct general policy would be concentrated in a national legislature. At the same time, he favored what he called administrative decentralization by which the power to direct purely local issues would be concentrated in the communes. In order to give them even greater freedom of action he urged the dismissal of all prefects, and the enlargement of the authority of elected mayors and municipal councils. This local power, he argued, would encourage the people to take a more lively interest in affairs directly concerning them, would give them political experience, and would make for a more active, creative citizenry, ready to oppose any tendency toward despotism on the part of the state. He wanted the communes to develop into fraternal associations, to become the civil equivalents of the social workshops, where men would act together and acquire the habit of co-operation. Communal administration would become a kind of school in which citizens prepared themselves for life in a socialist society.[13]

Blanc also favored endowing the social workshops with a large measure of autonomy, and he limited the state's role to that of originator and legislator. After a year of probation, each workshop was to fall under the direction of competent men elected by the workers. Direct control by the state would then come to an end, and as society progressed toward a perfect social democratic structure, its role would decrease proportionately. This two-way evolution, Blanc averred, would prevent the state from assuming absolute mastery over society.[14]

Of course, he did not really expect the state to disappear. It is true that once, in 1851, when disgusted with the Republic that had driven him into exile, Blanc admitted that all political organization might prove useless once society arrived at a condition of perfection.[15] However, in all his other writings he stresses the immortality of the state, the perfect state existing as a natural part of the perfect society.[16] It cannot disappear lest society cease to exist, for the state is the source of creation and regulation in which the progressive impulses arising out of the popular will are filtered, shaped, and given meaning as law. The people are the heart, the emotive source of inspiration; the government is the head, the reasoning source of organization and order. Society, like each person composing it, contains innate instincts which spread outward in a prodigal manner; the government is the *tabula rasa* of Locke, acquiring ideas through its close contact with the people. Unwittingly, Louis Blanc combined Descartes and Locke.

His arguments in support of a democratic regime were not original save as an eclectic amalgam drawn from three currents of political thought: Rousseau's ideal of popular sovereignty, Jeremy Bentham's ideal of manhood suffrage, and Robespierre's ideal of a republic of virtue.

Following Rousseau, Blanc predicated that the state is not sovereign. It is the head of the body politic, possessing considerable power, above all the right to act, to inaugurate; but it does not have—must never have —the power to control which resides in the ultimate sovereign, the people. Here, it should be noted, he blandly cleared away much of the verbal hocus-pocus he resorted to when defining the state. The mystifying oneness between the state and the people now fades as Blanc concentrates upon the true master. The people are the bearers of a new way of life, and their will and sovereignty therefore must triumph by means of the vote.

This ideal of democracy stirred within his imagination both a buoyant optimism and a somber caution. Full of trust, he championed giving the vote to all men, a proposal he called "universal suffrage." But in precise terms, he stood for adult male suffrage, since he observed among most women an outlook far too clericalist and conservative. Women, above all, must undergo a long period of democratic indoctrination before they might be trusted with so precious a responsibility as the right to decide on the destiny of men.[17] A typical radical, Blanc never took up with his usual gusto the feminist cause, not in the field of politics at any rate. A typical Frenchman, he reserved that field for men, however illogical this reservation left his arguments in defense of popular suffrage.

This defense is basically utilitarian. Like Jeremy Bentham he held that each man, aware of his particular needs, and also affected by the laws as a member of society, must have the right to choose the delegates who make these laws. He admitted, of course, the existence of "fictitious needs," and stressed that education would make each person aware of his "true needs." But he also intended granting some concessions to the "egotistical aspect" of man's nature which would find satisfaction in voting and in a system of proportional representation.

Proportionality results from a democratic system permitting every interest to be represented by a group of delegates whose size depends upon the number of like-minded voters. This form of representation stabilizes the government, for, unlike a monarchy which necessarily excludes certain interests while it favors others and thereby drives the neglected to revolt, a democracy admits all interests, giving each of them a proportional voice in the making of laws. Blanc categorically rejected any system based on the dictatorship of one, of a few, or of a class. "The truth is" he insisted, "a government must ally itself equally with the strong to be powerful and with the weak to be always just. We go further, and we assert that the mission of the central power is precisely to try at all times to re-establish the equilibrium between the strong and the weak." [18] "Democracy is like the sun, it shines for all." [19]

All forms of tyranny, then, must end. Tyranny, Blanc explained, comes from two directions: from above, from one man in power, or from below, from the people acting tyrannically through their representatives. The first is the tyranny of an individual; the second is the tyranny of the multitude or what Blanc called the "tyranny of law." The first is the lesser of two evils. The tyranny of an individual is less constant in its application and more easily abolished, whereas the tyranny of the multitude is translated into popular law and, like the multitude, is omnipresent and far more difficult to abolish.[20]

From his description of popular tyranny Blanc would seem most fearful of the people. But his faith in the rectitude of the masses was, before

1848, generally unclouded with doubts; indeed, he insisted that democratic government obviates popular oppression by engendering "social virtue." [21] This he saw as a reconciliation between egotism or love of self and socialism or love of mankind. Because no interests are excluded, a democratic regime creates an environment favorable to co-operation. Men learn to strike a balance between their own needs and the needs of others, and in fraternal harmony they seek to realize the goal of justice: the greatest happiness of the greatest number. There is, at this juncture, a shade of Cartesian mechanism in Blanc's approach. Manhood suffrage seems to function like a well-oiled machine, and Blanc, modifying the well-known phrase of Descartes, might have said: "I vote, therefore I am free." He even insisted that democracy obviates tyranny before man's social virtue comes into full bloom. Unlike a government based on limited suffrage a democratic regime is the expression of the voters; it is a *résumé* of all the interests composing society. Naturally the government will not become tyrannical because the people will not tyrannize itself.[22] Here, again, is Blanc the political mystic, and yet, the political Aquinas too, who must support his faith with rational argument.

To his dialectical chain, fastened with the scholastic subtlety he had learned in Rodez, Blanc added another link when he reasoned that the intimate bond between government and people can exist only if full political power becomes concentrated in a unicameral legislature. The balance of power between executive and legislature makes for conflict and inertia. To prove his argument, Blanc pointed contemptuously to the July Monarchy's legislative immobility which resulted from the struggle between king and chamber. Neither did he accept the argument that a ministry can serve as mediator between executive and legislature, an impossible role, he felt, in that neither branch trusts a ministry not entirely subservient to it. Since the natural rivalry between two chambers leads to the same inertia, Blanc saw no solution but the concentration of full power in a single chamber. In fact, he concluded that only a unicameral government with a weak executive, the radical's dream, may identify itself with society, may become the "résumé" of the popular will demanding reform.[23]

Louis Blanc did not doubt during the 1840's that the majority of Frenchmen desired some sort of political reform. At the same time he realized that this same majority was not ready for profound social reform. The peasants were backward; their ignorance kept them submissive to the clergy who hindered the inculcation of progressive ideas.[24] Nevertheless, Blanc believed that democratic notions were rapidly spreading throughout France. Inaugural action had been taken. Like the *philosophes* of the eighteenth century, whose writing Blanc regarded as the basic cause of the Revolution of 1789, the democrats and socialists of the nineteenth century were rapidly expanding their influence. The workers were avidly reading their books and rallying to their principles. Indeed, many ideas that would shape the future were being developed by the workers themselves. Change was in the air; democracy was popular and therefore inevitable.[25] This was particularly true in Paris, and Blanc was most concerned with public opinion in the capital. He did not want her to dominate France; nevertheless, he looked to her for the inspiration and leadership that would motivate the rest of the nation.

In this situation he brooked no opposition to the will of the majority. He vehemently attacked François Guizot's thesis that minorities must be safeguarded from domination by the greatest number. Blanc associated the majority with the "people," with democracy and freedom, while he identified the minority with the bourgeois oligarchy that controlled the constitutional monarchy. In his thinking, it was logical that minority rule must be tyrannical: the minority is compelled to silence the "public voice" in order to conserve its own power. The majority, then, once it assumes control, must not be restrained by the narrow egotism of the few; it must be free to act. Inspired by democratic ideals the majority personifies true liberation, acts in the name of the people, and cannot be oppressive.

Before 1848 Blanc made no distinction between the majority and the people, and in the final analysis, his ideal of popular sovereignty attributed full power to the majority. He therefore did not hesitate to stress that all laws emanating from the will of the greatest number required obedience; indeed, the popular origin of laws in a republic added to their strictly juridical force the awesome power of public sanction. Those who willfully and actively opposed the new regime must either emigrate to another country or suffer the legal consequences.[26]

Yet Blanc did not favor a popular despotism: he never advocated the abolition of the basic liberties of speech and thought, and he did not imagine that the majority would suppress them. As a guarantee against any such oppression he advocated a supreme court, vaguely similar to that of the United States, to decide on the constitutionality of legislation. Although he failed to state whether the court was to be appointed or elected, he did not feel that the role of the court would destroy unity in government. Its role was purely negative and offered no danger to political stability.[27] Blanc did not believe that the court or any small group of wealthy men could hinder the advance of socialism. In fact, he never paused long to weigh the possibility of minority opposition. Resistance to the popular will, he felt, would simply wither away, like the Old Regime in 1789, but without the ensuing dictatorship of the Terror.

CHAPTER FOUR

The Philosopher of Socialism

I

𝕰 L O U I S B L A N C convinced himself that it was possible to achieve broad reform without resorting to a Reign of Terror. One had merely to describe social evils to move men's hearts and then to explain the means of erasing such evils to inspire their reason. With this self-granted mandate in mind he put forth a socialist program intended to complement his political ideas. It appeared first in June and August, 1840, as a series of articles in his review, then in September as a book entitled, *Organisation du travail.* The book was just a slight expansion of the articles, and yet, it brought him greater fame than all his multivolume histories. The workers who printed the original edition of three thousand copies became so enthusiastic they carried its message into the streets, a sort of publicity that was most helpful. Within two weeks three thousand additional copies were needed.[1] By 1847 it was in its fifth edition, and doubled in size by the author's rebuttals to his critics.

The disapproval of other theorists did not constitute a danger to Blanc's publication, but the government did. Immediately the original copies appeared, the police took alarm. September was a month of workingmen's strikes and the agents of Louis Philippe must have regarded the book and the pickets as cause and effect. Although this linkage was without foundation, the ministry of interior accused Blanc of "exciting class hatred" and the ministry of justice alerted the public prosecutor. Only the prefect of police appeared relatively undisturbed; the book, he asserted erroneously, was a mere pastiche of Fourier. However, the bureaucratic machinery of the monarchic police state, once set into motion, could not be halted until the first edition was seized.[2] This act probably had the effect of publicizing the book and of augmenting its sale in subsequent editions. It certainly competed successfully with the subversive literature which issued forth in a reformist torrent during 1840.

II

Blanc began his little opus with an unrelenting attack on competition. The competitive system, he argued, makes it impossible to obtain the desirable balance between production and demand. However, the

distressing result of this inbalance is not overproduction but undercon-
sumption, a seemingly economic malady that is, in truth, a grave social
one affecting all classes. For while the struggle for jobs keeps labor's income low, the struggle for markets is gradually depressing the middle
class to the level of the proletariat. In order to lower costs aggressive
capitalists tend to concentrate and rationalize their industries, putting
smaller firms with higher costs at a disadvantage. In time, medium-sized
plants destroy small ones, only to be destroyed or absorbed in turn by
those few giant organizations able to win control of the market. Prices
then will mount while the bankrupt producers will sink.[3]

Blanc was not the first to observe this tendency. He was influenced by
Jean Simonde de Sismondi who explained it but hoped for return to
artisanal production. He was also influenced by Fourier who, warning
against economic individualism as a cause of the new industrial feudalism,
called for voluntary co-operation to combine harmoniously capital, talent,
and labor. This co-operation would bring about the sublimation of
man's passions which, Fourier argued, were of divine origin. Karl Marx,
a relative latecomer on the scene, saw the same defects of competition and
predicted increasing misery ending in revolution, a necessary step toward
a new order. Before Marx, Blanc also warned that a terrible revolution
awaited in the future; but unlike Marx, he hoped to prevent the final
catastrophe by inducing the bourgeoisie to favor reform. He therefore
appealed to their self-interest by sowing the seeds of alarm, by warning
of impending depression and the loss of cherished property. To substantiate his predictions he often drew up long lists of bankruptcies,
holding aloft the specter of poverty as the inevitable end for all but the
giant producers. There was, he wrote, "equality of suffering." [4]

Competition, Blanc argued, has also led to moral decay, for individualistic rivalry desiccates man's sense of public duty as well as his humanitarian instincts. Moral decay is not a future threat, but an established
fact. Its consequences are already patent. Crime has increased to mass
proportions and armies of assassins roam in search of victims. Ironically,
without the organization of work there is the organization of crime.
Another symptom is the crass materialism of the rich and the poor.
"Love of money has entered into the mores; the tyranny of money has
passed into institutions." [5] The result has been the withering of all affection, even filial affection. Among the rich, skeptical materialism transforms the son into a vulture-like creature awaiting the death of the father
and the reading of the will; the son exploits the parent. Among the
poor, however, the father exploits the son. Unable to earn a sufficient
wage, he is compelled to send his child, as well as his wife, to the factory.
His daughters, unable to marry wealth, will seek it in the dark corners
of the streets.

Such exploitation has been steadily undermining the family as an
institution, a result that can lead only to the decline of man. Destroy the

family, Blanc warned, and man will cease to be human, for "what best characterizes the human species, what most completely distinguishes it from the brute species is the family." [6] Unlike the Saint-Simonians and some other socialists who favored the abolition of the family, Blanc cautioned against even the precipitate destruction of inheritance rights. It was not that tampering with these rights would necessarily weaken family ties; on the contrary, he saw no natural relation between them. He reasoned, rather oddly, that they were absolutely distinct, the family being of divine creation, a "natural phenomenon" carrying "within itself its own reason for being," and inheritance being man-made, a mere "social convention" whose disappearance would in no way violate the laws of nature. In fact, as a mere social convention inheritance must disappear eventually when the rights to work and to education would be universally put in force. Consequently there is no need to rush, to change so abruptly that a temporary reaction results. A more tactful method, he concluded hopefully, would be the termination of inheritance in the collateral line of each family.

A corollary to his defense of the family was his championing of the rights of women. Undoubtedly he was led into the feminist movement by his admiration for George Sand and Flora Tristan; however, unlike Sand, Mérimée, Vigny, Hugo, and Sainte-Beuve, he refused to exalt adultery. Tolerant and yet profoundly moral, Blanc took part in the movement, not to free women from the dictate of the seventh commandment, but to decry those laws and mores which drove them to violate it. He was particularly vehement in his condemnation of the marriage of convenience whereby greedy fathers literally sold their young daughters to aged wealth. These victims, he argued, unable to free themselves, yet bored and frustrated, were more easily tempted by illicit passions whose attractions soothed their worried consciences. The first error of these marriages is made worse by the impossibility of divorce: "failure to consecrate divorce has legalized adultery." The deep sense of satisfaction that women crave, and which is their destiny, can be found only in the "circle of the domestic hearth." "A word," he sang on, "sums up all the poetry of their existence: LOVE! A word expresses all their duties: FAMILY!" [7] But the real defense of the family lay ultimately in the hands of men who must create a society based on love rather than distrust, on co-operation rather than competition. Then feelings of kinship would sink deeper roots, growing like natural, vigorous sentiments, making their contribution to a new way of life.

This new way of life could not come about at once. As Blanc looked back over the centuries, studying the brutalities and aggressions men committed against one another, he consoled himself that "every revolution is useful, . . . in that it absorbs a baneful eventuality. . . . In the decrees of God, good would be, alas, only the exhaustion of evil." [8] Each abortive upheaval of the past, then, was a testing of a solution that failed, but not wholly. Each trial eliminated an error, and from the cruel interplay of revolution and reaction would laboriously emerge the just solution. Blanc's historical studies aroused within him a sense of travail, of bewilderment, and a fear of those too simple formulas that lure men into fatal action. Hence his warning: "The problem is obscure. It is terrible. We must approach it with fear and modesty. No one person can resolve it, . . . Let us seek truth with slowness, with prudence, with diffidence even; this is best." [9] And yet he also displayed impatience common to the visionary reformer and advised against "restraining the temerities of the mind," as well as against the fatalistic acceptance of so much social injustice, which, after all, resulted from an "error so easy to correct." [10]

III

Louis Blanc saw in cheap credit a powerful instrument for effecting change. Here too, he had predecessors. He revealed an open admiration for John Law, arguing that the unfortunate financier had been the first to recognize that the state must become the source of credit.[11] Saint-Simon and his disciples had the greatest influence on Blanc in this respect, arguing that cheap credit was the very life blood of a progressive economy, and that the state was to be the source of all credit. And Pierre Joseph Proudhon saw in cheap credit the means of preserving petty capitalism. It was Constantin Pecqueur and Blanc, however, who were the first to see in it the means of abolishing capitalism.

Blanc constantly warned against the perils of private credit. He accused the financial oligarchy of stifling industrial expansion, and argued that everyone will benefit when the state enters the lending trade by setting up an official money market. It will then force downward the high cost of capital in private banks, and before too long these banks will peacefully disappear as their reason for being ceases to exist. The government, as the source of credit, will obtain large sums of money more quickly by borrowing than by taxing. To be sure, Blanc favored a heavy tax on the rich, as well as high tariffs, but he never publicly called for a comprehensive extension of taxes. In fact, he opposed amortizing the public debt precisely because such a step would compel the government to resort to taxes. "This would mean," he argued, "taking money from those who want to keep it in order to give it to those who do not ask for it; this would mean taking from agriculture, industry, and general production which uses in a fecund manner the capital that those for whom it is destined will squander in unproductive consumption." [12] He was not much concerned with a mere reform of taxes or a displacement of their burden; his panacea was credit. Opposed to violent expropriation, he wanted capitalists to continue investing in government bonds; hence, the source of state capital is low-interest borrowing, not really taxation.[13] Ironically enough, the

rentier class is to help destroy the institutions which guarantee its existence.

If the *rentier* class decides to transfer its capital from the state to industry, it will soon find this source of return closed off. However, Blanc cautioned, this closing off must not be brought about too quickly by the
willful and sudden destruction of private industry which, for the sake of
justice and expediency, may be allowed to survive for a time. He even
considered seriously the scheme of setting up transitional workshops,
half capitalist, with a system of private investment, and half socialist, with
a co-operative organization. Hoping to win over persons with surplus
capital and humane hearts, he urged, during 1847, the founding of an independent committee to seek out anyone desirous of placing money in
these precursory workshops.[14]

Here is Blanc the Utopian in lock step with dreamers like Fourier,
who also wanted model associations, and who looked to beneficent capitalists to set them up. Most early nineteenth-century reformers held to the
belief that model communities, where everyone lived happily ever after,
would persuade men to discard the old economic systems in order to imitate the new. But unlike Etienne Cabet, Blanc never desired to isolate
his ideal workshop which must both produce for a large market, and compete against private industry within the market. He also differed from
Fourier in insisting that the investors who perform no work are not to
share in the profits. Investors, being lenders rather than shareholders,
should receive only a fixed interest, nothing more. When the shops are
able to finance themselves, they must amortize these loans, so that the increasing socialization of industry will close the outlets for private investment, thus bringing about the gradual fading away of capitalism. Expanding socialization, of course, cannot result from mere expediency, and
Blanc always argued that real changes must await the founding of a republic. It is state, not private, credit which he called *crédit véritable,*
and which he believed to be the only effective means of transferring the
"instruments of work from the hands of those who possess them without
using them, to the hands of those who know how to use them and do
not possess them." [15] The latter were Blanc's economic dependents, the
people. Soon the capitalist class, like the landed nobility, will cease to
exist. It will be absorbed "fraternally" by the people, a process resulting
in a classless society in which everyone works.

IV

Work, for Louis Blanc, is more than mere labor or physical exertion, it
is an integral part of man's experience. Unlike Guizot, he did not see in it
a restraint upon man's passions; on the contrary, it is a creative outlet for
human energy and, properly organized, an aid in man's fullest develop-

ment. Blanc was a firm advocate of the right to work, and for him, this right meant work appropriate to one's temperament and aptitudes. Gregarious by nature, men will work happily together, each doing that for which he is best fitted. Work will become a pleasure. It seems drudgery in a capitalist society because skills are subordinated to the hazards of circumstance, and the freedom to choose a profession, so vaunted by the liberals, is a mere abstraction in the experience of the poor. Too often a man of genius, born in poverty, is compelled to labor twelve hours a day fashioning pin heads. Consequently, one of the major goals of socialism is to transform this abstract right into a real liberty, the "liberty of vocation." This necessitates universal, gratuitous education, with all children up to a certain age exposed to a common program, after which they are to study in those professions for which their temperament and ability fit them.[16] In this fashion, equality of opportunity will engender liberty of opportunity, which all men will continue to enjoy after leaving school and entering the social workshops.

V

In Blanc's system the social workshop is far more than a unit for production, a mere assembly of men to share in common labor; it is, rather, the economic equivalent of the local administrative unit, serving the same purpose, that is, as the place where men come together to learn how to live fraternally, as well as how to produce.

There is some uncertainty as to whether or not Blanc favored voluntary or forced association. Louis Garnier-Pagès asserted that in several meetings at the home of Alexandre Marie during 1847 he defended "obligatory" association. Blanc's chief opponents in the debates were Claude-Anthime Corbon of the *Atelier* and Ledru-Rollin of the *Réforme* who, wrote Garnier-Pagès, defended "voluntary" association.[17] After the publication of this assertion, Blanc specifically denied that he had ever taken the stand attributed to him.[18] At any rate, he never used the term *association forcée*. He called, rather, for volunteers of proven morality and probity to organize the first experimental workshops. These early establishments were to be "rigorously circumscribed" in number and confined to industries of national importance such as textiles, metallurgy, and printing. Before long, however, the whole national economy would become socialized, and the question of free or forced association become meaningless as the alternatives disappeared.

Expansion will result from competition between privately and fraternally organized industries. This competition will not be ruthless but "saintly," with the government serving as a sort of referee to keep the struggle clean and aboveboard. Transformation must be orderly and gradual. However, Blanc did not envisage a very long period of transition, for the social workshops will have over their adversaries the ad-vantages resulting from communal living and a mode of organization which stimulates all workers to produce quickly and well. After a relatively short resistance, capitalists and workers will flock to join state-supported co-operatives. Blanc passed over in silence the fate of independent co-operatives which might resist absorption into his pattern of socialism; that is, they must disappear, but he did not explain in what manner.

He applied the term workshop (*atelier*) to both local and national establishments. The local establishment will be a sort of cell composed preferably of men of the same profession, although, on occasion, diverse professions may be included. During the first year of each shop's existence the state appoints and regulates its administrative hierarchy. Afterward, when the workers come to know one another, the hierarchy is to be chosen in shop-wide elections, because the workers, well qualified to choose good deputies for a national assembly, will also prove their capacity for selecting capable directors. Frequent personal contact will offer them the occasions for becoming acquainted with one another's capacities, and their own interest will urge them to vote wisely. The elective principle, in the shop as in the government, will produce a hierarchy of ability, and banish forever the inefficiency resulting from the privileges of birth and inheritance.[19]

Elected managers will oversee both the running of each association and the distribution of income. If there are private investors their interest payments will form part of the budget; if the state has financed the enterprise it too must be reimbursed, so that it can eventually amortize its bonds. At the end of each year, Blanc went on, the net profits will constitute a capital belonging to the workers collectively, not to each individually, a scheme that resembles P.-J.-B. Buchez's notion of an "inalienable capital." This sum is to be divided into several parts: one which the workers share equally, another which will provide for sickness, accident and old-age pensions, and another destined to finance new equipment and expansion. Again like Buchez, Blanc proposed self-financing associations; however, the author of *Organisation du travail* went considerably beyond Buchez in his ultimate goal, having planned for a central workshop in each industry and a national system of interrelationships binding all industries. The shops, then, would enjoy limited autonomy, not complete independence. Blanc's objective here was to eliminate competition among them, hence his insistence that they owed aid to one another when in distress.

Some regulation is necessary, in his opinion, because of the need to adjust more accurately production to demand. The consolidation of industry-wide central workshops is desirable as a means of achieving this end. What control exists, then, will be ultimately vested in an economic hierarchy; however, the hierarchy must not interfere excessively in each local workshop which, like the administrative commune, needs to defend its autonomy. Central organizations must limit themselves to laying down general principles and policies; local units will apply these in accordance with local needs. The same system holds good for commerce, with each industry providing for its own stores and warehouses.[20]

Although influenced by the centralist ideals of Saint-Simon, Blanc was not a "disguised Saint-Simonian." [21] His ideal economic structure, like his political structure, was clearly pyramidal, but loosely centralized and firmly democratic. He warned that centralized control of every detail of production, which the Saint-Simonians approved, would lead to inefficiency, weighty bureaucracy, and lethargic output. It would also increase the possibility of tyranny, with the state becoming the "pope of industry." [22] Blanc, on the contrary, did not want the state to become even the proprietor of industry, hence his demand that workshops amortize their debts to the official bank as quickly as possible.

Unfortunately, he never discussed the relation between the political and the economic hierarchies. It seems fairly definite, however, that he invested greater importance in the legislature chosen on the basis of electoral districts than in the central workshops chosen by the local units. It is doubtful, then, that he envisioned a corporate state; he certainly never wrote in favor of one. He preferred, rather, two hierarchies with specific functions, with the legislature enjoying ultimate control. When he spoke of the state's being immortal, he was thinking of the political state. It is curious, however, that while he firmly opposed a bicameral legislature, he consciously proposed a bicameral hierarchy, and the objections he raised against the former could serve equally well against the latter. Might not the central workshops, chosen by the same voters who elected the legislature, challenge the authority of this latter body? Who is to mediate here? The supreme court seems useless, and there is no strong executive. Perhaps Blanc would have argued that as society progressed, the role of central agencies, whether political or economic, would diminish to the point where such conflicts became meaningless. For all his supposed étatisme, he clearly displayed the petty bourgeois distrust of an omnipotent political agency, and dreamed of a society in which centralized powers interfered as little as possible in local affairs, serving rather as symbols of unity and planners of purely national policy.

Unfortunately, Blanc never convinced the orthodox radicals, the moderate republicans, and the co-operators of the Atelier that he was not an étatiste in the clothing of an autonomist. His failure to do so resulted perhaps from their different attitude toward competition. For Buchez, moderate competition is a stimulant, although he does not explain how it might be kept moderate. For Blanc, it cannot be kept moderate, save by official intervention during the change from capitalism to socialism, after which such intervention diminishes. A mixed economy, as desired by the Atelier, is merely a perpetuation of what should be a transition, and a perpetuation of necessary state control. Therefore, the very principle of competition must vanish, for to retain it even among co-operatives will eventually bring about the same ruthless rivalry among them as among private concerns, and the same state of injustice. Some associations will prosper, others will not. Business will be concentrated in an increasingly smaller number of shops at the expense of the rest, and in time there will emerge two new classes: a bourgeoisie of workers and a proletariat of workers, two new classes whose mutual animosities will destroy all fraternal spirit. The only means of avoiding this catastrophe is to make it incumbent upon the workshops to aid one another and abolish, in the early phase of the revolution, the practice of competition, incompatible as it is with real fraternity. "The grafting of association on to competition," Blanc warned, "is a poor idea, like replacing eunuchs by hermaphrodites. Association constitutes progress only on the condition of being universal." [23]

VI

The diffusion of the spirit of fraternity, he reasoned, requires substituting the idea of social duty for that of personal self-interest, the practice of mutual aid for that of general rivalry. Substitution here means complete change, since there exists, he stressed, no permanent middle way, no possibility of durable compromise between these opposites.[24] Having taken this dogmatic stand, Blanc was inevitably forced into the corner of compromise. As his concept of "social virtue" was intended to balance the two extremes of human nature in the field of politics, a similar proposal called "fraternal emulation" was intended now to make adjustments in the field of social organization.

In reality, "fraternal emulation" allowed for competition, not among the workshops, but within each shop. Blanc was forced to accept modified rivalry because he rightly perceived that men are not equal in talent, initiative, and inclination. He did not conclude from this that men are unequally good. He was content to emphasize that these inequalities are not harmful; on the contrary, they are necessary to the proper functioning of society. "What is society," he asked, "if not a mutual exchange of services founded on diversity of forces, aptitudes, needs and tastes?" Men therefore cannot live isolated or self-sufficient lives. "Nature created men unequal precisely because she made men social." [25] There must, then, be rivalry to do good; men of different tastes and abilities must compete to produce more, not so that each may enrich himself, but so that each may contribute toward improving the condition of all men. This is "fraternal emulation." Louis Blanc admitted that even a socially educated man needs some stimulus and the answer to the problem of inducement he found in his old master Mably, and in a man who influenced him more than he ever admitted, Napoleon I. Mably had written of non-pecuniary distinctions. Reasoning along similar lines, and recalling Napoleon's

Legion of Honor, Blanc conceived of a Legion of Honor of Work. No longer the activities of war but those of industry would elevate natural leaders to heroic action. Those with great capacities would be stimulated to achievement by a cross and the honor of having their busts placed in a Pantheon of Labor. What Blanc proposed was a kind of Stakhanovitism; but given his idealization of the French character, glory rather than money was to furnish the motivation.

Yet, the problem of material recompense could not be waved away and gave him considerable difficulty until he hit upon the idea of "proportional" equality. This notion was the end result of a rather long evolution of arguments which began in 1834 when he first broached the problem of equality. His early idea was expressed in a vague formula: "equality of all interests in the inequality of all positions." [26] Not until 1837 did he become more explicit when he wrote of the "organization of work, with a view to equality, that is, scientific fixing of salaries, and certitude of job or bread given to the worker; the admission of all to the benefits of credit by the possibility given to all of making economies and of reaping the fruits of an honest and wise life." [27] It is apparent that his idea of equality now contained definite economic and social substance. Two years later, in the first issue of his *Revue du progrès,* Blanc was concerned even more specifically with the rewards of work, and wrote of the "regular distribution of the fruits of common labor among those who have contributed to it, and according to the contribution of each." In this same issue he called for "equitable distribution between capitalists and manual workers." [28] During the summer of 1839 his ideas on equality had hardly gone beyond those of the Jacobins. In June of that year he explained: "Nothing is more opposed than our opinions to those ideas of the agrarian law, the abolition of property, dreams of some wounded souls or of some delirious minds." He continued, writing in capitals: "I consider whoever would destroy property in France as a counter-revolutionary. . . . Equality of fortune is a chimera without doubt, but what is not a chimera, what God wished, what constitutes the real progress of societies, is the equality of rights and of the means of development in the inequality of conditions and of fortune, and this equality is neither less equitable, nor less precious than equality before the law." [29] In 1840, when he first published his famous brochure, his idea of equality had a definite Saint-Simonian flavor. He did not yet call for the abolition of salaries, nor their equalization. Rather, he wanted them "graduated according to the hierarchy of functions." [30] He did, however, insist that even the lowest wage must suffice for a worker's needs, and that all the active members of each shop were to receive equal shares out of a fixed portion of the net profits. Not until the 1847 edition of his work did he explicitly demand equal salaries. [31] The next year he abandoned this plan.

Because of these shifts, some writers have felt that Blanc was inconsistent. It is possible that he was more hesitant than inconsistent. In 1840 he explained: "It is not as unjust that we condemn, for the present, equality in salary, but as striking too sudden a blow at habitudes that only education, according to us, will have the power to change. The equality that we admit in the distribution of profits is a sufficiently discreet transition between what is and what ought to be." [32] Against his equalitarian critics, he leveled the charge of impracticality; even the venerable Robert Owen was gently chided for not being a "practical reformer when he demanded the distribution of the fruits of labor according to needs, in a society where they are not yet founded on services." [33] There was, then, a marked strain of opportunism in both the writings and action of Louis Blanc, which perhaps explains his defense of property in 1839. Undoubtedly during that year he looked forward, perhaps vaguely as yet, to the eventual disappearance of private ownership, but reasoned that an immoderate and hasty demand would terrify the petty bourgeois whose support he solicited. Extreme claims, as impolitic as violent action, only aided the reactionary by alienating the undecided, a consequence Blanc seriously wished to avoid around 1840. This was the year of reinvigorated reform movements whose success, he realized, depended on the support of everyone opposed to Louis Philippe's personal rule.

Yet he did not water his socialism to the extent of destroying its essentially collectivist nature. Nor did he let up in his attacks upon capitalism or in his defense of fraternity, and in his *Histoire de dix ans,* written during the early 1840's, he condemned as unjust the watchword of the Saint-Simonians: "From each according to capacity; to each according to work." [34] Beneath a panoply of moderation, he steadily moved toward a more equalitarian position, a progress which his socialist critics, who accused him of retaining the salary system, seem not to have noticed. What he was cautiously seeking was a principle of remuneration compatible with his notion of fraternal emulation. The Saint-Simonian motto, which he accepted in the first edition of the *Organisation du travail,* already appeared unjust to him. In fact, in the same edition of his famous book, as well as in his review, he hinted at his ultimate goal when he wrote: "A day shall come when it will be recognized that he who has received greater force and greater intelligence from God owes more to his fellow men. Then it will behove the genius, and that is worthy of him, to declare his legitimate authority, not by the importance of the tribute that he will levy on society, but by the grandeur of the services he will render. For it is not in the inequality of remuneration that the inequality of aptitudes should end: it is in the inequality of duties." [35]

But not until 1848 when he was a member of the Provisional Government and president of the Luxembourg Commission on labor did Blanc decide the time was at hand to proclaim his revolutionary scheme. True equality, he explained then, is not "absolute" but "proportional." That is, it is proportional between man's needs and faculties. "By his needs, man is passive, by his faculties he is active. By his needs he calls his fellow men to his succor; by his faculties, he puts himself at the service of his fellow men. Needs are the indication that God gives to society. So, more is due to him who has the greatest needs, and it is permissible to demand more from him who has the greatest faculties." [36] Blanc also found the aphoristic formula to express the notion of proportional equality: "Let each produce according to his aptitudes and his force; let each consume according to his need." [37] He undoubtedly borrowed the expression from Morelly. Marx, who used the same watchword, probably borrowed it from the same source. For all three reformers it meant the end of salaries. Blanc was quite explicit when he wrote: "The truth is that the wage-earning system is a regime to be completely destroyed." [38] It must give way to fraternal emulation and proportional equality, whose happy union would produce a system of perfect justice. But even in the midst of the revolutionary movement, speaking to the Luxembourg Commission, Blanc warned that the moment had not yet arrived to apply this formula. It was still impossible to measure man's faculties and needs, a perverse civilization having obscured the laws of nature by substituting privilege for capacity in rulership, and depraved tastes and false desires for true needs in society.[39] The triumph of justice presupposed a new system of education.

VII

Louis Blanc never wavered in his conviction that the well-being of a society ultimately depends on its system of education, and as a socialist he stood firmly in favor of a system emphasizing social unity. He never wanted to crush those traits which distinguish each person, lest there prevail an intellectual homogeneity fatal to initiative, a violation of proportional equality. But he did want a system that would involve the genius in society. The chief failing of pedagogy, he warned, has been its unconcern with preparing men to live fraternally; methods and subject matter have exaggerated individualism. Therefore Blanc's ideal system would be a highly centralized one. "In the matter of education," he affirmed with great Jacobin faith, "centralization cannot be too strong. To permit, in a country torn by factions, the absurd competition of private schools, is to inoculate in new generations the venom of civil discord, it is to give the rival parties the means of continuing and perpetuating themselves in the midst of a growing confusion of opinions and of principles, it is to sow chaos." [40]

Of course, centralization meant state control, and if the political theorist sought to modify his *étatisme* by defending certain local rights, the educational theorist showed himself an unmitigated exponent of all-powerful government. The schools, under the scrutiny of an argus-eyed ministry, would adopt a common program emphasizing militant patriotism along with fraternity, for the coming generations must love not only the "useful" and the "beautiful," but above all, *la patrie.*

This goal required a tight censorship of all textbooks to eliminate those attacking the basic premises on which the new society rested. "Let the people," Blanc urged, "learn how to read in good books, let them be taught that what is useful to all is most honorable; . . . that nothing is worthy of scorn save what is of a nature to corrupt souls, to pour in them the poison of pride, to estrange them from the practice of fraternity, to inoculate them with egoism." [41] In his system education existed less to stimulate critical minds than to indoctrinate future citizens. These, broken of the habit of asking too many questions, and willingly elevating the principle of fraternity above criticism, would debate within the framework of the accepted regime. He never claimed the need to censor all reading matter, and in spite of his narrow vision, he acted most energetically in 1848 to protect freedom of the press. His serene opinion was that properly educated students, after leaving school, would simply not turn to "bad" books, and these would cease to appear. The future society, he argued, would not be intolerant; intolerance does not exist where all men voluntarily favor social unity based on a universal ideal.

Attaching this importance to education, Blanc naturally demanded a gratuitous and obligatory system, with strict uniformity of subject matter at the primary level to insure equality. He also favored improved standards for teachers whose profession he placed among the more exalted pursuits, such as journalism; it too, is a "sublime priesthood." The teacher is to become a lay missionary, part of the intellectual élite, serving as a "second father" to the pupils in his charge and replacing the priest as the bearer of a new dispensation.

VIII

Blanc looked upon religion as a spiritual force natural to men and necessary for the attainment of socialist aims. Hand in hand with education, it must prepare man for a happy life in this, the secular world. Blanc was not vitally concerned with the world beyond, with the supernatural. Only once, in 1877, after the death of his wife, did he even mention his belief in life after death, and he expressed it briefly then in a private letter to a friend. [42] And yet, like most of the visionary reformers of his period, he was religious in temperament, and found in the Bible the origins of the principle of fraternity. Once he asked: "What is socialism?" and then answered like a catechist, "It is the Bible in action." Curiously enough, he had first learned to read the Scriptures under the guidance of the clerics at Rodez, a beginning which did not prevent him from rejecting Catholicism during the 1830's, or from becoming fixed in an outlook strongly anti-clerical. He found incompatible with social progress the church's fatalism, its glorification of poverty, and its doctrine of "meritorious suffering" which it taught to those it would not liberate.[43] On the other hand, he was just as critical of paganism which glorified brute force, and of atheism, which exalted the individual. Happily, he did not follow Rousseau to the extent of calling for the execution of non-believers, but orthodox theists, like skeptics, would certainly find no comfort in his social regime.

His god is that of Rousseau, a pantheistic deity, defined as "the universality of creatures." Existing in all beings, he binds them intimately into a vast fraternity and his sublime doctrine teaches love, unity, and justice. "Pantheism," Blanc explained, "is the religious aspect of human solidarity." [44] It was in people, then, not in material things, that he found the proof of God. God exists in human sentiment, and this sentiment is the source of inspiration which brings men together and strengthens them in their service to justice. Indeed, religious feeling is the well-spring of all poetry, of all grandeur. Blanc, as a religious thinker, placed feeling high above reason, seeing in the latter the source of skepticism that atomized humanity. At times he came close to asserting that the man who thinks is depraved. And yet, he generally struck in his philosophy a balance between faith and reason.

Following Saint-Simon, he also sought to create a new Christianity stressing equally man's spiritual and physical needs. Too great emphasis on the spirit, he cautioned, leads to the degradation of the flesh, and so weakens the desire for social reform; while too great emphasis on the flesh gives rise to vile hedonism and to materialistic determinism which destroy man's freedom and sense of responsibility. The desire for this sublime balance suggests why Blanc, although a moralist, was not Puritanical. Unlike Rousseau, he was not a narrow-minded Genevan, or a bigoted peasant. He was a Parisian who enjoyed the good life in both the spiritual and physical sense, and who saw no basic contradiction between the two.

Yet there was an authoritarian streak forming part of his psychological make-up, and he sounded a sinister note when he insisted that man could and should arrive at absolutes.[45] Blanc insisted that the absolute validity of fraternity is a sacredly revealed truth and that any hypothesis to the contrary is heresy. His marked dislike for dissent and his exaggerated desire for solidarity led him to envision a society in which non-conformity becomes anathema. His educational system is designed to blot it out, so is his religious system; therefore the role of his priests is identical to that of his teachers. Like Rousseau, he desired a civic religion to which everyone would voluntarily belong, and like that of Saint-Simon, his priesthood would consist of intellectuals, artists, scientists, and industrial leaders. These men are to form a "sacerdotal corps" whose mission is the kindling of the sacred fire of common beliefs. They will be elected, but completely subordinate to the state, for "the state must direct the moral interests of society just as it directs the material interests of society. If it declares itself indifferent, it abdicates." [46]

The keynote of Blanc's system is not only unity but also considerable uniformity. He was a prefiguration of the rabid patriot and anticlerical of the Third Republic. Would not Combes carry out with ruthlessness certain of the policies he proposed? But long before the ex-seminarian attacked the church, radicalism adjusted its conscience to the sacrifice of some of the Rights of Man in the interest of social solidarity. This tendency is discernible also in Blanc's literary views.

IX

His ideal in literature was an amalgam of classical vigor and romantic sentimentality. He considered the classical form an effective one for conveying an idea, for teaching a lesson in social morality. However, in order for literature to leave a strong impression it must appeal to the heart as well as to the mind, a dual strength that would produce a style suitable for "useful" literature. The notion of "useful," that is, didactic art is one of the oldest in French literary tradition, and Blanc, immersed in that tradition, repudiated the concept of art for art's sake. Soon he was scolding the romantics, not because he opposed sentiment, but because he could not stomach their "sweet moan" which, in his opinion, was the rhymed emanation of egoism, a regard only for self. Romanticism, he declared, is the literary facet of individualism for its voice is an unpleasant dissonance of particular men. In contrast, he desired a more harmonious, moral, and fecund style, a literature of the people. Men of letters must adapt themselves to the rise of the lower classes and take their place in the struggle to edify them. "Woe betide the poet," he warned, "who does not understand that love of men is the most noble, the most virile of inspirations! Woe betide the poet who does not learn from the study of the past and meditations on the future that the old world has had its literature, and that the new world must have its own!" [47] The most impressive medium for carrying out this function is the theater. In consequence he insisted upon state control of the theater and censorship exercised by an elected, temporary, and responsible jury that would be "truly national." [48] Discussing books, however, he spoke out forcibly for intellectual freedom, and emphasized the all-important didactic role of the writer who "must rise above the prejudices of men, and have the courage to displease them in order to be useful to them." [49]

This courage required not only a most exalted sense of mission but also considerable independence, and it was to provide writers with independent means that Blanc proposed the organization of literature. His aim was the abolition of the traditional rights of authorship in order to destroy the poison of literary commercialism. The first step toward this goal is the establishment of a "social publishing house" similar to the social workshop, and dependent on the state without being enslaved to it. A select committee of enlightened, unpaid experts will choose the manuscripts to be printed from among those writers, beginners in particular, who desire to elevate rather than degrade the public. All printing costs will be met by the house, and all member-authors will share in the profits, but prices must remain under state control and be kept low so that good books can reach the widest possible audience. In exchange for their authorship rights, members will enjoy the exclusive privilege of competing for "national recompenses," the monetary awards drawn from the government's budget and granted by a national committee of experts in various fields to thinkers who have "best served the country." [50] Eventually, the most gifted authors will be drawn toward social publishing houses, literature will cease to be a source of loot, and private publishing houses will be put out of business by "saintly" competition.

There is no doubt that Blanc's ambition was to have a completely socialized society: collective ownership, communal living, unity in outlook. He did not desire to impose his new system by force; he wanted no reign of terror to eliminate his opponents (he even favored the abolition of capital punishment for political crimes), and no brutal dictatorship of a class. He imagined that his aim might be achieved peacefully, persuasively, democratically, and yet, despite all his good intentions, his system makes no provision for the existence of a minority championing a principle other than democratic socialism. He expected, he desired free discussion, provided it remains within the framework of the accepted principle. The basic characteristics of his future society are both uniformity and conformity.

X

When the liberals denounced him as the enemy of freedom, Blanc in turn accused the capitalist system of having created a worse tyranny: impersonal economic authority. "It is a mysterious tyranny," he explained, "which is everywhere and shows itself nowhere, which closes around the poor man, crushes him, stifles him, without letting him see whence comes the evil against which he struggles miserably and succumbs." [51] He saw clearly the menacingly impersonal character of industry, and he realized that machines contributed to this character. However, he did not, like Simonde de Sismondi, urge a reaction against them, because he felt that not machines as such, but capitalistic ownership of them, was at fault. Having been too much influenced by Saint-Simon to repudiate science and its application to manufacturing, he could sympathize with suffering craftsmen but not with Luddite riots. What he taught was not hatred or even distrust of machines, but the reorganization of work in order to use them as instruments of liberation from drudgery. Machines, he wrote enthusiastically, are labor-saving devices, making possible greater production, higher living standards, and yet, shorter hours. With a reduced work-day the division of labor, necessitated by machines, will not be oppressive. For just as "liberty of profession" is a system to spare the genius the monotony of mechanized production, the proper use of machines is a means of granting the less gifted more leisure to develop their mental capacities. Under socialism, mechanization will *"benefit everyone."* [52]

In this attitude he did not resemble his contemporaries, William Godwin, Buchez, Fourier, and Cabet, who in varying degrees accepted the belief that men were destined to scarcity and therefore would have sufficient food, clothing, and tools, not because they produced more, but because they lived simply and without ostentation. Louis Blanc, on the contrary, displayed the entrepreneurial spirit: men would have more by producing more and sharing their produce equitably. Once, in 1849, he wrote lyrically of a happy future in which produce would be as plentiful as air. In that economic paradise men would consume as they breathed, according to their needs.

XI

Concentration, enlargement, mechanization were also Blanc's answer for agriculture, but prior to 1848 he had very little to say about the organization of work on the farm. Here too, he distinguished himself from Fourier in particular, whose phalange was primarily an association to produce succulent food and fragrant roses. Recognizing the entrenched conservatism of peasants and the powerful influence of priests in rural regions, Blanc suggested postponing the socialization of land until after the movement was well under way in industry. He believed that since 1789 France had become an industrial nation and that the organization of industrial production should come first.[53] This belief did not induce him to sacrifice agriculture to industry, a tendency already apparent in England and against which he warned: "The commerce of a people cannot remain prosperous for long unless it rests on a solid base, and . . . this solid base is agriculture." [54] Industry and farming must complement rather than weaken each other. As in industry, he desired in agriculture the organization of large co-operatives, because individual exploitation and small-holdings discourage efficient utilization of the land and retard economic growth. Therefore, Blanc advised, let the state abolish succession in the collateral line and transfer uninherited land to the communes. This procedure will make possible the scientific development of large public estates, raise living standards, encourage farming, prepare the raw materials industry needs, and enhance the prestige of the provinces. Peasants will happily remain on the land; provincial genius will find an outlet at home and cease flocking to overcrowded Paris which already dominates France in an unhealthy fashion.[55]

It is perhaps in his desire to benefit everyone that Blanc may rightly be classed as a Utopian. Thus far he has seemed to be a peaceful one, a man of gentle, humanitarian manner, seeking to persuade, and distrustful of violent revolution. This view, however, does not encompass the whole man. Intertwined with his reformist beliefs was a patriotism so belligerent in it scope and form that it is difficult to realize that both his socialism and nationalism emerged from the same mind.

CHAPTER FIVE

The Patriot

I

𝓥 AS A SOCIALIST Blanc was in advance of his generation; as a patriot, fully conscious of his country's interests, he was in lock step with the French nationalists of his day. In their memory historic France had not only enjoyed intellectual hegemony but also military grandeur. They fused idea and sword, the two instruments that were supposed to bring glory to the motherland and liberty to Europe. These two objectives went easily, if illogically, together for it was the republicans, ardent patriots, and paladins of freedom who took up the battle cry of the Jacobins: war against tyranny! This ideal of a crusade attained its most violent expression during 1830 and the two decades following. In consequence, international projects designed by the liberal economists and the socialists, François Vidal, Constantin Pecqueur, Victor Considérant and Charles Fourier, made little appeal to these jingoists.[1]

During the July Monarchy Blanc formed a connecting link between pacifistic socialism and militant radicalism, and his nationalism assumed two distinct yet related forms: on the one hand, he extolled France as the liberator of Europe and the leader in its socialization, while on the other hand, he called upon her to conquer a Mediterranean empire. The one ambition inevitably gave rise to the other.

II

Louis Blanc began his career as a journalist with strong pronouncements in favor of universal fraternity. The feeling of nationality, he wrote, was nothing more than the egoism of peoples. Like the liberal economists he desired as an antidote to national hostilities a universal division of labor, with each country producing its specialties for the free world market.[2] However, he soon arrived at the conclusion that the two breeders of war, monarchy and competition, had first to be abolished before France and all humanity would benefit from peaceful free trade. The task of destroying them he assigned to his motherland and his strong patriotic sentiments derived from his belief that France was more than worthy and capable of such a humanitarian mission.

His faith in France resulted from his belief that the French nationality was unique. In the course of history Frenchmen had acquired superior traits which fitted them for world leadership. Among their dominant characteristics were their progressiveness, their willingness and ability to ascend to higher levels in all fields, and their cosmopolitanism. France, Blanc insisted, was the most European of all countries and the only nation which might extend her influence abroad without arousing the xenophobia of her neighbors.[3] France's mission was further facilitated by the fact that she was governed from the "capital of civilization," for Paris was, he affirmed, the most European city: "there is not a people which, at the end of a certain number of years, has not made a sojourn within her walls, so that combining time and space, one might nearly say that the world is contained in Paris." [4] This mystical veneration of Paris was most popular among the radicals. Paris, the *Ville-Lumière,* was the democratic volcano that would erupt, setting the tidal waves of freedom rolling ever outward, sweeping over thrones and surging up the people from the lower depths. This fervor underscored another French trait: a sense of devotion and an eager willingness to share progress with all men. France was a "petulant nation, adventurous, expansive, quick to spread abroad, weakly attached to her traditions, prodigious of herself, of her blood as of her treasures, of her ideas as of her blood, . . . hardy enough to take the initiative in all great things, intelligent enough to exercise it, likable enough, finally, to found her triumph on voluntary obedience and sympathy acquired without effort." [5] Happily there was no chance that this vitality might die out. "There are societies, France for example, which, endowed with a facile genius, with a supple nature, carry within themselves the faculty of rejuvenating themselves, and if one may speak thus, of living several lives." [6] She continued in an age of egoism and love of wealth to represent the principle of devotion to worthy causes, in particular the cause of *le peuple.*

Blanc conceived of the French nation as *le peuple* inspired and armed. Clearly excluded from the sacred group were the upper bourgeois, and while he did not call for class warfare, he condemned them for their treasonable acts against the motherland. It was they who stabbed her in the back on three occasions: in 1814 when they delivered France to the allies, in 1830 when they prevented her from "fraternally" annexing Belgium because they feared economic competition from that quarter, and in 1840 when they deprived her of legitimate rights in the Levant. The decline of the *patrie* was thus apparent in every diplomatic crisis, for "France, land of warriors, could not renounce her genius without losing her virility, and she saw herself condemned to impotence the day she consented to be governed by merchants." [7] If France was to fulfill her mission she first must cast off the grip of bourgeois materialism; she had to overthrow the July Monarchy. In general, Blanc did not favor revolution; but in moments of tension, especially during the Near Eastern affair of 1840, he looked forward to the violent overthrow of Louis Philippe.[8] National revival, he insisted, could be undertaken successfully only by a democracy eager to act.

For Blanc the term *national democratic state* was a synonym for the term *nation*. "In a democracy" he wrote, "the State is society itself acting in this capacity through its responsible and revocable mandatories." [9] But a true nation is also society itself. Both state and nation, as concepts, include all nationals, and both come into existence as a result of free choice by all male nationals, that is, as a result of their will to create a democratic national state. Nationality is the product of time, of historical development. But democratic national organization results from the desire of all members of the same nationality to form a nation, and only such a nation can become a real motherland (*patrie*), because only under free rule can patriotism grow and flourish. And only such a nation is capable of great action since it not only engenders unity but also successfully elicits sacrifices from its members, sacrifices of comfort, wealth, even life for the greater glory of the motherland. Only a democratic nation inspiring each citizen by inspiring the entire national group may legitimately demand of each patriot: "Thou will die for thy country (*pays*), because it is thy property; for thy fellow citizens, because they are thy brothers; for thy motherland, because she is thy mother." [10] A true motherland is a "collective interest." This a monarchy can never become; it therefore must be replaced by popular government whose foreign mission is "to tear up the treaties of 1815 and remake Europe." [11] Blanc did not believe that this could be accomplished peacefully.

III

Before 1848 Louis Blanc accepted war as inevitable. He would have preferred peaceful change to violent action; but given the malevolence of those in power, their unwillingness to favor reform, he envisioned the French nation in arms surging forward like the earlier Jacobins to spread by the sword the gospel of liberty, equality, fraternity. The new dispensation must bristle with bayonets if it was to prevail. This was the tragedy of progressive nationalism in the nineteenth century. Its high ideals did not insure its triumph; it had to resort to force. A logical consequence was its acceptance of violence, indeed, its apology for violence.

Blanc's apology was based upon a clearly stated economic determinism. Modern war, he reasoned, is the fatal, ever-present concomitant of capitalism. Competition itself is a form of belligerence. As such it stifles humanitarian sentiment and justice while abetting materialistic egoism and distrust among states. Even more important is the unavoidable tendency toward overproduction in private unregulated industry. With home markets restricted because labor is too impoverished to constitute an important purchasing body, and with trade in Europe hampered by national tariffs, a condition engendered by competition, industrial states are compelled to seek consumers beyond the frontiers of Europe. The desire to obtain exclusive control in non-European areas leads to colonial organization and, hence, to colonial imperialism. Capitalist expansion, then, is directly responsible for colonial imperialism. It is consequently responsible for colonial warfare since expanding nations must necessarily clash in areas suitable to exploitation. Blanc's conclusion is that peace must remain an unfulfilled hope in a world dominated by bourgeois interests.[12]

On the basis of this reasoning he warned his countrymen that war between France and England is inevitable, even desirable, for as soon as France equals her traditional enemy in economic output there will be "one nation too many in the world. Either France must perish, or England be erased from the map." [13] Insisting that England was declining, he felt France should attack at once, because England's weakness promised certain victory, but also because capitalism and long years of peace were sapping the vigor of France. "Twenty years of peace" he warned, "have done more to exhaust the nation than fifty years of war could have done." "Let there be war then, since it is inevitable, and war today rather than tomorrow." And since military conflict is unavoidable pacifism is useless; in fact, it is even unprogressive. "So war then, and to conduct it, a revolutionary power: that is what we need." "War against kings is legitimate, necessary, inevitable, demanded by the principle of the solidarity of peoples." [14]

Blanc was not, so he claimed, in favor of a war directed by a nondemocratic state, lest the hero of the battlefield become the dictator of the state. Such ambitions, he argued, are frustrated by a free people organized as a nation in arms, master of their government, of their will, and of their destiny. Democratic France, aroused by propaganda, martial music, parades, made fully conscious of her great mission, can engage in war without fear of tyrants and also without fear of defeat. Europe, divided and weak, cannot halt her advance. The age of coalitions is past; the age of French hegemony is opening; the age of world unity lies in the future.[15]

This bellicosity approached fanaticism in Blanc during the year of 1840. This was the highpoint of the Near Eastern crisis when France, allied with Egypt, faced a hostile Europe. In the Mediterranean Blanc's urging of a humanitarian crusade was deeply shaded by his desire for French colonial conquest. Of course, in the back of his mind there always remained his country's civilizing mission; however, he insisted that France, before setting out upon it, had not only to become economically powerful, she had also to become economically self-sufficient by the acquisition of colonies. He perceived nothing immoral in colonization provided it was carried out in a humanitarian spirit. France, therefore, enjoyed a moral right to acquire colonies, a right which England did not possess: "The principle of egoism is incarnate in the English people; the principle of devotion in the French nation. England has put her foot in no country without setting up counting-houses. France has passed nowhere without leaving the perfume of her spiritualism. The one has lived by self-interest, the other by glory." [16] This idealization of his compatriots led him to declare that their colonial expansion was, in fact, a necessary part of their mission to civilize not only Europeans but also "backward" peoples. Backward peoples were the Arabs and Blanc vociferously demanded that France colonize all North Africa as well as the Near East, establish socialist co-operatives there, and replace Moslem culture by that of France.[17] The Mediterranean must become a "French lake." He even imagined that France might reach agreement with Russia by partitioning Turkey with her. Then, in alliance with Prussia, she could wage war against England and Austria in order to liberate and unify each subject nationality.[18]

This was the blatant Jacobin nationalism which characterized all of Blanc's writings before 1848. Since he was the leading spokesman of Jacobin-socialism, he injected a strong dosage of nationalist feeling into the movement. However, other exponents did not succumb to this intense love of country. François Vidal and Constantin Pecqueur, for example, were more in accord with the liberals in their internationalism. It was chiefly in the field of domestic reconstruction that they were in close accord with Blanc, and their studies prepared them for common action with him when he came to power.

CHAPTER SIX

A Few Years of Happiness

I

℘ THE DECADE beginning with 1839 marked a new stage in the history of Jacobin-socialism. Blanc founded his *Revue du progrès* and put out his famous *Organisation du travail.* Pecqueur published *Economie sociale* and *Traité des améliorations matérielles* and in 1842, *Théorie nouvelle d' économie sociale et politique.* In 1846 Vidal brought out his *De la répartition des richesses.*

As expounded in these writings, Jacobin-socialism was a compound of the two ideas, radical politics and socialist economics, already traced in Chapter II. The two seemed to become one, harmoniously blended and inseparable. Without the radical state there could be no co-operative economy, and without a co-operative economy political democracy would lose its reason for being; there would be neither equality nor liberty.

Like the two ideologies it combined, Jacobin-socialism was dedicated to the little people, petty bourgeois, and urban and rural laborers. It did not, however, seek to foment class warfare, preferring persuasive to revolutionary techniques. It appealed to the humanitarianism of the well-to-do. Yet it was in the lower classes, the virtuous poor, that its exponents discerned the wellspring of social morality, the primeval source of that goodness inherent in humanity. Emphasizing virtue, they tended to repudiate the pain-pleasure polarities as motivating forces and posited that pain or pleasure really resulted from the absence or presence of virtue in society. Now virtue did not have quite the same meaning for them as it had for Mably who dreamed of recreating another Sparta. Rather they conceived of it as the desire for social justice, as a willingness to struggle unsparingly for the benefit of the people whose will must be sincerely respected. Virtue was enthusiasm for doing good, a state of social grace, and hence, a complete absence of skepticism.

Again unlike their predecessors, whether radical or socialist, the Jacobin socialists had more of the entrepreneurial spirit. State aid was made necessary because they had in mind a socialist system involving extensive mechanization and large-scale production. Not all of them wanted to do away with peasant holdings, but they called for an economy in which all men would have plenty, not because men lived frugally but because men produced in abundance.

It might be said that because of their views on land, Pierre Leroux and Godfrey Cavaignac, formed the right wing of the group; [1] Blanc and Vidal, who sought to balance centralized and decentralized control, constituted the center; and Pecqueur with his belief that a democratic, centralized state must be the sole owner and organizer of all property formed the left wing. Pecqueur has been called the real father of state socialism.[2]

But for the immediate influence, Blanc was undoubtedly the most important of these theorists. Less profound than Pecqueur, less philosophical than Leroux, more readable than Vidal, he came to be in the public eye the incarnation of the doctrine. It was he above all who stimulated the already growing political consciousness of the workers. This was, perhaps, his major achievement in the 1840's, and he accomplished it through literature rather than organizational activity.

II

The revival of the Jacobin-socialist tradition in 1839 did not have an immediate impact on French politics and Blanc made no effort to organize or to establish direct contact with the workers. Rather, he urged during the reform movement of the following year the formation of a sort of popular front, not of parties, but of famous names. However, not even the brilliance of some of these reformers was able to penetrate the dark somnolence of France. Confronted with this situation, Blanc felt the need to awaken public opinion, and published in 1841 the first volume of his *Histoire de dix ans, 1830–1840*. He explained that it was to serve as a mirror reflecting the hideousness of monarchy and capitalism. The remarkable success of this volume spurred his historical labors, leaving little time for editorial duties. After the appearance of another journal of Jacobin-socialist leanings, the *Revue indépendante,* he terminated his fortnightly as of December, 1842, explaining that the new organ would carry on the task he had begun. He did not join its staff. Pierre Leroux was one of its editors, and Blanc's spirit penetrated its columns in the work of François Vidal who drew up a socialist plan quite similar to that of the *Organisation du travail.*

The Jacobin-socialist movement now possessed a historian and a sympathetic, serious review; however, it did not have an aggressive daily at its disposal until Blanc, Arago, Cavaignac, Ledru-Rollin, and others founded the *Réforme* in July, 1843. Although Ferdinand Flocon was editor-in-chief, Cavaignac's influence pervaded the policies of the paper. He was somewhat chastened since his return from an exile lasting several years, yet he was still a young man, tall, lean, with flowing mustachios, and with a passion, flair, and intrepidity which made him the incarnation of militant Jacobinism. Little wonder that Louis Blanc was drawn toward him. He found in him a sincere friend and in his mother a maternal affection and consoling spirit hitherto unknown to him.[3]

It was undoubtedly Cavaignac who persuaded the editorial committee to have Blanc draft the *Réforme's* program.[4] This arrangement explains why, in the first issue, the *Réforme* heralded itself as an organ with a Jacobin-socialist wing and, in the firmness of the tone with which it called for social reform, separated itself from the moderate republicanism of the *National*.

However, there existed no impenetrable wall between the two journals, the right wing of the *Réforme* being hardly distinct from the moderates. François Arago delighted in prescribing the organization of work, but he was hardly more advanced that the wealthy financier Michel Goudchaux, who also flirted with the famous motto. Ledru-Rollin, in his social views, was in almost complete accord with Arago, although physically and temperamentally the two were worlds apart. Arago was venerably old, straight, and lean; Ledru had a powerful frame, a Rabelaisian paunch, a massive head attached to robust shoulders by an ample neck and an angelically round face with a laurel of whiskers sweeping under the chin.[5] By temperament, Arago was closer to the *philosophes*, a benevolent Voltaire; Ledru was a latter-day Conventional, an agitating hulk, whose oratory bordered on demagogy, a penchant that made him appear farther to the left than he really was. Although more individualistic than socialistic, he favored independent workers' associations, modified competition, and at least a minimum of state intervention in the form of economic control rather than extensive ownership. He wrote for the workers: "I wish that by the regulation of salaries the worker acquire industrial property by peaceful means." Then he explained to the petty bourgeois: "In order to become a proprietor I do not wish that the worker despoil you of your property. This would be a theft."[6] He accepted the co-existence of private and co-operative industry and modeling his views on those of the Conventionals of 1793, he posited: "Property is liberty. . . . We therefore respect property, but under the condition that it will be multiplied endlessly. . . ."[7] Little property, then, was sacrosanct, a natural right; large property, which social radicals like Ledru-Rollin tended to equate with monopoly, must be subject either to control or compensated expropriation. Large property, especially the large industrial establishment, was not compatible with social and political equality, and the paring away of large holdings owned by individuals seemed the best means of destroying the privileges which perpetuated inequality. Therefore, most radicals defended the Civil Code which enforced the partition of property among all heirs, and saw no reason to abolish the right of inheritance. It was rather to be subjected to considerable control by means of graduated taxes. Most radicals favored an income tax, but whether orthodox like Armand Marrast, social like Ledru-Rollin, or socialist like Louis Blanc, they were most vague concerning the idea of a progressive income tax. Their inherent individualism was that of the typical Frenchman who refused to look approvingly upon the idea of an administrative prying into his accounts. His moneybags were as precious as his wife, perhaps more so, and fiscal control seemed a violation of some kind of purity.

And yet, the radicals of the *Réforme* stood for a central power possessing many of the characteristics of a welfare state. The right to work that they championed was the kernel from which the principle of social security grew, for Louis Blanc gave a very broad interpretation to the right when he wrote in the first issue: "To the vigorous and healthy citizen, the State owes work; to the old and to the infirm, it owes aid and protection." Adding to this the demand for government-supported, gratuitous, obligatory education, the radical state of the *Réforme* assumed the care of every person from early youth to old age, protecting him from the oppression of ignorance, the hard luck of economic recession, and the despair of ill health and senility. Even the moderates of the *Réforme* accepted the ideal of a welfare state that did not tamper excessively with economic organization but which sought to improve social conditions by assisting individual workers.[8] Consequently, there was general approval in November, 1844, when Blanc drew up a "Pétition des Travailleurs," demanding an official investigation of the condition of the workers. Reproduced in most left-wing papers, it obtained some 130,000 signatures from all social classes. Ledru-Rollin, as deputy from Le Mans, called the attention of his colleagues in the chamber to the petition; as he expected, he was ignored.[9] His motion found no support among men unwilling to enforce even the prohibition of child labor. But while repulsed in the chamber, he found that his ideas were gaining dominance among the staff of the *Réforme*. Blanc found his steadily losing favor.

Cavaignac's death in 1845 removed from the offices of the *Réforme* a certain spiritual *élan*, the force and enthusiasm of an apostle who, burdened more with faith than philosophy, could rally men of various shades of opinion and instill in all of them a feeling of brotherhood and common purpose. But after him the nuances tended to become sects. In a short time the right wing, led by Flocon, editor-in-chief, and Ledru-Rollin, financier-in-chief, assumed control of policy. Financial support lent importance and great power to whoever gave it, since the journal, never as popular as more moderate republican dailies, was not able to win a large body of annual subscribers. The number of readers fluctuated between two and three thousand, all of whom sympathized with its tenets but not all of whom paid its subscription price, with the result that the stockholders bore a heavy economic burden. Fortunately for them, Ledru-Rollin had both broad shoulders and an open purse. Even so, by January, 1846, that purse was empty, hence, so was the paper's treasury.[10]

III

Although Blanc's influence after 1845 declined slightly among the leading editors of the journal, a decline which explains in part his contributing fewer articles, he nevertheless strove to preserve the journal; it was a rallying point where his influence was still not inconsiderable. However, he decided that the negotiation of loans, necessary for the moment, could not place the journal on a sound economic footing. What it required to attract a host of paying subscribers, and with them the prestige it deserved, was a galaxy of famous names among its collaborators. Proponent of a great-man theory of history, Blanc had almost a mania for eminent personages, believing that any association might become powerful if its leaders were celebrities. Looking about for famous names he turned to that of Louis Napoleon, having concluded that the vastly popular name of Bonaparte, duly panoplied with republican symbols, would serve the cause well.

Blanc was certainly not a devotee of the Napoleonic Legend. In 1839, when the pretender had published his *Idées napoléoniennes,* he had reviewed this small work and had asked: Who then is this Louis Napoleon, this little man with a great name? And what will he revive? The achievements of his uncle, without war! "Ah, sir! but that is despotism without glory, the servility of the court without the exaltation of victory, the great lords all covered in braid without the soldiers all covered with wounds, the courtesans on our backs without Europe at our feet, a great name without a great man; it is, in a word, the Empire without the Emperor." [11]

The evening after this article appeared its author received his first lesson in aggression. He was struck down by an attacker with a large club, who then ran away through the narrow streets, leaving his victim prostrate. It has been affirmed that at this precise moment Charles Blanc, attending a soirée at Rodez, reeled back, exclaiming, "I've been hit!" [12] At once he returned to Paris where Louis slowly recovered, having saved his life by deflecting the blow aimed at his temple. Prince Louis Napoleon certainly was not the instigator of this villainy, and its victim never held a grudge against him. Mutually interested in one another for reasons of policy, the two men corresponded, the prince, a prisoner at the fortress of Ham, having taken the initiative in a letter thanking Blanc for his sympathy during the trial of 1840. There was no personal meeting until after Napoleon published four years later a little book, *L'extinction du paupérisme,* which combined the ideas of Saint-Simon, Fourier, and Blanc. Apparently the author of *Organisation du travail* concluded that his correspondent had rallied to the right cause, and a meeting was arranged by a pharmacist living near Ham.

Louis Napoleon lived in a fairly sizable cell, well-furnished, comfortable, and cluttered with numerous books. Seated in an armchair when his visitor entered, he rose, greeted him with a warm handshake and addressed him in French with a marked foreign accent. They began their discussion with a brief review of events of the day; they then shifted cautiously to the possibility of an alliance between Napoleon and the republicans. They were agreed in their opposition to the July Monarchy, but not in their choice of the regime that would replace it. The pretender spoke favorably of an empire which would represent the will of the people. Blanc argued that any kind of hereditary government violates that will; he reiterated with renewed emphasis the arguments set forth in his 1839 article: social and economic changes had made anachronisms of empire and monarchy. The man who would influence society must look ahead, not backward, must march abreast of events, not block the way.[13]

During this time the two had quit the room and were walking slowly along a narrow passageway where prisoners enjoyed brief constitutionals. They kept their voices low lest "traitorous" winds carry their words to the ears of jailers following close behind.[14] Napoleon would become "chief of the executive power" after the disappearance of the present government, but he must be subordinate either to the committees if the new government were "revolutionary," or to the national assembly if it were "normal." [15] The prisoner thought his future role considerably limited, and while not rejecting the offer, he clearly had no intention of becoming a parliamentary emperor. However, during the three-day visit there was no rupture, probably because each still had hopes of using the other's name. Their parting was cordial; indeed, if we are to believe Louis Blanc's later account, it was maudlin. The prince took the hand of his departing guest, and while shaking it, his eyes became moist with tears. If there were tears, however, they contradicted the opinion Napoleon expressed of Blanc in 1842: "Very clever, but too cold, too reasoning, incapable of moving his readers to tears." [16]

Their relation did not come to an end; on the contrary, in February, 1846, Blanc wrote Napoleon an extremely flattering and sympathetic letter, which was to prove quite embarrassing for him in December, 1852, when it was printed in order to win labor support for the *coup d'état* of that year. Moreover his visit, which was not a secret excursion, as well as his favorable presentation of Napoleon's Strasbourg and Boulogne fiascos, kept the name of Louis Napoleon Bonaparte before the public eye.

In his effort to win the support of celebrated names, Blanc was far more successful with George Sand than with Louis Napoleon, and he was dealing with a person too straightforward to dream of using him for a selfish motive. He had got in touch with her as early as November, 1844, after she had revealed her sympathy for his petition demanding a study of social conditions. In a most touching letter he urged her to put her pen at the service of the *Réforme*.[17] There followed a meeting in Paris during which he sought to win her over to his brand of socialism, but while certain of his ideas may be found in her social novels, she remained the disciple of Leroux, and like him believed that the "sense of property is so deeply ingrained in the human being that the child needs only four square feet of soil to learn to love the land he tills. . . . One has to recognize private property. . . . The land a man works with his own hands is as personal to him as the clothes he wears." [18] This was Sand, the mistress of the landed estate of Nohant, speaking the words any French peasant might have used had he the eloquence.

This difference of opinion, which, in reality, was the essential one between the right and center wings of Jacobin-socialism, did not dissolve the friendship that began between Sand and Louis Blanc. On the contrary, their mutual respect deepened during succeeding years, and in the summer, when the heat of Paris was most oppressive, the socialist was glad to put aside the weight of just ideals and to run away to Nohant in the pleasant province of Berry. Light-hearted, he went along on the little excursions around the countryside, and to the races at Mézières-en-Brenne. Then, in the evening, he was cleverly led to descant upon socialism, or other topics, which he did in a declamatory tone that was roundly but good-naturedly mocked by the audience. Blanc was undoubtedly hoping to catch the eye of Solange, Sand's daughter, with whom he played in pantomimes. Soon after he asked for her hand. Several years earlier he had proposed marriage to a young woman of noble birth, and was refused for he had possessed neither wealth nor particle. Mme Sand was not concerned with these but while well-disposed toward Blanc, she could not push aside a certain doubt that he would make a good husband for any woman. She referred to him with her usual candor as a "big ambition in a little body," and this conviction was confirmed in her mind by her friend, Latouche, who wrote:

> He [Blanc] has a noble soul and a fine talent. Of how many men can one say as much in society? But I believe he has little gift for loving, and in the career of ambition that he will follow constantly, ardently, sometimes imprudently shall I see completely reassuring conditions for the happiness of *our princess?* He will be estimable and worthy all his life, but preoccupied with succeeding more than with making others happy and being so himself. A mind turned outwards, desirous of fame, rather than resigned to devote himself to family interests, I believe he has a mind more rich than his heart, but I mean to speak only of the future of his affections, for he has been admirable in his devotion to his father and his brother.[19]

This is one of the most just estimates of Blanc's character that has come to light, and it is doubtful that the match with Solange would have succeeded. The plans were dropped, and Blanc abandoned the thought of marriage, having realized that he was affianced to a dream, a vision of social sweetness that perhaps he would never embrace. Twenty years full of intense activity, momentary success and frustrating failure would pass before he would find, in England, the country he detested, the woman who would really understand him. As for Sand, she remained his friend and perhaps unconsciously solaced him when she suggested that he write a history of the great Revolution. Possibly his ambition to undertake such a vast labor influenced the decision he made not to enter politics.

IV

Louis Blanc had not been able to follow in the early 1830's the advice of Pierre Béranger to enter politics; he had been too poor. His financial standing was quite changed by the mid-1840's when he had earned a considerable revenue from his publications, and paid a tax sufficiently high to qualify him as a candidate for the chamber of deputies. In fact, by 1848 he had purchased government bonds amounting to 17,000 francs.[20]

In 1845 the radicals of Villefranche-de-Lauraguais urged Blanc to seek nomination as a candidate in their department, the Sarthe. At first he seemed willing, and the *Emancipation* of Toulouse announced that his hat was in the ring. He even made a trip to Toulouse where he harangued a large crowd filled with enthusiastic students at the Hotel de l'Europe. However, he soon learned that in the *arrondissement* of Mamers where he intended to stand the reform party was not united behind him. The man who had invited his candidacy was acting in opposition to the incumbent deputy and a majority of moderate reformers. Fearing that a split in republican ranks would open the way for the official candidate, Blanc withdrew from the contest. Nonetheless, he was accused of base ambition and of pursuing a selfish policy, a charge which he refuted in the *Réforme* of April 1, 1846. Several reasons motivated his decision. Perhaps the most important was his fear of splitting the rather weak republican party that had already suffered several demoralizing setbacks, and against which the odds were enormous. However, almost as important was his fear of becoming so much involved in party machinery as to forfeit his freedom of political and social expression. Only two years earlier he had expressed his qualms, concluding that "being head of a party means depending on it excessively, and when commanding is no longer but a lofty form of obedience, there must be an abnegation of oneself, of one's thoughts, and, sometimes, a servility of ambition of which inspired men are incapable." [21]

This apprehension undoubtedly stemmed from his painful awareness that the republican movement was dominated by socially moderate men, Félicité de Lamennais, Armand Marrast, editor of the *National*, Dupont de l'Eure, Hippolyte Carnot, François Arago, some of whom had collaborated with him on the *Revue du progrès*, but all of whom viewed in him the traits of restless ambition aspiring toward dictatorship. Any thinker who openly took a stand for governmental intervention appeared to them a dangerous *étatiste*.[22] This was why, in 1848, Blanc would have to compel these cautious men to accept him as a political colleague, an insistence which only intensified their distrust. He was able to command at least nominal acceptance, however, because of his solid popularity among the workers in that year.

Unfortunately for him, the workers did not enjoy the suffrage in 1846; so that their allegiance as yet offered only promise for the future, not fulfillment for the present. But even among the workers he had rivals: Etienne Cabet, who probably had a larger following, and Philippe Buchez, with a limited but highly intelligent and devoted coterie. Unlike them, Blanc made no consistent effort to arouse a following, either among the journalists or among the workers, with the result that in 1848 he had no familiarity with the latter as persons. Indeed, he never met Albert *l'ouvrier* until circumstance threw them together during the February upheaval. Before 1848 he limited his labor acquaintances to a few highly skilled artisans like Martin Nadaud, whom he did not meet through his own initiative, and whom he invited, along with a few other "proletarians," to his apartment for discussions.[23]

Yet his preference for writing rather than political activity inevitably kept Blanc aloof from the labor movement. He was an educator, not an organizer, a thinker, not an activist. Consequently most of his mornings were taken up either by reading and research in the Bibliothèque Nationale or by long promenades along the streets or in public parks. He walked slowly, always deep in thought, his imaginative mind elaborating those historical events that he would describe with classical precision and romantic fervor when, after lunch in a nearby café, he would sit at his desk in the quiet of his apartment. Only in the afternoon could he bring himself to write. Laurent-Antoine Pagnerre, his publisher, urged, pushed, and threatened, but Blanc could not produce more than twenty pages a day, and these were scrupulously edited by Charles. Then, in the evening, there was a soirée to be attended or the Comédie-Française where the two brothers were well-known, especially among the players with republican sympathies. Charles eventually married an actress, a "daughter of the people." Louis remained unmarried, probably a fortunate turn of events considering the fate awaiting him in 1848. For during the previous year arose the winds of a new revolutionary period, gentle winds, growing in volume, and soon catching him up, carrying him aloft to the uncertain pinnacle of success.

CHAPTER SEVEN

Revolution Without Revolutionaires

I

❦ IN THE EARLY MONTHS of 1847 Louis Blanc made his most direct contribution to the political disturbance which was to bring him to fame. On February 6 there appeared in the bookshops the first volume, and later in the year the second volume, of his *Histoire de la Révolution française,* a work not insignificant either as history or as propaganda. Although the study was not brought to an end until fifteen years later, these early volumes, in which he summed up his philosophy of history, marked the completion of a literary triology. Its birthdate was 1840, the year of his *Organisation du travail,* when he annexed to the political revolutionary tradition a socialist philosophy, and popularized the watchword symbolizing their union. Shortly after, in his *Histoire de dix ans,* he dramatically pointed up all the evils of the July Monarchy; indeed, he posed as a socialistic Dante, conducting his readers through a vividly elaborate capitalistic hell. Finally, during 1847, in his study of the Revolution, he concluded that man's long pilgrimage through the sufferings of poverty and grinding labor was nearing an end; the day of popular judgment was approaching and after that day everyone would enter the social paradise.

To this revolutionary ring must be added the histories of Jules Michelet and Alphonse de Lamartine. They, too, glorified certain phases of the revolutionary movement of the 1790's, and fired the imagination of the reading public.[1] Of course, these books did not "cause" the February upheaval; it is highly doubtful if many of the workers who manned the barricades were aware of their existence. Yet, they all sold well, were widely commented on and condensed in the press, and probably popularized the idea of revolt among radical elements of the middle class, many of whom fought at the side of workers on the barricades. Blanc's works, in particular, helped to broaden the social basis of the democratic revolutionary tradition.[2]

Neither did deteriorating economic conditions during the "hungry forties" directly cause the Revolution of 1848. However, the financial panic, the commercial and industrial crises, and the poor harvests of 1845–46 aroused discontent among the lower classes, especially among the unemployed, and drove them to man barricades once the signal was given. The testimony of many workers proves that they turned to insurrection because of hunger.[3]

Notwithstanding these intellectual and economic causes, it was bourgeois reformers, frustrated in their demands for purely political improvement by the obstinacy of the king and his ministers, who set in motion the systematic pressure that would, to their surprise and horror, end in the overthrow of monarchy. Like the revolutions of 1789 and 1830, that of 1848 was, to a large extent, directly inaugurated by the upper classes. During the mid-summer of 1847 moderate political theorists— monarchists of the dynastic Left and the left Center—organized a series of reform banquets at which speakers denounced governmental corruption and proposed a slight extension of the suffrage.[4]

The coterie of the *National* tended to sympathize with these liberal monarchists; but not so that of the *Réforme,* which bitterly mocked their timidity, and soon organized its own gastronomic demonstrations, under the leadership of Ledru-Rollin. Blanc, busy with historical research, attended only one banquet, at Dijon on November 21, where he was a principal speaker. Seated with Ledru-Rollin and Flocon, he was "always laughing and showing his beautiful white teeth, always speaking and gesticulating, always casting over the audience his large black eyes full of hardiness and spirit." [5] The number of guests has been estimated between 1000 and 1300, including nearly 400 workers whose elbows rubbed those of industrialists, merchants, priests, and professors. Here, indeed, Blanc was in his element, surrounded by politically educated enthusiasts, and in the city whose academy had crowned Rousseau's first significant work. He felt unrestrained when he rose to speak, and gave a summary of both his political and social philosophies, concluding that the present regime could not last. "When the fruit is rotten," he warned, "it awaits only the passing of the wind to detach itself from the tree." [6] He did not specify whether this would be the wind of revolution or of propaganda.

Although very few of the banqueters were in favor of a violent uprising, the government abandoned its earlier complacency, especially after the frankly socialist gathering at Limoges on January 2, 1848. This banquet was organized by Théodore Bac, a lawyer and Jacobin-socialist who was very popular with the workers at Limoges. The toasts were perhaps no more extravagant than some of those raised even at conservative banquets. Practically all shades of opinion joyfully sipped a bit of wine in praise of the organization of work, or in denunciation of the exploitation of man by man. These formulas seemed innocent; indeed, they had become the vogue. The difference among the various groups mouthing them was that the banqueters at Limoges meant what they said. The ministry, closely informed by the police, was aware of this situation. Consequently, it took alarm when a banquet was scheduled to be held by the National Guard of the radical twelfth district in Paris.

Moderate deputies also took alarm, intervened, and cleverly took into their own hands most of the arrangements. They raised the price from three to six francs, invited only electors, and changed the location to the Champs Elysées, which was an open field at this time. They intended to transform the meeting into a symbolic act in defense of the right of public assembly. To lend it greater dignity, they planned a long cortege, eventually scheduled for February 22, and of course, invited only persons acceptable to themselves to march in it.

Meanwhile, a republican electoral committee met and delegated Blanc and two others to demand a special place for workers. Odilon Barrot firmly protested, not against the inclusion of a few workers, but against their forming a special group, for "a demarcation was a sign of division, an offense rather than an honor." [7] Blanc thought otherwise and would not give way, with the result that he obtained his demand. Although notices of the procession in the *Siècle, Constitutionnel, National,* and *Courrier français* failed to mention the workers, he obstinately urged them to select a number of delegates prepared to march. They therefore spent all day Sunday and Monday (February 20–21) rushing from workshop to workshop to make known this decision.

Given this turn of events, many deputies were relieved when the ministry formally interdicted both banquet and parade, and in a meeting of the opposition, only seventeen out of eighty favored defiance. However, the king's arbitrary decision aroused Parisian indignation. Until eleven o'clock in the evening of the twenty-first, crowds, undecided and without leadership, milled in the streets. Popular orators appeared on corners, and small groups broke off from the mass to listen to their reading of the government's proclamation. Not until midnight did the city settle down, but sleep did not fill the empty larders of the laboring class and the acquiescence of the politicians frustrated the hope of immediate remedies. Popular desperation was at the full, and it is in this desperation that one must seek the basic motive inducing many men to fight. After the retreat of the deputies the unpopular government stood face to face with the hungry and angry people of Paris.[8]

No one person set these people into motion. There were soapbox orators, public agitators, a few conspirators of the secret societies, but hardly any real revolutionaries. His majesty's disloyal opposition was as much in a quandary as his loyal opposition. This dilemma was clearly revealed during the evening of the twenty-first when about fifty Jacobin devotees, including Charles de Ribeyrolles, Marc Caussidière, Etienne Arago, Lucien de La Hodde, Ledru-Rollin, Edgar Quinet and

Blanc, assembled at the *Réforme*. No one had a concrete plan to present. Then Edmond d'Alton-Shée came in to report that the opposition deputies had defected. He went on to urge resistance, and several among the group supported him. At this point Blanc broke in, and according to the police spy, La Hodde, exclaimed, "After the deputies of the opposition have stirred the country to its very marrow, they draw back! I feel my blood swelling my heart, and if I heeded only my indignation, I should say to you at once, in the face of such a felony: let us shout the war cry and march! but human nature restrains me. I wonder whether we have the right to dispose of the generous blood of the people without profit for democracy. If the patriots move tomorrow, abandoned by the men who have urged them on, they will infallibly be crushed, and democracy drowned in blood; that is what tomorrow's uprising will be. And, do not fool yourselves, the national guard, which has worn its uniform in banquet after banquet, will mow you down with the army." [9]

This pessimism was largely the result of immediate circumstance, for in November, 1847, he had assured Friedrich Engels that the workers were revolutionary and awaiting an opportune moment to strike. They were also sufficiently grounded in social doctrines so that their uprising would bring about social changes and not merely effect a reversal of dynasties.[10] However, a very recent trip to the provinces, where Blanc undoubtedly encountered the lethargy of the peasants, reinforced the caution which had steadily qualified the revolutionary fervor of his writings and of his address at the banquet of Dijon, and perhaps induced him to recall a warning written several years earlier apropos of the uprising of 1830: "Woe to those who throw themselves at random into revolutions and who run into combat shouting unknown cries." [11] Of course, France might follow Paris; in the early forties he had practically convinced himself that she would. But now, face to face with possible revolution, doubts assailed him. If the rest of France chose to resist the capital, the men who seized power would find themselves ineluctably drawn toward another reign of terror "by the force of things." This thought undoubtedly had a most sobering effect on Blanc, not only at this moment, but during the entire spring and summer of 1848. He had convinced himself by his historical studies that a cause, however just, which must dip its hands in blood, is running ahead of the natural march of history, hence, rushing into a fatal trap that can only retard the destined forward thrust of progress.

He did not convince the extremists who urged action, arguing that if barricades went up radicals must man them. However, Ledru-Rollin and Flocon sided with him and they won over the majority. At once the editor-in-chief drew up a notice for the next day's issue, in which he emphasized the need for caution. The secret societies, represented by those who called for action, also tended to fear the perils of an unprepared revolt. In all the groups, factions, and assemblies the word of order for the next day was, "wait and see."

II

The next morning, the twenty-second, not even the day looked promising. The sky was hung with low, rushing, billowing clouds, it was cold and close to rain; in France successful revolutions had usually been arranged in warm weather. Along the streets people were moving toward the Place de la Concorde, across the Seine from the Chamber of Deputies. Here one saw clusters of men, women, and children, from all classes, in all types of dress, either garrulous and gesticulating, or mutely watching. There was practically no disturbance until the Municipal Guard, hated for their brutality, charged the crowd. Blood flowed and tempers flared. Soon barricades were erected along the Rue de Rivoli, but easily taken. The people were unarmed and unprepared for insurrection. Fighting became sporadic. The king refused to take energetic measures, the National Guard hardly responded to the *rappel,* its call to arms. At the offices of the *Réforme,* Blanc and others reiterated their warning against violence. However, Marc Caussidière urged action and fixed a rendezvous with like-minded men at the Carré Saint-Martin for the next day.

The twenty-third was a day of decisive change: the National Guard tended to side with the reformers, François Guizot was replaced by Louis Molé, who satisfied no one, and on the barricades the battle cry rapidly became, "Down with Louis Philippe." Fighting continued. Among the most determined combatants were the activist collaborators of the *Réforme.*

After the fall of Guizot a crowd assembled at the offices of the *Réforme,* appropriately located in the Rue Jean-Jacques Rousseau. There Ledru-Rollin put forward a program: amnesty for all political prisoners, unrestricted right of assembly and suppression of the electoral *cens.* This would have democratized, not destroyed the monarchy. The editors of the paper were more timid than its rank and file on the barricades. Blanc was hardly more advanced, as he revealed that evening in the meeting at the home of Durant Saint-Amande, where after considerable debate, he hastily wrote a petition for the Democratic Electoral Committee of the Seine. He denounced using the army for repressing civil discord and maintained that only the National Guard, composed of all the people, was capable of keeping order and of distinguishing "a revolution from a riot." [12] No where did he mention the word *republic.* In reality the petition was nothing more than a demand for the military evacuation of Paris and the reorganization of the National Guard, two measures which the Provisional Government would later carry out.

After the petition was prepared for publication, Blanc, in the company of several friends, went out into the streets. Paris seemed calm, almost festive. Gamins with lanterns darted from window to window shouting "Light up! Light up!" whereupon shutters were opened and buildings sparkled with lights. Yet, in the distance, firing could be heard as the fighting continued by torchlight. Arriving at a wineshop, Blanc was sickened by the sight of a corpse, its face pallid, lying in the gutter. He turned away. Then he learned that a large body of people had been cut down by a volley of shot on the Boulevard des Capucines. Knowing that Charles was in that vicinity, he went quickly to their prearranged rendezvous where he found his brother enraged and hoarse, having mingled with the crowd fleeing the massacre and shouting "They are assassinating citizens!" Soon he and Charles witnessed a hideous spectacle: a wagonload of lifeless bodies, drawn through the streets and surrounded by men with torches. All shouting had ceased. But the night air was still heavy with the sounds of weeping and muted anger. Of this scene Blanc wrote, "Paris, to enter into a rage, had need of the sight of only one corpse; in the evening, the firing of a platoon, . . . furnished a pile of them." [13] That night there was no sleep for the city. At the Tuileries the Adolphe Thiers-Odilon Barrot cabinet was formed, a move which might have saved the throne on the previous day. However, in the streets, working by torchlight, men built new barricades, strengthened older ones, and settled into the determination to overthrow the throne.

As early as six in the morning—a clear, crisp morning—determined radicals began arriving at the *Réforme*, which was no longer a journal but a revolutionary center. Blanc arrived toward seven-thirty, dressed in the uniform of a national guardsman. He and his colleagues now learned of the new cabinet. It was unacceptable, particularly because it contained Marshal Bugeaud, the man held responsible for the massacre of the Rue Transnonain in 1834. His appointment after the butchery in the Boulevard des Capucines had the appearance of a provocation, and Blanc's petition, written the previous evening and now passed from hand to hand, was widely interpreted as a protest against him. The government's tactics had failed. The insurrection began rapidly closing in on the Tuileries and other fortified places, with the result that Louis-Philippe's abdication in favor of his grandson failed to save the throne; already in the early afternoon the mob invading the royal palace had decided for a republic. Meanwhile, when the editors of the *National* learned of the king's abdication, a list of names to form a "committee of direction" was drawn up. Included were François Arago, Alexander Marie, Louis-Antoine Garnier-Pagès, Alphonse de Lamartine, Armand Marrast and Odilon Barrot.

Suddenly Louis Blanc, his brother, and several other persons entered the room where the editors were busy deliberating. Climbing onto a chair, from which he could be seen as well as heard, he summoned his audience to include his name. This the majority strongly opposed. The *Réforme*, they retorted, was already represented by Arago and the name of a socialist would frighten the middle class. A lively debate followed until men began to file out, whereupon Blanc too, quit the room, complaining that he had not been understood, and that this rebuff would leave a bad impression on republicans.[14] Nonetheless, the *National's* list was carried to the Chamber of Deputies where it was tentatively accepted by Marie and Lamartine. Most of the politicians, however, supported Barrot's demand for a regency; indeed, not even Ledru-Rollin came out openly for a republic until the hall was invaded by a mob of angry insurgents. Frightened monarchists fled and in the confusion the list, excluding Barrot but adding Dupont de l'Eure and Ledru-Rollin, was read and applauded. At once the men chosen departed for the City Hall while the mob, remaining in the chamber, let off steam by shooting at the portrait of the ex-king.

It was this mob which had repudiated Odilon Barrot in the chamber; earlier during the afternoon the crowd assembled outside of the *National* had also cried out against the inclusion of his name, and receiving no satisfaction, had marched hurriedly to the *Réforme*. There, from a point of vantage, Eugène Baune, a leader of the Lyons uprising of 1834, harangued them. By this time a few strong points had been taken and revolutionaries had gone in several directions: most to attack the Tuileries, some to invade the Chamber of Deputies, some to the *Réforme*. Therefore the crowd was now swollen by men blackened with gunpowder, dripping sweat, and enthusiastic with victory. They pushed their way into the offices, crowding clumsily into everdiminishing space. They listened as Flocon read the *National's* list, and shouted angrily at the name of Barrot. Martin de Strasbourg and Blanc, who had brought this list, explained that Barrot was an indispensable concession to the bourgeois of the National Guard. Exploiting the occasion to win popular support for his old tactic of an alliance between moderates and radicals, Blanc emphasized that since republicans were not numerous, they must minimize their differences in order to co-operate against a common enemy. The power of the *National* could not be ignored, and of especial importance was its great prestige in the provinces, which would facilitate the establishment of a republic.[15] From these statements it is clear that Blanc was striving to add to the *National's* list, not erase names acceptable to it. From the beginning, then, he was not an *exclusif*, a derogatory epithet stamped upon him by Garnier-Pagès. As a matter of fact, it was only when men like Garnier-Pagès attempted later in the day to exclude him from the Provisional Government that he began to act more arbitrarily.

The crowd at the *Réforme* was not convinced by his compromises and discarding the list with Barrot, drew up another that was practically identical with the one of the chamber, save for the absence of Adolphe

Crémieux and the addition of Blanc, Ferdinand Flocon, and Albert *l'ouvrier*, the latter having been put forward by the secret societies, who wanted a worker included. It does not seem, however, that Albert was present, and during the next two days he was nearly forgotten since he did not put in an appearance at the City Hall.[16]

IV

It was nighttime when Blanc arrived at the City Hall. The Place de Grève was covered with an impenetrable human mass whose myriad faces were sharply visible in the dancing glow of torches. Blanc stood helpless on the edge of the square until several workmen recognized their hero. "Make way! Make way!" they shouted, "Let a member of the Provisional Government pass." Several lifted him, and he was passed, like a cork on an active sea, from hand to hand, urged on with delirious shouts of joy, into the Salle Saint-Jean. Here was assembled a group of revolutionaries bent on establishing a republic. But neither official nor unofficial proclamation had been made, although the mob had taken over the City Hall earlier in the afternoon. At once Blanc assured the group of his desire for a republic, and one favorable to social reform. Flocon, now beside him, readily agreed. The resounding cheers revealed that in the crowd's mind Blanc was a member, indeed, the most favored member, of the Provisional Government.[17]

This was not the opinion of the parliamentary group acclaimed at the Chamber of Deputies. They had arrived earlier, taken over control, and distributed cabinet posts. Meeting now in a small room they displayed amazement and distrust when Blanc, Flocon, and Marrast were shown in. Adolphe Crémieux, newly appointed minister of justice, and defender of a regency until the last minute, asked Lamartine, "What have they come to do here?" With a shrug of his lean shoulders the poet said curtly, "I don't know." He had rejected Blanc's name in the Chamber of Deputies.

The newcomer, fully conscious of his popularity, advanced boldly toward the table where Dupont de l'Eure and François Arago were seated, and made the laconic statement, "Very well, messieurs, let us deliberate." Undoubtedly he had hoped for a welcome from Arago, who had offered him paternal affection in the past. However, the new minister of the navy replied, "Without doubt, Monsieur, we are going to deliberate, but not until you have left." [18] Blanc was hurt and angry. He asserted with pride that his powers came directly from the people who had delegated him, that the will of the people gave him a right to rule more legitimate than that of certain members delegated at the chamber. Without him, there could be no government. Shouts from without and violent banging on the door underscored his warning. At this moment Garnier-Pagès, provisional mayor of Paris, came forward, and referred to the three recent arrivals as "secretaries," a tag which apparently implied their acceptance into the new government, but left them without power. Blanc fully grasped the meaning and refused the offer. He threatened to call upon the people until Ledru-Rollin urged him not to create discord in a newborn republic. Flocon and Marrast accepted the "titles," and therefore Blanc, already fearful of what turn mob action might take, gave way, at least for the moment. On the twenty-sixth the word "secretary" was definitely dropped.[19]

When Ledru-Rollin implored Blanc's agreement in the name of the republic, he raised another issue: what kind of government did France now have? Since everyone in the room was republican, the issue would seem to be a minor one. But it was not minor; in fact, it was the first concrete issue which divided the members. Their intensity of feeling resulted, not so much from their views about the form of government as from their views about the role of Paris. The legalistic moderate republicans, Dupont, Arago, Marie, and Crémieux argued that Paris must not impose a government on France; the issue must be submitted to a national decision. From the liberal point of view, this argument was unimpeachable. But it is quite possible that other motives influenced their attitude. For them, the question was not exclusively political; it had social ramifications. An immediately established republic would fall quickly under the control of Paris, and therefore find itself driven, if it would survive, to carry out social reforms. This was clearly the intention of the mob shouting outside. Now these moderates were not opposed to social improvement and there is no reason to question their sincerity; but face to face with the crowd that would impose social measures, they stiffened in their distrust. For one concession would entail a chain of concessions, at the end of which awaited a Convention with Ledru-Rollin or Louis Blanc ready to play the role of Robespierre. To give way to the mob shouting for a republic would be to surrender moderation, excite inordinate demands, and encourage Utopians—as well as to violate the will of the provinces. As republicans, these men represented the Girondin tradition.[20]

At the other pole were Blanc, Ledru-Rollin, and Flocon who continued the Jacobin tradition, and were plagued with the same dilemma that had troubled their spiritual ancestors in 1793. They were, on the one hand, defenders of popular sovereignty and universal suffrage; on the other hand, they were fearful of the peasant majority. Wary of the backwardness of the peasants, they concluded that an enlightened Parisian minority possessed, "by the force of things," the right to speak and act for all of France. To those who denied this right, Blanc replied that "the whole of France coming to Paris, Paris is to the provinces what the sea is to the rivers which flow into it. Through Paris it is France which speaks, if by France you mean that which represents her veritable instincts and constitutes her genius." Here is the definite expression of a somewhat new direction Blanc was to follow: the defense of a militant minority, an inevitable course arising from his fear of a backward majority and also from the conclusions of his Jacobin logic:

"A republican government being that which draws its legitimacy only from the national will, expressed in a formal manner, . . . it is clear that 'sovereignty of the people' and 'republic' are terms which enter into one another. The entire nation cannot reject the republican form without giving up by this act its own sovereignty, without committing suicide; what's more, without scandalously confiscating the rights of future generations; hence the conclusion that in proclaiming the Republic, Paris is doing what France cannot undo by means of universal suffrage, save under the condition of destroying it.[21]

For the radicals the republican form of government was not a question to be brought up for discussion or for head counting. Blanc was particularly emphatic, and seeking to impose his views by the force of both argument and histrionics, he climbed onto the sofa, and with Gallic gesticulation, made his points. Arago, ill and irritated, threw at him, "Eh! Monsieur, I was a republican before you were born!" The old man then threatened to resign, a move bringing consternation to the moderates as well as to the radicals who were not really prepared for a proletarian dictatorship. Indeed, Ledru-Rollin and Flocon tended to distrust Blanc, and he, in turn, was not sure that he could control the mob. But the radicals knew that the crowd was on their side, so the debate went on within the room, with neither side willing to give way. At times Lamartine and Garnier-Pagès managed to temper the sharpness of verbal exchanges, but fatigue and excitement were wearing nerves thin.

The indecision of the government aroused the people crowded into every niche of the building. Reverberating through long corridors were cries of "Vive la République," punctuated by rifle shots which chipped plaster from ceilings and walls. As if by a miracle of strength a column of students, just arrived from the Latin Quarter, forced its way into the building and tried to penetrate the little room. At once Blanc took advantage of the interruption to apply pressure upon the moderates. Turning to the student leader, he said, "Now tell these gentlemen, you who come from outside, tell them what's taking place; they will believe you perhaps."[22] To parry this arbitrary move, Lamartine went to harangue the crowd which kept calling out for a republic. Blanc followed him, and mounted on a table set up before the building, cried out, "The Provisional Government wants the Republic!" A deafening cheer arose, emanating from "rough faces, . . . to which the light of torces lent something terrible." Others spoke, then they all assembled again in the small room. It was clear that further delay might prove fatal, not only to the moderates, but to the republican movement. "What can be more dangerous in the present circumstances," Blanc asked, "than leaving such a question undecided? This will be to put all interests in suspense, to unchain all passions, to encourage all ambitious desires, to open the way for thousands of intrigues. . . . Do you not hear, all around us, this loud noise of arms and of horses, and these clamors?"[23] Indeed, the deliberators were at the mercy of the revolutionaries.

Finally, admitting the legal correctness of Arago and Dupont, Crémieux suggested, "Let us proclaim the Republic, and leave to an assembly freely, and immediately convoked, the right to confirm or to annul the act." In reality, this proposal was identical to one put forward by Lamartine before Blanc's arrival; Lamartine had even drawn up a proclamation to which Ledru-Rollin had consented, but which had been withdrawn from the printers by Marie and Arago, with Lamartine's consent. Now he wrote out another manifesto: "The Provisional Government desires the Republic, save ratification by the people, who will be consulted immediately." Blanc read it, replaced the word *désire* by *veut,* and accepted it, as did everyone else.[24] Copies were hastily written out and thrown from the windows, like manna from the republican heaven.

Of course, this wording left the question open. The middle phrase, *sauf ratification par le peuple,* would lead to dissension over the date for holding elections, and the question of governmental form would again rear up. For in the popular mind of Paris, France was now a republic, and this was a victory won on the barricades, not a concession granted by the moderates. Therefore the possibility of rural France's reversing the *fait accompli* would not be tolerated.

Interestingly enough, Blanc seems to have glimpsed at this early date the means of influencing his moderate colleagues: mob pressure. And his tactics had certain characteristics of a Parisian plebiscite. However, he would on later occasions be as fearful of the mob as he was on the twenty-fourth, and would accept half-measures as he had on the twenty-fourth.

It was nearly midnight when popular agitation died down. Members of the government were exhausted and famished, for they had not eaten since morning. Searching for food, they found only a *pain de munition,* a few crumbs of Gruyère left by soldiers, a bottle of wine and a cracked cup. Someone furnished a pocketknife, and soon morsels of bread and cheese, accompanied by cheap wine, were passed from hand to hand.

Since Blanc had no cabinet post, he had no special duties for the moment. He left for home in the company of Charles and another friend. They made their way down narrow dark alleys until a huge barricade rose before them. In the blackness a cry rang out, "Halte-là!" followed by a demand for the password. Since none of the company knew it they were put under guard until Blanc was recognized and given a guard of honor to escort him. After a change of clothing he returned to the City Hall. He had to pick his way among revolutionaries sprawled out in the streets and on the Place de Grève. At intervals he heard the sentry's call passing from mouth to mouth, "Sentinelles, prenez garde à vous!" Sensing that all was well, he entered the dimly lighted building.

CHAPTER EIGHT

The Gentle Art of Dupery

I

❦ ON THE MORNING of February 25 the corridors and rooms of the City Hall were still crammed with armed men of every description. In the small room where the Republic had been born, Blanc and five other members of the new government sat busily drawing up decrees for the release of political prisoners, for the official adoption of the children of dead combatants, and for financial aid to the families of the wounded. Their pens scratched noisily in the silence of a city not yet fully awake.

This early morning calm was deceptive, for already there was a movement which intended to sweep the revolution on into radical social reform, and which manifested itself at about noon with the arrival of another wave of workers on the Place de Grève. Suddenly the door of the council room was flung open and a young worker, rifle in hand and chest bared, advanced and struck the tile floor with the butt of his weapon. Then in a highpitched voice he read a petition: "Citizens, the organization of work, the right to work in an hour! Such is the will of the people. It awaits!"

Marche's presence was tantamount to a shock treatment for the council. Even Blanc admitted that he was strongly offended at first. He was certainly not accustomed to dealing with revolutionaries like this one; the workers with whom he was most familiar were those like Martin Nadaud, who were skilled, scholarly and respectful. But his anger quickly changed to admiration and then to pride.[1] It was Lamartine, however, who first recovered his wits and, advancing toward the intruder, sought "to captivate him with oratorical caresses." Marche, however, had steeled himself in the determination to force the council's hand. He interrupted abruptly with the announcement that the people were now master and ordered again the immediate recognition of the right to work.

The details of what followed are vague, since witnesses do not agree. It seems that Lamartine finally managed to soothe the petitioner by playing upon a theme which became a favorite of liberal republican propaganda: hasty action in the field of social reform must be avoided because the republic was in danger. To which Marche is supposed to have replied that the people "put three months of poverty into the service of the republic." [2] Whatever his words, he apparently was not certain what Blanc's catch-phrase "Organization of work" really meant, and so it was possible for Lamartine to deflate his grand purpose for the time. However, the left wing of the government were determined to benefit from the occasion. Blanc, Ledru-Rollin, and Flocon had earlier gathered about a table near the window and drawn up a proclamation which, according to Garnier-Pagès, called for the compulsory establishment of co-operatives. Whether or not this was the content of the proclamation, Garnier-Pagès and Lamartine rejected it, whereupon Blanc reworded it, softening its tone. As published, it read: "The Provisional Government of the French Republic pledges itself to guarantee the existence of the worker by [providing him with] labor; it pledges itself to guarantee work to all citizens; it recognizes that the workers should associate among themselves to enjoy the legitimate profits of their labor; the Provisional Government returns to the workers, to whom it belongs, the million which is going to fall due from the civil list." [3]

Interestingly enough, no one signed this decree which was so controversial. The last sentence, inserted by Ledru-Rollin, was probably the least objectionable. It did not reiterate the two principles, the right to work and the organization of work, which the majority of the council accepted only under duress and which they would henceforth attempt to circumvent. The right wing certainly had no intention of using the million francs for social experiments; it was, rather, to be distributed as charity.[4] Furthermore, Lamartine had already convinced himself that these principles could not be applied without the use of violence.[5] And he had already assumed the role of the dissipator of violent action, which he played dramatically and effectively during the red flag affair.[6]

During the late afternoon another crowd of revolutionaries demanded the replacement of the national flag, the tricolor, with a pure red banner. In a remarkable burst of oratory, Lamartine hit upon the one chord that moved almost all Parisians: partiotism. Identifying the tricolor with French military glory and honor, he not only charmed the mob, he preserved the power of the moderates and greatly enhanced his prestige among them. Until the election of April, he was their chief spokesman, whose eloquence quite literally talked the workers out of renewing the revolt.

While it can be argued that he did not always use his particular genius to foster the social movement, Lamartine nevertheless was a firm believer in reform. He displayed this zeal during the evening council meeting when he put forward a proposal to abolish capital punishment for purely political crimes. The principle was approved by everyone present, but several objections were raised. Unfortunately it is not quite certain who raised them or why: the transcriptions jotted down on the spot have been destroyed, and all that remain are copies which, made at a later date, are not always credible. According to Daniel Stern, the pseudonym of Mme d'Agoult, who received her information indirectly, Blanc felt the proposal inopportune and impolitic, while Marie raised the scruples of a legalist.[7] Stern, however, was a strong admirer of Lamartine, from whom she probably obtained her information, and the poet later wrote in his history that Blanc had declared the idea "too advanced for the situation."[8] On the other hand, Blanc categorically denied the stand attributed to him by Stern.[9] In the 1862 edition of her *Histoire de la Révolution de 1848* she gave the impression that he warmly and at once supported Lamartine's proposal, but "secondary objections were drawn in by the superior considerations that Lamartine developed."[10] It seems fairly certain that Blanc did not at once respond with complete favor, and his repeated assertions that he did are suspect. However, it is not probable that he was the only one to doubt the feasibility of the motion, and he redeemed himself the next morning when he rushed into the council room, indignantly opened a royalist journal whose editor had predicted a new reign of terror, and breathlessly demanded a decree embodying Lamartine's idea. At once the tall, slender poet rushed from the other end of the room to embrace his diminutive colleague, and the two together drew up the proclamation which Lamartine read from the steps of the City Hall. It was received *comme un évangile d'humanité.* The age of terror was over, or so the government imagined.

On the previous day Lamartine had associated terror with the red flag. Now, reading the new proclamation, he was wearing a tricolor sash, the symbol of office. But the question of colors had not been definitely settled, for about the same time that Lamartine proposed the abolition of capital punishment, Louis Auguste Blanqui assembled his cohorts to lay plans for another demonstration in favor of red. The next morning, therefore, the Place de Grève was filled again with a great crowd, albeit not a very turbulent one. Within the council, Blanc was the only member to favor a change. He argued that the red flag was the banner of revolution; it had waved over the barricades; it symbolized a new era. He pointed out that the tricolor came into existence in 1789 as a compromise between the red and blue of the bourgeois and the white of the monarchy. With monarchy abolished, it was a false symbol, whereas pure red would represent the unity of classes. However logical, his argument did not convince the others. More convincing was the banker Michel Goudchaux, who suddenly arrived to warn that the red flag would frighten businessmen and harmfully affect the stock market. Since the moderates in the government planned to help the workers by first helping their employers to overcome the economic slump, the crowd's petition was rejected. However, the moderates were tactful enough to grant a decorative concession: a red ribbon was to be attached to each flag pole and red rosettes worn in the lapels of officials. Of course, these rosettes disappeared after a few days.

Several of the moderates hoped that Blanc's political career would last no longer; in fact, during the twenty-seventh, Eugène Bethmont, Alexandre Marie, Hippolyte Carnot, Armand Marrast and Antoine Pagnerre, all of the *National,* planned to oust the Jacobin-socialists of the *Réforme.*[11] Their aim was to remove Marc Caussidière from the prefecture of police and then set up a new government, probably without Ledru-Rollin, and definitely without Blanc and Albert who, on Blanc's insistence, had begun to attend the meetings. Lamartine was to be president of the new government; however, he failed to show up on the evening of the twenty-seventh, so the plot was put off until the next day.

Blanc was apparently unaware of these schemes, and his own intentions towards his colleagues were far less subversive. One can state with considerable assurance that he did not wish to destroy, or even to "purify" the government, but rather to enlarge it by creating new ministries with social functions. Early in the morning of the twenty-eighth, before the council met, he approached Flocon and Marrast with the complaint that neither they nor he, although carried to power by the people, had ministries. Of course, he admitted, the word "secretary" had disappeared but their position was inferior and unbearable. New ministries were needed, one of fine arts for Marrast, one of charity for Flocon, and one of progress for himself and Albert.[12] Marrast, impatient to eliminate Blanc altogether, naturally turned down the suggestion. So did Flocon, who, as editor of the *Réforme,* had never been particularly favorable to Blanc and who now came to fear the power that was slipping into his hands. Only the evening before Flocon had received a delegation of some forty workers who demanded a ministry of progress for the socialist. The petitioners, unsatisfied, withdrew, but not before warning that they would return the next day.

Therefore it was the next morning, shortly after Blanc's rebuff and while he was presenting the same idea in a council meeting, that a crowd of 2,000 workers tramped into the Place de Grève. They were dressed in their work smocks and many carried banners inscribed with "Ten-hour Day," "Ministry of Labor," "Organization of Work," or "Abolition of *Marchandage,*" a system by which middle men obtained labor for an entrepreneur at the cheapest wage possible. Now the moderates, sensing a counterplot, added the bitterness of their frustration to the debate. Lamartine was again Blanc's chief antagonist, insisting that a new ministry was not needed, and that he did not understand the meaning of organization of work. Moreover, the government, being only provisional, must leave such important issues to the decision of a national body representing all of France. Lamartine would find occasions to ignore this last argument, however: on the next day when the council abolished the nobility, later when it abolished the property right of slavery in the colonies, and again, when he defended the immediate nationalization of the railroads, all of which measures indicated that the moderates acted when action accorded with their program. When it did not, they simply emphasized the transience of their power and chose to wait. But Blanc desired to enlarge the authority arbitrarily limited by the Provisional Government. In this desire Ledru-Rollin tended to agree with him; however, Ledru acted to extend authority chiefly in the field of politics, and concentrated most of his time and energy in reorganizing the administration and preparing for elections. He offered the socialist little support; in fact, he grew suspicious of him and sided with Lamartine. Like Flocon and other radicals, he became increasingly moderate in regard to social reform, with the result that under the impact of the 1848 crisis the radical movement rapidly fell apart. Save for Albert, Blanc stood alone in the government when the issue at hand was basic social reform. Inevitably he turned to the sympathetic mob for support.

Outside the crowd had come to a halt. Marche was again the chief petitioner and this time his attitude showed clearly that he and the others were not prepared to be packed off with empty promises. Unemployment was widespread, the insurrection having aggravated an already serious economic crisis, and the decision of the government to undertake a small public works program—the origin of the National Workshops— had not seemed very enterprising. If need be, the workers were ready to suffer certain privations for a republic; however, they were not prepared to starve for it. They were torn between the desperation of their condition and their hope in Louis Blanc, in his motto and in his proposed ministry of progress. They saw these things as their cure-all. Blanc had taught them to look to a republic as a benevolent force; and they now came demanding benevolent action. Had they not fought on the barricades for a republic? Had they not compelled the moderates to declare France a republic? In their minds there could be no reversal of that declaration, and the Republic could not retreat or even hesitate in its foremost mission, the organization of work. A ministry of progress, then, would be a necessary part of it.[13]

In the council room Blanc, too, argued that the "revolution had a social meaning" which must be defined.[14] With this the moderates did not entirely agree, whereupon he bluntly threw out his intention of resigning. This came as a shock. All at once the plot to oust him evaporated before the realization that he was indispensable. Were he to walk out of the room and announce to the multitude that he, and therefore Albert, were no longer part of the council, a new insurrection would begin at once. With anxiety now the other members urged him to reconsider. Garnier-Pagès came forward with the notion of a commission to study social conditions and to prepare legislative projects for the future constituent assembly. In this way, until the council could hand over its responsibilities to a stronger national body, Blanc could be kept busy and the pressure for socialist reform be diverted into innocuous paths.[15]

Blanc saw through the subterfuge and declined. It was only after François Arago prevailed upon him, even offering to be a member of the commission, that he reluctantly consented. He drew up a proclamation which he read to Marche, who questioned him with puzzled eyes. The people outside, however, responded with shouts of joy, and, heeding his appeal that they set an example of orderly conduct, retired as he bid them, to return home or to work. The streets resounded with their marching and with their singing of the *Marseillaise*. Shortly afterward the Luxembourg Commission was founded.

II

What undivulged thoughts were rising up in Louis Blanc's mind at this critical moment? Why did he acquiesce in a stratagem that must have appeared to him a clumsy attempt to get around the social aims of the revolution? Was he the dupe of the situation, as certain writers have claimed, or did he consider the stratagem his own ultimately, one by which he might dupe the dupers?

Blanc was by nature optimistic, so that the establishment of the Republic seemed to him to herald a new age of well-being. He was not unmindful of strong opposition, but the almost universal enthusiasm for the Republic offered a guarantee of its permanence. Legitimists, Bonapartists, Orleanists, soldiers, bankers, clergymen, all the old enemies of popular government offered their services to the new regime. Almost overnight France became republican. Everywhere in Paris and in provincial towns trees of liberty were planted. On the twenty-seventh a huge celebration was held to honor the proclamation of the Republic. Blanc and his colleagues, dressed in black, with tricolor sashes and red rosettes, paraded to the July Column. Immense crowds lined the way, cheering and shouting, "Long live the Republic!" It seemed clear that the very idea of a republic, as Blanc had predicted, had taken root at all levels of society. Could he seriously doubt, during this early stage, that with popular government widely accepted, social reform would be postponed for long? All that he needed to hasten the inevitable consequence of political democracy was an effective means of popularizing the idea of social democracy.

As a firm believer in the power of ideas, he saw in the Luxembourg Commission a great rostrum from which he would elaborate his doctrines. This rostrum would be his compensation for the absence of a budget and legislative powers. Consequently, while the commission was supposed to be merely a study group, he refused to limit its activities as prescribed during its short history. On the contrary, he came to see in it the means of carrying out a great historic mission which he blandly assigned to himself. In 1844 he had written: "It is the nature of superior statesmen to give an impulse to things, to ennoble each situation, at the risk of bringing about obstacles and perils for themselves! Without forgetting to adjust themselves to the hour, great men fecundate the pres-

ent; they elevate history." [16] He would use the commission to fecundate
history with the idea of Jacobin-socialism, for "individuals are only instruments destined by God to consume and to break themselves in the
service of ideas." [17] He was prepared "to break himself" because he knew
precisely what he wanted. Here was his strength. "In order to make
revolutions," he reasoned, "you must know well what you do not want;
but a sure means of dominating them is to know better than anyone else
what you do want." [18] With the enrooting of Jacobin-socialism the "social meaning" of the revolution would be "defined," and all levels of
society would rally to the cause of fundamental reform. The bourgeois
would renounce their privileges. Already some producers had written
him, offering to turn over their workshops to the government.[19] The new
revolution, then, would take shape as a voluntary acceptance of social
equality. It would also be an orderly process. On the twenty-ninth, addressing a delegation from the Cour des comptes, Blanc said: "The
motto of the Republic will no longer be Liberty, Public Order; these two
things are inseparable. What we should have henceforth, is *Order in
Liberty*." [20]

Blanc certainly never intended the inauguration of a new reign of
terror; his basic mental attitude revolted against the cruel shedding of
blood. And yet, he was not a complete humanitarian, for there were
strong hatreds within him that, at times, almost balanced both his devotion to justice and his abundance of pity. His capacity for hatred most
clearly expressed itself as a form of jingoism, but it must be emphasized
that even this violence was always in the form of words, not of deeds. In
the final analysis, he reminds one of those moderate revolutionaries, the
Marquis de Condorcet, Friedrich Ebert, Alexander Kerensky, J. Ramsay
McDonald, Léon Blum, who ultimately failed because they were not
prepared to undertake the brutal measures that their opponents, either
of the right or the left, willingly resorted to.

Blanc was definitely not of a piece with Louis Auguste Blanqui; indeed, it was his deep-seated distrust of the *"Enfermé"* which helped to
compel his acceptance of the Luxembourg Commission. He used this
organization in his effort to win the workers away from fanatical revolutionaries. Like most moderate reformers, he was just as fearful of the
extremists on his left as of those on his right, and one of the forces
motivating his action during the spring of 1848 was his suspicion that a
renewal of civil war would either pave the way for the dictatorship of
Blanqui or cause a conservative reaction. Whichever the result, men like
himself would become the victims.[21] Consequently, on the twenty-eighth,
when the crowd of workers assembled to demand a ministry of labor,
Blanc suddenly found himself in an uncomfortable situation. For while
it is possible that he instigated this demonstration, at least indirectly
through his followers, in order to force the hand of the Provisional Government, he found that it would not be coerced. Momentarily a renewal of

civil war stared him in the face, a disaster from which the suggestion of Garnier-Pagès, the commission of inquiry, offered him an escape. He accepted.

Perhaps Blanc's gravest error was to give in so quickly. Later, he reproached the workers for having too easily accepted the proposal.[22] However, the crowd apparently considered itself at his orders, and did his bidding. Therefore, had he held out for a short while longer, he might have obtained his ministry. But it is doubtful that even with a ministry he could have accomplished much more than he did. Of course, the Luxembourg Commission did not have a budget, but money was not the only necessity lacking; it was time that Blanc needed as well. He soon realized this and therefore used the commission in a desperate effort to gain time by retarding the elections to a National Assembly. Thus, the commission became a fundamental agency in the move to establish a temporary Jacobin dictatorship.

III

Louis Blanc took up residence in the Luxembourg Palace on the twenty-ninth. Eighteen years earlier he had been brought to this same building, where he was presented to the grand referendary, Eric Decazes, and now, ironically, he would sleep in the same room Decazes had occupied during the interview. Before retiring Blanc roamed through the deserted chambers where Marie de Médici had once entertained, and where, during the July Monarchy, the friends of democracy had been prosecuted. Undoubtedly he compared his present position with the lowly one he had suffered when he first entered the palace for his presentation to the indifferent Decazes. His rise from obscurity to power certainly titillated his love of popularity. Yet, his rise and ambition had not hardened him: while he was a self-made man, he never forgot that it was the people who had brought him to power. There, in the rows of seats before him, he saw his real ambition coming true: "an aristocracy in white hair was going to be replaced by a people in rags." [23]

The next morning, March 1, not rags, but worker smocks were markedly present when at nine o'clock some labor delegates occupied the benches. Suddenly they heard a rumbling ovation that began in the corridors, increased in volume as Blanc and Albert passed, and attained a wild crescendo, counterpointed with "Long live Louis Blanc!" as the two men entered the large chamber, preceded by ushers and captains of the guard. They mounted the rostrum and faced the crowd. Behind them, in niches in the wall, stood the majestic statues of France's past heroes; before them, gesticulating enthusiastically, were France's future heroes, obscure men, many of whom would fall during the June Days.

Certainly none of the delegates dreamed of such an outcome on this first day of March. Their attention was focused on the diminutive man

wearing the uniform of a guardsman and surrounded by ushers dressed
in the traditional black uniform, white gloves and glittering sword.
They became silent. Then Blanc, in clear simple statements, emphasized
the historic significance of the occasion: for the first time in history manual laborers had been called upon to settle their own problems. He explained the purpose of the commission: the study of social conditions
and the elaboration of projects of law for the National Assembly. His
speech now grew detailed as he explained his scheme of organization:
each craft was to be entitled to three delegates, two of whom would form
part of a large committee meeting periodically, while the third would
belong to a small permanent body. He stressed the desirability of a small
manageable body capable of arriving readily at proposals which would
then be submitted to the large committee for discussion. The method of
election, he concluded, would be announced. He then urged his audience
to return to work.[24]

As a student of the Revolution of 1789, Blanc should have realized that
in his opening address he resembled Jacques Necker speaking to the
Estates General: nowhere among its many technicalities were those proposals the listeners really wanted to hear. Consequently, Blanc stood at
the rostrum, waiting for a dispersal which did not take place. Then a
worker rose to his feet, and in a determined voice stated that no one
would leave until two measures were decreed: first, a reduction of the
working day; and second, the abolition of *marchandage*. Blanc, rising
from the president's chair, countered this demand with a warning against
impatience. The commission must constitute itself before it could act.
There must be elections.

A clamor of discontent rose steadily while Blanc warned that the
lessening of hours would raise the cost of production and therefore of
prices, weaken consumption, favor foreign goods produced more cheaply,
and thus be a disadvantage for French workers. This sounded too much
like orthodox liberalism to satisfy the delegates and, for a while, it
seemed that the unhappy president would have a general strike on his
hands. Fortunately, François Arago entered at this moment and added his
popularity to that of his colleague whose determination to resist finally
reduced his listeners to obedience. They filed out shouting "Long live
the Republic!"

Before the hall was empty, Blanc sent horsemen to summon employers
to a meeting for the next day. The men who showed up were enlightened
enough to discern the urgency of the workers' demands and accepted the
argument that fewer hours for the employed would create work for the
jobless. It was decided to abolish the most oppressive type of *marchandage*
and to reduce the work day from eleven to ten hours in Paris and from
twelve to eleven in the provinces. The difference in standard between the
capital and other cities obviously resulted from the fact that the Parisians
were able to bring direct organized pressure to bear on the agents of

constituted power in the city. But the difference had little meaning inasmuch as the decrees were never put into effect. Sanctions were not provided for until it was too late to apply them. Blanc really did not come out strongly for enforcement, probably because he did not want to antagonize unduly the capitalists whom he hoped to convert and because he felt the reduction of hours inopportune. He repeated his warning against reduced hours in a speech he made before the commission on March 10, the day he explained that leisure would result naturally from the use of machines, and the termination of "industrial anarchy." [25] When the workers continued to complain about the violation of the new ten hour decree, he made a rapid appeal to the *patriotisme des citoyens*.[26] Other issues of reform were similarly forestalled. Apparently, Blanc intended to eliminate *marchandage* by the creation of municipal employment bureaus, but the proposal was never put into effect. The *livret*, the workbook which all workers were compelled to carry and in which employers might give their opinions of the worker, was not used in 1848 but not abolished. It was later revived. The same is true for article 1781 of the Criminal Code, which provided that an employer's statement would be given preference over a worker's statement in the law courts.[27]

Blanc's moderation resulted from his belief that at last society was suffering the sweet birthpains of socialism. Many workers, of course, looked forward to that birth; however, they wanted extensive relief as quickly as possible, and constantly pressed Blanc for more immediate reforms. He soon came to consider their demands exorbitant. In the meetings of the Provisional Government he complained of his difficult role, but found little sympathy there. In the Luxembourg, he emphasized that the commission was a study group existing to prepare legislative bills for the National Assembly and that the organization of work was too complex to accomplish overnight.[28]

At times his own patience wore thin from the constant harassment of friends and foes. He was overworked, and his near isolation in the council meetings, where Albert's support was more devout than dynamic, increased his anxieties. Happily, his robust health did not give way at this early date, as did Flocon's, but his fatigue mounted steadily. Evenings he often returned late from meetings and simply threw himself on the bed, fully clothed. On April 3 he was forced to remain away from his work.[29]

His time, when not interrupted by demands for this or that reform, was occupied with preparations for the first meeting of the commission, which he awaited impatiently. Elections were finally held, somewhat haphazardly because the old corporate organizations of each profession had practically disappeared and Blanc had decided too confidently to leave the task of reconstituting them to the workers.[30] On March 10, all the worker delegates met at the Luxembourg Palace. Blanc made the opening address and again emphasized patience, extolled machines and called for class harmony. His impassioned speech, as well as the novel solemnity of the occasion, had a marked effect on those present. When he was called away, the delegates rose in a mass and applauded wildly, so moved were they by an *émotion inexprimable.*[31] Then a permanent committee of ten was chosen by lot.

Not until the seventeenth was there a general session of 242 worker delegates and 231 employer delegates. The latter co-opted ten from their number to form a permanent committee which generally met separately from that of the workers. On occasion, however, the two met in joint session to discuss important issues affecting capital and labor, and when this occurred, Blanc presided. His presence manifested itself everywhere, and it was largely through his personal efforts that the Luxembourg Commission was now almost as fully constituted as it would ever be. Unfortunately, it was never complete, some crafts having sent no representatives, while enthusiasm could not overcome the negligence and ill will of most employers and even of many workers.[32]

Perhaps it was partly Blanc's fault that not all the schools of social reform were present, but on March 3 he certainly essayed to bring together a wide variety of thinkers: Saint-Simonians, Fourierists, Jacobin-socialists, and liberals sat face to face in another committee, one of experts chosen by Blanc. They were to present their ideas on social conditions, and to draw up a report for the future government. Blanc, too occupied with other pressing matters, was never able to play an active role in this committee; he therefore relied on Vidal and Pecqueur to take charge of the final report. Assisted by Charles Dupont-White, an *étatiste* liberal, they eventually drew up the *Exposé général des travaux de la Commission du Luxembourg,* published in the *Moniteur.*[33] The *Exposé* was by no means the work of the multifarious committee; it was rather an exposition of the theories Blanc, Vidal, and Pecqueur held in common, though its considerable attention to agrarian reorganization, which Blanc had almost ignored, particularly revealed the views of Vidal and Pecqueur. The report had no discernible influence at this time. It was an important landmark, however, in the development of Jacobin-socialism and later influenced men like Benoît Malon and Georges Renard.[34]

More effective was the part Blanc took in the Luxembourg where, during March and early April, he expatiated on his ideas before audiences of workingmen. He used the commission for indoctrination, not investigation. Of course, on every occasion when he counseled his audience to be patient, he stressed the need for study, for discussion, as a means of discovering solutions; but this was a tactic, not a goal. Why waste time investigating? He had already exposed the poverty of the lower classes. Why search for a solution? He had one.

Unfortunately for him, he could not inaugurate his socialist program at once. Having accepted the Luxembourg Commission he had given up the budget for the word. This was, perhaps, a catastrophe, because not all of the plans he put forward were Utopian. On March 5 he elaborated his plan for a workers' city, composed of large apartments, each housing some 400 families, with either communal or private kitchens and dining rooms. The cost of each building was estimated at about a million francs.[35] The construction of these apartments would have been a useful public works project, giving worthwhile tasks to the men in the National Workshops, and would have been effective in relieving the economic crisis. The plan was approved by both the commission and the committee of experts; however, neither the Provisional Government nor the National Assembly, when it met, would grant the required funds. The moderates, guided by Marie, preferred to use the National Workshops as a means of discrediting labor and of undermining the influence of socialism.[36]

The Luxembourg Commission, therefore, could not act, save in one field, industrial relations. It came to serve as the arbitrator in the disputes that broke out between capital and labor. After the February revolt these disputes were numerous, among the pavers who demanded higher wages to repair torn up streets, among the bakers whose hours were excessive, among the cabbies, and among the men in the smaller workshops. It was Blanc who usually sat as arbitrator and he was quite successful at this task, settling most of the conflicts. Indeed, the commission proved to be a far more just means of arbitration than the Prud'homme councils had been, since both employers and employees, rather than foremen, were represented, and Blanc, working directly for the first time with labor leaders, greatly expanded his popularity. In fact, it is probable that his role as an arbitrator was more appreciated by the workers than his part as a social theorist; immediate improvements were more understandable than abstract principles. For example, on March 15, some bakers of Paris turned out on strike, ran from shop to shop to urge other bakers to leave the ovens, and finally massed in the courtyard of the Luxembourg Palace. Apprized of the maneuver Blanc acted at once, realizing that without bread a large part of the city's population would go hungry and that a hungry mass might become a revolutionary mass. He rushed down to calm the crowd and, before long, brought together representatives of the bakers and their employers. These agreed upon a new salary schedule that Blanc read to the crowd which, overjoyed, surged forward to embrace him and ended by almost crushing him to death.[37]

Blanc was also active in protecting foreign workers whom his proletarian compatriots wished to expel because of the scarcity of jobs. For once, the *Atelier* and the Luxembourg acted in accord, both of them urging the government to issue the proclamations necessary to remind Frenchmen that the revolution had been fought to benefit everyone. At the same time the government took steps to prevent immigration and encouraged the departure of foreign workers who had formed themselves into revolutionary bands for the purpose of overthrowing tyranny in their homelands. This action of the government, however, created serious diplomatic problems.

Another provocative issue, magnified by unemployment, was the competition between private industry and the production located in religious houses and prisons. Workers complained bitterly about the nuns and criminals whose costs were minimal and who were able to undersell them. At once Blanc brought the matter up in the governing council, where measures were taken to regulate production in nunneries and to eliminate it in jails. At the same time both he and Albert demanded the abolition of imprisonment for debt. The moderates arrayed themselves in opposition, arguing that it was an indispensable weapon for creditors. As usual a heated debate ensued, ending only with a provisional discontinuance on March 9.

IV

This decision of the government, although temporary, emptied the Clichy debtors' prison. At once Blanc decided to use this place, the symbol of bankruptcy, as an experimental workshop where the remedy of socialism would be applied to the ills of capitalism. This dramatic, unprecedented turnabout struck him as being most auspicious, especially when he learned that the city of Paris was about to furnish the newly democratized National Guard with uniforms. There were some 100,000 men to outfit, and the government had intended, when acceding to the popular demand for free uniforms, to create a sartorial relief program. It was Blanc, however, who decided to use the plan as a means of fostering socialism.

He had heard about a tailor named Philippe Bérard who was a collaborator of the *Atelier*. Summoning him to the Luxembourg, he explained his project for a co-operative. Bérard asked if the government would advance the capital, an embarrassing question which the socialist hesitantly answered in the negative. He had also to point out that the commission did not possess a ministerial budget, so all that he could offer was the building and the plan of organization. Neither of the men allowed these obstacles to dampen their determination. Bérard got together a group of about fifty journeymen tailors and they obtained the contract, chiefly through Blanc's intercession. Their capital came from an unexpected source: 11,600 francs from the master-tailors who feared that the order might fall to the clothiers (middlemen) whom they despised.[38]

On March 28 Bérard and his small band moved into their new workshop. Before long, their number jumped to 800, then by mid-May to almost 1600 men. This rapid increase resulted from the willingness of the association to accept all who applied for jobs, even the unskilled, whose work had at times to be redone.[39] There was some inefficiency and waste, both inevitable, given the haste and novelty of the experiment. Organized in accordance with Blanc's ideal of a social workshop, the workday was limited to ten hours, and the salary of two francs was equal for everyone. The administrative hierarchy was elected. Bérard remained in charge and, although in ill health, proved to be a remarkably active and capable chief.[40]

One of his major obstacles was widespread opposition to the experiment. Although it was an independent co-operative, it was greeted with marked hostility, not merely by orthodox liberals, but also by the so-called friends of association, such as Lamennais, whose accusations of laziness and inefficiency were disproved by the administrators of the tailors.[41] Marrast, mayor of Paris, and the municipal council revealed their aversion by retarding as long as possible the payments due, refusing to advance a *sou* until the order was filled. The association attempted to get around this obstacle by issuing script (*bons*), which local merchants accepted in lieu of cash. Eventually all of these debts were paid in full. At the same time, many of the young hoodlums taken into the newly organized Mobile National Guard were excited against the tailors by equally exaggerated stories of their laziness and corruption and allowed to filch cloth from the workshop.[42]

The animosity which created these problems for the workshop had subtle causes. It reflected not only the intensified social conservatism of the republicans, but also their resentment of the close liaison between the Luxembourg and Clichy. The tailors had their delegates, Bérard, Leclerq, and Chalon, in the commission, while it in turn had a special agent, almost a sort of ambassador, Edmond Frossard, attached to the association. In the eyes of many republicans and orthodox radicals, Clichy was nothing more than an extension of the Luxembourg Commission, and their determination to destroy the latter naturally included the former.

The desire for associations among the working class was nonetheless fired by this experiment, with the result that Blanc was overwhelmed with demands for his aid. He was, in fact, so pressed that he had to announce once more in the *Moniteur* that the commission's chief task was the preparation of bills for the assembly.[43] Still, he helped to found other co-operatives: one of spinners, for whom he obtained another government contract, another of saddlers, and another of machinists. But these too were weakened by the lack of adequate capital, for while government contracts gave them a start, they received no subsidies from a government preferring to spend vast sums upon the unproductive National Workshops. The National Workshops, growing rapidly in size, offered fertile ground for antisocialistic indoctrination, whereas the co-operatives, whether or not directly founded by Blanc, were all inspired by his *Organisation du travail*. Even in the provinces, especially in Lyons, his ideas were dominant, the goal of the associations being social solidarity through the elimination of competition.[44] Cognizant of his own force as early as February 24, Blanc augmented it through his leadership in the Luxembourg and soon came to use it in order to influence the Provisional Government.

CHAPTER NINE

First Worker of France

I

☞ WHEN LOUIS BLANC entered, or rather, forced his way into the Provisional Government, he created the issue of socialist participation in a nonsocialist ministry. This issue would envenom the debates among socialists around the turn of the century, and he would be cited as its first example, favorably by Jean Jaurès,[1] and unfavorably by Paul Lafargue.[2] Revolutionary Marxians such as Lafargue would accuse him of having stupidly submitted to the machinations of bourgeois republicans who used him as a political opiate to benumb the revolutionary workers.

Now, in truth, his position within the council was most vague. He was a part of it, but not an integral part. He possessed voting rights, even when classified as a "secretary";[3] however, he never occupied a ministry or disposed of a budget. He consequently shared the responsibilities of the council without sharing all of its powers. This awkward position soon prompted him to use the Luxembourg Commission as a source of political power. He accepted the commission, at first to propagate his ideas and subsequently to set up precursory workshops. Yet, he never relinquished his belief that governmental aid was indispensable to the co-operative movement.

In the economic crisis, official assistance had become all the more necessary. By early March the question was posed clearly: which social force, capitalism or socialism, would receive this aid. Immediately after street fighting came to an end, Blanc and the workers of Paris demanded it for socialism and by means of threats they received a few palliatives. However, the moderates fully intended to use their political power to rescue capitalism. Indeed, among the most positive measures carried out by the Provisional Government were precisely those which strengthened French capitalism. The moderates where neither cruel nor indifferent to the hardships of labor. But they concluded that the only way to help the workers, so many of whom were jobless, was to stimulate the economy and thereby recreate the jobs that had disappeared in the economic depression.[4] They chose the famous banker, Goudchaux, as finance minister, a choice as much intended to reassure the middle class, as was their refusal to accept the red flag and a ministry of labor, even when they were vio-

lently threatened by the mob. Goudchaux warned that the flag would
frighten the bourgeois who were already hiding their money and so
threatening to dry up the source of both credit and government revenue.

Here were the two chief economic problems, credit and revenue, facing
all members of the council. Goudchaux, in hope of restoring confidence
in the government, urged it to meet all its usual obligations. Unfortunately, it had not only inherited an economic crisis and a considerable
debt from the July Monarchy, but also a near-empty treasury. Nonetheless, it announced that interest payments would be made in advance of
the date they were regularly due. Blanc accepted this proposal, though
his acceptance did not reduce the anxiety felt by financiers and business
men about his presence in the government. Credit continued to dry up.[5]
In despair Goudchaux resigned in early March. Garnier-Pagès replaced
him and in the midst of a worsening financial crisis proved to be fairly
resourceful. While Lamartine played the part of hero of the bourgeois
and captivator of the mob, the finance minister undertook the less dramatic task of saving capitalism. He had already revealed his resourceful-
ness on February 28, when, to appease the crowd, he had substituted the
idea of a study commission without a budget for a ministry of labor with
one. In charge of the government's money, he now made every effort to
thwart the commission.

Under the guidance of its president, the Luxembourg drew up its own
plan for relieving the crisis. It called for the issuance of paper money
whose value would be based on produce deposited in large stores set up
by the government. The plan was frankly inflationist and Blanc hoped to
use inflated paper to pay off the public debt, buy ruined industries, and
set up workers' co-operatives. However, when he made known his proposals in a council meeting, Garnier-Pagès flatly refused even to consider
them. He later explained why: "This was the maximum with its sequel,
ruin and the scaffold—pitiless logic deduced by history! . . . legalized
theft." [6] The moderate majority voted against Blanc and the same refusal
awaited his plan to nationalize the Bank of France in order to destroy the
financial oligarchy. Garnier-Pagès was not a warm friend of this oligarchy, but instead of seeking to destroy it, he acted rather to broaden
the sources of credit which it controlled. To achieve this end he founded
the *Comptoir National d'Escompte,* a sort of unofficial adjunct to the
Bank of France, serving to loosen credit and thaw frozen paper by guar-
anteeing loans made by private banks. He was not opposed to the lending
of money to co-operatives by the branches of the *Comptoir,* a "benefit
which would assure pacifically the true organization of work." [7] However, apart from a loan at the regular interest rate to one of the associations founded by Blanc, the *Comptoir* did nothing directly to aid the
workers. Indirectly, of course, it aided them by contributing to the economic revival and the creation of jobs. Curiously enough, the finance
minister provided for the creation of "general stores" where capitalist

producers might deposit produce, receive a receipt, and use this paper as security for loans. A socialist idea was put at the service of capitalism.

Economic Revival did not come about at once and the treasury remained lean, its outlays having increased while its income diminished. Early in its career the government, under pressure from journalists and popular agitation, had rescinded the generally detested imposts on periodicals and salt. Soon, its income from other indirect taxes grew less with the decline in consumption. This loss was certainly not compensated by the "patriotic gifts" flowing in after the revolution, and the move to raise a new loan by selling bonds proved sterile. Frankly desperate, Garnier-Pagès decided to raid the popular savings banks, the *caisses d'épargne*, and issued a decree proclaiming that all deposits over a hundred francs would no longer be redeemed in currency. The depositors received state bonds, which rapidly depreciated from 25% to 40% below par. This act was not only confiscatory, it was a flagrant violation of the March 7 decree lauding both the *caisses d'épargne* and the ideal of saving. Prior to 1848 Blanc had been a persistent critic of these savings banks, though he had affixed his signature to the March 7 degree.[8] Since the finance minister's present expediency was in accord with his old hostility, he more readily accepted it, apparently failing to realize in the present situation the political implication of this act. Those who stood to lose were chiefly petty merchants and highly skilled workers, the backbone of radicalism, if not of pure socialism. While Blanc was not the advocate of the act, antisocialist publicists, as well as his socialist opponents, sought to cast the blame for heavy expenditures upon him, arguing that excessive outlays of money for his socialist experiments necessitated heavier impositions.[9] It was widely believed that he was the creator of the National Workshops which voraciously devoured the public revenue.

To offset the draining of the treasury all members of the government accepted a new land tax of forty-five *centimes*. Blanc and Ledru-Rollin urged the exemption of small farmers, but their proposal was not written into the decree of March 16. It might have been had they insisted more vigorously, because their proposal was not opposed. On this occasion, as on others, Blanc by-passed the opportunity to win peasant support. His earlier inflationist proposals would have been a boon to the peasants, giving them an opportunity to pay off heavy mortgages. His lack of political force here, and the above charges of heavy expenditure, undoubtedly weakened further his position in the country at large.

It was not known that the amount of public money Blanc really spent was insignificant, since all of his measures calling for considerable outlays were defeated. For example, he urged the nationalization of the railroads whose completion would take the unemployed out of the National Workshops, where they spent half the day and more in idleness, and give them useful jobs. The moderates also favored nationalization, and Lamartine, who was far more responsive than Marie and the extreme right of the council, issued the decree of April 4 sequestrating two companies. In the council meeting, Blanc had favored the move, but argued that it treated the companies too leniently by over-valuing their stock, thus placing too heavy a financial burden on the state. In the end, however, moderates chose to leave the issue for the National Assembly. It is possible that this timidity resulted, in part, from their fear that immediate development of the railroads would empty the National Workshops and increase Blanc's popularity. By this time the moderates were too deeply committed to his destruction, and the National Workshops were part of their plan to effect this goal. Their republican vision had so focused itself that socialism appeared to be the chief if not the only enemy of the liberal Republic. Believing the end worthy enough, they resorted to most dangerous means for achieving it. For in their purblind use of the workshops, they laid the seeds of the June Days, after which the republic of their plans became impossible. Their mistake proved fatal in the end. Blanc's mistakes during March and April, however, hastened the day of reckoning.

II

Louis Blanc's action during March and April was determined by his belief that Jacobins, preferably Jacobin-socialists, must obtain positions of control in the chief branches of government, including the National Guard. That he intended to destroy the Provisional Government, or even to purge it, is highly improbable; his action suggests, rather, he sought to exploit his popularity among the workers in order to compel the government by threats to move in the desired direction. However, unless the National Guard of Paris favored this tactic, it might react adversely and strengthen those who opposed Blanc. He feared the guard; on February 22, he had warned against undertaking a revolt because he believed the guard would fire on the people. Therefore he desired subsequently to infuse it with radicalist sentiments. The enlisting of workers in the guard was the first step in this direction, and accomplished shortly after the February revolt. The next step was to provide for the election of workers to officer posts. Registration lists were drawn up, and on March 3 it was announced that they would remain open during the next ten days, elections in Paris and the suburbs having been scheduled to take place on March 18.

Meanwhile, elections of officers in the guard became inextricably bound up with elections for a National Constituent Assembly. Ledru-Rollin and others having prepared the decree regulating the latter, the government decided on March 5 to accept their plans and to announce that the consultation of the nation would take place on April 9, just about a month away. Already, however, a clamorous debate was underway over the timing of these elections. Within the council, the moderates had decided upon early elections, wishing to turn over their powers as soon as possible to a national body. They were far more embarrassed than Louis Philippe for having derived their rulership from the barricades. Outside of the government they were supported by Lamennais, Raspail, and Caussidière, who called for early elections before republican fervor began to cool.

However, most of the revolutionary republicans, particularly those in the clubs, demanded postponement, asserting that the peasants, who would enjoy the vote, were ignorant, dominated by royalists and priests, and easily impressed by anti-democratic propaganda. There was need for time "to educate" the masses, asserted Barbès, Cabet, and especially Blanqui, who were the chief spokesmen for this view outside of the council. On March 7 Blanqui arrived at the City Hall with a large body of followers bearing a petition. Lamartine received them, listened with patience, but refused their demand.

Within the council, it seems that Blanc was the first to take up the arguments favoring postponement of the officer corps elections, as distinct from national elections. Meeting with his colleagues in the Petit-Luxembourg during the evening of March 13, when at midnight the registration rolls were to be closed, he contended that many persons had not yet registered, either from lack of time or as a result of the obstructionist tactics of certain district mayors. Moreover, time was necessary to allow the recruits, workers for the most part who had not belonged to the guard during the July Monarchy, to become acquainted with one another. Otherwise the bourgeois who had been officers would surely be re-elected. Blanc's arguments made little impression, because the moderates were aware that the majority of the old officer corps was mildly republican, not at all radical, and firmly antisocialist.

Almost as a last resort, Blanc warned that unless delay was accorded, a solemn demonstration of over 100,000 citizens would make known the popular will. This news caused an angry stir among his colleagues; they boldly asserted that they would not give way to mob pressure. At this point Blanc sought to clarify the aim of the manifestation. It was not to be a threat, but "a simple notification of the intentions which have been communicated to me and which deeply move me." [10] The others finally decided on a twofold compromise: the registries would remain open through the sixteenth, and the élite companies of *grenadiers* and *voltigeurs,* composed of the wealthiest citizens in costly uniforms, would be dissolved.

During this time Blanc was in very close touch with the labor leaders of the Luxembourg. Through them he was apprized of the activities of the clubs—hence his knowledge of the planned demonstration, the idea for which, it seems, had originated in Cabet's club on March 10.[11] Whether or not Blanc may have hit upon the same idea, he had again used the menace of a demonstration in his arguments with the moderates, as he had on the twenty-fourth and the twenty-eighth of February. Perhaps he did not intend that the demonstration take place, hoping merely to force his colleagues into acquiescence by means of its threat. However, his technique was undoubtedly the outcome of a conviction arrived at some eight years earlier when he had written that unless the government was controlled by social reformers, it would stifle all efforts to improve society, because "not to seize power as an instrument is to find it in one's path as an obstacle." [12] Now in the late winter and spring of 1848, his problem was to discover the method of putting this maxim into effect. Undoubtedly he was familiar with Robespierre's famous statement that in time of peace, reason should serve as the basis of government, while in time of trouble, reason must be supplemented by intimidation. Without a Paris Commune to carry out this intimidation, Blanc resorted to the Luxembourg Commission; it put him in contact with the clubs, of which he was not a member, and with the workers, few of whom he knew personally. This is probably one of the reasons why he hardheadedly insisted, when the delegates called vociferously for immediate reforms, that the commission first organize itself as quickly as possible. For the same reason, he had not abandoned the Provisional Government, whose meetings he attended regularly,[13] for the impotent commission. His tactic, of course, was designed to reinforce the radical minority in the council. He all but openly revealed it when he wrote about the manifestation that eventually took place: "The influence of March 17 has, since then, remained alive in the Council. There were always seven voters on one side, four on the other; but behind the four, the memory of March 17 brought forth a fifth voter . . . the People." [14]

There were several flaws in Blanc's plan, probably fatal ones. First, socialism was not nearly so strong as he imagined, not even in Paris, and by April there were workers who became fearful of the audacity of their diminutive leader. Particularly those in the National Workshops, plied with anti-socialist propaganda, came to look upon the Luxembourg as a rival organization, and held back to a large extent from taking part in the popular movements in March and April.[15] The creation of the workshops had split the labor movement, weakening the socialist by limiting the popular basis on which he could establish his power. Secondly, the use Blanc made of the Luxembourg gave it a new role; it became what he himself referred to as a second people's chamber.[16] Thus Blanc, the defender of unicameralism, really brought into existence a power challenging that of the council, producing something like a bicameral legislature. But having no way of creating a definite, regular relation between the two bodies, he was finally driven to exert pressure, not in a constant, subtle fashion, but by a series of shocks in the form of popular demonstrations. Finally, and this was Blanc's most serious miscalculation, the moderates in the council resisted the pressure of these shocks, for while they seemed to retreat, they really took one step back and two forward. Not on any occasion, February 26, February 28, March 17 or April 16, did he wring from them what he really sought: ministerial power for himself within a pliable, provisional dictatorship of a committee of public safety.[17]

Pierre Joseph Proudhon was surprised by him and Marx critical of him, the "little sultan," for not setting up a personal dictatorship. Neither of them understood his dilemma. He was impeded by his loathing of terrorism. Being fully aware, long before 1848, that Jacobin-socialism had no deep roots in most areas of France, he desired to placate the middle and peasant classes with the presence of moderates in the government, while he gradually acquired the means of implanting socialism throughout the country. Eliminate the moderates at once, however, and the bulk of France would react against the capital, so that the radicals, if they would keep power, would find themselves compelled to inaugurate a new reign of terror, an eventuality by no means appealing to Blanc.[18] He did not possess the fanatical will necessary to overcome his humanitarian scruples. Moreover, he feared that terrorism in turn would open the way for Blanqui's rise to power. On one occasion, when the pallid, uncompromising revolutionary sought to establish an alliance with him, Blanc flatly refused, holding that a member of the government must not compromise himself by entering into relations with the chief of a sect.[19] He was more squeamish in this respect than Lamartine.

Indeed, the thought that Blanqui might profit from the demonstration planned by the clubs and the Luxembourg aroused his anxiety, and by the fourteenth he was troubled by the very audacity of his plan. His fears were apparently exaggerated, since Blanqui, at this early date, chose much the same tactic as Blanc himself: popular pressure rather than a *coup de main*.[20] Nonetheless, Blanc felt that he was playing with revolutionary fire and he was not entirely sure that he could control the flames. Therefore, remaining in close contact with his men in the commission, he instructed them to beware of any effort to enlarge the limited role he envisioned for the demonstrators.

That same evening he, Ledru-Rollin, and Albert made a sincere and determined effort to convince the moderates of the danger their intransigence might entail. But by a vote of 8 to 3—Flocon voted with the majority—delay of the elections was rejected, even though the mayor of the wealthy first district doubted that the lists would be completed in time. Not until the next day, the fifteenth, when Marrast admitted that the registers could not be completed as planned, did the council decide to extend registration until the twenty-third and to postpone the elections until the twenty-fifth. Blanc, motivated perhaps by information that the Blanquists were organizing, accepted this palliative, this one step backward. At once the decision was made public.

Probably the demonstration of the clubs and the Luxembourg would now have been called off had not another been organized by the élite national guardsmen, who strongly protested against the dissolution of their companies. On the sixteenth they marched, dressed in their costly uniforms and tall shakos, the *bonnets à poils,* and halted before the City Hall. There they thundered against their decreed demise. Probably they were protesting not only against the decree, but against the entire left-wing of the council.[21] The threats which proliferated from the mass of black shakos, and the roughing of Ledru-Rollin, certainly left the radicals with little doubt as to the intent of the petitioners. The radicals' concern was heightened because this was the second hostile demonstration on the part of the wealthy middle class, the first having occurred only five days earlier. Moreover, Blanc was well aware that the protests against post-ponement of the elections came chiefly from middle class groups, organized in electoral committees, such as the Central Republican Committee, which had branches in the suburbs and departments and was in a position to swamp the government with petitions opposing delay. These petitions, either mailed or ostentatiously delivered by numerous delegations, had the effect of stiffening the moderates' resistance to the left.[22] The keen opposition to an immediate election, emanating from the radicals, the Luxembourg and the clubs, only increased their desire for haste.

Blanc must have suspected that this was the view of the employer delegates who were to meet at the Luxembourg on the next day, the seventeenth. How then, could he impress them with his theories, how could he call for action, if they shared the belief that the voice of all France would probably order him out of power in the very near future? The tactics of his moderate colleagues would become theirs: no action until after the vote. Blanc must have believed that the vociferous demonstration by the élite guards had stiffened the obstinate moderation of his colleagues.

Inevitably, therefore, he proposed a more extensive delay when he met with the council that afternoon, the sixteenth. To the numerous objections raised he admitted he wanted a dictatorship, albeit one of progress, not of reaction. He averred that no one had more respect for popular sovereignty than himself; what he dreaded was its falsification. According to Garnier-Pagès he reasoned that it would be a crime to deliver the Republic over to the eternal enemies of the people, who would then take advantage of their riches and influence in order to procure the people's votes and to perpetuate the people's enslavement. The first day these enemies had been supple and flexible; but now they had just risen up, deceiving and exciting the National Guard by a pretext. It was not logical or prudent to expect anything from men who used professions of faith and oaths only to mislead the country. If the elections were not delayed they would assuredly be reactionary. Then one would find oneself at the head of a doubtful majority confronted by an exasperated people. All the caution of the government would end only by throwing the National Assembly into a conflagration that nothing could extinguish, and there would follow a popular Brumaire.

There is every reason to believe that Garnier-Pagès faithfully transcribed, if not the exact words, certainly the thoughts of Louis Blanc. Blanc had earlier admitted that when he had visited Louis Napoleon at Ham, he had argued that "universal suffrage must not be a loaded pistol in the hands of a child. The sovereignty of the People implies in no way whatever the intellectual abdication of those who are in a position to impress upon the public will, either by their writings or by their discourses, a generous and enlightened impulsion." [23] As early as 1846 he had begun to doubt that various groups could automatically harmonize their differences within the unifying walls of a single chamber. By 1848 he feared that "social virtue" would not hinder the conservative provinces from dealing rigorously with radical Paris. As in 1793, the struggle between rural and urban France must be resolved by the dictatorship of the capital, that is, by the "dictatorship of progress." [24] Therefore Blanc was not willing to surrender to the argument of Garnier-Pagès who pointed out that immediate elections would return "esteemed republicans" and "famous liberals." Blanc did not want a national assembly dominated by such moderates, and warned again that such a gathering would drive the workers to rebellion. Paris, that is, the Jacobin-socialists of Paris, must educate the peasants while at the same time retaining control of the Provisional Government as well as of the administration, the judiciary and the military, all of which must be "purified." [25]

This Jacobinism, however, only aroused the resistance of the moderates, and Blanc found himself thwarted when Lamartine, the would-be disciple of the Girondins, and Dupont, deeply angered, threatened to resign. Such a step would destroy his carefully laid plans. Hence, he desisted and even signed a proclamation drawn up by the towering poet, extolling the beauties of popular sovereignty and, by implication, calling for early elections. Assuredly by now the thought could not have been absent from Blanc's mind that the appearance of the élite guards had encouraged the moderates and weakened his position. Thus a counter-demonstration was not only desirable, it was necessary, in spite of Blanqui.

III

We do not know the extent to which Blanc participated directly in the preparations carried out at first by the corporations of the Luxembourg. These were represented by fifteen delegates, who joined during the stormy, wind-swept night of March 16, with a like number from the clubs. This committee of thirty, in which the club delegates quickly assumed leadership, drew up a proclamation, posted on the walls of Paris in the early morning, calling upon the workers' corporations to meet at the Place de la Révolution at ten o'clock.[26] Then, an hour before the scheduled assembly, it prepared a petition containing three demands: withdrawal of all troops from Paris, adjournment of the National Guard elections to April 5, and adjournment of the general elections to May 31. These dates had been set by Cabet, not by Blanc.

At the appointed time and place, about 150,000 workers assembled and were formed into ranks by the Luxembourgers, who were under strict orders from their president to beware of extremists.[27] With the clubbists at their head the corporations marched in a long, almost silent column toward the City Hall, arriving at about two in the afternoon. As they spread out over the Place de Grève they sang the *Marseillaise* and, unappropriately, the *Chant des Girondins*. Between these they interspersed vivas for Blanc and Ledru-Rollin. The Jacobin-socialist had just arrived from the Luxembourg where he had been discoursing on the evils of competition before an audience of employers. Their response, more polite than fervent, had been as nothing compared to this massive ovation in the streets which, he hoped, would spread like a joyous wind and settle over France. His spirit would have been much less elated had he observed Buchez and Lamartine watching in disquiet from an upper window. On an impulse Buchez urged the poet to invite the leaders in, arrest them, then to harangue the crowd and send it off.[28] Lamartine refused, and descended to the first floor where the committee of thirty and ten others presented the petition. As Louis Blanc listened, his emotions were now mingled. He saw in the delegation "strange faces," men of Blanqui, whom he distrusted. With one shout, he reasoned, these few men could transform a completely peaceful crowd into an insurrectionary mob.[29] On the other hand, he was content to realize that he was the real intermediary between this fragile government and the politically carnivorous mass, momentarily tamed by the gentle music of promises.

The reading over, Blanc stepped forward, praised the people, and invited the delegates to depart. He and his colleagues would take up the people's will but they could not deliberate under pressure. The calmness of the people, he said, was the majesty of its force. Then, the most unexpected happened. Several delegates roared, "We'll not leave here without an answer to transmit to the People." But Joseph Sobrier relieved the tenseness with assurances that the people had confidence in all members of the council. "Not in all! Not in all!" warned several voices. "Yes, yes, in all! In all!" shouted the majority, drowning out the Blanquists. Seizing a propitious moment Lamartine stated that there were only a few troops in Paris. After him, Ledru-Rollin suggested putting off a definite decision until the reports from his agents clarified the attitude of the provinces, and went on to point out that Paris was not all of France.[30] This was the argument of the moderates and was probably Ledru-Rollin's first step in the direction of moderation. Although the final decision of certain clubbists to hold a demonstration resulted in part from the abuse Ledru-Rollin had suffered at the hands of the élite guards on the previous day, and although he was hailed by the crowd, he was to become increasingly suspicious of Blanc, of the workers, and of the clubs. At any rate, the crisis was over, for the time being. Blanc and his colleagues and the delegates now moved toward the massive front stairway. Suddenly, a partisan of Blanqui grabbed his arm and hissed close to his face, "So you're a traitor, you too!" [31] Without turning Blanc joined the others outside where the crowd was clamoring to see all members of the council. The members therefore climbed onto a long table, as shaky as their nerves, and around them gathered Sobrier, Barbès, Etienne Arago and others to form a protecting circle. At a command the host of men filed by in a narrow column, with banners floating in the bright sun, singing patriotic songs and shouting vivas whose echos grew dim as the public square was vacated. When the last of the men moved out, night had fallen and their torches, fading into the twisting streets, abandoned the empty square to the dim glow of the lamps.

IV

The crowd had marched away filled with both the confidence of victory and the belief that its heroes, Blanc, Ledru-Rollin, and Albert, now had the force to impose their will on the moderates. Blanc, too, as he made his way to the council meeting, imagined himself reinforced. But during the debates that evening the moderates apparently did not recognize his new strength; by a vote of seven to three, they held to the date already fixed for the National Guard elections, and their firmness here precluded even a discussion of the general elections. At once the two socialists threatened to resign, a step which clearly suggests a preconceived pattern of coercion. Their tactic of March 17 is identical to that of February 28: first a mass demonstration in favor of a particular objective, during which Blanc assumed the role of savior, and then the threat to resign. He thus left the moderates face to face with a frustrated mob, not an unorganized mob like the one demanding the red flag, but rather one which he had shown to be fairly pliable to his will.

On this occasion it was Ledru-Rollin, a somewhat embarrassed hero of the day, who appealed to the angry socialist. He argued that a definite date for the elections need not be fixed at once, the question being still open. After him Marrast proposed sending for delegates from the Luxembourg and the clubs in order to ascertain whether or not a delay was really needed. Blanc therefore withdrew his resignation and the next day, not the workers but a somewhat confused Barbès informed the council that a delay of eight days was desired, a request so modest that the right-wing readily acquiesced, and it was printed in the *Moniteur* that the elections would be held on April 5.

On the seventeenth, the government appeared to bow to the will of the workers; on the nineteenth, it seemed to acknowledge the mastership of the Luxembourg. Blanc summoned a meeting of the commission for the latter date. Entering the large chamber, Blanc was greeted with so vigorous an ovation that the very walls, accustomed to the infirm declamations of aged peers, must have shaken. It was a long while before he was able to obtain silence. Then, in a voice that was elation made audible, he said:

> My dear friends, this welcome that you give me hardly allows me to overcome my emotion. Thank you for your acclamations; they are a sweet encouragement for us in our perseverence to do good.
> We shall have your co-operation, shall we not? (Yes! Yes!) We shall found the Republic. (Bravo! Bravo!)
> My friends, elected of labor, representatives of those puissant corporations which, during the immortal day before yesterday, gave to the capital such an imposing spectacle, the members of the Provisional Government, my dear colleagues, and, at their head, our venerable president Dupont (de l'Eure) are going to come in a minute into your midst . . . to express their deep sympathy.[32]

When his "dear colleagues" made their entrance, Blanc offered the "venerable" Dupont his arm to assist him in mounting the high rostrum. Arago then gave a brief address in which he thanked his audience for the *"magnifique, . . . imposante manifestation d'avant hier."* After a few more banalities, the meeting was adjourned.

During these few days, Blanc was at the summit of his political career. His name was known throughout France. No evidence has been found to indicate that his following in provincial towns was large, and the election of April 23 made it clear that socialism of any sort was hardly known in the countryside. Yet, Blanc more than anyone else infused political democracy with the idea of social reform. He came to personify, despite his diminutive size, the massive hopes and lofty goals of a growing segment of society. It was appropriate for a group of laborers, joyous in the expectation of well-being after the hard years of the hungry forties, to dub him and Albert the "first workers of France." The occasion was the planting of a tree of liberty in the Luxembourg garden. A frolicsome crowd arrived, with wreaths of foliage, a scattering of priests, a band, and an enormous tree, for which Blanc broke the ground. In a brief allocution, he denied that the tree of liberty must be watered with the blood of kings or of any man.[33]

The next day, a Sunday, he was too busy with the organization of the Clichy tailors' co-operative to attend the council meeting. He was certainly informed that the question of electoral postponement would be taken up, yet he stated that he would defer to the decision of the majority. Perhaps he too was beginning to wonder if a brief delay was desirable. It was clear to him by now that the moderates could not be swayed by *la douce violence* to retain power for a long period, that they had been throwing him mere crumbs of time, and that the only alternative to elections within the near future would be a bloody dictatorship. The latter he rejected even more definitely since the seventeenth when the Blanquist had called him a traitor.

Except among the extreme left, there occurred a noticeable slackening in the demand for delay, probably a result of numerous reports sent in by Ledru-Rollin's agents in the provinces warning that conservatives were reasserting themselves and that time would benefit their schemes. On the other hand, the agents admitted that preparations were not complete, that delay was necessary.[34] The council perused these reports and reluctantly decided to postpone the parliamentary elections until April 23, Easter Sunday. On this issue, Ledru-Rollin had joined the moderates who believed that political equality would end class divisions, and that once the "election belongs to everyone without exception . . . there will no longer be any proletarians in France!" [35]

Ledru-Rollin and Flocon on the one hand, and Blanc and Albert on the other, envisioned a broad program of change, but found it difficult to agree upon a minimum program. Of course, they were both busily engaged in the estimable task of spreading democratic ideas, Ledru-Rollin in the provinces, Blanc in Paris. But even in their common effort they were not above nipping at one another, as in the council meeting of March 29 when Blanc accused the interior minister's agents of antagonizing provincials by using their official positions to favor themselves as candidates in the coming elections. It was at Blanc's request that a circular was sent out prohibiting this practice. Yet, he was on Ledru's side, especially when the agents were criticized for their radicalism; he had convinced himself that it was necessary to speak firmly and to act vigorously against royalism.[36] He was aware that his influence amounted to nothing in the radical's ministry, the important posts being staffed by men fundamentally moderate, like Favre and Landrin, who would attempt to destroy him in early June. On the other hand, Ledru-Rollin had no influence in the Luxembourg; in fact, he became as afraid of the commission as the liberals in the government. However, it was not until the street demonstration of April 16 that the reservoir of mutual suspicion overflowed.

Unlike Ledru-Rollin, the moderates had been deliberately plotting the downfall of Blanc since late February, and after March 17 they hastily completed the web in which they would trap him. There was no one mastermind directing the work. In fact, the moderates were not all of a piece. On the one hand, there was Lamartine whose romantic temperament fed readily upon the intrigues he concocted. By no means a brutal man, nor even a consciously deceitful one, he nevertheless fancied himself as the savior of society, and to carry out this self-appointed mission he was prepared to use both force and negotiation. He sought force in the army. With General Négrier he drew up plans for troop concentrations in the provinces, so that the moderates, were they driven from Paris, would find asylum at Lille, where they would await the recapture of the capital. Ensconced in the Girondin frame of mind, he was quite proud of this "antisocialist and antianarchic federation instituted and mobilized in advance under the control of the departments." [37] Within Paris, he, Marrast, and other moderates, in concert with Generals Bedeau and Changarnier, organized a Mobile National Guard, composed of young unemployed workers, whom they indoctrinated with a hatred for their own class and incited against socialist co-operatives. The young hoodlums, eager to strut about in colorful new uniforms, were told that they had none because of the laziness of the Clichy tailors, whereupon they began the practice of raiding the Clichy workshop, stealing cloth or finished tunics.[38] Lamartine's scheme for negotiations called for wooing Flocon and Ledru-Rollin, as well as the leaders of the clubs. He was in contact with Barbès, Joseph Sobrier, Cabet and Alton-Shée, and even had a secret, nocturnal, and most melodramatic meeting with Blanqui, in order to win his support.

The extreme right of the council, whose mastermind was Marie, also sought to weaken Blanc by dividing the labor movement. In accord with Emile Thomas, director of the National Workshops, he sought to turn the men on relief away from the Luxembourg. A club was established for them, and in its meetings Blanc and his followers were described as a sect of impractical dreamers.[39] Blanc was certainly aware of this maneuver and tried to counteract it. Through the delegates of the commission he maintained contact with some of the men in the workshops. An inner group was led by Gustave Robert, Jacquet, and Auguste Dehaut, who were under the influence of the Luxembourg and acted in accord with that body during the preparations for the manifestation of April 16.[40] However, it does not seem that they managed to extend their control among the thousands of men under the rule of Thomas, at any rate, not before May 15, and perhaps this is why Blanc attempted to win Thomas away from Marie, but with no success. Thomas remained under the orders of the minister of public works, at least until he fell under the influence of Louis Napoleon, and all the while acted with sufficient vigor to dampen considerably Blanc's *mystique*. Also acting in concert with Marie was the minister of education, Hippolyte Carnot, who arranged for the distribution of textbooks describing Blanc's system as the tyrannical destruction of freedom.[41]

By the end of March the forces opposed to socialism began to swell their ranks, to leave the obscurity where they had hidden since the demise of the July Monarchy, and to hurl their anathemas against the Luxembourg and the clubs. Inevitably the very concept of the organization of work came in for rough treatment in the columns of the conservative and liberal press. Léon Faucher in the *Journal des économistes* came to the defense of competition, while the ex-Saint-Simonians, Prosper Enfantin, Michel Chevalier and Louis Reybaud, a member of the Luxembourg study group, avenged their first master for Blanc's criticisms in his *Histoire de dix ans*. These writers, although they sometimes distorted the socialist's ideas, at least kept the debate clear of scurrility.[42] Not so the vile-minded Auguste Villemessant, whose "rag," the *Lampion,* specialized in calumny, asserting, for example, that the socialists at the Luxembourg enjoyed a luxurious existence, dining upon succulent dishes served in silver, all at the taxpayers' expense. In truth, the president and vice-president cut the cost of their meals from six to two francs fifty, and received not one *sou* in remuneration.[43] Louis Blanc, now often called "Louis Blague" (Louis the Joke), was also depicted as the owner of sumptuous houses in the Faubourg Saint-Germain, where he refused to lodge workers. There was, in addition, the popular assertion that he went about preaching socialism for the sole purpose of stimulating the sale of his book. These attacks increased in May and June and overflowed the brink of villainy when Blanc was accused of having abandoned his aged, demented father.[44]

The attacks from the right were reinforced by those from the left. Buchez and Anthime Corbon in the *Atelier* depicted the Luxembourg as the source of all trouble, while Lamennais in his *Peuple constituant* saw in the Clichy association the seeds of materialistic communism. During 1848 the nascent Christian socialist movement, fearful of the "spectre of communism," allied itself with anti-socialist forces, and after the passing of Buchez, became a right-wing movement directed even against republicanism. Blanc later found himself under a torrent of abuse emanating from Proudhon, whose virulence had all the characteristics of the petty bourgeoisie when its traditional individualism rears up against the new forces of collectivism.[45] The attacks of Proudhon represented a class favorable to a republic responsive to its needs, a republic that would control the financiers, the big industrialists, merchants and railroad magnates, but a republic generally hostile to Jacobin-socialist experimentation. Although suspicious of the state, the petty bourgeois, if not Proudhon, looked to it as the agency capable of regulating capital, not as the agency intended to inaugurate socialist co-operatives. Jacobin-socialism had no deep roots in French society; the sociological soil in which it sought to grow was as granite-hard as the peasant's mind against change, and as tight-closed as the bourgeois' purse against the tax collector.

Small wonder, then, that Blanc found relatively few defenders among the publicists. Among these were Cabet, George Sand, Pierre Leroux, Charles Robin, his first biographer, and Théophile Thoré, editor of *La vrai république,* a Jacobin-socialist journal. The influence of Blanc's ideas was markedly visible in the program of the Club de la Révolution.[46] Barbès, an old friend of his, was president of this club, and among its officers were Leroux, Théodore Bac, Théophile Thoré, Pierre-François Landolphe, Marc Dufraisse, and others who were Jacobins and socialists.

The most significant group devoted to him without hesitation consisted of the labor delegates in the Luxembourg. Theirs was almost a personal attachment which took umbrage when he was defamed; indeed, on one occasion they set out to break the presses of the *Charivari* because it satirized their hero. Happily, Blanc was informed, saved the presses and gave the crowd a lecture on freedom.[³¹] Undoubtedly he was secretly pleased with this demonstration, for he could not place himself above the criticisms directed either against his person or his system, or distinguish between the two, having come to view even mild attacks upon his socialism as personal affronts. He identified himself with the socialist movement and reasoned that open hostility to him would embolden the moderates in the council. Therefore, unable to postpone the elections indefinitely, he concluded that the Luxembourg must be used to impel the moderates toward *une généreuse initiative* before April 23.

V

The occasion for another demonstration came about in mid-April when Blanc was informed that fourteen posts in the general staff of the National Guard were to be reserved for workers elected to them. The earlier election of line officers had been disappointing, bourgeois candidates having won most of the votes. Probably the laborers from the National Workshops, enrolled in the guard through the efforts of Marie, helped to counter-balance the influence of the worker guards from the Luxembourg and the clubs. In order to avert another electoral defeat, Blanc decided to call a mass rally at the Champ-de-Mars at which his men could influence the choices. The date was set for April 16, a Sunday one week before the general elections. The assembly, of course, was to be far more than an outdoor caucus; it was to be another demonstration to strengthen the cause of socialism, that is, Louis Blanc's brand of socialism, for the corporations would march afterward to the City Hall to bring not only their sympathy and a patriotic gift, but also a socialist petition.

Undoubtedly Blanc was still concerned about Blanqui, but probably less so than on March 17, because on March 22 Ledru-Rollin obtained a document which could serve to place the arch-revolutionary in the position of having been a police spy in 1839. It was published in Jules Taschereau's *Revue rétrospective* on March 31, for the express purpose of destroying the leader of the extreme left, hence, Blanc's consent to its publication. Blanc perhaps concluded that this maneuver had been effective; Blanqui had not yet disproved the implications of the document, and seemed less of a menace than when panoplied in the pure but unwashed raiment of an unimpeachable insurrectionary.[⁴⁸]

Moreover Blanc had considerably tightened his control over the Luxembourg delegates. The original committee of ten, chosen by lot, apparently had no real power. Blanc now worked through a hand-picked *comité d'action* which met privately, sometimes in the Luxembourg, sometimes, it seems, in the apartment of George Sand situated near the palace.[⁴⁹] In the nocturnal assemblies of April 14 and 15, Blanc laid out plans for another march on the City Hall. A petition was composed which clearly reflected the anger that the attacks upon him had aroused: "The reaction raises its head; calumny, that favorite weapon of men without principles and without honor, pours out from all sides its contagious venom on the veritable friends of the people." [50] The petition went on to demand a democratic republic, an end to the exploitation of man by man, and the organization of work by means of association. These latter were the mottoes that the corporations would place on their banners. Certainly behind these rather vague formulas was couched the desire for a ministry of labor, with the socialist as its incumbent. Unable to put off the elections, he was undoubtedly seeking to ensconce himself in power, a position which would be presented to the assembly as a *fait accompli*. At the same time, he was eager to strengthen the determination of the Luxembourg to put up a bold front in the face of a possibly conservative assembly, so that the politicians would not only accept his ministry but also bow to the will of the worker delegates. Thus he told the delegates during a secret meeting: "Your co-operation can be useful to us by the force that you communicate to us; a moral force which must put us in a position to say to the Assembly: here are the projects of law that we present; these projects of law, it is not Albert, it is not Louis Blanc who present them; it is the people represented by their delegates. Treat with them, and now that they are organized, repudiate them if you dare!" [51]

During the late evening of the fourteenth, after he quit the comfortable company of his disciples, Louis Blanc went to the finance ministry for a meeting of the government. There, in conformity with his usual tactic, he solemnly announced that a new manifestation was pending. This news was frankly disturbing, and Marie, Marrast, and Lamartine sought to parry his maneuver by frightening him with the spectre of Blanqui. Already, they warned, the radical clubs were sitting *en permanence*. Before long the exchange of words became *âpres et vives,* but the socialist would not give way.

He soon began to suspect that the moderates might be correct, and that the demonstration which he had planned as a means of merely pressuring his moderate colleagues might end as one bent upon eliminating them from power. Such, it is likely, were the intentions of Blanqui and perhaps of Caussidière, and in the separate headquarters of each of these men, lists for a new council were prepared.[52] In spite of these clandestine activities, Blanc apparently concluded that too much was at stake to abandon his plan, and in a council meeting held at noon the next day, the fifteenth, he sought to reassure his colleagues with the promise that the workers were concerned only with the general staff elections. But his colleagues refused to be reassured.

On the same day appeared the sixteenth *Bulletin,* written by George Sand and published, like all of them, by the interior department. Prob-

ably influenced by Barbès and radical clubbists, she wrote in substance
that if rural France chose candidates hostile to a social republic, Paris
would have to renew the revolution. Ledru-Rollin was as dumbfounded
as the others, for he had not read Sand's manuscript prior to its publication.[53] Probably the anxiety caused by it prompted him to suggest
Blanqui's arrest, a proposal rejected, not by Louis Blanc, but by Lamartine who early in the morning had engaged in a secret rendezvous with
Blanqui, and now imagined the conspirator under his power. In fact, it
was perhaps Lamartine who countermanded the order, drawn up by
Favre, to arrest Albert, Blanc, and Blanqui.[54] At any rate, Lamartine
quickly emerged as master of the situation, with carefully laid plans
and a strengthened determination to resist the advancement of socialism.
In another meeting held that evening he made it clear to Blanc and
Albert, who were now isolated in the council, that he was not prepared
to tolerate another march on the City Hall, for however pacifistic the
workers' intentions, "violence was in the crowd itself." [55] Now there was
ample reason for fear, because once the news of the demonstration had
got out, there were numerous plots to "purify" or overthrow the council.
Lamartine was especially concerned, his noble, agrarian background
having led him to despise the mass following of the popular leaders who
"could recruit their forces only in the deepest and the most noxious slime
of the population of the big capitals." [56] The Girondin now prepared
against another June second, and during the night the City Hall was
transformed into a fortress.

The next day began with a clear, bright morning. As the church bells
rang for Sunday mass, many workers made their way toward the Champ-
de-Mars where elections were to be held. The turnout was not tremendous, for the moderates, probably Lamartine, having warned Cabet
and Barbès that Blanqui was preparing a *coup de main,* persuaded
them to restrain their followers from taking part. All the delegates of the
Luxembourg were there, but probably not more than 13,000 workers
who were under their orders, and 12,000 to 15,000 members of the National Workshops who were not.[57] There were also many laborers at the
Hippodrome where, it seems, they had been summoned by Caussidière,
but a large number of these were more faithful to Thomas than to Louis
Blanc.

While the crowd assembled at the Champ-de-Mars accomplished the
meeting's ostensible purpose of choosing workers for the general staff,
Blanqui appeared among them, and began distributing copies of his
refutation of the Taschereau document. At the same time, Luxembourg
delegates moved about collecting a *don patriotique* which they, leading
the crowd, were to bring to the City Hall, along with their petition. In the
late morning the column began to move out, and swelled by the multitude from the Hippodrome, followed the Seine toward the City Hall.
When it was almost abreast of the Louvre the relative calm of the city

was disturbed by the sound of drums beating the *rappel*. At once there was consternation and indecision. Most, but not all, of the members of the National Workshops, instinctively responding to the appeals of Thomas' lieutenants, scurried away to join their regiments.[58] The rest of the column filed on, unarmed save for their banners and their hopes. When they arrived, they found the Place de Grève covered with guardsmen, and conspicuous atop a black horse was none other than Barbès at the head of his twelfth legion!

Meanwhile, at the ministry of interior some distance away, all the moderates save Lamartine were awaiting news. Ledru-Rollin was also there, basking in the congratulations of Jules Favre, his aid, for it was he who had first given orders to beat the *rappel*. Presumably it was the vivid imagination of Lamartine, conjuring up pictures of a new terror, which prompted Ledru's decision.[59] His break with Jacobin-socialism was now complete. Henceforth he and Blanc, not to mention Blanqui, would be enemies, and the hostility between them became a concrete wall that not even their common fate in exile could tunnel. Of course, when Blanc and Albert rushed in, Ledru essayed to dispel their fury by explaining that he had acted to weaken Blanqui. Unconvinced, the socialist strongly urged his colleagues to follow him to the City Hall. They refused, whereupon he and Albert departed.

His numerous histories reveal the infuriated consternation Blanc felt when he came upon the solid mass of guardsmen blocking the entrance to the City Hall. This time there were no cheers, as on February 24, no brawny laborers' arms to pass his little body triumphantly overhead into the building. Rather, he and his companion had to push their way through a jungle of flashing bayonets. Everywhere there were hostile murmurings, relieved by only a few greetings from guardsmen who were happy to see him alive. These had rushed to his defense after hearing rumors that he, Albert, and Ledru-Rollin had been murdered by enemies of the people. Like Barbès, they had confusedly come prepared to defend the republic against Blanqui.

Inside the building the uniform of the Mobile Guard was now as conspicuous as the workers' smock had been during the night the republic was proclaimed. And Lamartine, rising to his full height when the diminutive socialist came demanding an explanation, retorted angrily. He consented, however, to allow a small delegation of workers to present their petition and their patriotic gift. It was now Blanc who parried the fury of his followers with the explanation that the beating of the *rappel* had been an error (*malentendu*). "Fiery men," he went on, "extremists have been mixed into this movement in order to cause it to end in disorder. . . . The *rappel* was ordered against these men and not against you." [60] He then obtained permission for the workers to march in review, but the close-packed guards opened only a narrow passage through which his followers passed two abreast. Standing at a window, he could see no more than their banners, waving arms and agitated caps, and hardly hear their vivas, drowned beneath the thunderous shouts of the stationary guards, "A bas Louis Blanc! à bas Blanqui! à bas Cabet, à l'eau les communistes!" Without weapons the workers could do nothing but return home; they were no longer masters of the Place de Grève. When night fell, the guard was passed in review by all members of the council, for Lamartine's colleagues had put in an appearance to share in the acclamations that bordered on delirium. Without doubt, the poet was the hero of the day, "the most beautiful day of his political life." [61]

Lamartine was hardly aware that this day marked the beginning of his decline. He had played the role of the savior of society, that is, of bourgeois society, which, however, was not really threatened, either on March 17 or April 16. He did not realize that on both occasions the Luxembourg delegates had the unarmed workers well in hand, that the reports of his agents and of Ledru-Rollin were grossly exaggerated; that neither Cabet nor Barbès, and probably not Caussidière, were really plotting to overthrow the council, or even to "purify" part of it. Like Blanc, they were too fearful that the extreme left would profit from disorder, and it was Lamartine who excited their fears. Egoistic, he fancied himself a messiah,[62] the son of a god called Order; he also created a devil, Blanqui, and at the same time that he tried to convert this revolutionary satan, he blew him up to exaggerated proportions. However, Blanc, too, was weakened at this juncture. From this time on the revolutionary movement was really no longer under his control; it gradually passed into the hands of men more determined upon action, a turn resulting in the fiasco of May 15 which undermined Lamartine, and which could never have occurred had Louis Blanc retained his earlier prestige. The electoral victory of the poet was the last brilliant glow before a setting sun, for he failed to realize at a crucial moment that without Blanc as a foil there could be no Lamartine as a leader. When bourgeois society would find itself really threatened, the bourgeois would turn to generals, not to poets.

On the other hand, Louis Blanc had acted from the start upon the assumption that without the moderates in the council there could be no peaceful revolution. But displaying a Jacobin distrust of the very god he had adored, universal suffrage, he sought to bully the moderates, driving them not to the left but steadily to the right. He ended by incurring their absolute hostility and, worse, by splitting the left in the council. Flocon and Ledru-Rollin also were frightened by the "fifth voter" whom Blanc called out of the Faubourg Saint-Antoine like a menacing spectre. In the end, he destroyed both himself and the program he stood for, the "days" that he organized, March 17 and April 16, leading to the "days" that he did not, May 15 and June 22, and eventually to the long days of exile.

During the week following the aborted demonstration he received a sort of forewarning of things to come, for there took place, beginning on the evening of the sixteenth, a small-scale bourgeois reign of terror. Extremists in the guard promenaded in the street shouting "Death to communists." A crowd of them gathered before the innocuous Cabet's residence, chanting in chorus, "Cabet à la lanterne." The excitement did not abate rapidly, and no one dared speak openly in praise of socialism or the organization of work. Some working-class guardsmen who defiantly did so were pushed about, beaten, even threatened with death.[63] The middle class was limbering its muscles for the June reckoning.

Fearful of these early excesses, the moderates in the council recoiled. They addressed a letter of felicitation to the clubs: "April 16 has revealed how unshakable are the foundations of the Republic." [64] The words, of course, lent themselves to a double interpretation. The moderates also abolished internal duties on meat, reduced those on wine, and promised new taxes on luxuries, but these measures, which might have appeared as concessions, had been accepted in principle before April 16.[65] They also conceded Blanc's demand for an inquiry into the events of the day. But Auguste Portalis and Armand Landrin, given the task, used their information against the socialist. The concessions were hardly significant.

More significant was the council meeting of the nineteenth. Caussidière brought the disturbing news that he was on the track of another plot launched by Blanqui. It has been claimed that Blanc, along with Ledru-Rollin, proposed the arrest of the arch-conspirator.[66] However, there is testimony to the effect that Blanc did not sign the order of arrest.[67] At any rate, Blanqui was not apprehended. The moderates had a better plan: recall the army. Over the protests of Blanc and Albert, this was precisely what they did, using as an excuse the Festival of Fraternity for which five divisions were brought into the capital. But whatever fraternity was felt during the celebrations of April 20 was that which brought together the army and the guard. From this alliance, Blanqui warned, a Saint-Bartholomew massacre of proletarians would result. Blanc too, was cognizant of the dangers implicit in this alliance, and his awareness produced a revision of his plans. Open pressure was no longer feasible; everything now depended on the organization of the labor vote for the elections.

CHAPTER TEN

Les Illusions Perdues—Presque

I

℣ THE WEEK of April 16–23 was a crucial one for Louis Blanc. He knew quite well that his ideas had not penetrated provincial France, even though the Luxembourg Commission had received, it has been claimed, over 100,000 francs from the government to cover the expenses of hustling votes for worker candidates in the departments.[1] This sum, if really given, was probably a concession in return for Blanc's approval of the final election date, and perhaps a sop for the defeat of his voting plan. On March 5 the moderates had adopted the *scrutin de liste* or departmental slate, rather than the *scrutin d'arrondissement,* or single member constituency. Blanc and the left had argued that the latter made for a more intimate relation between the candidate and the voters whose number was limited. "True and obscure merit," they asserted, "will stand out more easily. The man of devotion, the honest cultivator, the capable worker, will find as lively sympathies as the rich egoist or as the large proprietor." [2]

Blanc's failure to influence the moderates led him to realize that men of wealth and local fame would be at a great advantage. To counter this situation he pursued two policies: one sought the indefinite postponement of all elections; the other looked toward organizing, indeed, regimenting, the labor vote in Paris. The essential failure of the March 17 demonstration persuaded him to put aside the first plan. Having failed to obtain the period of grace he deemed indispensable for educating France, he now feared that the social revolution would be stifled by the very institution which should guarantee it. This fear, latent in his writing since 1840, now took possession of him, and guided his action. Well before the April 16 reversal, he sought with resolution to transform the Luxembourg Palace into a nocturnal caucus room. By day, in the general assemblies, the keynote of his perorations was moderation: he dilated on his theories for everyone to hear, and published them in the *Moniteur* and in broadsides for everyone to read. Before the public he was an educator. In the meetings from which the public was excluded, however, his tone changed. Before a select audience of devoted followers he revealed, beneath an appearance of calm, the near reckless determination animating him during March and April. His statements before the secret sessions were so fiery in tone that he decided against inserting them unrevised in the *Moniteur.*[3]

Undoubtedly his impatient determination was increased by the discouraging reports from Ledru-Rollin's agents in the provinces. He therefore set about consciously to forge the commission into a permanent political weapon. Of course, he had already used it on March 17 as a pressure group, but he was now preparing to make it much more than a lobby marching in the streets. His plans clearly called for its organization as an elected assembly for labor. During the secret session of March 28 he said, "We are talking of having to form an assembly of deputies; you are an assembly of deputies; you are the assembly of the deputies of the people, and whether the National Assembly is installed or not, this one, I am confident, will not perish. . . . There were two chambers, the chamber of deputies of the bourgeoisie, and the chamber of Peers. What did the provisional government do? It suppressed the chamber of Peers: it was good that the place was occupied. The People are there, it is up to them to decide on the way to remain there." [4] He frankly expressed his fear that the future assembly "will recruit in the provinces none but the representatives of old ideas, and perhaps many enemies of the people will enter it." He explained that the representatives from Paris, although in a minority is the assembly, would enjoy the domination which comes from the "moral force that will be lent them by the people who will name them." Thus, "by having the elections of Paris," he told the workers, "you have, I swear, the elections of France, and although Europe has not been called to an election today, you have the elections of all Europe, because what Paris wants, France wants, and what France wants, the entire world will end by wanting."

To accomplish this grandiose objective, two things were necessary: the masses of Paris must be encouraged "to bring to these elections all their solicitude and all their heart"; and "you must adopt a system that necessarily causes the triumph of the popular choices, you can do it. Numbers are on the side of the people. . . . I urge you, then, most passionately and with all the ardor of the patriotism which inspires me, to undertake a system which makes for unity in your choices, and which, by unity, inevitably produces their triumph."

Since the department of the Seine, of which Paris was a part, was entitled to thirty-four representatives, Louis Blanc suggested that a committee of delegates draw up a list containing this number of names. When completed, it would be submitted for the approval of the general assembly of the Luxembourg. The slate must have the approval of every delegate in order that it might win universal acceptance among the workers; it must possess the authority needed to regiment the labor vote. Blanc was quite explicit on this point: "The names which will be submitted to the approbation and decision of the people must have been definitively decided on by you, so that, when you have discussed them, they may no longer be discussed elsewhere." "Let one sign then, and not discuss!"

A voice from the delegates called upon Blanc to draw up the list. He answered that he could not, that he called the meeting only to proffer the plan and to suggest certain procedures. He strongly advised against choosing laborers exclusively; twenty would suffice, thereby leaving place for fourteen non-worker friends of the people, that is, intellectuals. These latter, he insisted, must be selected from "those who can prove a long attachment to the proletarians," and not from "those who rallied to their cause the day after the Revolution." This automatically eliminated most of the moderates in the government.

Once more several voices called out for Blanc to compose a list unofficially. The delegates had become quite dependent upon him; they willingly submitted to his leadership; many of them worshipped him as a savior and his long discourses on Jacobin-socialism had become their bible, their revelation. For his part, Blanc delighted in his role, and, at times, this adoration inflated his ego and occasioned a degree of demagogy which cheapened his innate political decency. During this meeting, apparently the only one whose minutes were totally excluded from the *Moniteur,* he appeared at his worst, with such outbursts as, "If there is someone among you who dares say that he loves the people more than Louis Blanc, let this man rise, because Louis Blanc is going to refute him. One can love the people as much as [Blanc], but more, I swear, that's impossible." That the workers applauded this with almost frantic exaltation reveals their political immaturity, a result of their hitherto complete exclusion from governmental matters. In the Luxembourg they found compensation for years of indifference. Probably Blanc did too. He had been praised as an author, cordially saluted as a reformer, but never before had he enjoyed the intoxication of mass adulation. Of course, he had loved the people, but the people as an abstraction, whose conditions he expatiated on, whose poverty he had experienced, but whose intimate, personal being was foreign to him. In fact, he had finally to decline the suggestion to draw up the electoral list on the grounds that he was not sufficiently acquainted with the workers. And yet he saw their many faces, felt their hopeful eyes focused upon him, and heard their thunderous applause greeting him and his socialism. Being only human, he succumbed to the enjoyment of the popularity that was, after all, largely his due.

Finally two committees were set up within the Luxembourg assembly. One, the Central Committee of the Workers of the Department of the Seine, had as its mission the political organization and guidance of the workers, and therefore was a committee of action. It became the liaison between Blanc and the masses and outlived the larger commission from which it was recruited. At once it established relations with the Revolutionary Committee of the clubs, intending thus to win wider acceptance for the Luxembourg list. The names that were to compose the Luxembourg electoral list were to be chosen by an eleven-man Committee of Elections which established headquarters at the Sorbonne, in rooms furnished by Dumas, a chemistry professor. That it should not sit at the Luxembourg was Blanc's idea, for he wished to parry all accusations that he was influencing its decisions. The conservative journals, having learned of the committee's activity, accused it and Blanc of electoral corruption.[5] Whereupon the Central Committee replied that "the citizen Louis Blanc took no part, in any fashion whatever, in the designation of the candidates that we, men of the people, have chosen after mature examination and with the most complete independence of our judgement." Blanc and Albert, the committee affirmed, only approved "a regulation designed to prevent the dispersal of popular votes, . . ."[6] It is probable that Blanc drew up the regulations governing the procedure of the Committee of Elections; however, there is reason to doubt that he influenced to any appreciable extent the final choices. Indeed, he was not satisfied with them.

The Committee of Elections began its work on April 5. Having invited each corporation to designate a candidate, it scrupulously questioned the seventy men who appeared before it about their views on taxes, religion, the organization of work, the army, divorce, political institutions, Franco-European relations, and so on. On the seventeenth, a general assembly of the Luxembourg met to form a definite list. This was the day after the April 16 fiasco and the workers were in a defiant mood. Therefore, after favorably receiving the twenty worker candidates recommended by the examining committee, they rejected every popular leader who had criticized the Luxembourg, such as Proudhon, Lamennais, Buchez, Lamartine, and others. Indeed, so systematic was the elimination that Blanc complained that their list would be weakened by its exclusiveness. Yet, when selecting men from the government, the delegates were only following his earlier advice, for, reproving the moderates, they accepted none but Blanc, Ledru-Rollin, Albert, and Flocon. To these they added Barbès, Sobrier, Deplanque, vice-president of the Comité Revolutionnaire, Vidal, Etienne Arago, Thoré, Caussidière, Leroux, François Raspail, and Napoléon Lebon. These men were socialists for the most part. Pecqueur, whom Blanc wanted, was not included. Before April 16, Blanc's "advice" might have weighed more heavily; after that fatal day, the delegates manifested a new spirit of independence. They were beginning to look to themselves rather than to middle class intellectuals for inspiration and leadership. This change undoubtedly resulted from their latent impatience, suddenly brought to the surface by the resistance of the moderates which Blanc could not overcome. Through the Central Committee they established closer contacts with the clubs—most of the intellectuals on their list being leaders in the clubs and less given to thought than to action. Furthermore, the Luxembourg Commission had undoubtedly stimulated their class consciousness. It brought about the rejuvenation of decayed craft organizations thus facilitating the grouping of workingmen, while at the same time it made them aware of their strength and their unity of purpose by bringing them together in one large assembly through which they could establish mutual relations and seek out their natural leaders.[7] That the spokesmen of the middle class attacked the commission so vehemently and at times so perniciously, sharpened the members' feeling of difference between the workers and the bourgeois. When the middle class politicians began their aggressions against the National Workshops, these two groups of workers, previously hostile, were thrown together before a visible enemy.[8] Thus, the very existence of the Luxembourg Commission, created as an expedient by bourgeois republicans and presided over by Louis Blanc, served as a seed bed for the growth of the class consciousness they all deplored! Small wonder, then, that Blanc's influence declined after April 16. But it remained for the elections of April 23 to undermine that influence further and nearly to isolate him.

II

The Luxembourg list was apparently not made public until the eve of the elections, at about the same time that the Central Committee issued a proclamation calling the workers to the Champ-de-Mars early the next morning. The purpose, in both instances, was to assemble the workers, distribute a prepared list and urge them to vote "labor." [9] The turn-out was evidently not up to the expectations of the Central Committee, and worse, a large number of agents from the National Workshops and from the Ecole Central, paid five francs a day by Thomas, moved among the workers, distributing another list, printed on pink paper, without Blanc's name. They told the workers that this list, which had been drawn up by Buchez and Marrast, was the Luxembourg slate.[10] After the meeting, these hired agents, who were some 800 in number, went about like goon squads to break up labor meetings and to spread the pink list.[11] However, the moderates of the *National* issued another list which included the names of Blanc and Albert as members of the Provisional Government, and Daniel Stern has asserted that it was their inclusion in this slate which saved them from defeat.[12]

Even so, Blanc suffered a severe moral setback. The seven moderates of the council headed the list of successful candidates in the Seine department, and to Lamartine's 259,800 votes, Blanc received only 121,140, not even half. Indeed, he was behind Buchez, Anthime Corbon, Albert, and Caussidière, arriving twenty-seventh out of a total of thirty-four successful candidates, and it was small consolation that Lamennais, enemy of the Clichy tailors, was at the end.

The blow that must have struck hardest was the essential conservatism of Paris. Blanc had no doubt that socialism would lose heavily in the provinces, as it did. On the other hand, he had told the workers that if they won the capital, they would control France; therefore, their defeat seemed catastrophic. And yet, the rout was not by any means complete. It is true that only six of the Luxembourg candidates won seats, and their success resulted partly from their inclusion in other lists. However, excluding two Luxembourgers whose names were not among the candidates, the men of the Commission accumulated 1,736,125 votes out of a total of 8,306,609 for the department. Inasmuch as there were in 1847 only about 204,000 adult male workers,[13] the votes indicated that within the city of Paris the strength of Jacobin-socialism was by no means negligible, and by no means confined to the working class. Undoubtedly the labor vote was split, for even though the men of the *Atelier,* Buchez, Corbon, and Alexandre Peupin, were on conservative lists, they certainly attracted considerable support from the skilled workers, as did Lamennais, Joseph Guinard and Cabet. There were, in addition, six non-Luxembourg worker candidates who together obtained 222,326 votes. Finally there were the men in the National Workshops, a number of whom probably rallied to the moderates, although Emile Thomas was among the defeated with a total of only 26,166. At one point, the president of the central committee, Lagarde, perhaps advised by Blanc, had tried to form an alliance with Thomas, but obtained for his effort only a rebuff and a lecture against socialism.[14]

The Central Committee had done yeoman work to get out the labor vote and had allied with the Revolutionary Committee, which was the chief electoral agency of the clubs, in a move to unify the left-wing. There was here the raw material for a Jacobin-socialist party which did not develop, for the plans and the efforts to unify labor came too late to take effect at such short notice. During the 1840's Blanc believed that ideas as such were the prime forces in history and that the true reformer must be a preacher rather than an organizer. When he wrote of organization, he meant that of work, not of workers, and he had given all of his time to the former, none at all to the latter. As a romantic individualist, he held to a great-man theory of history, and appropriately felt that the strong sentiments, the puissant ideas stirring within his mind were signs designating him as the hero of the age, around whom men would rally. There was no need for a party; parties gathered in small groups, became closed sects, and communicated only with the faithful. The hero of the age, standing above partisan intrigue, must speak to all humanity.

Blanc's weakness resulted from another cause: the class structure of French society in 1848 precluded the victory of Jacobin-socialism. The peasantry, the bulk of the population, while not anti-republican, was definitely anti-socialist. It was not the 45 centime tax which induced them to vote for conservatives and moderates, it was their deep-felt individualism, their distrust of urban movements, and their love of private property.[15] The petty bourgeois and many artisans also voted as moderates in April. Inasmuch as many of them had manned the barricades two months earlier, their vote revealed that they desired and fought for essentially political goals. However much they detested the wealthy, they rallied to moderates and conservatives when the Jacobin-socialists of the Luxembourg and the ultra-revolutionaries like Blanqui appeared as a threat to private property. As Flaubert rightly observed, property became more than a principle; it became a god.[16] Therefore Jacobin-socialism, conceiving of the "people" as a fraternal amalgam of the lower middle and the working classes, was doomed to failure. The widening split between Ledru-Rollin and Flocon on the one hand, and Blanc and Albert on the other, was really a reflection of the split between petty bourgeois radicals and proletarian socialists. Undoubtedly the "days" of March 17 and April 16 deepened the cleavage; the small merchants, the salaried clerks, the little producers increasingly distinguished themselves from the men in laborers' smocks and for about the same reason that Ledru-Rollin drew apart from Blanc: ingrained social conservatism activated by fear. Of course, Blanc was further weakened by divisions within the working class and it was small consolation to realize that Buchez, Corbon, and Peupin, each of whose total votes surpassed his, were aided considerably by the moderates who voted for them in order to weaken the candidates of the Luxembourg. Small consolation also was the inclusion of his name on an electoral slate in Corsica where he failed to win enough votes to obtain a seat.[17]

On the twenty-seventh, the day before the successful candidacies were announced at the City Hall by the jubilant Marrast, Louis Blanc mounted the rostrum of the Luxembourg, surveyed his audience, and said: "My friends, I come before you with a somewhat saddened heart, and yet full of ardor, of courage, of hope. No, whatever one may think, I swear that the genius of France, the genius of the revolution shall not perish." His listeners responded with shouts, "No! No!" He has been accused, he went on, of wanting twenty workers in the assembly; if this was a crime, he readily accepted the guilt. He has been accused of falsifying the workers' cause. Admitting that he was not a worker, like Albert, he pointed out that he too, had "lived by the sweat of [his] brow," that he too, when young, had borne "all the weight of an iniquitous social order," and that he had taken an oath before God, before his conscience that "if ever I am called upon to put in order the conditions of this iniquitous society, I shall not forget that I was one of the unhappiest children of the people, that society weighed on me. And I took, against this social order which makes unhappy such a large number of our brothers, the oath of Hannibal." [18] Carried away, he continued, "They have proclaimed universal suffrage.—Is it the expression of the will of the people? Yes, in a society where all conditions will be equal; yes, in a society where each will enjoy the free development of his mind and of his heart. In the present society, no! no! a thousand times no!"

These were incendiary statements, and when the speech was published in the *Moniteur,* they were either modified or eliminated. However, Blanc had not become a fanatic screaming for violence; rather, he revealed himself as an orator of consummate skill counter-pointing excitation and moderation, fire and water. Like a verbally gifted maestro he orchestrated his address so as to elicit both determination and patience from his audience. Thus, he intercalated at appropriate intervals statements like: "I do not come here to bring you irritating words, I do not wish to appeal to your angered impatience; the very way in which I pose the question tells you sufficiently that the crime here is not attributable to such and such a man, but to the situation. It is the principle which is guilty. . . . You suffer, but do not be too impatient, let your indignation be directed to ideas rather than to men. . . . Wait and know how to suffer." He fortified himself and his listeners with the view that individuals are broken for the benefit of indestructible principles. "Courage then! In spite of everything, equality shall triumph, . . . The secret of the Revolution to maintain, to save, to bring about the abolition of the proletariat, the enfranchisement of the people, is union, more union and still more union!" When he concluded, amidst a roar of applause and *vivas,* Lagarde presented him with a massive bouquet of flowers and embraced him.[19] In the dark recesses of disillusion he found the brightness of gratitude. And for another such moment of exaltation he must wait nearly twenty-two years when, back from exile, Paris would place him at the head of her lists of representatives. But the interval between April 27, 1848, and February 8, 1871, was to be one of defeat, frustration and sadness.

Even before the twenty-seventh reached its close his horizon darkened. Amidst the jubilation of the national festival for the distribution of flags, Blanc could not help but notice the large number of regular troops which fraternized with the National Guard. He also learned that in Rouen, troops and guards had joined forces to suppress the workers who revolted after learning of their electoral defeat. In an evening meeting of the government, both he and Ledru-Rollin vigorously demanded that the general in command of the troops be summoned to Paris. Arago, minister of war, categorically refused, and Blanc could do nothing.

III

His impotence, as well as that of the left, was clearly revealed when the National Constituent Assembly held its inaugural meeting on May 4. As he entered, supporting the aged Arago, he had already concluded that most of the representatives were hostile toward him, and indeed, he was not in error. The men composing the assembly were mostly wealthy bourgeois. Of the nine hundred representatives, at least three-quarters could have met the high property qualifications of the July Monarchy. Yet, there was little thought of a restoration, at least for the present, and the assembly unanimously proclaimed France a republic. Shortly afterward, it also voted that the Provisional Government merited the gratitude of the country.

This unanimity was short-lived and divisions appeared as groups formed. On the highest seats were the radicals led by Lamennais, and the Jacobin-socialists led by Blanc, Barbès, Albert, Félix Pyat, and Jean-Louis Greppo. As of old, they called themselves the Mountain, and were the first to form a rudimentary political party, with their headquarters in a house in the Rue des Pyramides. When, however, the May 15 affair brought about a division, the Jacobin-socialists began meeting regularly at Blanc's apartment in the Rue Taitbout.

Dominating the Center, and therefore the assembly, were some three hundred representatives of the *National* nuance. On the Right were Catholic conservatives and Orleanists, whose meeting place in the Rue de Poitiers eventually became a center of anti-republicanism. For the moment, however, they deferred to both the moderate republicanism and anodyne reformism of the Center, with the result that on May 6 the men of the *National* and the *Atelier* won most of the commanding posts in the Assembly. Buchez became its president.[20]

After the verification of credentials on May 6, each member of the Provisional Government except Albert mounted the rostrum to give an account of his policies since February. Blanc undoubtedly made the poorest showing, unable to conceal for the occasion the discouragement stifling his usual flourish of spirit. When he spoke of the economic impotence of the Luxembourg and the great burden put on his and his colleagues' shoulders, which they bore like "soldiers of society," he certainly did not win the sympathy of his listeners.[21] The majority was determined to put him out of power, with the result that three days later when Barbès proposed maintaining the Provisional Government, "in order that the socialist element be represented there," the assembly's vote went overwhelmingly against him. Immediately afterward, it voted for the creation of a five-man Executive Committee, and on the next day it decided that the socialist element would not be represented. In fact, it would have also eliminated the radical element had not Lamartine used his personal prestige in favor of Ledru-Rollin, whose lone voice, however, would adequately be controlled by those of Arago, Garnier-Pagès and Marie, the other members of the committee.

It is possible that Blanc had imagined that he would be elected. On the previous day, before the assembly had voted for the committee, he had announced his resignation from the Luxembourg.[22] Was this step taken in disgust or hope? Whatever the reason, the vote of May 10, which left him without any official position, was interpreted by him as a personal affront. He had grown too accustomed to the adulation of his listeners at the Luxembourg and had come to regard himself as the sole incarnation of the socialist movement. He therefore interpreted an attack upon socialism as an attack upon himself. This self-absorption is clearly recognizable in the speech he made shortly after the creation of the Executive Committee. After assuring his audience that he was happy to be relieved of the burdens of office, he came to his own defense against those who reproached him for posing the labor question. A voice cried out that there was no reproach. Ignoring it, he defended his work at the Luxembourg for which he had been vilely criticized. "A great deal of bitterness," he said, "has entered my heart, but I was expecting everything that has been done." Although a deputy shouted, "You have merited the gratitude of the country," he went on to explain his sadness arising not from the attacks against his ideas, but from the questioning of his intentions. Another deputy reassured him that his system and not his person had been the target of criticism.

But no words could check the flood of bitterness and thwarted hope that poured forth now in such volume that his friends began to squirm and his opponents to smirk. With amused smiles the latter urged him to leave himself out of the debate, and when he implied that he, above all others, represented the people, the Right and Center shouted, "We have all come in the name of the people." He had become the butt of their humor. He had also aroused the suspicion that he was trying to identify himself, and no one else, with the socialist movement in order to overshadow men like Buchez, a suspicion confirmed in their minds when Barbès impetuously came forward to defend the Luxembourg and to motion for the passing of a decree stating that Blanc merited the gratitude of the country. Pierre Freslon interjected his disapproval at once, and with consummate oratorical skill praised Blanc's intentions and his work, but warned against allowing any one man to personify the social question. In the end, Blanc's self-pity weakened his proposal for a ministry of labor and progress, and his denial that he wished the office for himself rang false. The issue was hardly debated. Unfortunately, the majority also refused to heed his sound warning that unless it undertook measures for social reform it would find itself faced with a "revolution of hunger."

Curiously enough, Blanc's proposal had been brushed aside by Peupin, disciple of Buchez, who light-heartedly assured the deputies that a ministry of progress would become a "ministry of routine." In its place he called for a parliamentary labor committee to undertake a large-scale study of social conditions. Count Frédéric de Falloux and all the antisocialists were delighted with this motion. Their plan was to drag out the investigation as long as possible and thus bottle up the labor issue in a committee they could control. The majority, preferring study to action, readily approved. They wanted to discover, wrote Louis Ménard, if the poor were really poor.[23] Of course there were many who naively imagined that the investigation would steal the thunder of reform from the socialists, that it would unmask the nullity of the demands for change, and that at its completion all society would settle down in peaceful unanimity. Therefore, when Jean-Jacques Vignerte, addressing the assembly, spoke of classes, a chorus of voices blandly sang out, "There are no classes."

The workers of Rouen and of Lyons had already revealed that they were of a different opinion, and the overwhelming defeat of Blanc's proposal had a marked effect on the entire lower class of Paris. The labor editors of the *Atelier,* becoming suspicious of the social moderation of Corbon and Peupin, turned more toward Proudhon.[24] The next day the delegates of the Luxembourg drew up a protest against the assembly's rejection of a ministry of labor, and proclaimed their refusal to take part in the Festival of Concord, scheduled for May 14. The association of ex-political prisoners sent out a similar proclamation.[25] This concerted action revealed that the Luxembourg was allied to some degree with the men of the old secret societies: Théophile Kersausie, Paul Flotte, and Aloysius Huber. That the last two had been included in the Luxembourg electoral list indicated that the rapprochement dated back at least to April. In fact, shortly after the creation of the commission, many of its members were affiliated with the clubs, while laborers in the clubs had been elected as delegates to the Luxembourg, and by late April these advanced elements were growing impatient. Before Blanc's resignation from the presidency he had acted as an essentially moderating influence, using the organization to exert pressure upon, but not to overthrow the government. He had also been a stable source of hope for the workers; but that hope was now being snuffed out by the new strength of conservatism. Men who had called for renewed fighting if the elections proved antisocialist, found it increasingly easy to assume greater control as members of the Central Committee.[26] The Jacobin-socialist press also took on a more threatening tone. In the *Vrai République,* Thoré wrote on May 10 that the republic would be perverted unless God or the people intervened.

IV

Inasmuch as the entire Parisian left-wing, explosively patriotic, had assigned to the republic the role of democratic liberator of all Europe, the parliamentary debates on foreign affairs became the catalyst activating its extreme opposition. When news of the failure of an expedition of Poles to liberate their homeland reached Paris, the men of the Luxembourg and of the clubs composed a petition calling upon the French government to aid Poland. In his club, Huber laid plans for a popular demonstration to carry the petition to the assembly. Called for the thirteenth, the undertaking proved abortive.

Although Blanc had probably been apprized of it, there is no factual evidence to prove that he was involved. The act of accusation drawn up against him in March, 1849, asserted that on May 13, 1848, he had attended a secret meeting at the Luxembourg where he urged the workers to keep their arms and to make certain that they were loaded.[27] There is no evidence either to substantiate or to refute this assertion. It was the accusation of a government fundamentally committed to the destruction of socialism and prepared to use most questionable measures to achieve this goal, as is attested by the creation of a special court at Bourges posterior to the events in which Blanc was accused of involvement. However, his fiery speeches in the secret sessions of the Luxembourg when he was its head, suggest that he well may have advised the workers to keep their arms loaded. And yet, this advice need not be interpreted, as some historians still do interpret it, as a call for revolution.[28] It is just as probable that this counsel resulted from his fear that an assembly containing many monarchists might attempt to abolish the Republic. In fact, Blanc supposedly warned the delegates on May 13 that such a reaction was well underway. In his mind, as in those of all Jacobin-socialists, the "betrayal" of 1830 must not be repeated, not even by a democratically elected body. The Republic was a fact and any move to destroy it appeared a violation of the people's sovereignty. The workers of Paris, who had become the guardians of the Republic, must therefore remain armed. Of course no one can deny that at times Blanc allowed himself remarks which seem full of the impatience of a demagogue ready to resort to force. And between March 17 and April 16 the Luxembourg showed many of the signs of an insurrectionary center dominated by a fanatical agitator. It was during this span of about a month that Blanc passed through his most revolutionary phase. But even during the secret session of March 29, when he bluntly emphasized that Parisian workers would probably have to "support from outside" their deputies inside the future assembly, he spoke only of "moral force," not of physical action. Soon after, the events of April 16 had a marked sobering effect on both his oratory and his action. The elections a week later left him disillusioned as to his strength even in Paris, and his assertions in the Luxembourg to the effect that "the Revolution will not perish" were far more probably intended to encourage the morale of his followers than to incite them to revolt. Nonetheless, fear of him as a labor leader came to dominate the action of many of his colleagues. In his deposition of July 7, 1848, made to a parliamentary committee investigating the May 15 uprising and the June Days, François Arago asserted that Blanc had once spoken of his project "to overthrow the moderate part of the Provisional Government, and, as a last resort, the National Assembly itself." [29] Arago claimed to have obtained this information from Garnier-Pagès, who got it from

Eugène Duclerc, who was told it by Blanc. Blanc denied its veracity; Duclerc could not recall it; [30] and Garnier-Pagès never mentioned it in his testimony. In general, Arago's deposition contained too many errors of fact and was too infused with hatred for the socialist to be trustworthy.

One is therefore inclined to doubt the truth of another episode that the investigating committee blew up to menacing proportions. Ulysse Trélat, minister of public works, testified that on May 26, when he dismissed Emile Thomas, head of the National Workshops, Thomas bitterly ejaculated, "Ah! this would not have happened, if I had accepted the proposals of Louis Blanc. . . . I don't know if I was right. . . . I had an army of a hundred thousand men. If it had acted, things would have perhaps turned out differently on May 15." [31] Now Trélat had come in for a good deal of criticism for his ineptitude in the dismissal of Thomas. Was it possible, then, that the minister of public works was deliberately trying to associate Thomas and Blanc in order to pass off his blunder as a necessary move in the weakening of socialism? At any rate, Thomas categorically denied the validity of this testimony. A third person present, Boulage, although a rather noncommittal witness, admitted he did not recall that anything about May 15 or an army of 100,000 entered the rather heated exchange. [32] Even were Thomas trying to exculpate himself, there is every reason to believe that if he had information proving Blanc's guilt, he would certainly have included it in his book, Les Ateliers nationaux, written to glorify himself as well as to execrate both the socialist and the Luxembourg. But there is nothing of the sort in his book. And the committee's testimony concerning Blanc is so vague as to be useless.

More explicit was the testimony of Blanc's friends, the chief delegates of the Luxembourg, who were not consulted by the investigating committee, and who denied his involvement in a letter they sent on August 11 to aid his defense. [33] Of course this letter, like Blanc's sworn denials, is far from sufficient as evidence. But even Lamartine later came to the conclusion that the socialist "sowed errors, not conspiracies." [34]

Perhaps this is a better epigram than a statement of fact; yet there is ample reason to believe that Blanc was innocent of any scheme to overthrow the assembly. Notwithstanding his Jacobin tendencies, he was always cognizant of the ineluctable outcome of a popular insurrection in Paris, that is, another reign of terror. Both his humanitarianism and his fear of the extremists caused him to put firmly aside the appeal of such desperate measures. It is possible that his fiery elocution of April 27 left the worker delegates with the impression that he was prepared for desperate measures. But after the defeats of April 16 and 23, he had come more and more to accept the veracity of his own aphorism: "The enemies of a revolution cannot have more useful accomplices than those who exaggerate it." [35]

Aloysius Huber and his club were prepared for extreme measures, and probably during the night of May 13 laid out plans for another demonstration on the fifteenth. Some delegates of the Luxembourg, from which Blanc had resigned several days earlier, were actively involved in this planning and must have informed him of it. During his deposition before the investigating committee he admitted having "heard vaguely" about it.[36] Later, in his histories of the Revolution of 1848, he wrote that he acted to prevent the carrying out of Huber's plans; however, in his testimony before the investigating committee he tried to disassociate himself almost entirely from the whole affair, either as instigator or opponent. This tactic undoubtedly resulted from the deliberate attempt of the investigators to prove by circumstantial evidence that the overthrow of the assembly was planned during a conclave at his apartment on the fourteenth.

When Blanc resigned from the Luxembourg, he moved back into his apartment where Charles had lived during his absence, and after the extreme Left of the assembly discontinued its meetings at the house in the Rue des Pyramides, it decided to assemble periodically at his place. A meeting was planned for noon on the fourteenth. Invited were Barbès, Hippolyte Détours, Charles Gambon, Jacques Brives, Albert, Esprit Doutre, Jean-Louis Greppo, Félix Pyat, Vidal, Charles, and several other representatives. The subject of the meeting was not the overthrow of the assembly, but the selection of their candidates for the parliamentary committee on the constitution. In his first deposition before the investigating magistrate, Blanc could not recall that the demonstration planned by Huber had come up as a topic of conversation. Not until after the meeting, at about 4:30 P.M., did he and Barbès take up the issue and decide to take steps to oppose the demonstration energetically. However, Greppo reported to the magistrate that while the Polish affair was not the subject of the meeting and did not enter into the general conversation, it was a topic of several particular conversations and that Barbès, when leaving, said that he was going to his club that evening to dissuade his followers from participating. Détours testified that both Blanc and Barbès said that it must be prevented at all costs. They also denounced Blanqui, and feared that he would profit from the agitation.[37] However, his own testimony indicated that Blanc did nothing to prevent the demonstration. At six o'clock he dined in a restaurant with Albert and several other representatives, after which they all went to the *Variétés*.

The next morning, May 15, Blanc left his apartment at 9:30 in the morning, accompanied by a cousin, Lucien Delacroix, by Charles and by two secretaries of the assembly. Percheron, owner of the Café Tortoni, located in the same building, and his *garçon limonadier* later testified that the group departed "as in the direction of the Bastille." [38] In truth, anyone coming out of Blanc's apartment on the Rue Taitbout, had to choose between two directions, north or south. Because the men walked south, Percheron concluded that they were going to the Place de la Bastille, the point of assembly for the demonstrators. Blanc, on the contrary, testified that he and his companions went to breakfast at the Café Véron. In his report to the legislature several months later, Alexandre Quentin-Bauchart cast doubt on Blanc's account and asserted that some sixty persons entered Blanc's apartment before he left it.[39] But no testimony supports that of Quentin-Bauchart, and curiously enough the investigators did not attempt to question the proprietor or the waiters in the Café Véron. Moreover, no other witness observed the sixty persons entering Blanc's dwelling. At about 10:30 the owner of the Café Tortoni saw some two hundred persons "descend from the Rue Taitbout onto the boulevart [sic]," shouting "Vive Louis Blanc." He also saw some men assembled "beneath the carriage-entrance of M. Louis Blanc" at about noon; they had flags and banners, and an hour later left to join the parade. But all this took place during Blanc's absence.

He arrived at the National Assembly about 11:30. He climbed to his usual seat, high up and to the left next to Barbès who was waiting for him. They spoke about the agitation on the boulevards and then turned their attention toward the rostrum where Louis-François Wolowski was earnestly speaking for the cause of Poland.

Outside the people's column approached, led by men of the clubs and delegates of the Luxembourg. Practically unopposed by the National Guard, it made its way into the outer hall of the assembly building where it raised an immense volume of sound. Frightened representatives jumped to their feet; others shouted, "Keep your seats!" Wolowsky resumed his speech. Suddenly the mob swarmed into the public galleries, sending the elegantly dressed ladies screeching for safety. More men climbed down among the benches while reinforcements waving flags and red caps poured in from every door. The great hall was literally inundated with noise, dust, stifling heat, and sweating men, who pushed their way along the aisles staring menacingly at the politicians. The menace, however, was in their eyes, for no one was visibly armed. In the president's chair Buchez was powerless. Raspail went up to the rostrum to read the petition, but no one could hear him.

All this while Louis Blanc remained in his seat, refusing to heed the ushers who begged him to speak to the crowd as a means of calming it. A representative, Albert Huet, who had tried to harangue the crowd in the outer corridor but who had been shouted down with the demand for Blanc, urged him to act, whereupon he sternly replied, "My place is here, on my bench, I do not wish to leave it." [40] Soon the rumor spread that he had been arrested, and several of his colleagues supplicated him to show himself for such a rumor might cause a real revolution. Lucien Murat warned that the flow of blood would rest upon him.

At last Blanc rose and pushed his way down; he would not utter a word without authorization from the chair. Buchez, hoarse and wan, hardly knew what to answer, and only after a moment of debate with himself, replied, "As president, I cannot give you this authorization, for the session is interrupted; but as a citizen, I urge you to do everything that your conscience suggests." In the midst of this bedlam, the scruples of legality gripped both men. Blanc would not speak without official permission and Buchez would not give it. In despair, Corbon, vice-president, cried out, "Very well, the chair permits." [41]

Blanc then scampered onto a nearby desk, raised his little arms and called for silence in order that the right of petition might be consecrated and that the people might not violate its own sovereignty.[42] He claimed that he wished to proceed at once with the reading so that the people might be induced to retire. During a moment of relative quiet, however, Raspail, who was not a representative, rather than Blanc, began to read, but before he was well started, the cacophony of many voices drowned him out for the second time. Numerous would-be orators now struggled for the rostrum.

Meanwhile, ushers and other persons informed Blanc that a huge crowd had gathered in the courtyard outside and was calling for him. They led him up to a window, where Barbès, posed on a small balcony, was passionately haranguing the crowd. It seems that he had already announced to his noisy listeners that they would be allowed to parade before the assembly. Just inside, Albert listened and said nothing, and only when Blanc arrived did he climb onto the balcony. He and Barbès then pulled their tiny comrade up by the arms, placing him between them. Blanc, too, made a speech, but we have no certainty of its content. According to one witness, he said, "My friends, your action has won full success, but do not withdraw before having forced the Assembly to pronounce definitely on the question of war." [43] But no other witnesses summoned by the committee attributed to him such an incendiary statement, even though most of them revealed marked hostility toward him. Judging from the general content of the testimony, it seems that Blanc thanked the crowd for bringing the petition and for fulfilling a lofty duty. Their manifestation did them honor. He then referred to the right of petition as "imprescriptible," and glorified another, "the right to enjoy all the benefits of society." [44] In his own deposition, Blanc swore that he said, "The demands of the workers for the amelioration of their condition, are legitimate; their feelings for a friendly people are noble and touching, but, in order that their wishes may be usefully heard, it is necessary to leave the representatives full and complete liberty to discuss them." He then requested everyone to retire.[45] Among the witnesses, only one, Boski, who was an exiled Pole, swore that he heard him summon the crowd to retire.[46] However, this testimony is also suspect. In a letter to the committee Boski asserted that Blanc openly deplored the fact that the original intention of the manifestation, aid for Poland, had been used to lead the people into error, and he therefore urged the people to retire.[47] But this letter, like all the sworn statements, is suspect to a cer-

tain degree. No witnesses agreed, yet even those summoned a month after
the fatal day of May 15 insisted that they recalled Blanc's exact words.
Given the applause, the vivas, the shouting, the general hubbub, no one
could conceivably have obtained a wholly correct impression of his entire speech.

On the other hand, everyone agreed that a Polish flag was passed up to
the trio who had taken one another's hands and who were now draped
in the colors of the abused state. The crowd was hysterical; it was apparently full of exiled Poles who were impatient to be off to liberate their
homeland. Suddenly the big doors were opened, by whom no one knows,
and this mob swirled into the assembly which was already packed by its
earlier invasion. Chaos reigned.

Before Blanc could descend from the balcony several husky workers
seized him, raised him to their shoulders and paraded him around the
Salle des Pas-Perdus. For a while, he too, became intoxicated with the
madness, the abandon of this people's Sabbath. When he was placed
feet-first on a chair, he apparently launched another speech: "The revolution of February will have a necessary and decisive influence on the future of the entire world, for a revolution of this kind is not one of those
that merely shakes thrones, but which overturns them." [48] After a few
more remarks, probably just as incendiary, he was snatched up again by
the workers. Several times his little body nearly slipped from their shoulders, and a Hercules who came to boost him with big sweating hands,
showed him a clenched fist and said, "Ah! little rascal, if you wished—."

Suddenly Blanc seemed to realize the immense folly of the whole affair. He squirmed and struggled to get down, but the crowd was solid
and from its motley surface arms reached up to embrace him, pulling
him forward and backward. Some feared for him and warned, "Take
care not to smother him." Then, from the assembly room the chant, "We
want Louis Blanc," made itself heard above the din. In response his bearers brought him there. By now he was struggling vigorously to get down,
but he could not disengage his little legs from the vicelike grip of his ad-
mirers. His voice was gone; he was exhausted and covered with dust,
his face was red and his hair in wild disorder.

Then, like the rumbling of a distant earthquake, the beat of the *rappel*
was heard. Fear and confusion took hold of the mob. The men carrying Blanc quickly put him down on a bench. He was in a frenzy, and kept
mumbling, "They're crazy, they're destroying the Republic." [49] Since he
could hardly speak any longer, he sat down to write a sentence beseeching
the people to retire, when he heard the fatal one pronounced by Huber,
"The Assembly is dissolved!" Although many cried out, "No! No!"
others gathered around Blanc, urging him to lead them to the City Hall.
This he refused to do, although lists for a new government were hastily
drawn up and his name stood with those of Barbès, Blanqui, Albert,
and Caussidière.

As the crowd surged toward an exit, he was carried along, his minute figure almost lost in the mass. Those around him kept insisting that he lead them to the City Hall, but according to one witness, Olivier, who was beside him, he "energetically rejected the propositions that were made him, arguing that it was a question of public tranquillity and of the interest of the people itself."

Outside, the crowd with Blanc helpless in its midst flowed toward the Boulevard des Invalides. There were many who still wanted to carry him in triumph and who ignored his admonitions. Fortunately Charles and an artist friend, Nanteuil, rushed to his rescue, warding off his too-eager disciples while trying to make them realize that they were compromising him. As they neared the Invalides, the artist spied a cabriolet, stopped it and hustled Louis Blanc into a spot just behind the driver. A passer-by, Bergounioux, testified that when he himself tried to climb aboard, he heard someone cry out, "To the City Hall!" Several other persons tried to mount the little carriage and would have crushed it, had the driver not got away.

Lemaigre, a wine merchant who had originally hired the cabriolet, testified that he offered to take Blanc home, but the little socialist, sitting almost on the driver's back, kept mumbling that he must go to the City Hall in order to prevent bloodshed and a new civil war. Blanc later denied that the City Hall was his intended destination; however, it seems quite possible that in spite of his exhaustion, there was a force within him perhaps unconsciously impelling him in that direction, and for the explicit purpose the merchant revealed. Since the cabbie would not risk such a trip, he dropped his fare at the house of Arnaud, a friend of the merchant. There Blanc asked for a flannel undershirt lest he catch cold. None could be found, so after sipping a little wine, he and Charles hurried away to a nearby bookstore owned by Masson, a friend, where he obtained his flannel.

It was after five o'clock when they went off in search of a cab. They made their way toward the Quai des Fleurs without so much as seeing one. The investigating committee emphasized that this itinerary indicated that the Blancs were headed for the City Hall. A legal agent of the government also testified that at the quai he saw them in the company of armed men. As it turned out, a man named Redon, who had gone to join his guard regiment at the City Hall and who was now returning after failing to find it, spied Blanc and came up to him to inquire about the events that had taken place. He carried his carbine, and was with another man bearing no arms. The meeting lasted no more than a few minutes, after which Louis and Charles found a cab near the prefecture of police.

At this point it is not certain whether or not the brothers separated. Louis insisted that Charles never left his side. On the other hand, a coachman testified that he drove Charles to the assembly, while Louis

remained behind. But it is important that the man testified a full month
later, on June 16, that he did not know the Blancs, and that at the time
he was "half asleep." The committee used his testimony in order to imply
that Louis, left alone, must have hastened to the City Hall. Another
convenient witness was a lieutenant-colonel in the National Guard,
Watrin or Vatrin, who swore that he had bravely entered the City Hall to
arrest the conspirators, but had become separated from his troops. Alone,
he heard voices coming from behind closed doors. He quickly opened the
doors, saw some three hundred conspirators, with Blanc conspicuously
seated at a table in their midst, and then closed them, decamping at once
to seek help. This testimony figured conspicuously in the committee's report. What the committee failed to notice was that the conspirators at the
City Hall were arrested at about five in the evening, when Blanc was either drinking his glass of wine or changing flannels! Not long after, Blanc
produced letters from the national guardsmen who made the arrests.
They affirmed that Watrin did not enter the building until after it was occupied by them, and that posted outside of the doors supposedly opened
by the self-made hero were several sentinels who would have prevented
his approach.[50] And a year later, when Watrin was again called as a witness for Blanc's trial at Bourges, he admitted that he was nearsighted!
The committee also played up a letter supposedly found in the room
where the conspirators were gathered, which read, "I am writing you
this word so that you will not worry; I am with Albert and Louis le
blans [sic], and we and the Sembly [La Samblé] is dismissed. We hold a
meeting tonight at the Lux sambour. I greet you: your husband." [51] That
the committee accepted as valid evidence a letter that was not signed and
that did not contain the name of the addressee, reveals its own partisan-
ship more clearly than it proves the presence of Blanc among the conspirators. By August 25, the president of the committee, Odilon Barrot,
confessed that he was convinced that Blanc had not gone to the City Hall
on May 15.[52] But as early as August 11, Blanc had produced significant
evidence proving his innocence. This Odilon Barrot and the committee
had chosen to ignore in the final report.

Instead of rushing to the City Hall, Blanc found a cab near the prefecture of police and went home. According to his *concierge,* he and Charles
arrived together between seven and seven-thirty. He rested, washed,
changed clothes, and then hurried back to the assembly.

He was alone when he entered the vestibule where several national
guardsmen recognized his little form and with angry shouts seized him.
Several pulled his hair and ripped his clothes, while one, unable to grip
him, tried to pierce him with a bayonet. Another twisted his fingers.
Furiously he fought back, shouting in a strident voice, "Cowards!
Cowards! You're cowards!" Had the commotion not attracted several of-
ficers and representatives who rescued him, he might have been killed.
His reception inside the assembly room was not much better. The sight

of his bloodied face and torn clothes only antagonized the representatives who cried out, "Arrest him!" Fortunately, the more fanatical among them had earlier satisfied their lust for violence by maltreating General Courtais, and the others wished to hear Blanc's explanation. He was given the rostrum, and he was so upset that he failed to demand the little stool on which he usually stood in order to bring his chin above the banister. Not amused and pitiless, someone shouted, "He's an insurgent."[53] There followed an explosion of voices, and Buchez rang his bell angrily before the chamber settled down.

Blanc began: "Citizens, it is your liberty, it is your right, it is your dignity, that I come to defend in my person."

"You insult the Assembly!" "Get down!" "Come on, now!" "You have never had any courage!"

These interjections completely unnerved him. His defense became a jumble of words, of sentences that had no end, save when he offered: "I am not among those who approve the steps taken by the Assembly. . . ." The hall was filled with angry murmurs, which became, in the words of the *Moniteur*, "violent insults."

"I sense by the exclamations that I cause," Blanc replied, "that I have here many convictions against me."

"More than that!"

"There cannot be any hatred for me."

"There is only contempt!"

These exchanges, which lent a bit of comedy to a tragic situation, grew more menacing when Blanc said, "I swear by all that is most sacred in the world that I have done nothing, absolutely nothing to bring the people here." And he brought enraged deputies to their feet, when he defiantly repeated, "I swear by what is most sacred in the world that I share completely the sentiments that the people manifested. . . ." At once he was drowned out. The general animosity was somewhat sated when Marrast announced the arrest of Barbès and Albert, taken while trying to set up a new government at the City Hall. Blanc at once came to their defense, and for a brief moment he found the eloquence that had enchanted the workers at the Luxembourg. But the men of the assembly shouted him down with such acrimony that he finally abandoned the rostrum.

CHAPTER ELEVEN

The Tiny Titan Falls

I

℘ LOUIS BLANC'S FIRST EXPERIENCE of violent persecution occurred in 1839, when an outraged Bonapartist tried to lay him low with a big stick. That was an isolated attempt carried out by a fanatic. But on May 15, 1848, and during the months following, he found himself the victim of class hatred and of systematic persecution; neither in the streets nor in the assembly could he enjoy the sense of security that the average man takes for granted. His enemies were now ubiquitous.

This experience was to have a marked effect on the general development of his thought, an effect revealed in his beginning to shed most of the Jacobinism which he had imbibed in Rousseau and Robespierre, and which he had allowed to exist like a menacing shadow even among his most exquisite paragraphs in praise of liberty. Having come face to face with those hatreds that stifle freedom, he emerged now as one of freedom's most heroic defenders.

The first notable step in this direction was taken by him on May 26 when he voted openly against the perpetual banishment of the Orleans family. Although he did not speak on this occasion, he later explained that "every penalty inflicted on one man for the crime of another man is a gross iniquity . . . ," that "reason of State is a sophism which must be left to tyrants, and that for true republicans, reason of State is justice. . . ." [1] The same inspiration motivated his opposition to the banishment of Louis Napoleon Bonaparte on June 13. With firm conviction he announced: "Republican logic, which rejected hereditary solidarity in the exercising of power, cannot admit hereditary solidarity in the application of punishment." [2]

Meanwhile the moderates revealed a spirit far less tolerant. With Marrast apparently serving as chief instigator, they prepared to do away with Blanc. Ironically, their liberal principles prompted them to seek legal means, and Armand Landrin, the district-attorney, aided by Auguste Portalis, the attorney-general, drew up an indictment against him and Caussidière, accusing them of instigating the May 15 affair. Although Ledru-Rollin, sensing here a dangerous precedent, interposed his veto, the two officials appeared before the assembly on May 31, where they asked for the lifting of the accused's parliamentary immunity.[3]

Blanc had felt ill in the morning and arrived late for the session. As he entered he noticed that Pierre Piétri, a fellow Corsican, was in the tribune. Suddenly he heard his name mentioned and was dumbfounded to learn of the indictment. He had not been notified! This shock was slightly mitigated by the firm oratory of Piétri who was speaking in his behalf, insisting that he had seen the accused trying to calm, not excite the crowd, as the prosecutors claimed. When Blanc entered the tribune and mounted his little stool, he explained that he would defend himself, not as an individual, but as a representative of the assembly. He began by expressing his fears of a new era of proscription and the restoration of capital punishment. After this introduction he absolutely denied the charges. No one, he asserted, had greater respect for a democratically elected assembly, and therefore he had unsuccessfully sought to prevent the demonstration before it took place.[4] His address was brief, to the point, and quite effective.

Following him, five deputies testified that he had obstinately refused to leave his seat and that he did not utter a word to the invaders until permission was granted. Buchez verified their statements. However, representative Gabriel Milhoux insisted that Blanc began by calling for proscriptions and that he "wished to cut down the assembly." At about this time Crémieux decided that the debate was going about in a circle, so he motioned for the creation of a special committee which would decide in the calm atmosphere of its office the issue of Blanc's indictment. His proposal was almost unanimously accepted, after which the accusations were read again.

Only now was Blanc fully acquainted with the charges against him, and realizing their gravity, he rose to point out certain fallacies. The indictment stated that he spoke on two occasions; it did not even imply that he had permission to do so. Was this a crime? Then why was Ledru-Rollin not included in the indictment for having spoken without permission? Blanc was accused of having been carried about the assembly; but there was ample evidence to prove that he was the unwilling victim of popular emotion. Finally he was accused of inciting the mob with the words, "I congratulate you for having reconquered the right of bringing your petitions to the Assembly, henceforth no one can challenge it." He denied having made this statement. At once his enemies rose to their feet, clamorously insisting that the words were his. The president called for order, but the assembly was in a tumult, with threats and insults passing from Right to Left and back again. Unable to make himself heard, Blanc angrily took his seat. But now numerous voices called upon him to complete his testimony. Back in the rostrum he admitted that he had spoken of the "right of petition," but in an entirely different sense. He had in the *Moniteur* an irrefragable witness.[5]

The special committee was not much concerned with irrefragable witnesses. It ignored not only the *Moniteur,* but also the *procès-verbal* of the assembly, and the letter sent by Barbès in which he admitted having made the statement with which Blanc was charged. By a vote of 15 to 3, the committee declared in favor of removing Blanc's inviolability. Jules Favre reported its decision on June 2—a fatal Girondin anniversary.

Favre's report was a revealing one. Most of it consisted of a lengthy eulogy upon parliamentary immunity, followed by an explanation of the present problem which emphasized the committee's fair-mindedness. Favre referred to Blanc as "a man who, attacked in his theories, has none the less been respected and honored for the generous sentiments that his economic errors have not effaced." [6] Undoubtedly, the anti-socialist Marie Larabit was correct when asserting, a day later, that the reporter revealed his and the committee's prejudice when he referred to Blanc's "economic errors." Even Maurice Reclus, Favre's apologetic biographer, admitted that he was preoccupied above all with destroying socialism. [7] It has been suggested that Favre was impelled by personal spite growing out of the harsh criticism to which he was subjected by Blanc in the *Histoire de dix ans.* But it was Blanc's system he mainly fought and it is highly probable that he was prepared to sacrifice its chief in order to destroy the system.

The report stirred up a lively debate precisely because both the friends and some of the enemies of Jacobin-socialism had an inkling of Favre's objective, and saw in his methods a most dangerous precedent for a newborn Republic to establish. The security of the individual would dissolve in the heated struggle of the systems. These men, apparently better read in the history of the Convention than those who drew up the report, came forward not to defend Blanc's system, which some of them openly criticized, but to defend a principle. Like Dreyfus, half a century later, Blanc became for a time the living symbol of the principle of justice for the individual, a situation which considerably modified his own political thought.

The great debate began on June 3. Pierre Mathieu (de la Drôme) and Paul Laurent (de l' Ardèche) pointed up the report's omission of known evidence favorable to the accused. The committee's reporter, said Mathieu, "has told you only one thing, that is, that he can tell us nothing." [8] Théodore Bac, who spoke for the committee's minority, made clear that the testimony on which the original indictment was based was known neither to the committee nor to the assembly. He did not call for its revelation, but denounced the use made of it by the justice department, and the committee's willingness to acquiesce in the department's request. Recalling Blanc's warning against a "conspiracy of falsehood" he put the assembly on guard against a "conspiracy of silence." Following him came Blanc's old friend, Dupont (the lawyer) who counseled his audience: "You are going, by this decision, to make an article of your future constitution. It is as though you were now placing the precedent which you are about to establish in the constitution that you are going to vote upon in a month." Before long, the argument turned in a different direction. It was well known that Marrast had spread the rumor that Blanc had gone to the City Hall with Barbès and Albert on May 15. Raynal summoned Marrast to answer. There was a moment of tense silence before the editor of the *National* admitted that his information had proven to be false. It was significant, however, that he refused to reveal the truth until driven into a corner from which there was no escape.

Also significant was the final vote on June 4: 369 to 337, a majority for Blanc which was alarmingly slim, and which impressed upon him the realization that a democratically elected assembly was not of necessity the birthplace of "social virtue." It offered not even the certainty of real justice, for some of the votes favorable to the socialist were cast for the sake of political expediency. Crémieux, for example, took his stand for Blanc out of fear that if Blanc were finally tried and acquitted, his popularity would be increased.[9] The vote also clearly revealed that Blanc and others of the Left would enjoy relative security only as long as the Center remained strong. Indeed, the existence of the Republic depended on the Center's serving as a buffer between the Right and the Left. But the elections of June 4-5 reinforced the two wings. Thiers, Moreau, Changarnier, Hugo, Boissel took their seats on the Right, while Caussidière, Leroux, Legrange, and Proudhon went to the Left.[10] Only Goudchaux came to the Center and during June and July he inched toward the Right, as did many others. The question of the National Workshops destroyed the Center and proved too hard a problem for the weak attachments to the Republic.

II

The liberal republicans of the Center differed from the monarchists of the Right chiefly in political ideas;[11] in economics, they were practically all disciples of the laissez-faire school, stanch defenders of private property and avowed enemies of anything resembling the welfare state— save at election time, or when the state's fortune was to be distributed among employers in the form of subsidies. Now to these men the National Workshops appeared a menace to everything they held dear; they were determined to abolish them, and the quicker the better. Unfortunately for the Republic, the task of abolition was placed in the hands of the parliamentary labor committee. Blanc had been appointed to this committee but its minutes show that he never attended any of its meetings and he soon resigned his post. Before long it was dominated by Falloux and its moderate majority. Their policies reflected the wishes of most representatives: dissolution of the Workshops with all possible speed.[12]

The Executive Committee also favored terminating the experiment but was divided over the question of speed. As might be expected, Marie was at one with Falloux. However, the entire burden of responsibility for the destruction of the workshops cannot be placed on his shoulders. He once confided to Thomas that his policy after the revolution called for a governmental subsidy to industry in order to hasten its revival and thus to create jobs for the unemployed. Fear of the workers, however, had caused the moderates to subsidize labor as well by means of a relief program.[13] By implication, Marie threw the guilt for the workshops on Blanc, and it was widely believed at the time that the National Workshops had been created by him, and were an experiment in socialism. Although Thomas correctly denied this, the myth was cultivated by Blanc's enemies to emphasize the need for hasty dissolution. Like most myths which serve men in power, this one lived on and is not extinct today. In fact, it has appeared in a new, more subtle form. Blanc is no longer passed off just as the father of the workshops; rather, he is accused of "moral complicity" in forcing the government to recognize the right to work and, therefore, in forcing it to establish the workshops.[14] No doubt he compelled his colleagues to accept the above principle; it is not so certain, however, that the relation of cause and effect was so simple. The government had already inaugurated a very moderate program of public works on February 25, the day before the setting up of the workshops, and undoubtedly, with or without Blanc, it would have been compelled to expand public relief, for with a nearly empty treasury it could not have subsidized industry to the extent necessary for solving unemployment.

Even granting that Blanc's pressure forced the government to resort to public relief, no argument can hold him directly responsibile for the transformation of a simple relief program into a political weapon designed to destroy his power.[15] Indeed, he was very foolish to allow this shift to occur. But without him in the council the recourse to violence might have come in March rather than in June. And if the moderates had given more attention to the pressing needs of the workers and less to undermining the socialist leader, the recourse to violence might never have occurred. Had Marie acted vigorously to limit the size of the workshops instead of urging Thomas to build them up as an anti-socialist army, the issue they created in June might have been more easily resolved, even by the ill-willed Falloux and his labor committee. The "army" of workers was the creation of the moderates, not of Blanc. That the army went into action was largely the fault of leading moderates and conservatives who were determined to crush the labor movement. Their insistence that the cost was too great appears as a badly veiled strategem, possibly to provoke the combat, for certainly Falloux was not ignorant of the fact that between March 5 and May 31 the National Workshops received only 7,240,200 francs while the army obtained 120,705,419 during a shorter period of time.[16] Indeed, the total cost of the workshops was only 14,493,-

250 francs.[17] This sum is meager when it is contrasted with the cost of suppressing the June insurrection, some 60,000,000 francs.[18]

Aware that precipitate action would cause violence, Garnier-Pagès, Lamartine, and Ledru-Rollin, although wanting to abolish the workshops, hoped to ease the transfer of thousands of laborers by nationalizing and expanding the railroads, thereby creating employment for them. But the Executive Commission was not only divided, it was practically powerless. Too many representatives opposed transferring the railroads to the state, an experiment that smacked of socialism. Therefore, Trélat, minister of public works, was acting under the pressure of definite orders when he dismissed Thomas and shipped him off to the South. Trélat was nevertheless responsible for much of the distrust of the workshops, since it was he who whetted the desire for their immediate abolition by constantly asserting that the workers had become saturated with Blanc's socialism. Now it is true that the doctrines of the Luxembourg influenced some of the workshop men as early as April 16, probably earlier, and about twenty thousand of them took part in the May 15 demonstration.[19] Although the outcome of this fatal *journée* was the termination of the commission, its permanent committee in charge of the delegates remained in existence.[20] It soon tightened its relations with a similar committee in the workshops. According to Pierre Carlier, director of police in the ministry of the interior, the members of the permanent committee and other ex-delegates became officers in the official committees of the workshops.[21] But in spite of this undeniable rapprochement, it is possible that both Trélat and Carlier exaggerated the penetration of Blanc's socialism in an effort to make the June Days appear as a socialist uprising instigated by the former president of the Luxembourg. Curiously enough, Carlier insisted that the Bonapartists were in no way acting to stir up the workers, a palpably false assertion. Even Thomas became influenced by the Bonapartists, and certainly his summary dismissal stands out as one of the factors causing many in the workshops to turn to the well-indoctrinated men of the Luxembourg.[22] The men in the workshops grew hostile toward a government threatening to destroy not only their means of existence, but the man whom they regarded as their leader; the men of the Luxembourg came to oppose the assembly which refused to take seriously the leader they adored and to implement the reform system they believed in with religious zeal.

However, Blanc does not seem to have maintained his former control over his disciples after the end of the Luxembourg. When, in June, they founded a paper, the *Journal des travailleurs,* he took no part in it.[23] In fact, it published only two issues, then died. Had Blanc acted with greater vigor, he might have maintained his position, serving now as a beneficent force restraining the workers from threatened catastrophe. But attacked by the moderates, he turned all his energy and attention to the task of defending himself, probably believing that at the same time he was working for the salvation of socialism. Since many Luxembourgers has taken part in the May 15 fiasco, he certainly realized that his own prosecution was, in reality, a prosecution of the labor movement. He defended himself and his cause; then he became silent.

In the assembly it was Leroux, good-hearted and humane, but confused, incapable of brevity and precision, who took up the cause of reform.[24] In the secrecy of conspiratorial conclaves, it was Louis Pujol who assumed leadership, rallying the men of the workshops and of the Luxembourg to a lost cause. On June 22 he and the leaders of these two organizations brought a petition denouncing the resolve to abolish the National Workshops. The insolence of Marie, the intransigence of Pujol created the friction needed to ignite again the smoldering revolutionary movement. Before long, barricades were erected, and while most who manned them were driven by sheer hunger, many others took up arms to defend both the right to work and the organization of work.[25] Blanc's ideas helped to motivate the June insurrection, which, as a protest against an antisocialist assembly, was a defense of socialism. As an individual, however, Blanc had not in any direct way instigated the revolt.

On the morning of June 23, he went to breakfast at the Café Foy, where he remained to read the newspapers until 11 A.M. He then returned to his apartment where his janitor informed him that barricades had risen, news which caused Blanc great consternation. A Corsican compatriot, Paul Savelli, testified that upon arriving for a visit, he found Blanc deeply distressed.[26] Apparently the socialist was quite out of contact with the course of events. Apprized undoubtedly of the general mood of discontent, he did not know that the "revolution of hunger," predicted earlier by him, was on the point of breaking out. The moment, he realized at last, was crucial, yet he could not bring himself to take a positive step. When several workers appeared to seek his advice, he asked if there was a general meeting place? They knew of none. Thus the movement seemed amorphous, impalpable. As on February 22, Blanc could do no more than warn the workers that the opposition was too powerful, that if fighting began it would end in the defeat of labor and of the Republic. After urging them to make this known among the other workers, he left for the assembly.[27] He took no more action to halt the insurrection of June than he had to prevent the demonstration of May 15. Yet he did not bless it; curiously, the only revolutions he approved were those without definite socialistic aims: August, 1792; February, 1848, and September, 1870. Those which did have marked socialistic overtones, the uprisings of September, 1796, June, 1848, and March, 1871, seemed to him aberrations from the lofty goal he had set out to achieve: social unity. To attain it he incited the workers, intimidated the Provisional Government and reasoned with the National Assembly. Then, when most of the representatives turned thumbs down on significant social improvement, he did nothing. The workers, however, responded with the only weapon they really understood, direct action, their *Realpolitik*. The revolutionary tradition, with its emphasis on an urban élite of activists and its scorn for the routine-ridden peasants, was more deeply enrooted than the democratic tradition.[28] And yet the workers of Paris, regarding themselves as the true proponents of democracy, denounced the moderates as reactionaries, for Blanc had succeeded more than he imagined in imprinting on the popular mind the essential oneness of democracy and social reform. And his teaching had been reinforced by practically every writer and orator within the Republican party during the 1840's. Ledru-Rollin, François Arago, Goudchaux and Marrast had all emphasized that political power was merely a means of achieving social reform.[29] For the workers, therefore, the new government must be a *République démocratique et sociale*. When, in June, the moderates pretty clearly rejected the second of the two adjectives, the workers resorted to barricades to defend, not to destroy, the Republic. The men in power appeared to them as representatives of social reaction, and hence, antirepublican.[30]

The balance between excitation and moderation with which Blanc had orchestrated his oratory was upset, and a split occurred between leader and followers. Blanc would not man the barricades; he was not prepared to die in order to live in proletarian legend. He was not a coward. On the contrary he chose his own arena, the assembly, and it required all his courage to take his seat on June 23 among men who possessed the power to crush him, and who would soon exercise that power. But having chosen the arena, he did not assume the stance of a defiant gladiator, but rather that of a broken, lame warrior. For all practical purposes he was a prisoner, and a most silent one, for it was the impetuous Caussidière who alone essayed to call to the assembly's attention, preoccupied as it was with railroads, that men were dying in the streets. He was shouted down. Amidst this abuse the organizer of work sat silent and aloof. He was not a Prometheus; his spirited will had melted into sadness. Later, when Marie would cry out against the insurgents, "It is not the Republic that has combatted the Republic; it is barbarity which has dared raise its head against civilization," and when Lamartine would characterize the June Days as an "explosion of servile war and not of civil war," Blanc would reply with the simplicity that anguish inspires, "You have sought the causes; there is only one, it is poverty."

Finally, on the twenty-fifth, Paris was made safe for "civilization," and Blanc left for home late in the evening. As he was making his way, several guardsmen spied his little figure. At once they ran at him, one with sabre raised. Their ferocious shouts attracted some representatives and officers who rushed to his defense. They formed a protective ring around him. Undaunted, an assailant thrust a pistol at his temple, but Greppo knocked it away. The shot went wild. Blanc's rescuers pushed him into

a nearby café, to which his attackers laid siege. At last, Bouillon, lieutenant-colonel of the second legion, took him under his great arms and es-
corted him out, commanding the enemy authoritatively, "Respect for the
National Assembly!" At this moment, another representative Jean Du-
tier, happened by in an open cabriolet, took Blanc in, and fled away.[31]
The next day, he was offered a room in the Palais-Bourbon, which he
refused. However, he was induced by Charles and others to share the
apartment of a colleague who lived near the assembly, and when he went
out, his brother and friends went along to protect him. Their protection, however, was useless against the real menace which came from
within the assembly. On June 26 a committee was set up to probe the
causes and events of May 15 and June 22.

Meanwhile, Cavaignac's government, which had replaced the Executive Committee, prepared a Draconian decree to punish the rebels. Particularly harsh was the first article which provided for banishment to
penal colonies, those "dry guillotines" preferred by the men who condemned the fanaticism of Robespierre. Once more the burden of opposition and the call for clemency were placed on the shoulders of Leroux
and Caussidière, neither of whom was an effective orator. The decree
passed with a heavy majority, as did the one leveled against the clubs.
Blanc voted with the minority on both occasions, but did not speak
against the bills.[32]

On August 7, however, when a bill providing for the re-establishment
of *caution* on the press was introduced, he came forward, not, he explained, to defend scurrility, but to champion a principle. If a republic
wished to be based on justice, it must place the principle of free press
alongside that of popular sovereignty. Universal suffrage, Blanc argued,
gives that force to law which compels obedience. But it is the majority
which profits most from a democratic franchise and the majority can err.
Therefore the minority must have both the right and the means to protect itself, or the tyranny of numbers will perpetuate itself. The means,
the counterweight to the great force of the majority, is freedom of the
press. "Universal suffrage, there is the principle of order; the press, there
you must admit liberty." *Caution* will lead to centralization, with the
big papers profiting at the expense of the small, of the poor. The vast
power of the press is a reality too frightening to be ignored:

> Since the press has replaced books, since it has become the preferred aliment of
> our hours of study and even of our hours of leisure, the press has acquired a
> power, an incomparable domination, . . . which, overly concentrated, would
> be terrible, because exercised on the best parts of man, his intelligence, his
> heart. To submit everything to a permanent, indefatigable control; to make
> and unmake reputations, direct progress, public affections and hatreds, impro-
> vise history, create a series of judgements accepted, most of the time with confi-
> dence, [by] that irresistible sovereignty of modern times, opinion: that is the
> role of the press, and certainly, there is none other more imposing.[33]

Concentrate this power in the hands of a few, Blanc warned, and society will suffer from a lack of information, and those enjoying power will become corrupt and the press become perverse. What he was really combatting was the emergence of a journalistic feudalism, concomitant of what he and others had called the "industrial feudalism."

Undoubtedly this was one of his best speeches, intelligent, moving, and incisive. Yet it was hardly applauded. Léon Faucher expressed the opinion of the majority when he concatenated *caution*, respectability, and moderation. And to be sure, many of the extremist papers, both of the right and left, had covered themselves with the yellow mud of infamy during the spring and summer of 1848. Blanc, however, did not feel that to punish them with added financial burdens would solve the problem. Although some of the moderate republicans agreed with him, the law passed with a heavy vote, for it revived the old interdictions against the criticism of private property. However, the law, for all its interdictions, did not succeed in enforcing journalistic moderation. Encouraged by it, Cavaignac suspended on August 21 the last surviving organ of Jacobin-socialism, the *Vrai République,* along with three other left-wing journals. Four days later debates began on the report drawn up by the committee to investigate the events of May 15 and June 22.

III

The reading of the report, requiring four hours, had already taken place on August 3. On this day it was clear to the entire Left that the report was part of the reaction which had been mobilizing its forces since May 15. The president of the investigating committee was Odilon Barrot, who no more could have been just toward Louis Blanc than Blanc toward him: they were implacable enemies. The reporter of the committee was Alexandre Quentin-Bauchart, the man who on June 24 had proposed dictatorial powers for Cavaignac.[34] He would soon rally to Louis Napoleon. His animosity toward Blanc, which destroyed all sense of impartiality, was clearly revealed in 1848, and was still vigorous in the 1870's.[35] As for the committee, it was overwhelmingly Orleanist, with only two members, Charles-François Woirhaye and Louis Latrade, sincerely republican. And even they became increasingly moderate after the June Days. Thus the entire committee was openly intolerant, not only of socialism but even of social reform. Moreover, not one member represented Paris. Like the peasant and village guardsmen who had come to fight the workers in June, the committee represented the socially conservative provinces. Inevitably, therefore, its report was so grossly unjust as to make that of Favre seem a model of objectivity. Favre, at least, was a firm republican. The report read by Quentin-Bauchart was based almost entirely on testimony adverse to Blanc, Caussidière, and Ledru-Rollin. The statements of witnesses in their favor were practically ignored, or if brought up, they were mentioned merely in passing, while adverse testimony, although contradictory at times, was expatiated upon. In the printed report, the committee stooped to the tactic of italicizing hostile accusations that were patently exaggerated or false. No effort was made to determine the attitudes of witnesses, most of whom were of the middle class, or to throw light on their personal reliability. Unfortunately, the conservative press, after the publication of the report and the testimony on which it was based, followed the example of the committee and played up every sentence which put Blanc in the role of a conspirator.

On the twenty-fifth, the assembly decided to hold the debate in one meeting, even if it lasted two days. Troops were stationed outside, and in the president's chair was Marrast, now Blanc's enemy, who nevertheless presided with impartiality and noble consideration for the accused. Ledru was the first of the defendants to mount the rostrum, and both his delivery and his factual evidence were sufficiently well developed to exculpate him in the eyes of his fellow representatives.

Then came Blanc who mounted his little stool. He began with a general defense of his socialism, his idea of liberty, and his speeches in the Luxembourg. Concerning the last, he admitted that when improvising he had at times been carried away, making certain statements which, while not going beyond his idea, were a little too vivid. These he modified for publication. His discourse of March 28, he continued, was not published because it offered electoral advice to the labor delegates and concerned only them. Thus far, his defense had the ring of sincerity, but his denial of participation in the March 17 and April 16 *journées* was dubious. Rather, he was most convincing when he tore into the report, and with the scalpel of an acute historian, cut it apart. He produced conclusive and damning evidence about the characters of two adverse witnesses, one being a well-known drunkard and wastrel, and the other an imposter who often tried to pass himself off as a representative.[36] As Blanc spoke his colleagues were generally silent, save for one seated on the right who impatiently tapped his desk, and murmured: "Go on, go on, talk as much as you like; you're no less *foutu!*" [37] It was eleven at night when he finished, and in spite of eight lamps and seven chandeliers the great hall was half dark and the atmosphere heavy with emotion. Blanc felt the charged intensity as he took his seat and listened to Caussidière who spoke until one in the morning.

Then Marrast broke the train of events by reading an indictment, drawn up by the attorney-general, which demanded the raising of Blanc's and Caussidière's parliamentary immunity so that they might be tried in court. It accused Blanc of having taken part in the May 15 violation of the assembly, and Caussidière of having participated in both that and the June uprising.

At once the Left came alive with loud and vigorous protestations, since it perceived that Cavaignac's government had injected a new element, a judicial indictment, into a purely political debate. It was known that the justice department and the parliamentary committee had undertaken investigations simultaneously, but it was not realized by many that the report of the investigating magistrate was contained in the same volume as the committee's report, for the two were almost identical, not only in their conclusions, but even in their wording.[38] Cavaignac defended the interpellation of the indictment with the bland assertion that the assembly could discuss it and the committees report simultaneously. But a voice cried out, "This is political assassination!" And Laurent protested against "a monstrous union of a political act with a judicial act." Cavaignac stood his ground, even though he was convinced, if we are to believe Emile de Girardin, that Blanc was innocent.[39] As a matter of fact, he hated Blanc for having criticized his cavalier treatment of the Provisional Government in February. It was difficult to realize that his brother, Godfrey, had died in the arms of the man he now accused. Naturally he had his way in the deferential assembly, for, as Blanc later said, "A majority, become tyrannical, does not discuss, it votes." [40] The vote was against him, 504 to 252. The left Center, which had stood by him on June 3, had deserted to the Right (Marie, Buchez, Marrast), or abstained (Arago, Crémieux, Favre, Garnier-Pagès, Lamartine). Chiefly the radical Left stood by him, with a few from the Right such as Louis Napolean, Victor Hugo and Pierre-Antoine Berryer. The votes of Marie, Buchez, Marrast, Trélat, Cavaignac, and Goudchaux were, perhaps, motivated by a certain amount of personal animosity, but the votes of the majority who had no personal acquaintance with Blanc were undoubtedly acts of faith against socialism which he had consciously sought to personify. To destroy the system they were not only willing to deport thousands of unknown men, but also to sacrifice two of their own numbers.

It was not until six in the morning that Blanc's immunity was lifted, but before this fateful hour, he had been urged by Charles and friends to escape. The large majority, the hostility carved on the faces that seemed impatient to be done with him, perhaps revived the memory of his parents' fate in 1794. Although of the mental firmness of his grandfather, he grasped the fatality of the situation and, like his father, fled. He did not have a taste for martyrdom if it meant imprisonment.

It was still dark when Blanc took refuge at the home of a colleague, Charles d'Aragon, where he threw himself fully clothed across the bed. He was exhausted and fell asleep at once. Meanwhile, Charles went to find money and to save his brother's personal papers. Two hours later Blanc was awakened by Felix Pyat and Eugène Duclerc who urged him to hurry his departure. D'Aragon, a moderate republican, thrust a roll of bills into his hands, while Pyat obtained a carriage and accompanied Blanc to Saint-Denis where he boarded the train for Lille. When bidding him farewell, Pyat prophesied, "Adieu, but for a short while. You open the way; other republicans will follow; we'll be going to find you again over there, all of us, all of us!" The prophecy was more accurate than he could have imagined even in this moment of extreme pessimism. Blanc was merely one of the first to flee northward to Belgium, and the Paris-Lille line would become one of the main arteries of exile for the persecuted of the Second Republic and Empire.

Aboard the train, Blanc squeezed into a compartment. He was not recognized. The talk of his fellow travelers centered on the nocturnal session of the assembly, and conspicuous was a handsome young woman who, after hearing of the final vote, displayed her approval with such exaltation that twenty-two years later Blanc could still recall the impression her outburst made on him. "This bitter tone from lips that seemed made for consoling and blessing," he wrote, "pierced me like a poignard in the heart." He said nothing, but eventually he was recognized, for unlike many famous escapees, he had not stooped to disguise himself. No one moved to apprehend him; the curious contented themselves with a good look and many seemed to sympathize with him. Even the young woman, when she quit the train, offered him her hand, and added, "May you be happy!" [41]

Shortly after Blanc arrived in Ghent. He was arrested, held overnight, and released early the next morning when he took ship for England. [42] As the shore of Europe disappeared from view, the most decisive phase of his life came to an end. His flight marked not only his own fall, but the defeat of Jacobin-socialism as a movement. Once more, as before 1848, it became a force confined to a handful of ardent, brilliant leaders, who had practically no following. The brief period of action, greatly limited as that action had been, came to an end. Once more Blanc returned to the strategy at which he was far more adept, education of the masses.

CHAPTER TWELVE

Socialism Versus Radicalism

I

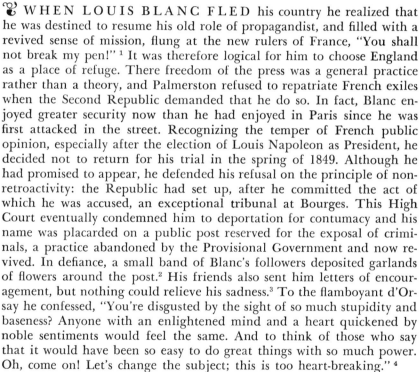

☙ WHEN LOUIS BLANC FLED his country he realized that he was destined to resume his old role of propagandist, and filled with a revived sense of mission, flung at the new rulers of France, "You shall not break my pen!"[1] It was therefore logical for him to choose England as a place of refuge. There freedom of the press was a general practice rather than a theory, and Palmerston refused to repatriate French exiles when the Second Republic demanded that he do so. In fact, Blanc enjoyed greater security now than he had enjoyed in Paris since he was first attacked in the street. Recognizing the temper of French public opinion, especially after the election of Louis Napoleon as President, he decided not to return for his trial in the spring of 1849. Although he had promised to appear, he defended his refusal on the principle of non-retroactivity: the Republic had set up, after he committed the act of which he was accused, an exceptional tribunal at Bourges. This High Court eventually condemned him to deportation for contumacy and his name was placarded on a public post reserved for the exposal of criminals, a practice abandoned by the Provisional Government and now revived. In defiance, a small band of Blanc's followers deposited garlands of flowers around the post.[2] His friends also sent him letters of encouragement, but nothing could relieve his sadness.[3] To the flamboyant d'Orsay he confessed, "You're disgusted by the sight of so much stupidity and baseness? Anyone with an enlightened mind and a heart quickened by noble sentiments would feel the same. And to think of those who say that it would have been so easy to do great things with so much power. Oh, come on! Let's change the subject; this is too heart-breaking."[4]

He could not change the subject which gnawed at him mercilessly, for in the attacks upon his socialism were innumerable attacks upon Blanc himself which grossly distorted his role in 1848. To justify himself he published in the spring of 1849 two books, *Appel aux honnêtes gens* and *La Révolution de Février au Luxembourg,* which were combined in the next year as *Pages d'histoire de la Révolution de 1848.* He held no illusions as to their effect, and confided to his old friend, Hippolyte Lucas, "You are perfectly correct in saying that logic and evidence are useless against political parties. Also, I have no illusions regarding the present effect of my last book. I wrote it for history." [5]

Yet, there was a resilience in Blanc that the murderous thrusts of his enemies could not destroy. In July he mustered up what little money he had, and founded a new journal symbolically named the *Nouveau monde*. Drawing a new breath of determination, he introduced the first number: "I write this journal from London, that is, from exile. As for my friends, some are in prison, others are on foreign soil. The cause to which I belong has become for a host of deceived men a subject for scandal and fear. The party which I serve has lost one by one its leaders; its journals have been suppressed; it is perhaps on the eve of losing its very existence. . . . This is certainly a great disaster. Very well, with a clear conscience I declare: never, no never before have I felt my heart more filled with hope, courage and confidence." [6]

This manifesto, like the founding of the monthly review, was an act of faith, and as such, both were purely personal. Blanc bore the cost of publication and he wrote all the articles, few of which were original. Drawing from his plentiful memory his journalistic sallies against the July Monarchy, he launched them against the Second Republic, by now an almost phoenix-like resurrection of the defunct kingdom. Of course, there were new events which came in for his new denunciation: Louis Napoleon's Roman expedition, which Blanc held up as a violation of France's civilizing mission; and the Falloux law, which he viewed as a sly encroachment of the clergy upon elementary education, the level at which democratic dogma must be vigorously inculcated. [7]

Although welcomed in France by Jacobin-socialists like Faure and Greppo—who would soon share Blanc's exile—the *Nouveau monde* had little practical effect. Its circulation was severely curtailed by the prefects who were instructed to apply thoroughly the press law of July, 1849. [8] The journal was slowly strangled until the new press law of July, 1850, dealt it the death blow by raising the *caution*. The review was affected because it was printed in France, and Blanc was called upon to increase his bond. To raise the money he attempted to sell his remaining government bonds, which now amounted to about 600 francs. The police, having opened his mail, learned of the transaction and confiscated the bonds to defray the expenses of his trial at Bourges. [9] The review ceased to appear in March, 1851. Blanc also met insuperable difficulties in the publication of his books. The appearance of *La république une et indivisible* occasioned the arrest of its publisher. Parisian printers were so intimidated that they came to insist on the right of censoring the manuscripts of exiles before signing contracts. [10] Not even in Belgium was Blanc able to find competent printers, with the result that his published works were not always free of grave textual errors. [11]

Blanc's writings were not the only victims of the new press law. Pierre Leroux's *Revue sociale* failed because sufficient funds were not available for bond and Cabet's *Populaire* was dangerously in debt and hounded by the police. The realization was therefore brought home to each socialist editor that his journal, solitary and dependent upon the limited resources of his particular following, could not hope to survive. If the united forces of conservatism were to be effectively withstood, the hitherto divided ranks of socialism had to seek a counterbalancing unity. The most effective means of achieving this solidarity was to establish a single journal representing the several schools and so enable the scattered forces of socialism to create a kind of journalistic directory which would foster both alliance and leadership. During January, 1850, shortly before Blanc's review disappeared, the editorial staff of Cabet's *Populaire* suggested the publication of a doctrinal manifesto signed by the leaders of French socialism. The founding of a paper was to follow, similar to the *Populaire*, but broader in scope and under a new editorial board composed of Cabet, Leroux, and Blanc. All necessary concessions were to be made to obtain Blanc's co-operation.[12] Negotiations began, went on without decision for over a year and finally failed when Blanc refused to form part of the editorial board.

His ostensible reason was the necessity to publish the third volume of his history of the Revolution.[13] This, however, was not the main reason. Blanc realized the rigor of the new press law and the ubiquity of the police. More important, he could not accept Cabet's integral pacifism. During the spring of 1850 he had written to a friend: "How right you are in not finding to your taste the ultra-pacific policy of some of our colleagues! I see with anxiety that they are trying to enervate the party, to eliminate its vigor, its originality. They compromise it in alliances without honor, in which it will be lost if we do not take care." [14] Here he was probably referring not to Cabet but to Michel de Bourges, who had taken Ledru-Rollin's place and under whom the Mountain had rapidly become a mere hill. The socialist concluded that the violent methods of reactionaries must be met, if necessary, with counter-violence. In August, 1851, he spoke at London before a group of French workers who, at the initiative of the ex-Luxembourger, Pierre Vinçard, had invited him to dine with them, and he prophesied that the reaction would not lay down its arms, prepared as it was to call upon Russia for aid against the "red spectre." A last combat being inevitable, the time was not ripe for "the apostolate of peace." And to Mme d'Agoult, he wrote, "I fear that in the presence of oppression, our hearts might be softened too much." [15]

His fears were justified in December, 1851, when Louis Napoleon resorted to a *coup d'état* as a means of preserving his power. Learning of this action, Blanc and other exiles thought only of returning to take part in the resistance, but few of them had the necessary passports and fewer the money for the voyage. Blanc was equipped with both, and carrying a forged passport bearing the romantic name Edward Reyloff, he managed to reach Ostend on December 6. By this time the *opération de police un*

peu rude was over, and the failure of a general uprising to materialize
thwarted Blanc's plans. To make matters worse, the Belgian police were
belatedly on the alert and arrested him on December 10. He then wrote
for permission to quit the country, which the harassed cabinet quickly
granted.[16] Bitter in heart, he again boarded the ship for Dover.

Five months later Cabet, now in exile, joined Blanc and Leroux to
establish a *Union socialiste.* Their purpose was: "To light in the land
of exile a flame that can be seen from afar, from the depths of the shadows where our brothers are plunged. . . ." [17] The movement published
its manifesto, then died, as one by one the organs of democracy were
scattered and suppressed.

II

The condition of life for the French exiles was far from easy. Intellectuals like Blanc, Ledru-Rollin, Pyat, Hugo, and Victor Schoelcher, who
had achieved wealth and reputation prior to 1848, left France with
enough money to withstand the severity of the early years of proscription.
Louis Blanc had 2,000 francs in his wallet when searched by the Belgian
police. But soon the costs of printing his journal and brochures nearly
depleted his cash, and when the government expropriated the revenue
from his bonds, he suffered again those rigors of penury which had tor-
mented his early years in Paris. Similarly, his colleagues found their reve-
nues curtailed but they still had sufficient money. Not so the majority of
those stalwart workers who fled the homeland with their pockets empty
and now found themselves greatly handicapped in their search for work
by their not knowing English. Jobs were not plentiful and cautious English employers, like organized labor, looked with a suspicious eye on these
revolutionaries.[18]

Blanc tried to help some of these men, but individual assistance could
not relieve the mass of exiles in London, more wretched from the material point of view than those in Belgium and Switzerland. In order to
bring some economic assistance Blanc and others founded in September,
1850, The Fraternal Society of Democrats and Socialists of London. Several committees were created to receive and distribute food and money
and to find work for the unemployed.[19] But the society remained too
impecunious to solve the problem of economic distress for the 900 exiles
in London and its vicinity.[20] Moreover, it was soon rent by internal conflicts.

III

The discord which at intervals ruptured the Fraternal Society was the
extended result of doctrinal conflicts among the French exiles, with Blanc
and Ledru-Rollin as the chief antagonists. Well informed of the situation

although imprisoned at Vincennes, Barbès explained to George Sand: "Democrats, socialists, and socialist democrats are more concerned with destroying one another than with defending the Republic against the common enemy. . . ."[21]

The nature of the conflict was curious. Considering the fact that Blanc remained a defender of socialism while the radicals had become antagonistic to all socialists, one would expect their quarrel to be filled with high-explosive social theories. The struggle did begin in this way. Ledru-Rollin, perhaps with Proudhon in mind, accused the socialists of betraying the revolution. Yet the ideas he went on to develop were not basically in conflict with those of the *Organisation du travail;* they were rather not so complete, and included the right to work, free credit, voluntary association for the workers, and a single, proportional tax.[22] When he demanded only free and obligatory education, however, Blanc complained in a private letter to Barbès that the radical had omitted the word "uniform" from the educational formula, which according to the socialist, should be "uniform, gratuitous and obligatory." He was willing, he went on, to sacrifice his personal feelings and to put aside the fact that Ledru-Rollin had not aided in his defense before the National Assembly in August. But the real difficulty was "in the *nonidentité* not only of opinions but of principles." Yet he hoped that it would be possible to agree on a minimum program as a means of establishing unity of action.[23]

Blanc's letter to Barbès was his reply to the effort of George Sand to mediate between the socialist and the radical. Like Barbès, she sided with Blanc, and while doubtful that a reconciliation with Ledru-Rollin could be achieved, she made the attempt. When it was clear that not even a *modus vivendi* could be found, she was relieved and explained to Joseph Mazzini that if Louis Blanc knew the antipathy of Ledru-Rollin, not only for his socialist ideas but also for his person, he would never try to act in concert with him.[24] A curious fact is that she insisted on placing Mazzini beside Blanc, apparently unaware of the hostility between the Frenchman and the Italian. Mazzini had already joined with Ledru-Rollin, Arnold Ruge, a German radical, Louis Kossuth, a Magyar nationalist, and Charles Delescluze, a French Jacobin, to form a European Democratic Central Committee. This organization, radical in its program rather than socialist, immediately aroused the hostility of Blanc and other socialist proscripts, for they were not apprised of its formation until the news was given to the public at large, and it seemed a usurpation of left wing leadership since the radicals asserted that it was the true voice of democracy.[25]

As time passed, the conflict between Ledru-Rollin and Charles Delescluze on the one hand, and Louis Blanc on the other grew more bitter. But this conflict never entered deeply into the realm of social ideas: the right and left wings of Jacobin-socialism were no more distant from each other in social ideas after 1848 than before. Delescluze even took up

Blanc's educational program, insisting all the while that he too was a socialist.[26] He apparently never convinced Blanc, whose letter to Barbès is clear proof that differing social ideas influenced the polemic, but mainly indirectly, abetting mutual distrust. The main conflict was almost exclusively confined to the field of political doctrines. The effect was to debilitate the Jacobin-socialist movement, for this was the chief area where socialists and radicals had forged their bonds prior to the February Revolution. The point at issue here was the radicalist ambivalence toward the state. An extreme individualist, the radical distrusted the state, seeing in it the source of political tyranny; but as a spokesman of the petty bourgeois, he also distrusted the capitalist plutocracy, seeing in it the source of economic tyranny. In despair he looked to the democratic state as the only agency powerful enough to curb the rich, but in striking down one evil, he aggrandized the other. The role of the state became more than ever the central theme of the polemic.

IV

These political ideas were considerably influenced by the course of politics in France. The Second Republic, having dispersed or imprisoned practically all active reformers, followed the logic of its action and abolished most reform measures during the authoritarian rule of General Cavaignac and the presidency of Louis Napoleon. The hopes of the Jacobin-socialists disappeared, as manhood suffrage proved to be no panacea against the evils of the times. The voice of France, a babel of provincial dialects for the most part, pronounced categorically against a socialist republic in April, 1848. In later elections it even opposed one favorable to mild social reform.

This manifest failure of the democratic process to strengthen the position of the progressives led them to modify their earlier political ideas. The Jacobin radicals were the first to publish their modifications when Ledru-Rollin joined Charles Delescluze to establish in 1851 the *Voix du proscrit,* a journal in which they elaborated a system of direct government. This system marked a great change in their ideas, for in the 1840's they had demanded that full legislative power be given to a unicameral body elected by manhood suffrage. As it turned out, the Second Republic consisted of unicameral legislatures elected by manhood suffrage, and yet these were the same bodies that had turned against the most advanced progressives. So in the eyes of the proscribed radicals, the deputies had betrayed their popular mandates, the bulk of the voters, insisted the radicals, being opposed to the reaction. The editors of the *Voix du proscrit* searched now for a political system that would prevent such a betrayal. The system they adopted was direct government: "Today . . . we say: 'No more representatives, but only delegates, commissioners if not to say agents, appointed simply to prepare the laws which the people will vote:

in other words, Direct Government of the People by the People.' " [27]

These articles and the doctrinal publications of Moritz Ritting-hausen [28] and Victor Considérant [29] induced Louis Blanc to enter the arena of political debate with a lengthy brochure entitled *Plus de Girondins,* published in the spring of 1851. It was an adverse criticism of direct government in general, but as the title implied, it was aimed particularly at the radicals and their proposal to organize all male adults into small local councils for the purpose of voting on legislation. Blanc readily perceived that such a system would mean the end of his cherished political centralization.

The doctrine which he opposed to that of direct democracy had been turning in his mind since the beginning of his exile. Like the editors of the *Voix du proscrit,* he was a disciple of Rousseau and Robespierre; however, while the radicals chose those sections of the revered apostles which supported direct government, the socialist chose those which underlined the need for a democratically elected body to act as legislator. Even so, the socialist did not entirely reject the principle of direct government. In fact, he preferred it, while insisting, nonetheless, that it could work effectively only in the society of the future when public opinion would be characterized by fraternal unanimity. "But are we on the eve of the establishment of this ideal society?" he asked. "No; there are only a very few upright and intrepid thinkers who can understand it, and an abyss separates us from it." [30] This was an open confession of disillusionment which he had scrupulously avoided until now. He was led to this revelation by his growing distrust of the attitude of the French electorate, a distrust which determined the nature of his political philosophy after 1848.

In exile Blanc did not abandon his democratic beliefs. As before he insisted that only a government based on popular suffrage was capable of inaugurating social reform. The radicals naturally concurred with this premise. The conflict between them lay rather in their different attitudes toward the progressive capacity of the voter, and toward the nature and purpose of government. That the radicals no longer favored a highly centralized regime resulted from their persecution, as well as from their essential individualism, which limited their aspiration to the harmonious existence of workers' co-operatives and small private enterprise for industry and a land-owning peasantry for agriculture. They desired a minimum of governmental intervention, and that chiefly in the form of economic controls rather than ownership. They were more melioristic than socialistic. In the mind of Blanc, however, there could be no amelioration without public ownership, by which he meant a basic renovation of society in conformity with his own ideas. Looking to the state as the prime mover, he expected far more from it than did the radicals, and while oversimplifying the tasks it must perform, he was keenly aware of the complexity of social renovation. He consequently wanted a government of experts, in short, democratic technocracy. He realized that the devoted experts formed only a small minority, but the well-being of society depended on their rule:

> Is it true, yes or no, generally speaking;
> That enlightened men are fewer in number than ignorant men?
> That devoted souls are fewer in number than egotistical hearts?
> That friends of progress are fewer in number than slaves of habitude?
> That propagators of just ideas are fewer in number than those who spread, or accept, or are disposed to accept false ideas?
> Thus, generally speaking, to demand that the greater number govern the smaller number is to make a demand contrary to the interests of all, of all without exception, contrary to the interests of the people:
> That ignorance govern intelligence;
> That egotism govern devotion;
> That routine govern progress;
> That error govern truth![31]

Consequently it was not proper for the less enlightened people to govern directly by voting on all the complicated laws drawn up by the experts. Recognizing a division of labor, Blanc held that it was the experts' task to govern, while it was the people's task to choose the experts, no easy task to be sure. Nevertheless, he believed that the voters were capable of singling out intelligent men for office. He recognized that they could be misled, as, for example, in their choices in 1848–49, but these aberrations, he willfully insisted, were rare instances. On the other hand, the people would always fall into error when confronted with highly complicated legislation. So direct government would lead not to a better world but to utter chaos.[32]

Louis Blanc had always desired government by experts, but he had never before stressed so unequivocally the ignorance of the masses, a conviction born of the disappointing conservatism of the voters in 1848. In exile he was therefore led to place a new emphasis on the role of the forward-looking minority both in and out of government. He now recognized a progressive will distinct from the conservative will of the masses. As before, he urged the few to lead the campaign for reform, they must educate the popular will, but he now urged the minority to stand by its principles, to brave the temporary displeasure of the majority, and at no time to submit its will to the backward will of the masses.[33]

The socialist, when developing his new ideas, had constantly in mind the conditions then prevailing in France. He did not elaborate a universal system but one destined for the unique French scene. Unlike the radicals, he now feared the majority. On August 7, 1848, shortly before he left France, he extolled universal manhood suffrage, but he was aware by then of what latent dangers might accompany its application if the bulk of the voters were not progressive. Give the vote to all men, he told his fellow deputies, and the government will be stabilized. Yet he warned:

"Universal suffrage is less a principle of liberty than a principle of order. . . . Universal suffrage represents only the opinion of the majority. Now it can happen that this majority errs, and that certain interests are unjustly sacrificed by this error." [34]

These statements marked a turning point in his thinking. He continued as before to favor universal suffrage, which he never dropped from his program, but he now placed a new emphasis on minority rights. In 1839 he had attacked Guizot's thesis that minorities have certain rights to freedom which the majority must not violate, for at this time he denied that majority rule could be tyrannical. If a man, he reasoned, rejected the necessity of obedience to the majority, this man denied the very basis of democratic society. Such a man had one of two choices: he must submit to the will of the numerically dominant group or leave the country. The man who did not obey the will of the majority forced it to obey him. Then on which side, Blanc asked dogmatically, was the tyranny? [35] At this time he was practically convinced that oppression always came from above, from the dictator or the oligarchy in power; to prevent oppression, he demanded that the government, by the inauguration of universal suffrage, be placed under the control of, and become identified with, the people. In this way oppression would be obviated because the people would never oppress itself.

Blanc was just as sure that his concept of "people" included the vast majority of Frenchmen. He distinguished between two classes, the bourgeoisie and the people: "By bourgeoisie I mean all those citizens who, possessing the instruments of work or capital, work with their own resources and depend on others only in a certain measure. These [citizens] are more or less free. The people are all those citizens who, possessing no capital, depend completely on others, even for the prime necessities of life. These [citizens] are free in name only." [36] He drew class lines, then, on a purely economic basis, and he mistakenly regarded this second class as a united whole, motivated by the same impulse for reform. What he apparently did not recognize were the deep divisions within the working class. Urban artisans hardly shared a common social program with the urban proletariat and while the artisans made up the majority of the working class, there were many of them, probably most of them, who were more inclined to follow liberal republicans and orthodox radicals than the socialists. And, of course, there were the petty bourgeois, often economically dependent, politically radical, but socially moderate. Blanc as a social theorist recognized classes while as a political theorist he tended to ignore them, just as he had ignored the rural population prior to 1848. He had imagined that France, since 1789, was really an industrial country.[37] Not until the elections of 1848–49 did he recognize the great force of the peasants and he then concluded that their backwardness vitiated the vote: "Is it not true," he asked, "that apart from the people of the principal cities the bulk of the population in France is steeped in ignorance? Is it not true that thousands of the inhabitants of the countryside live beneath the baneful and obstinate rule of prejudice?" [38] Since he regarded himself as the leader of the minority urban group who had been forced into exile because of his leadership, he now turned his attention to developing a system of guarantees for this group.

He began by reinterpreting his earlier ideas of popular sovereignty. Before 1848 he had asserted that the people constituted the true sovereign. However, by his definition of people, this meant that only the economically dependent members of society, the majority according to him, formed the true sovereign. And he emphasized that the majority had to be obeyed. After 1848, when he took up the defense of the minority, he radically modified his earlier premise by distinguishing between legitimate and illegitimate sovereignty:

> Sovereignty, being the supreme power upon which all depends, is in essence absolute. But if, being absolute, this power were not incontestably just and considered by everyone to be infallible; far from being legitimate, far from constituting a right, it would have the odious character of a brutal fact (*fait écrasant*), and sovereignty would be infamous. Yes, let a single interest succomb, let a single will be suppressed, and sovereignty disappears as a right and subsists only as a force. For it is certain, it is historically proved that one man can, at a given moment, be in the right as against one thousand men, as against one million men, as against all men save himself: for example Christ when he began preaching. Thus sovereignty, from the point of view of right, implies necessarily the idea of universality and cannot cease being an abstraction until the day when there will be established, should that day ever come, a government of *All* by *All*. Without that, instead of a people governing itself, we have a certain part of the people governing another part. Who will dare, in this case, certify that every act will always be just? Where will be the proof of infallibility of decision? Is right a mere number (*chiffre*)? [39]

At an earlier date he had denied that any sovereign was infallible. But now, by cleverly bifurcating the idea of sovereignty, he posited that the sovereignty of all the citizens was infallible and therefore legitimate, whereas that of the mere majority was fallible and therefore illegitimate. Certainly illegitimate, for how could a government rule without sacrificing certain interests? Hence Blanc was really asserting that there could be no absolutely lawful rule until the advent of his fraternal society in which the popular will would be unanimous. This would also be the advent of infallible government because the "sovereign, composed of all citizens without exception, cannot be unjust, since one is not unjust toward oneself; . . ." Blanc recognized the right of the majority to govern, but refused to accept their claim to full sovereignty: "The right of the greatest number," he argued, "is never more than a convention, it is not, properly speaking, a right; it is only a *means of ending a conflict of wills;* it is justified only because of the *impossibility of other solutions.*" [40]

He did not reject majority rule for minority rule, but aimed rather at safeguards for the minority, because secure in its rights, it could then continue educating the people until the backward majority was transformed into a progressive one. Accordingly he outlined a series of inviolable liberties for all men, which no group might abrogate without losing the right to be obeyed by the rest of the population. These liberties were already classic: freedom of speech, of conscience, and of assembly, and the right to live by working. Hence a constitution which included these was the foundation of free government.[41] Blanc's chief criticism of the Second Republic during 1849–50 was that it violated the constitution by depriving the minority of these basic privileges, and since there existed no recognized legal agency to check such abuses, he emphasized again the idea of a supreme court. Prior to 1848 he had favored a supreme court as a means of preventing the legislature from suppressing basic law. In exile he reiterated his earlier proposal, again asserting that such a court would not constitute a second chamber. Strong enough to protect the constitution, it would not be strong enough to combat the law-making body in the manner of an upper house. But since Blanc now added to his earlier proposal the idea of a court elected by universal suffrage, one might wonder whether the court would accept the modest role which he planned for it.[42]

In regard to the executive branch of government, Louis Blanc had practically nothing to say until after 1848. Before his exile he had spoken of putting a "consul" in the place of the king, without indicating, however, whether this consul was to be chosen by the people or by the legislature. He did not fear that the "head of the state" (*chef de l'Etat*) would become tyrannical in a democracy: "The idea of his [the consul's] responsibility, interposing itself constantly between him and despotism, holds him beneath the law of an incessant menace. The idea of the brief duration of his power compels him in spite of himself to practice simplicity of manners, modesty of language, prudence of desires, and moderation of authority. He knows that if he rules today he must obey tomorrow. Authority is a yoke that is not in his interest to make heavier because he will probably have to submit to it." [43]

In 1849 Blanc reversed his position, now maintaining that a fixed term of office, instead of abating the executive's ambitions, would only stimulate them: "To mark the limit at which the power of the president must end in order to make place for that of his successor is to proffer to the chief of state the most dangerous temptation; it incites him to conquer, with the force of his office, the permanence that is refused him; it creates for him a reason to overthrow the constitution, or, at least, to desire its overthrow." [44] This change of opinion undoubtedly resulted from the fact that in December, 1848, Louis Napoleon was elected President of the Second Republic. Napoleon had been preparing for this victory as early as August, when Blanc arrived in London, and had sought to win him to his cause. The socialist had realized at once that the pretender would not rest content until he restored the empire. Since he had been elected by manhood suffrage, Blanc now proposed certain constitutional changes. He called for an executive branch consisting not of a président but of a council of ministers, chosen by and completely responsible to the uni-cameral legislature.[45] With this proposal a curious contradiction in his thinking arose: his acceptance of a popularly elected court and his re-jection of a popularly elected president. The argument he advanced against the executive, that a popularly elected president or council would destroy unity in the government, was equally valid against the court. An elected court might easily play the role of a second chamber, might try to expand its jurisdiction, and would offer only a flimsy defense against con-stitutional violation since it was chosen by the same voters who elected the deputies.

Blanc's fear of the conservatives led him a step further in his defense of minority rights: he recommended non-obedience on the part of the few should the majority turn to oppression. Particularly if the latter voted the Republic out of existence, the democratic minority had the right to reject the will of the majority by the rule of non-obedience. Like Rous-seau, Blanc posited that the people could not legally alienate its sover-eignty, but the reasoning he used to support this assertion was closer to the traditionalism of Joseph de Maistre. Any majority, said Blanc, was only a majority at a given moment of history, not a majority of the peo-ple of past and future generations, of the people considered in the "suc-cession of ages." Consequently, if the majority of one generation or age substituted an hereditary monarchy for a republic, it illegally abolished the rights of the following generations. Thus, the existence of the Re-public, he implied, and the basic Rights of Man, he asserted clearly, were sacred, instituted by God and therefore inviolable. If then, the greater number voted for the abolition of these, should the few obey? He an-swered with an emphatic no.[46]

In later years Blanc became an advocate of the Hare system of propor-tional representation, which he learned about from John Stuart Mill, and as a correspondent for the *Temps* in France, the *Etoile Belge* in Belgium, and the *Europa* in Germany, he used the columns at his dis-posal to describe the details of this system.[47] Proportional representation remained thereafter on his political banner.

He took his last thrust at the radicals for the year 1851 in a brochure entitled *La République une et indivisible,* in which he again denied that direct government was an effective means of preventing political reaction. If the power of the deputies, or mandatories as he now called them, was limited to one year and if the electorate was a vigilant one, the politicians would not dare repudiate their mandates. Rejecting the argument that annual elections were inconvenient, he contended that, quite to the con-trary, frequent elections would dissipate the tendency toward violence and partisan passion common to such events. What troubled him was that frequent elections might diminish the public concern necessary to sagacious choice. But the press and political meetings could carry this danger. Pursuing this argument, Blanc preferred re-election to referendum: "I have proposed," he explained, "an assembly of mandatories of the people to make the laws that the people may change at the end of a year if they believe these laws inadequate, by naming new mandatories to improve them." [48] He accepted the principle of referendum for a constitution and for amendments. He also accepted it for bills already passed into law if a sufficient opposition to the law was assembled, since in this case the people acted as critics or judges, not as legislators. Even the referendum, then, was preferable to direct government.

Louis Blanc went to dangerous lengths in his opposition to the radicals. His aversion for the secret ballot was hardly in conformity with his desire to safeguard minority rights, yet he cast this precious principle into the limbo of "degrading expedients." [49] Prior to 1848, when he was explaining the excellence of democracy, he had regarded the vote as an individual's right. Each person was to choose those representatives who would defend his own interests. The socialist imagined that those interests could be reconciled in a unicameral legislature and laws promulgated which would be beneficial to society as a whole. But after 1848, when he clearly discerned the divisions of majority and minority, he came to regard the vote less as an individual and more as a social privilege. Most of the laws passed by the Second Republic had not proved beneficial to society as a whole; consequently, Blanc seems to have concluded that by open voting some sort of moral pressure could be exerted on the electorate, moral pressure that would compel them to think in terms of social interests rather than in terms of personal interests. But he was too blinded by his cherished principles to realize the necessities of the times.

Another dangerous step was his demand for the abolition of parliamentary inviolability.[50] Such a step would have removed one of the safeguards protecting the delegates of the minority from the animosity of the delegates of the majority. As a student of the Revolution of 1789, Blanc should have remembered that the lifting of inviolability by the Girondins had exposed them to uncalculated excesses on the part of their opponents, and indeed, his own experiences in June and August, 1848, should have forcefully reminded him that such immunity had become a principle invaluable to a reformist élite.

V

The intellectual differences which divided the exiles proved effective in preventing a rapprochement on the level of organization, so that failure dogged every attempt to unite the forces of democracy in exile. Until the summer of 1850 most of the French émigrés belonged to the Society of the Democratic-Socialist Exiles, to which the conflict of doctrines brought an early demise. Ledru-Rollin and the social radicals were the first to withdraw; then Blanc and the Jacobin-socialists, who felt no sympathy for the Blanquists, made their exit.[51]

In accordance with their doctrinal predispositions the exiles soon formed into loosely knit small groups. The Rollinists, or followers of Ledru-Rollin, formed an organization called the Society of the Revolution, whose organ was the *Voix du proscrit*. Allied with the European Central Committee, the Rollinists were revolutionary, but not actively socialist, being more concerned with overthrowing the government in France than with seeking the bases for a new social order.

The Revolutionary Commune was the organization of the extreme left which was subdivided into two groups: the Pyatists, named for Felix Pyat, and the Blanquists. Forming a somewhat amorphous center was a host of so-called Independents, consisting of men like Pierre Landolphe, Jules Leroux, and Martin Nadaud, who recognized Blanc as their leader, and also of men like Gustave Lefrançais, whose sympathies were divided between Blanc and Blanqui.[52] The Revolutionary Commune and the Independents represented French socialism in exile; neither, however, managed to become an effective organization. The Barbès-Blanqui feud, dividing into violently hostile factions the socialists imprisoned with the two leaders at Belle Ile, had the same effect on the exiles. Blanc, being a warm friend of Barbès, naturally took his side, a stand which, added to the Taschereau document, envenomed the antipathy Blanqui and his comrades felt for both men.

The occasion to celebrate the third anniversary of the February Revolution did not ameliorate the situation, but rather deepened the animosities. Radicals refused to join with socialists, the former celebrating the occasion with a banquet at Saint John's Institution where they toasted direct government and international revolution, the latter meeting at Highbury Barn Tavern for their Banquet of Equals. For the socialists this was an opportunity to solidify their ranks, but unity was not written on the bill of fare. A Blanquist in the group had written to Blanqui for a toast to be read at the banquet, requesting him to spare Blanc, who presided over a committee charged with editing the toasts in order to tone down inflammatory phrases. To this the prisoner replied with a denunciation of Blanc as a traitor to the socialist movement.[53] According to Maurice Dommanget, Blanqui was amazed that his followers presented this *aide-mémoire* to the examining committee at London, which, innocently thinking it a toast, rejected it. When it was subsequently published by the prisoner's brother-in-law, the committee members were enraged for they were put in the position of having censored the statement. Blanqui next drew up a more clearly written supplement which called for a complete rupture between his group and the "bourgeois socialists."

Because the conservative journals rejoiced over the defection, Blanc felt compelled to reply. In a letter to the *Times* he denied that Blanqui's toast represented the attitude of all the political prisoners at Belle Ile, where many inmates, he explained, had refused to calumniate the exiles. As for Blanqui, he was "one of those unhappy beings who, in their rage, attempt violence against renown, and who would lose the best of causes if it were possible to lose them." [54] Despite the mutual distrust which dogged the socialist leaders, the Banquet of Equals passed off well enough. Blanc and the Blanquists warned against direct government which "would only lead to a war against Socialism." [55] The appearance of socialist unity was achieved as a result of common opposition to the ideas of the radicals; even Blanqui could find a good word for Blanc when deprecating Ledru-Rollin and Mazzini. But the solidarity needed for positive enterprise was still lacking, both among Frenchmen and among other nationals.

The German refugees, like the French, were unable to unite, the so-called Utopians gathering around August Willich, while those favoring the *Communist Manifesto* followed Marx. Although Blanc had remained in contact with Marx until 1847, he never consented to see in the class struggle a beneficial evil, and therefore, after a peremptory rebuff from Marx, he would have nothing more to do with the communist during their common exile in London.[56] Rather, he associated with Marx's opponents who were trying to bring together men of similar ideals in the Union of Socialist Democrats of Germany and France. Founded by Willich in November, 1850, this organization returned to the tenets of 1847: brotherhood of all men and parliamentary democracy. Nationalist distrust, however, was stronger than the feeling of brotherhood and the union was short-lived.

Another attempt to unite all French exiles in London, socialist and radical, came from the initiative of the Revolutionary Commune. On June 13, 1852, Pyat, Blanc, Leroux, and Ledru-Rollin, with many others, assembled in a hall on Little Dean Street where they essayed to find a common ground on which they could rally. But none of the leaders would make concessions and the effort failed. Another attempt was made toward the close of the 1850's. Blanc, Ledru-Rollin, Barbès, Charras, Greppo, Hugo, and Pyat formed a Republican Union. The central bureau was at London, with branches at Guernsey and Jersey. The members at Jersey, apparently under the influence of Mazzini, called for action, while the Londoners, guided by Blanc and Ledru-Rollin, emphasized the efficacy of propaganda, and insisted that the "idea alone stirs the world." [57] Since the occasion for action did not exist and since the idea of a republic was hardly stirring the world, and not stirring France at all, the union was impotent and soon died. It did not unite the refugees, many of whom profited from the general amnesty of 1859 to return home, and their repatriation further weakened the influence of such organizations.

VI

Louis Blanc harbored no illusions about the political situation in France. Napoleon had solidified his regime by brutally crushing his opponents, and under his rule the country continued politically lethargic. The socialist had this depressing picture before him when he rejected the amnesty of August 15, 1859. Considering the situation at home, he argued, the leaders of democracy in exile will further weaken their cause by an acceptance of the Emperor's sly generosity, an overt acceptance of the amnesty being a tacit indorsement of the Empire.[58] There is, he reasoned, a European democratic faith to strengthen and a conservative propaganda to combat; therefore, both a protest against and a rejection of the amnesty are the duties of all exiles, and "an act eminently republican." He did not object to the repatriation of the rank and file of the democrats. They would, at least, carry home an indomitable faith in democracy. But he remained opposed to the return of the leaders, the destined, who must continue to suffer exile in order to carry on the work of propaganda. Although Blanc had refused to accept the martyrdom of prison in 1848, he was obsessed by the idea of martyrdom, and looking upon his exile as a sacrifice advantageous to the democratic cause, he wrote, "There is, in every great immolation to a great principle, a secret power that nothing counterweighs, that nothing replaces." [59] But he preferred the sacrifices of exile to the martyrdom of imprisonment, since to be effective, the martyrdom must be an outspoken public action. The activity of the immolated of the July Monarchy—Rodde, Carrel, Cavaignac—had been known to all and brought forth loud protests, and by these protests the people took a stand against oppression. The Empire, however, frustrated public martyrdom. Pasquier's police force worked at night; it arrested in dark alleys, hidden from the public eye. Its victims simply disappeared, without the public's realizing what happened. This type of martyrdom, while heroic, did not effectively arouse the people. This was not only a sacrifice without gain, but good men lost to the cause. Moreover, the press was now muzzled even more tightly than under Louis Philippe. The debates in the chamber were not published, so that opponents of the Empire spoke only to four impenetrable walls. And the printers were so intimidated that they refused to publish brochures for the opposition. Blanc admitted that in 1857 he had taken a stand against abstention in the elections; but now, in 1859, he would not return to France where he would have to abstain from public resistance or go to jail. "Prison," he had written in 1849, "is a tomb." [60]

When the amnesty of 1869 raised the question again, Blanc's position remained unchanged. He was not opposed to the return of those in economic distress, but he would not, and he hoped that the other leaders would not, succumb to Napoleon's pardon. This time the chiefs were agreed. But there were many Frenchmen who wished to return, and among these were some who did not have enough money to pay the passage back. To help them, a fund was raised to which Blanc contributed 20 francs.

In 1859 he had seen a wave of his fellow exiles take the homeward journey. As the years passed he watched the ranks of the refugees thin out as men one by one or in small groups trickled back into France. But he only watched, as he watched the Channel from Brighton, realizing that his homeland was barred to him by an unscalable wall of principles. However admirable his decision, it was of little consequence, not only to French politics, but also to the labor movement. For the lofty and determined vindication of his principles did not sustain his position as one of the leading socialist theorists.

CHAPTER THIRTEEN

Louis Blanc and the Labor Movement in France

I

℘ THE SUDDEN DECLINE in Louis Blanc's influence after his escape from France seems incredible, especially when one considers his popularity in Paris and the general elation of the workers in the spring of 1848. One of them had joyously exclaimed to Garnier-Pagès, "I don't know what's happening inside me since the Revolution of February. I earn ten *sous* less per day, and that's all the same to me, for I understand that from nothing I've become something." [1] After June, this spirit ebbed precipitously, and Blanc, who had risen upon its crest, was soon stranded in a foreign country, weak and forgotten. His very popularity and the irrational effervescence of his following were his undoing.

As one of the first to approach the relations between a socialist society and a democratic state, he had taught labor to utilize the government as a means of establishing a new fraternal order. A large segment of the urban working class not only accepted his motto, Organization of Work, but also, on February 28, petitioned the government to undertake this organization. In the minds of these men Blanc represented the new benevolent state; it was chiefly to him that they addressed this particular petition. His name was the concomitant of the loaded phrase which his book, *Organisation du travail,* had popularized during the 1840's. Consequently, his standing with labor depended on whether or not the ideas behind the phrase would be successfully implemented.

The National Workshops resulted from the popular demand for governmental action, and while Blanc had nothing officially to do with this project, which in no way resembled his scheme for social workshops, it was assumed by many that the project under the direction of Marie, minister of public works, was based on his doctrines. He did practically nothing to dispel this misconception until it was too late, and his negligence in this regard contributed to his eventual loss of leadership. The National Workshops constituted the flaw in the armature of the social revolution. Their maintenance, draining the monetary resources of the government, was used by their opponents as a valid reason for abolishing them. But since business was at a standstill, thousands of laborers depended on public works for their existence, a situation which determined these men to oppose the abolition by revolt on June 23. Their defeat by Cavaignac broke the back of the social movement. Blanc deplored the June revolt, and he apparently tried to remain neutral during the struggle. This was impossible. He was too deeply involved. For the moderates and the conservatives, his socialist program was behind the workshops and therefore the direct cause of the unheaval. For those workers and socialists who also believed that his ideas were at stake, he was a quitter when the time came for real action. Earlier abandoned by Ledru-Rollin and the radicals, he now lost an important part of his labor support, so that except for a moderate number of artisans who remained faithful, he stood alone.

From exile Blanc continually denied that his ideas were involved in the workshops; however, he could not effectively eradicate the mythical bond growing between them and himself. Blanqui, who had a following among the skilled and unskilled workers of Paris, believed that he was a traitor to the social revolution, a refrain taken up by Lefrançais, who rallied to Blanqui and depicted Blanc as a traitor associating "with a light heart in all the reactionary intrigues of his colleagues of the Provisional Government." [2] In the minds of the Blanquists, the National Workshops, which they did not distinguish from Blanc's social workshops, had been used to weaken and divide the proletariat. The publication of a history of the National Workshops by Marie's assistant, Emile Thomas, seemed to justify their suspicions. Blanc quoted Thomas to prove that the workshops had no relation to his socialist schemes. But by this defense of his socialism he inadvertently demonstrated his inability as a politician, since he admitted that he had allowed the plot of the workshops to be hatched under his nose. He was in a dilemma from which he could not escape without sacrificing either his principles or his reputation for wisdom.

The attacks of the extreme left were reinforced by those of Proudhon who condemned the Luxembourg Commission for squandering France's wealth, and accused its president of aiming at personal dictatorship.[3] Blanc defended himself in the *Nouveau monde* against these grossly unjust accusations, but his review was hardly distributed in France. Some of his faithful followers of the Luxembourg sought to defend his reputation and ideas, but they were without an organ. It was rather the disciples of Buchez and of Proudhon who were listened to, and they tended to throw the burden of failure on the exile's shoulders.[4] Indeed, even a sympathetic biographer like Charles Robin took him to task for the unhappy turn of events.[5]

The undeniable fact was the failure of the social program in 1848. The workers, who had fought for its success, asked why. Blanc's enemies explained and their voices drowned out his distant defense. Belief in his personal incompetence as a leader and in the inadequacy of his system had taken deep root by the 1850's, and was the accepted belief by the 1860's.

II

This belief contained a certain amount of truth; Blanc was not a particularly effective leader, and the calculated risks he took merely antagonized his opposition. But the criticism of his system was more often vicious than accurate. Proudhon, in particular, was demoniac in his misrepresentations, which were perhaps envenomed by Blanc's refusal to allow him to take over the Luxembourg as the seat of power in the reform movement.[6] Moreover, Blanc was not without justified apprehension when he warned against the Buchezian type of co-operative with its *mystique anti-étatiste* and its emphasis on competition. In July, 1848, three million francs were made available for the encouragement of co-operatives, and the disciples of Buchez, dominating the committee set up for disbursing the funds, loaned them at a 5% or 6% interest rate, and imposed their ideas on all applicants. The result was the encouragement of a form of co-operative egoism rather than co-operative fraternity; the associations, or those which survived, became closed capitalist enterprises, benefitting only the few original founders.[7]

The Provisional Government never offered the degree of assistance to Blanc's co-operatives which he had recommended in his doctrinal writings, and after the June Days, it suppressed all his experiments except that of the tailors. The city of Paris then terminated its contract for uniforms, claiming that the tailors had taken part in the revolt, which they had not.[8] Considerably reduced in numbers, the tailors liquidated, paid all their debts, as well as a dividend of seventy-five *centimes* to everyone who had been employed during fifteen days, and then set up a new shop in the Rue Saint-Denis. Soon the practice of equal salaries was dropped, but the sartorial co-operators remained attached to Blanc, and defended him against the often false charges of his enemies. This loyalty perhaps explains why they were refused a loan from the three millions of the Constituent Assembly, in spite of the old connections of Bérard with the *Atelier*. Reduced to forty members, the association came to its end in 1851, the victim, like so many of the co-operatives, of political oppression; Louis Napoleon's police equated economic associations with political societies, applying the laws against the latter to the former. In all, about fifteen associations in Paris and Lyons managed to survive the *coup d'état* of December, 1851.[9] One cannot claim that Blanc's system was a success or a failure, since there was no experiment in the Jacobin-socialism he championed, but only the creation of a few isolated co-operatives launched like fragile boats in a time of storm. What, one must ask, would have been the fate of capitalism had it not encountered the benevolence of feudal monarchs and the active assistance of mercantile states? And what would have been the fate of individual producers and merchants had they not unified themselves in the old guilds?

Always aware of the necessity of unity, Blanc, soon after fleeing France, sought to keep alive the spirit of solidarity that had animated the Luxembourg Commission. In his ephemeral organ, the *Nouveau monde,* he devoted a special section to producers' associations, in which he not only gave advice and encouragement, but also distinguished between associations that were fraternal and those that were not. He was advised in this matter by the still functioning Committee of the Delegates of the Luxembourg, and to one of its members, he wrote: "The essential is that our great family of the Luxembourg continue intact and maintain its fraternal union. The delegates of the Luxembourg must remain what the Revolution of February made them, that is, the intelligent, pacific, and courageous advance guard of the workers." [10]

He advised his disciples to present a united front to government intolerance by forming a Central Committee of Associated Workers. This committee was to form the directing bureau of a vast federation of producers' co-operatives, and from each local organization it would collect a fixed sum of money, the total of which was to form the "Budget of the Workers." A delegate from each member association would sit on the central committee which was to oversee the general interests of the co-operative movement, verify statutes of new organizations, build worker-cities, form special committees to find markets, and serve as an agent of exchange and publicity for all member groups. The Budget of the Workers was to be supervised by this directory which would use it to establish new co-operatives. Female workers in particular, whose salary was at a starvation low, were to be assisted to organize. The budget would also serve to set up temporary bazaars where produce could be displayed, and to build permanent stores where articles could be put up for sale.[11] Blanc here revealed an important innovation in his thinking: he called on labor to act independently of the state, not by setting up a few precursory shops but by creating a vast network of interdependent associations. If he had maintained this position, he would have anticipated the evolution of French co-operation. But for him this project was only an expedient to be tried in the face of a hostile government. The idea of a paternal democratic state inaugurating the socialist society remained fundamental in his system.

In spite of the criticism of the disciples of Buchez, Corbon in particular, the desire for federation was strong. Even before Blanc went into exile a Society of United Corporations had been founded by the Luxembourgers, Pierre Vinçard, Dupas, and Auguste Blum, with the aim of creating a center of action capable of solidifying the co-operative movement. At first principally inspired by Blanc, the society later allowed the mutualism of Proudhon to creep in. But it was, at any rate, short-lived, the repression that followed the June Days cutting its strength. The repression, nevertheless, could not eliminate the desire for federation. Several organizations of painters, bakers, binders, cooks, and barbers formed alliances. The most important federation to cut across professional lines was the Union of Workers' Associations, founded between August and November, 1849. Blanc was notified by its central committee which declared itself to be the continuator of the Luxembourg and the parliamentary committee on labor.[12] The Union was somewhat Proudhonian with its motto of "reciprocal exchange," but Blanc favored it, probably seeing in it a justification of his call for solidarity.[13] In reality, any theorist could find satisfaction in its program which ran the gamut of contemporary socialistic principles from Saint-Simon to Blanc and Proudhon. That 104 associations joined, did not insure its viability, for the police, present at every meeting, succeeded in finding among its papers an innocuous letter from Blanc, and used this as an excuse to suppress it in May, 1850.[14]

Consequently, the workers, ardent supporters of state intervention on February 28, 1848, grew antipathetic to the very idea of the state. Freed from their illusions by the turn of events, they saw that state intervention at this time, and perhaps for all time, meant only fraud, as in the National Workshops, or anti-revolution, as in the June repression. Given this distrust, it was impossible for Blanc's abstract defenses of state socialism to take root. Disenchanted with the government, the skilled urban working class, the real protagonists of the revolutionary tradition, eventually turned to a form of revolutionary *anti-étatisme,* compounded from the *émeutisme* of Blanqui and the anarchistic mutalism of Proudhon.[15] In particular the mutualism of Proudhon, with its call for bazaars, stores, mutual exchange, and free credit, was the solvent of the radical state as conceived by Blanc, the republic one and indivisible. The economy was to be organized around centers of exchange free from the control of any central power which might exist. Proudhonism found fertile soil in the disgust which labor felt for the imperial government, basically hostile as it was to both co-operatives and *syndicats,* two organizational forms widely popular in the 1860's.[16] The conflict of repression by the police and of syndical activity by the workers, along with the desire for independent action, awakened in the minds of workingmen a class-consciousness which intensified as industry expanded in France.

This increasing class-consciousness also contributed to alienate the workers from Louis Blanc, since he had called for the co-operation between bourgeois and labor, and never accepted the doctrine of class struggle. After 1848, intelligent followers of Proudhon like Henri Tolain and Benoît Malon realized that the upper classes had no intention of uniting their efforts with the proletarian movement in order to better social conditions.[17] Capitalists might combine with workers in order to overthrow a regime palpably reactionary, as they had in 1830 and 1848. But once the narrow political objectives of the bourgeoisie were attained, the union of expediency was dissolved under the pressure of divergent class interests. No longer capable of acting in accord, the capitalists turned against those workers who called for broad social reform. This lesson was impressed with increased conviction on the minds of the workers in 1863 when Tolain and several other labor candidates, in spite of Proudhon's disapproval, entered the general electoral campaign. They were decidedly defeated. In 1864 appeared the *Manifesto of the Sixty,* which called for the formation of a labor party. The defeat of labor in the supplementary elections, however, squashed the plan. Labor learned that it could look neither to the state nor to society at large for sympathy in its effort to ameliorate social evils. It could look only to itself. These experiences, more than Proudhon's writings, led the workers to realize the need for autonomous action.

Even Blanc came to realize the inadequacy of his ideas in relation to the conditions then existing when he wrote: "Centralization in France is so all-pervasive, official intervention weighs down so heavily on the free impulse of the mind and soul, that a reaction in favor of individual spontaneity was inevitable. This reaction is legitimate. From many aspects it is beneficial." [18] He also gave his endorsement to the short-lived Workers' Credit Society of J. P. Beluze, which had as its purpose the making of loans to co-operatives, and which had no relations with the state.[19] In spite of this concession, Blanc never dropped his *étatisme.* He continued to insist that in a truly democratic regime the state would be the very essence of society; it would not be a force directed against individuality and therefore opposed to spontaneous initiative, but rather an instrument which offered this initiative the power, as distinct from the mere right, to act. But on this point Blanc found no support.

Realizing the impossibility of serious class co-operation on an extended scale, labor girded itself for the class struggle by closing its own ranks, first at the national level by the federation of co-operatives and *syndicats,* and then at the European level by the founding of the International Workingmen's Association. The men who founded the French section were disciples of Proudhon and so bent on keeping the working class entirely independent that they moved to exclude all but true salaried laborers from the International.[20] Here was the germ of French *ouvriérisme* which, as an outgrowth of a developing class-consciousness, sought a complete separation of labor from the bourgeoisie, especially from "bourgeois" intellectuals. Given this attitude the French delegates were hardly eager to invite Blanc to join. In fact, the delegates from Paris revealed a marked dislike for most of the exiles.

Blanc, as it turned out, was invited by the English general secretary to attend the inaugural conference at Saint Martin's Hall, and while he chose not to attend, he approved of Marx's opening address. It seems that the English delegates sought his adherence. This he would not give, preferring to be inscribed only as an honorary member, whereupon Marx, who considered the ideas of "the little Sultan" to be "bourgeois," had a by-law approved which forbade the acceptance of honorary members.[21] The result was that Blanc never formed part of the First International. He was also apparently unaware of the renascence of the socialist movement in 1868, when a new law provided for the toleration of public meetings. Or perhaps he refused to recognize the movement as genuine, for in the meetings the *anti-étatistes* dominated, and neither his name nor his work was mentioned.[22]

Debarred from the true labor organizations, he was exiled not only from his homeland, but also from the social movement. Either consciously or unconsciously, he sensed his isolated existence, even more oppressive since his removal to Brighton. There he came into contact with Arnold Ruge, one-time leader of the anti-socialist European Central Committee. In desperation, Blanc approached him with the hope of reviving this long defunct organization which he had denounced so bitterly when it was founded by Ledru-Rollin, Ruge, Mazzini, and Kossuth. The German exile, sensible enough to realize the futility of such a hope, dismissed the proposal.[23] Blanc was sinking into a deadly passivity which imprisoned his mind in the past. His historical research concentrated his thought almost exclusively on the Revolution of 1789 and his memories did not permit him to move far beyond 1848.

CHAPTER FOURTEEN

The Philosopher of History

I

℘ DURING THE EARLY YEARS of his exile Louis Blanc was too preoccupied with *émigré* politics in England and labor developments in France to resume work on his study of the great Revolution. It was only after the *coup* of 1851 that he recognized the futility of his efforts to influence events in his homeland. Disgusted and frustrated, he became less and less active in *émigré* organizations and sought solace in the past. This does not mean that he wrote history merely as an escape; in large measure he took up his work now for the same reason as before 1848: Jacobin-socialist propaganda. His philosophy of history, among the numerous aspects of his general thought, was, in fact, the least affected by his experiences in 1848.

Blanc's philosophy of history grew out of the democratic idealism of the two decades preceding the Revolution of 1848. Democracy as a movement was still very new and its champions were filled with that youthful ardor and intemperance which send men out to topple the windmills of conservatism. This mission came to dominate Blanc's philosophy of history, with the result that history became educational in a far more utilitarian sense than can be accepted by an objective scholar. For Blanc, it served as an instrument of propaganda, and the study of the past for its own sake made little appeal to him, the past being important only as it offered him information in bulk from which he might select those facts which gave deep roots and a sense of inevitability to his socialist doctrines. This use of history was a tendency among many writers of this period. Louis de Bonald, Augustin Thierry, François Guizot, Adolphe Thiers, and even Jules Michelet worked more or less the same way. Like them, Blanc approached the study of the past, not as an objective historian but rather as a subjective moralist unencumbered with the rules of what was already called "scientific history." To be sure, he insisted that he was impartial, and his prefaces generally ran like this: "I am going to write the history of the affairs of my time, a delicate and perilous task. Before taking up the pen I severely interrogated myself and as I found in myself neither partisan affections nor implacable hatreds, I thought that I could judge men and things without being unjust and without betraying truth." [1] But he rejected what he labeled "cold impartiality" and proudly stated: "You are, moreover, perfectly correct to feel that I am not a man who hides my sentiments. Whoever will peruse my book [*Histoire de dix ans*] will know who I am. Yes, I wrote with a definite goal in mind; yes, I took up the pen to exert as strong an influence as possible on the mind of my readers; . . . yes, the historian is in me a man with a cause; I not only avow it, I am proud of it. I consider this cold impartiality which leaves the reader undecided between glory and shame, between oppressor and oppressed, to be a violation of the eternal law of justice and of the most sacred duties of the historian. I *favor* what I feel is good; I *oppose* what I feel is bad. In this sense I have not been impartial; but, I swear, I have always been sincere." He went on to insist that a man's sense of justice need not lead him to alter facts.[2]

Throughout his life as a writer, Blanc took this attitude of involvement. The historian is not merely to relate facts, nor really to give an impartial interpretation of them; he is to judge on the basis of strict morality, to condemn or to praise. However, his judgment is to rest on irrecusable documentation, for Blanc wanted his preferences and aversions to receive the sanction of footnotes. Even in regard to the nascent science of political economy he held that it was not to describe "how events take place in our present society," but rather "how events ought to take place in a society organized on the basis of justice."[3]

Justice is a word that appears often in the socialist's writing, his concern having centered itself about that rather vague ideal men call social justice. But for the author of *Organisation du travail* the ideal was not vague; it was precise and, above all, absolute, since justice could not be relative lest it cease to be just. The past was full of horror and war, and there was not an ideal of justice appropriate to each historical period; justice was rather an immutable final condition toward which society must progress. Consequently, Blanc looked confidently ahead, convinced that society was moving toward a socialist paradise. And it was his discovery of the unswerving current of man's growth that had revealed to him this glorious destiny.

Naturally this vision influenced Blanc's interpretation; it also influenced, but less so, his methods of research. These were generally valid. He did not accept a document at its face value, and he made some attempt to evaluate his sources.[4] He collated documents, studied the predilections of witnesses, and took into consideration the parts they played in the events they described.[5] He used preferably those witnesses closest in time and place to the events under discussion. Assured of the solidity of his research for his *Histoire de la Révolution française,* Blanc proudly footnoted his facts. Michelet referred to this as a "vain ostentation" and insisted that source citations hindered the reading. Alphonse Aulard later disagreed: "We read Louis Blanc with no less pleasure and all in a breath. These notes, which Blanc was the first to use effectively in this manner, are an aid rather than a hindrance for the reader."[6] This documentation, of course, must not blind one to the fact that Blanc's history is essentially subjective; it is colorfully written, but often declamatory, the product of much labor, nevertheless inadequately supported by primary sources. His generalizations were not really intended to serve the cause of history, but rather that of Jacobin-socialism.

Louis Blanc published two important historical works. The *Histoire de dix ans, 1830–40* was the first to reach the public, a volume appearing each year from 1841 to 1843, and two volumes in 1844. This work is a description of the upper bourgeoisie in power and might rightly be called a political pamphlet in five stout volumes, its author having directed his scathing criticism against every facet of the July Monarchy. Because of its polemical character and limited scope, *Dix ans* is not important as an essay in the ideas of history. It is mostly descriptive, and while it is rich in Blanc's socio-political concepts, it contains little of his interpretation of historical forces.

The second work, the *Histoire de la Révolution française,* is another matter. This twelve-volume study is Blanc's major contribution to the philosophy of history, and it resulted from his endeavor to explain those forces which influenced the evolution of French society. Concerned primarily with the rise to power of the middle class, it should logically have preceded the *Histoire de dix ans,* which is a partisan description of that class already at the peak of power. More vast in scope, the later work falls into two parts: the first two volumes, written before 1848, deal with the pre-revolutionary period and, in a certain sense, are an attack upon the institution of monarchy; the other volumes, fruit of exile, deal with the revolutionary period and, in a certain sense, are a defense of democracy.

The Ancient Regime found no sympathizer in the Jacobin-socialist. In his thinking, kingship was the moribund remnant of the Middle Ages, and he used history as a propagandistic medium to expose all its evils. He was no more sympathetic toward constitutional than toward absolute monarchy. The Revolution of 1789, he felt, had mated a parliament to a king, producing that political androgyn known as parliamentary monarchy. This was the futile mating of two principles, authoritarianism and individualism, both of which were doomed to death by the ineluctable laws of history.

In Blanc's philosophy, principles constituted the chief source of action, and he viewed history as an evolutionary process determined in its course by a succession of ideas. Seeking a doctrinal framework within which to explain this gradual movement, he formulated a kind of dialectic. He compared three historical periods, each of which was governed by an idea, and each of which had characteristic political, social, and economic structures.

First there was the medieval period during which the idea of authority predominated. Less concerned with the period than with the principle, Blanc described the latter as the principle "which causes the life of nations to rest on beliefs blindly accepted, on superstitious respect for tradition, on inequality, and which, as a means of governing, employs constraint. ¹ This period and its doctrine formed the thesis of Blanc's triadic division of history, mainly French history.

The growth of a capitalist class undermined the social basis of the principle already in power when this class, emerging as the champion of individual freedom, inevitably came to grips with the feudal aristocracy and a class struggle resulted. Blanc was less concerned with the struggle between classes, however, than with the struggle between ideas which reflected the interests of the classes. What was important was the contest between the principle of authority and its antithesis, the principle of individualism. The latter he defined as the idea "which, detaching man from society, makes him the sole judge of all things and of himself, and gives him a magnified opinion of his rights without indicating his duties, and, for all government, proclaims laissez faire." ⁸ By the eighteenth century the middle class was ready to assume political control, for the principle with which it would mold society in accordance with its interests was already progressing from the second to the third and final stage of development.⁹

According to Blanc, all ideas must pass through three phases of growth. First, there is the phase of combat, when an idea is strongly opposed by the group in power; secondly, there is the stage of active discussion, when the idea, if it is serious, is given a wide hearing; finally, there is the phase of triumph when the idea, if it is just, is universally accepted by society.¹⁰ Now this last qualification, "if it is just," is disconcerting, since Blanc posited that the Revolution of 1789 marked the final stage, the triumph, of individualism. Yet he constantly emphasized that individualism was never based on justice, but on unjust egoism, and always argued that its triumph, while inevitable, was a necessary evil. It did not inaugurate the era of justice. On the contrary, it bred so much injustice that man would eventually turn against it.

This reaction against individualism would then lead men to favor the principle of fraternity, the synthesis of Blanc's dialectic. This new idea, involving the reorganization of society in accordance with the ideal of social harmony, he defined as the principle "which, considering all members of the great family to be interdependent, seeks to organize society, the work of man, on the model of the body, the work of God, and bases the power to govern on persuasion, on the voluntary consent of all hearts." ¹¹ During the 1840's he believed that the new principle had attained the second stage, possibly the third stage of development. He sketched its growth from its beginning in the sermons of Jesus Christ, through its propagation by the Albigensians, John Hus, Michel de l'Hôpital, Rousseau, Morelly, Bonnot de Mably, and Robespierre. However, the failure of the 1848 Revolution led him to believe that the new idea, in spite of its impressive lineage, was still only in the stage of combat.

The regnant principle during his own lifetime was that of individualism. Its birthdate as the dominant ideal was 1789; its deathdate was still uncertain. But its decline was as inevitable as its rise, because each principle and the society based on this principle contained the germs of their own destruction. At least the societies founded on the thesis and antithesis contained these germs; Blanc was silent as to whether or not his fraternal society of the future would contain them.

He was not silent, however, on the issue of the inevitability of the Revolution of 1789. This fateful year did not witness a mere change in government but a destined change in principles, a clear victory for the bourgeois and their ideal. There could be no compromise of principles. Once completely elaborated, a principle had to live or die in its entirety. Therefore the Old Regime, authoritarian as it was, could not have reformed itself in accordance with the demands of individualism without repudiating its philosophical integrity and thus destroying itself. The Revolution was inevitable because the champions of individual liberty were forced to abolish the prevailing ideal and its general structure in order to gain ascendency over society.[12]

It is apparent from these general statements that Blanc's knowledge of what Marxians call a "dialectical situation" was incomplete. He clearly perceived the opposition but not the interaction among triadic phases. He failed to explain that in a true dialectic each phase, while exhibiting "something qualitatively new, preserves some of the structural elements of the interacting phases, and eliminates others." [13] However, this interaction is implied in his philosophy, at least in regard to the synthesis. The principle of fraternity involved a rehabilitation of authority as well as the preservation of many of the basic liberties found in liberalism. Blanc, however, lacked subtlety in his explanation of these principles. Seeing absolutes rather than nuances of change, he tended to make too sharp distinctions. For him, papal authority was pure oppression and bourgeois individualism was complete anarchy. Also too sharp was the line he drew between 1789 and 1793.

He distinguished between two revolutions because he found two principles combatting the traditional system. The first, that of 1789, represented the triumph of individualism over authority, and it was successful, not only because it served the interests of the dominant capitalist class, but also because its chief ideal had over a long period of time taken root in the minds of men, having been effectively propagated by the great thinkers from Luther to the *philosophes* and the *économistes*.[14] The second revolution, that of 1793, failed because society was not yet ready to welcome its ideal, fraternity. The first revolution was influenced by Voltaire, the second by Rousseau. But Rousseau, like Hus, was only a precursor of future needs, not a representative, like Voltaire, of present needs. While Lafayette and Mirabeau were the continuators of Voltaire, Robespierre continued Jean-Jacques. Danton stood vaguely between the two, in an indefinable position, a sort of no-man's land between principles. Blanc had a vague admiration for Danton, but insisted that he did not measure up to the lofty purity of Robespierre. And yet, he had to admit that while the Incorruptible personified fraternity, his ideal was not socialistic. The revolution of 1793 sprang from Rousseau, not Mably, and since not even Robespierre understood the socialist implications of the great principle, it was impossible for socialism to triumph at this early date. Blanc was often accused of transforming Robespierre into a socialist. To this he replied, "You are wrong in saying that I attribute what you call my communist ideas to Robespierre and to the Mountain. I state just the opposite. Throughout the entire course of my book I maintain that the hardiest minds of the Revolution had only a vague idea of what constitutes the socialism of our day." [15] In fact, he strongly insisted that the victory of the synthesis had to await the further education of society, when it would be welcomed by all men. Were this not true, the Thermidorian reaction, which signaled the reassertion of individualism, could not have occurred.

Blanc went on to show that the Terror, concomitant of the fraternal revolt, also caused its defeat, the excesses of terrorism having broken the back of the revolutionary movement. However, the Terror was not to be wholly condemned because it saved France from reaction and invasion. Unprepared by propaganda, the second revolution and the Terror were necessitated by *la force des choses*. There would have been neither the one nor the other had it not been for the intrigues of the court, the clergy, and the *émigrés*, and an invasion of France by foreign armies bent on reversing the work accomplished. Because of these circumstances France, to save herself, submitted to a form of dictatorship, and Robespierre accepted this rule only because of these conditions. For him, the rule of the Terror was temporary, not a system to be continued. Only a strong centralized government, he felt, was capable of organizing the democratic resistance to royalist intrigue from within and invasion from without, and of equalizing among the various social strata the burdens of resistance. So if the Girondins represented clemency, Robespierre and his followers represented preservation and justice.[16]

This notion of a society which creates the instruments required for its salvation seems particularly inept, denying as it does the problem of individual responsibility. Given Blanc's thesis, a Barras, and even a General Cavaignac, infamous for his brutal repression of the workers in June, 1848, can be represented as men destined to save society. Blanc failed to perceive that the notion really weakened his demand for a society based on justice, for the chief question logically becomes one of salvation, not of justice. Hence the Thermidorian reaction, like the reaction following the June Days of 1848, is acceptable as an instrument necessary to social preservation. One might ask then, by what right did Blanc thunder against these reactions and against these mere mortals who were, to use his own words, only the "puppets" of destiny? [17]

Since he was supposedly interpreting the Revolution from a socialist point of view, why should he insist that the fall of Robespierre marked the end of that historic event? He saw two revolts; but why did he not perceive a third, the one represented by Babeuf and the Conspiracy of Equals? After all, Robespierre was only a precursor of fraternity, just as Luther was only a precursor of individualism. Real fraternity was socialistic just as real individualism was capitalistic. Certainly, then, he should have devoted his attention to Babeuf, far more representative of socialistic fraternity than the petty bourgeois Robespierre. However, he closed his study with the year 1795.

III

Now it is apparent that Louis Blanc, like his contemporary, Karl Marx, was a determinist. The historical evolution of society followed a definite path from which it could not swerve. However, Blanc was hardly a precursor of Marx as certain Germans erroneously believe.[18] To be sure, the French socialist elaborated a dialectic; but it is possible that he took the idea of triadic growth either from Saint-Simon or from German political thought. He met Arnold Ruge as early as 1843.[19] He was introduced to Karl Marx toward the end of the next year when they formed a "kind of friendship, if not a specially close one." [20] It was certainly after 1845 that he first used his faulty—or perhaps Gallicized—dialectical method to explain the evolution of French society. Nowhere in his *Histoire de dix ans,* the last volume of which was published in 1845, is there an indication of a dialectic.[21] Nor did he even mention the Hegelian dialectic in an article, "La France et l'Allemagne," which he published in 1843.[22]

At any rate, Marx certainly did not discover a materialist interpretation in Blanc's history, because the French socialist was fundamentally an idealist. Furthermore, Marx could have found relatively little that was really novel in Blanc's study of pre-revolutionary France. Blanc's study of the class struggle between the feudal aristocracy and the middle class was pretty much of a socialistic pastiche of Guizot's history of French civilization. Blanc differed from Guizot chiefly in that he did not accept the rise to power of the bourgeoisie as an end, but rather as the means toward the establishment of a fraternal society. In this respect, he went beyond Guizot, less as a historian than as a prophet. He was equally weak in his explanation of dialectical evolution. He did not fully understand the mechanism of the dialectic, and therefore fell into inconsistency in his use of it.

Blanc clearly perceived the struggle between the feudal and the capitalist classes, and he maintained that the transition from thesis to antithesis was partly motivated by this struggle. He also realized that the struggle had economic implications, although he did not emphasize them. However, in his study of the motivating force from antithesis to synthesis he ignored the class struggle; this later transition, he insisted, would result only from the union of the bourgeois and the people. This union did not suggest that the principles in question were reconcilable; for Blanc they were not. Logically, he should have concluded that the class protagonists of these principles were also irreconcilable; however, he never sought to draw from his ideas all the conclusions possible, and firmly insisted that while a wall of hostility separated doctrines, the classes involved might become fused. In this instance, as in others, his political philosophy hindered the logical development of his philosophy of history. He had elaborated his socio-political ideas before working out a theory of socio-political growth, with the result that the latter served as handmaid to the former.

Blanc placed his greatest faith in the persuasive power of ideas, never doubting that the principle of fraternity would eventually gain the approbation of all men. The triumph of this new principle, in accord with the philosophic needs of an increasingly industrialized society, was as inevitable as the victory of the idea of individualism during the eighteenth and early nineteenth centuries. He clearly explained the relation between philosophic ideas and philosophic needs; however, he was vague in his explanation of the origins of those principles or ideas which dominated the three main phases of his dialectic. The problem is roughly this: Do ideas arise out of the philosophic needs of society as a whole, or out of the needs of a particular class? Blanc seems to have been unaware of the problem he was skirting and in a most vexatious manner used the words *society* and *class* synonymously. And again, it is not easy to determine precisely the role he attributed to ideas. He generally posited that ideas guided society from one stage of development to the next stage. But an idea, it seems, did not come into play until a class was well enough advanced to favor it. The rise of the middle class began before Luther, but it was Luther who first gave voice to the principle of individualism and only later did bourgeois intellectuals expand this doctrine. Blanc implied, then, that while ideas guided society, they did not necessarily determine the direction that society would take. Principles arose out of a need; they did not create that need. This need was given substance by the growth of a new class, which, as it gradually developed, began the transformation of traditional structures, thus bringing about new philosophic requirements and the birth of a new principle which came into conflict with the old one, a conflict that could only result in the destruction of the outmoded principle.

However, an idea might exist independently of these particular requirements or, at least, need not necessarily grow out of them. This was true of the principle of fraternity which, according to Blanc, was first formulated by Jesus Christ. It consequently antedated both thesis and antithesis. But this principle would not dominate society until the necessity for it was widely felt both by the people and the bourgeois. For it was not any ideal that served as guide to men groping their way forward. The influence a concept exerted depended in part on its relation to the social and economic conditions, so that only when a class arrived at a certain stage of development did it come to favor that principle which conformed to its particular needs. Then a principle entered the first stage, that of combat, and came to serve as guide to social evolution.

It is apparent, then, that the attitude of the capitalists was determined in part by economic changes. But while Blanc observed the close rapport between the material conditions and the philosophic ideas, he rejected an outright materialist interpretation, running counter as it did to the prevalent idealism of his generation. So he gave little attention to the economic conditions and concentrated on the ideas, with the result that his history was essentially a treatment of the evolution of ideas. "It is not force," he wrote, "which guides the world, no matter what appearances might say: it is thought; and history is made by books." [23] He had a certain knowledge of the historical forces which led men to write these influential books, but he did not adequately explore the social and economic factors involved.

Another weakness of his history, considering his desire to interpret the past from the socialist point of view, was the meager attention he gave to the lower classes. In reality, he did not break away from that tradition which regarded history as fairly well limited to the fields of politics and diplomacy. He gave far more attention to the struggle among principles, the rise of the middle class to political power, and the corruption of monarchy, than he ever gave to social and economic conditions. This neglect was only natural, for in his view these conditions played only a secondary role in historical evolution.

The major force dominating all facets of history was God, and like Blanc's political doctrines his religious beliefs strongly influenced his view of the past. They certainly kept him from putting forth a mechanistic interpretation that was purely materialist. His determinism was mechanistic, of course, but in the Cartesian, not the Marxian sense. Society, he explained, followed a path traced out for it by the hand of God; like the planets in space, principles and the individuals who propagated them, as well as the society in which both existed, were subject to a divine plan, or preferably, to a divine law of progress manifesting itself in the form of contrasting principles. A necessary part of the plan was an intellectual élite, existing to fill out the philosophical content of the principles.

Blanc explained that there were two types of men. On the one hand, there was the average man who, with his equals, formed the bulk of society. The will of the average man was free, that is, non-determined, there being no force compelling him to act in a certain way. He was free because he exerted no influence upon the evolution of society. On the other hand, there was the great man who, with his equals, formed the élite. He was not free, being destined to act upon society and direct it along the path traced out for it by the hand of God.[24] This person Blanc called the representative man (*l'homme représentatif*), for he was a "concentration of the collective life." He did not create the principles he propagated; rather he perceived and formulated them to guide his contemporaries. Therefore, Blanc wrote, there was "operating in the depths of societies a slow mysterious continual labor that prepares the phases through which civilization must pass. There are first vague instincts, then incomplete and badly defined feelings. Comes a man who finds a formula for these feelings and transforms them into ideas, he is a great man." [25] The role of the great man was not an easy one. Each of these heroes was nothing more than an instrument destined by God to exhaust and break himself in the service of ideas. Even the power he possessed came not from within himself but from his "milieu," for he was only the personification of that milieu. In him the "principles were made flesh." [26]

Blanc's representative man cannot, however, be identified in any way with Carlyle's hero. Blanc emphasized the dependence of the great man on his milieu, really his human milieu, the source of his ideas and of his strength. He refused to elevate this thinker above "humanity" lest the towering individual seem to serve as arbiter of human destiny. Such an elevation would have meant essentially that the servant was usurping the rights of the master. Hence Blanc wrote: "I am not one of those who, to make certain men greater, will willingly make humanity smaller. . . . I know that historic personages, even the most illustrious, are, after all, only ephemeral actors in a drama composed by the society which contains them." [27]

Blanc was not given to religious speculation, and his religious sentiments and ideas were more instinctive than cultivated. However, his pantheism, the romantic naturalism he inherited from Rousseau, was modified by his equal adherence to classical humanism and to Catholic theism, and this eclectic faith makes for considerable confusion in his writings. For example, he once defined God as the "universality of all creatures," by which he really meant all human creatures, or humanity. Thus the gifted individual was the creature of his human environment, and the voice commanding him was the voice of God, that is, the voice of the people. On the other hand, Blanc also conceived of God as a theistic divinity, distant in his heaven, and directing society by mysterious impulses coming from "on high," which inspired the élite. For example, he wrote of Richelieu: "There is a man for whom God reserved the mission of clearing the route by which the bourgeois would advance in France. For great men are only blind powers. The role they play is not of their own making. A contemporaneous event dazzles them, it uses them, while the sovereign regulator of causes decides the final consequences and future repercussions." [28] It would seem then, that the élite, although a phenomenon of secular society, existed only to do blindly God's will. They were not so much "principles become flesh" as they were God's will become flesh. The great man was even less than an instrument, he was a mere "puppet" in the hands of the almighty.

But for all this fervor, Blanc was not conspicuously religious in his interpretation of history. He was chiefly concerned with the life of man in this world and his concept of fraternity was basically secular. Like his spiritual forebears of the eighteenth century he was bent on teaching man how to attain happiness in a future society on earth. The guiding hand of an omnipotent god assured a certitude of direction to historical evolution. But so did the dialectic. And this certitude was probably the chief importance of both. For Blanc's history was not a study of the past for its own sake; it was a description of society's progress from an unhappy past to a felicitous future. History was filled with tyranny and injustice; but it was also the source of hope, indeed of faith. It was the story of the birth pains of justice that must emerge from the womb of all humanity.

CHAPTER FIFTEEN

Let Us Cultivate Our Garden

I

❦ IN THE RESEARCH for his study of the French Revolution, Louis Blanc nourished his spirit upon the documents revealing France's past greatness, and in the writing of history he found the hope and inspiration that relieved his frustrated ambition. Possessing a Balzacian ability for identifying himself with the events and persons he revived, he often slipped willingly into the past, and contentedly isolated himself there in the company of his heroes. In this way he momentarily escaped his exile. He found it extremely difficult to adjust to the English way of life which he had long condemned for its "vulgar materialism." When he first arrived he received sympathy from only a few persons, such as Ernest Jones, the Chartist, and George Jacob Holyoake, the famous co-operator and free-thinker.[1] Thomas Carlyle was another who welcomed him, their mutual dislike of capitalism bringing them together; and although no real friendship grew between them, the generally satirical Englishman was most tender when he set down his impressions of the exile: "A pretty little miniature of a man, well shaped, long black head, brown skin; every way French aspect; quick, twinkling, earnest black eyes; a smallish, melodious voice, which rather quavers in its tones; free, lively, ingenious utterance, full of friendliness, transparency, logical definiteness, and seeming good faith; not much vanity either; a good little creature, to whom, deeply as I dissented from him, I could not help wishing heartily well." [2]

In fact, Blanc was more appreciated by the English socialists than by the French. In March, 1854, at the time of the strike at Preston, he was invited by Ernest Jones and his committee to be an honorary delegate to the Labor Parliament assembled there to decide what action to take.[3] The failure of this well-organized strike, incidentally, convinced Blanc of the futility of labor agitation for purely economic motives and in the face of a hostile government. No matter how well organized, he felt, strikes were doomed to failure. Not so the activities of English co-operatives, which he admired, seeing in them an efficacious answer to labor distress.[4] Nonetheless, he was critical in his writings of the British workers: even after winning the vote, they continued to choose bourgeois or noblemen in preference to labor leaders for parliament. British labor, he concluded, was too infected with British egoism and materialism, too purblind in its concern for such narrow objectives as higher salaries and shorter hours, to undertake the leadership in a vast socialist movement.[5] The French workers were, for all their shortcomings, still his heroes. He had created in his mind an almost divine image of the French worker, who, possessed of all the virtues that make for the superman, was the zealous, if sometimes misguided, leader of modern socialism.

Yet Blanc admired the English, praised the freedom he found there, and with great sincerity wrote, "England, at this moment, is the supreme place of refuge for the victims of civil dissension; she is the last great sanctuary open to the human mind."[6] Once he privately admitted that "London remembers the 'Marseillaise' that Paris seems to have forgotten."[7] But this admiration was not the true stuff of his attitude. English fervor, he recalled to himself, did not extend beyond the frontiers; it was not a herald of universal reform. It was nationally egoistic, and could not be otherwise. There were too many contradictions in the English people to allow them to concentrate their full force on the energetic, broad effort for reform.[8] In return, the English never fully trusted Blanc or his socialism and closed him off from their national affairs. John Stuart Mill once confessed that "his name is associated in the vulgar English mind with everything that can be made a bugbear of."[9]

However, the British public was most favorably responsive when he turned to public speaking as a means of livelihood, under the sponsorship of the Marylebone Literary and Scientific Institute. His two topics were innocuous enough: "The Workers of Miracles in France at the End of the Eighteenth Century," and "The Salons of Paris in the Eighteenth Century." Chosen to appeal to sophisticated middle-class audiences, his topics, as well as his oratory, became quite popular, drawing hundreds of applauding listeners.[10] His financial situation was considerably improved, for he received twenty-five pounds for each appearance. Yet, as he wrote to Madame d'Agoult in April, 1863, his purse was by no means full, with the result that he could afford neither a summer vacation nor the leisure which might interrupt the daily grind of making a living.[11]

When the lectures were over, Blanc again turned to journalism, and became the London correspondent for the *Temps*. The articles he sent to Paris were in the form of letters in which he claimed to describe life in England. Unfortunately he never really understood the English way of life for he rarely traveled beyond the suburbs of London. Characteristically, he was far more interested in England's politics than in her society and the bulk of his letters dealt with the parliamentary scene.[12] Although his observations there were by no means lacking in criticism, he wrote with the precision, comprehension, and sympathy which caused the English press to welcome him as a friendly critic.[13]

And he was basically a friend of England, although he never became, as the *Daily Mail* had claimed much earlier, "domesticated." To him, his residence was never more than a sojourn. In the 1860's, however, Blanc found a certain contentment, an outlook combining both lofty disdain and Voltairian skepticism. Thus he wrote to Madame d'Agoult in 1862 that having entered public life with no illusions, he was not now bitterly disenchanted. "I am now in a state of mental disinterest and calm which I will not willingly exchange for the troubles of an ambition vulgar in appearance, and for an activity always exposed to calumny, unless the duty to do so were imposed upon me by the conviction that this sacrifice would be useful." [14] His serenity, however, was tainted with a deep bitterness, and in the small garden behind his house in St. John's Wood, where he cultivated his flowers, he pondered, not the advice of Voltaire, but the words of Danton: "Humanity bores me!" [15] In his mind he also cultivated memories of a sweeter past, not historical, but personal: Paris and its boulevards, parks, cafés, theaters, and old friends who were in prison or dispersed in exile. His deepest pleasure was to meet a visitor from France. When the sculptor Jules Salmson came to London with a letter of introduction from Charles, he received him with warmth and with a barrage of questions about affairs in France. Then, after the sojourn, he accompanied his returning compatriot to Charing Cross station. He was silent, jealous, and mournful as he helped the lucky man board the train and as he stepped away, his emotions, overcoming his taciturn melancholy, filled his eyes with tears.[16]

Exile had not only separated him from his country but also from his brother Charles. The love which had bound these two since their school days at Rodez did not diminish following their separation, and on only one occasion was a strain put upon it; Charles, after Louis fled to England, decided to continue in the government. The younger brother, however, remained faithful to the elder. He acted to throw the police off Louis' tract at the time of his flight and to save his papers from seizure. He also fought a duel, wounding the editor of the conservative *Assemblée nationale,* who had printed a false citation in which Louis called for erecting a guillotine and for cutting off heads.[17] Charles' dependence upon his brother's direction had, in fact, been too great, and he suffered from its loss. He was on the verge of a nervous breakdown soon after the separation when a friend hurriedly sent him to London, and warned Louis of his brother's condition. The friend felt that the separation might later prove beneficial to Charles, but that for the present, Charles needed to be close to his brother.[18] The prognosis was accurate. Louis' long absence did affect the fraternal relations; love grew as influence diminished. By the 1860's Charles had abandoned the ideal of "useful" art, he had become a famous art critic in his own right, and Louis, the former mentor, gladly became Louis the attentive host when his brother visited him for at least one month out of each year.

Among the French exiles, with the exception of Nadaud, Blanc found no intimate friends and more indifference than sympathy. Not until the first decade in England came to a close did he mingle more freely with others. He then found hospitality at the home of the Russian émigré, Alexander Herzen, whose little daughter was enchanted by the French socialist not much taller than she. Upon entering, he immediately asked for his little friend, with whom he chatted and played for hours. He was very proud of his "conquest," and it really vexed him when a Frenchman snapped, "My God, Louis Blanc, you're not going to imagine that this child likes you? It's your blue coat and yellow buttons that she likes." At Herzen's he appeared démodé, both in attire and ideas. He exposed his theories eloquently and, for the more or less unsympathetic listeners, verbosely. Incapable of simple intimate conversation when there was more than one person in the room, he declaimed with ringing, revolutionary phrases.[19] His conduct was quite different when he visited Henri Ernst, the famous violinist. They often passed the entire night together, crouched over the chess board, eying with intense concentration the little figures which brought defeat or victory. Mme Ernst decided to present them with an enormous board, whose chessmen were appropriately large. With the board spread before them like a battle ground, each player sat in a large chair, from which he ordered the moves, and the amazingly sympathetic Mme Ernst acted as official mover. When the violinist returned to Paris, he and Blanc continued to play by mail, for the game had become for Blanc "a wretched passion." He took on good, mediocre, and hopeless players, and generally lost.[20] Always a lover of good company and brilliant conversation, Blanc did not hesitate to accept invitations to dine among the members of English high society. The cosmopolitanism of their dinner parties was an exhilarating pleasure, and he appeared at them, wrote Carlyle, "looking as neat as if he had just come out of a bandbox." [21] He certainly found little sympathy for his doctrines among his fellow guests, or with Carlyle, who now referred to him as the *"philosophe gamin,"* but he basked in an atmosphere that removed him from the drab daily existence of exile.

Although he moved at times in the circles of high society he no longer pretended to the hand of a rich young lady, as he had in the 1840's. When Blanc finally married, in October, 1865, he chose rather a "girl of the people," a Hessian, Christina Groh, the niece of his landlady, whom he courted for about five or six years. Although he was fifty-four and she was only thirty, their marriage was blissful, for she brought him as dowry "a treasure of charm, devotion and goodness." She possessed, he affirmed, a genius of the fingers whose creations threw him into fits of ecstasy, he, who hardly knew how to put on his tie. This simple woman brought, at last, tenderness and regularity into his life, which sweetened the last years of exile. After marriage he arose every morning at eight o'clock. At nine he breakfasted on the "eternal" soft-boiled egg and the "semi-eternal" cup of tea. From nine-fifteen until five he worked. Then came an hour's walk, followed by dinner, during which he drank beer instead of wine, his one national peccadillo. The evening was given over to relaxed conversation, or, if an opponent was on hand, to a game of chess. In 1866 Blanc and his wife went to live in Brighton. The move was made with reluctance, for he preferred large cities with crowds, lights, and action about him. But his wife, whose health was delicate, suffered from a chest disease and her doctor suggested this change. Blanc himself suffered from rheumatism, but nowhere in the British Isles could he find relief.[22]

When the cold winds of winter blew down from the North and the damp fogs shifted in from the sea, he must have longed more than usual for the clear crisp air of Paris. Certainly the thermometers of that Northern city registered winters as bitter as those of England, but life in the French capital seemed warmer to Blanc, and there was always the fire of politics to heat a man's soul. Undoubtedly the political thermometer rose several degrees in 1869, for that was the year of the general elections. Hot words and hotter passions chased the lingering winds of winter. Spring came early and democrats throughout France awakened from what had seemed a hibernation of almost twenty years.

II

Louis Blanc's long isolation from France undoubtedly influenced his views on the stand democrats should take for the general elections of 1869. Like a prophet of old, he cloaked himself in the doctrinal righteousness of '48, condemned the heresy of Bonapartism and cast his anathemas against those men of the younger generation who spurned his advice in the sacred ritual of electioneering. Earlier his advice had been of little consequence because there was no serious democratic opposition to Napoleon. In 1851 he had called for complete electoral abstention, a position he reversed six years later, since universal suffrage, abolished in 1850, had been restored by the Emperor. He now warned against taking the oath of fidelity to the Emperor, so that successful candidates might be expelled from the assembly and the empire exposed as a government not based on the will of the people.[23] The republicans in France, however, paid no attention to this advice, and their few delegates prepared to fight the regime as a parliamentary opposition within the assembly. For Blanc, this was cheap opportunism, and not even the political awakening of France during the 1860's moved him deeply. Fearing that renewed activity would strengthen the tendency toward opportunism among young men, he returned to a policy of complete abstention. It was not his desire to reform the Empire, but to destroy it. Most of the young generation of democrats, also eager to do away with the Empire, would have none of his abstentionist *mystique*. They referred to him, Hugo, and Quinet as "ankylotic sectarians" and "old beards," and followed Léon Gambetta, who would not be reconciled to Napoleon, but who was ready to take the oath in order to amplify the voice of opposition within the legislature.[24] The exiles lost most of their influence, with the result that the republican revival was not accompanied by a Jacobin-socialist revival; it was primarily a political movement.

However, within France there were certain democratic groups who, disgusted with the methods of the radicals, turned to the irreconcilables in exile. In the spring of 1869 the democrats of Saint-Etienne offered Blanc a candidacy for the elections of May. He would not accept. "There is no discourse delivered from the tribune against the Empire," he insisted, "which is an *act* as completely an *act* as the refusal to compromise, in whatever fashion it might be, with Napoleon." [25] Although the elections of May, 1869, showed an outstanding increase in the strength of the opposition, Blanc refused to believe that the Empire could be reformed from within. The so-called evolution toward liberalism was deceptive. Napoleon still possessed the veto, and France still had a master.

Blanc's attitude towards the elections of May, however, was inconsistent. Having refused to run himself, and scorning those who urged participation and the oath, he nonetheless gave both his blessing and support to the *assermenté* Henry Rochefort. Descending from the lofty sphere of principles where he had erected his tribune, he entered the political campaign with a public letter to François-Victor Hugo's *Rappel*, in which he co-opted for Rochefort, opponent of Jules Favre.[26] Many wondered why the exile took such a step, which was a contradiction of his avowed purpose. Undoubtedly he had no fear that Rochefort might be contaminated by the opportunism of the *assermentés,* and Rochefort was among the few candidates who advocated energetically both political and social reform rather than merely the liberalization of the Empire.[27]

For his decision Blanc was widely criticized, especially because Favre had been the spokesman in 1848 for the parliamentary committee which called for his prosecution as an instigator of the May 15 demonstration. Blanc had realized the delicacy of the situation, which caused him to deny that he had been moved by personal resentment. Yet it seems improbable that he was entirely free of rancor when making his choice. How else explain the contradictory position of this doctrinaire who denounced contradiction and held so tenaciously to his principles? Furthermore, he cast away his principles for a useless cause: Rochefort lost the election. But he received over 14,000 votes, a great many of which, he asserted, were given him because of Blanc's letter.[28]

As a matter of fact, Blanc's support of Rochefort brought criticism chiefly from moderate republicans. The socialist opponents of the Empire congratulated him and the Socialist Democratic Committee of the eighth circumscription of the Seine offered him a candidacy for the supplementary elections in November. He again refused the candidacy for he would not take the oath. The democrats of Paris, however, were not easily discouraged. Hoping to force Napoleon's hand, they were determined to present the exiled *inassermentés* at the polls. On November 7, 1869, a meeting of the radicals of the first, third, fourth, and eighth circumscriptions of the Seine was called. The caucus decided to invite Blanc, Barbès, and Ledru-Rollin to return, and dispatched a committee to persuade the exiles that they were needed in the fight against Napoleon. Their presence, it was hoped, would discourage the *assermentés* from running in the supplementary elections of November, and they would also form a powerful group of candidates opposed to the oath.

The illness of Barbès prevented his return. Ledru-Rollin felt that his presence in France would only lead to his arrest, for he had never been amnestied, and give Napoleon an excuse for clamping down on the meager liberties won by the democrats. No such imperial condemnation prevented Blanc's return. He asked for time to decide whether or not to run in the third district, and finally he chose not to. If he had been among the first candidates chosen in committee, he explained, he would have quit exile; but since he was not, his return to Paris to pose his candidacy would have been an act of antagonism toward those candidates already acclaimed by the voters, an act of protestation against a choice already decided upon. It was necessary, he went on, to affirm clearly the principle. But once this was done the question of the candidate was of no more than secondary importance. Blanc also advised against the democrats' marching en masse to the Palais-Bourbon in order to protest the prorogation of the old assembly.[29]

If there were electors willing to follow Blanc this far, not many accepted his notion of open voting at a time when secrecy was indispensable to free choice. He urged that electoral lists be drawn up on which each voter would write his name, address, and the candidate he preferred. The publication of these lists would constitute the popular counting of the vote. To those who feared open voting, he replied: "In general, in a country which desires liberty and which, consequently, ought to be worthy of it, each man must have the courage of his opinion. The right to vote implies the duty to vote. By exercising your right of suffrage, you contribute to send to the chamber a man who will share in the making of laws which I must obey. You owe me an account of the use that you make of your power to influence to this extent my destiny. For this use you are responsible to society, whose existence it will affect for good or for bad. Your vote belongs to all. If it belonged to you, you could sell it."[30] Like the issue of direct government, Blanc might well have saved this idea for the future fraternal society. It was a most curious proposal for a man safely outside of France to make to those who were well within the reach of Napoleon's police. There were, of course, few who favored the notion, for even those who agreed with Blanc in principle, like Charles Chassin of the *Démocratie,* concluded that the scheme was foolhardy. Naturally the moderate republicans, whose organ was the *Siècle,* decried bitterly the entire program of the exile, and asked where was the utility in electing Blanc, Ledru-Rollin, Barbès, and Hugo? Since they would not take the oath, they would be excluded from the chamber, and four good republicans in the legislature would more quickly reform the Empire than a hundred thousand votes of protest which left those four seats vacant.[31]

Although Blanc and the men of '48 were cheered in the third district of Paris and the candidacy of Barbès was unofficially posed in the fourth, the supplementary election was not fully favorable to the Left, for while Rochefort won his seat, Barbès was defeated. Blanc immediately wrote to Holland where Barbès lay on his deathbed, hoping to soften the blow of defeat, which, perhaps, he feared would be his own fate should he return. He lamented: "There's the outcome of the substitution of tactics for principles! That breaks my heart! And Paris! Paris siding with the *cunning ones* without seeing the lack of intelligence in their pretended cunning! It's not with impunity that a people remains enslaved for almost a quarter of a century. The general abasement of human character, that's what I consider the greatest crime of the Empire." [32]

The campaign occasioned by the plebiscite of 1870 brought no change in Blanc's position. If he did not regret his support of Rochefort, he was determined to make no more exceptions, and he now went a step beyond the measures suggested by many of the opposition. A large number of democrats called for either a negative vote or a blank ballot. Blanc, on the other hand, demanded that no ballot be deposited, that is, that there be complete abstention. He insisted that the plebiscite was a mockery of free choice, for in a democracy a constitutional convention, not an Emperor, must draw up or amend the constitution. He warned those who were ready to cast affirmative ballots that the acceptance of the puny reforms would hinder the passage of more radical measures.[33]

Although the number of abstentions surpassed by over 300,000 the number of negative votes, the plebiscite of May returned an overwhelming majority for the liberal Empire. But the whole affair soon became meaningless when France went to war against Prussia. Now Blanc once again added patriotism to his politics.

CHAPTER SIXTEEN

The Patriot Returns

I

❦ THE OUTBREAK of the Franco-Prussian War in 1870, re-
newed the bellicose nationalism of Louis Blanc's younger days.[1] Between
1848 and the rise of Germany as a threat to France in the 1860's, he had
become increasingly pacifistic. His assumption of power in the Provisional Government of 1848 had turned his attention away from international affairs to concentrate it on domestic difficulties. Even on May 15,
when the National Assembly had been invaded by crowds demanding
the liberation of Poland, he did not call for a crusade. As it turned out,
the only wars of the Second Republic were waged first against socialism
and then against democracy itself. A world of illusion began to crumble.
Too many of the heroes who were to have marched in the ideological
crusade were bowing before Napoleon, the anti-crusader, the man who
had perverted France's mission by butchering democrats in Paris and
Rome.

Blanc had not always been on such acrimonious terms with Louis
Napoleon.[2] In fact, before 1848 he had been fairly sympathetic toward
him. And he perhaps made some slight contribution to the spread of the
Napoleonic Legend. Certainly, he offered no significant opposition to its
growth. On the one hand he accused the first Napoleon of tyranny, but
on the other, he lauded him as the sower of revolutionary ideas throughout Europe and the personification of the French martial temperament.
No doubt Blanc looked back with some nostalgia upon the Napoleonic
era. In his eyes the July Monarchy was a crass reminder of his country's
downfall in 1814, and he often compared the unsoldierly Louis Philippe
groveling before England and Austria with Napoleon bringing honor
to France by bringing Europe to her knees. In this way Blanc's political
attack on Bonapartism was considerably mitigated by his patriotic sentiments. What he failed to realize was that his compatriots might go even
further than he in condoning autocracy, that they might prefer national
glory to political democracy. He also failed to realize—and here was his
greatest error—that Napoleon's nephew, whom Blanc considered a naive
politician, could successfully combine the ideals of glory, democracy,
and governmental stability in a political program.

France's endorsement of the *coup d'état* of 1851 bitterly disappointed the socialist, and the 1850's were years of disillusion for him. Renouncing the political world, the crestfallen crusader retired to the British Museum where he obtained vicarious excitement by studying the Jacobin crusade of 1793. He did not emerge until the beginning of the 1860's. Then he found little change in his homeland. France, who was to free the world, seemed scarcely concerned with freeing herself.[3] It was largely this frightening apathy which induced him to become a pacifist: just as he had often preached war for the greater glory of France, so he now professed peace for the salvation of France. He came to fear for the very existence of his homeland when in the rise of Prussia he perceived a new enemy beside which England paled. In fact, he dropped his extreme hostility toward England after he found refuge there. He continued to distrust her, but he now recognized that the downfall of England would be the downfall of political freedom.[4] Therefore he sought to foster good relations between his native country and his country of exile. As part of this effort, he omitted from the 1850 edition of his *Organisation du travail* the incendiary chapter entitled "Competition Leads Necessarily to a War to the Death between France and England." His series of articles for the *Monde,* too, explained English life critically but sympathetically to his compatriots. But when he turned to the subject of Prussia it was to warn them against the menace looming on their eastern frontier.

This warning marked a deep change in Blanc's earlier attitude. In the 1840's he had urged Germans to accept unification under Prussian leadership. The vigor of German thought, if guided by France, he reassured, could resist Prussian militarism and popularize democracy throughout the Bund. By the 1860's, however, he perceived that the Germans had gone their own way and were moving not toward real democracy but toward unity under militaristic Prussia and hegemony in Central Europe. In fact, Blanc glimpsed the frightening possibility of Teutonic domination over all of Europe. The central geographic position of a united Germany awakened his anxiety. A Prussian Napoleon, and he had Bismarck in mind, could easily invest all the capitals of the Continent, Rome excepted. If Germany were militarized on the Prussian model and supported by a strong navy, she would be closer to universal domination than France had ever been under Napoleon. The intensification of Italian nationalism with which Blanc had earlier sympathized, also frightened him. A strong Germany and an expanding Italy meant France closed off from the Rhine and her supremacy contested in the Mediterranean.[5]

As Napoleon steered France farther into a diplomatic impasse, Blanc found himself caught in a dilemma. If France were dragged into a war, whether she won or lost, democracy would be destroyed in France and in Europe. Should the Emperor emerge victorious he would consolidate his regime. All the efforts put forth by republicans in Paris would meet with failure. And until free government was firmly established in France, Blanc saw little hope of its spreading through Europe. He still believed that the spark of freedom which would ignite the Continent had to be struck first in his homeland. But he no longer spoke of a crusade, and he was convinced that a war led by Napoleon would be one of conquest, not of liberation. And worse, Napoleon's success would arouse the animosity of other nationalities with the result that France's prestige would decline. On the other hand, should the Emperor fall in defeat, the revolution that would follow would render France easy prey for a Prussian invasion.[6] Blanc, doubting if mere revolutionary fervor was capable of parrying the aggression of a modern army, found the only escape from his dilemma in pacifism. Only if a war were avoided might the forces of democracy within France continue their peaceful encirclement of Napoleonic autocracy. Blanc therefore adhered to the peace movement founded in the later 1860's. However, he did not attend the congress held in Geneva and he was disappointed with the assembly, filled as it was with moderate liberals who drew back when Michael Bakunin vigorously expressed the need for social reform.[7]

In Blanc's opinion the delegates failed to attack the basic cause of war which he now found in the definition of dictatorship. Sword rattling and military glory were the natural complements of empire. Autocrats were impelled to seek military glory in foreign lands in order to keep the populace docile in their own lands. But this militarism caused other nations to take alarm; they in turn rattled their swords while forging many more to brandish. Tension grew until the slightest incident, easily created, brought on a state of belligerency.[8] Undoubtedly Blanc still believed that economic competition incited war, but he no longer emphasized this theory. Rather he stressed the political cause, the conflict resulting from dynastic ambitions. This shift reflected his change of interest during his second decade of exile. He of course remained a socialist, but he rarely expatiated on social problems. He now devoted most of his time to discrediting autocratic government, and he therefore tended to view world problems more in the light of politics than of economics. Partly for this reason, he shifted his hostility from England, the economic menace for France, to Prussia, her political menace. And with the same ardor that he had desired a conflict between his country and her Channel neighbor in the 1840's, he now desired peace between France and her Rhine neighbor in 1870. In a desperate hope to prevent hostilities he signed, along with Michelet, Marx, and other exiles, an appeal for peace. It of course had no effect.

As Blanc feared, the war came, and there was no doubt in his mind that the bellicose diplomacy of the Emperor of France was its chief cause. When he learned that his beloved France, "capital of modern civilization," was being invaded, he mourned her great error: "There is the fate reserved for nations who let their destinies depend on the will of one man."[9] And yet he insisted that the genius of France was invincible; she had not lost the habit of *levées en masse*. Victory was attainable if she was ready to cast off both the paralysis which the Empire had imposed on her, and imperial rule. The weakness of one man had to be replaced by the strength of all men, united and ready to do battle, no longer for the glory of a single person, but for the life and glory of the nation. Until now the nation had disappeared behind a man; the hour had come for the man to vanish behind the nation. Only in a new burst of the will to be free would France find the power to repulse her enemy.[10]

Before the outbreak of hostilities, Blanc had feared that a revolution during wartime would weaken the French resistance. His pessimism led him to the demand for peace. But once the Germans took the route for Paris, he apprehended that the very war he had feared offered the conditions for revolt against the Empire. Ready to throw himself into the battle, he waited anxiously the occasion to return.

II

The moment the Franco-Prussian war began, Louis Blanc, observant, expectant, brooding, waited like a ship delayed by adverse winds. For when on September 4 the news of Napoleon's surrender at Sedan became generally known, he left at once for his homeland, reaching Paris during the night of the fifth. There he learned that on the previous day the crowd had shouted for his inclusion in the Government of National Defense, and that he had been rejected by the moderate republicans, the *assermentés,* who were no more sympathetic toward him now than they had been in 1848. This time, however, he was not prepared to force his way into power. Twenty-two years of exile had not deadened the memory of his unenviable position in the Provisional Government. He chose to remain an "independant" and not to force the issue of social reform as long as the war continued. He urged all Frenchmen to rally in support of the new power.

He viewed the situation of 1870 as one similar to that of 1814, and his ardent patriotism dispelled momentarily whatever doubt he had entertained in exile about the ability of a revolutionary power to stand up against a modern army. If Paris was not betrayed, as he believed she had been in 1814, she could stop the Prussian advance. Seeking to rouse the populace, Blanc wrote broadsides full of the Jacobin fury of 1792. Deep within himself, however, he recognized early the menace of Prussian technology, and with blended disdain and apprehension, he referred to the invaders as "Mohicans who had graduated from the polytechnic school." [11]

For all his patriotic fervor, Blanc recognized the military weakness of France, and, quite realistically, hoped to awaken the interest of foreign powers, especially England, with his articles warning against a Prussianized Germany whose victory over France would enable her to dominate the Continent. He also hoped to influence England by affirming that his country now stood for peace and freedom, that her struggle against the

aggressive Germans was made legitimate both by her right to defend herself and by the need to safeguard the heartland of a revived democratic
movement.[12] Frenchmen, including most socialists, would repeat these
principles in 1914 and 1939 with greater success. But in 1870 most Eng-
lishmen were far too skeptical to be impressed. Possibly supposing that
this skepticism characterized the government rather than the people,
Blanc decided upon a dramatic return to England to arouse the public,
a decision that the British cabinet could hardly have viewed with equa-
nimity. The would-be Citizen Genêt, therefore, received no official encouragement from either side of the Channel. His own government, refusing to invest him with an official title, consented merely to wish him a
successful journey.[13] It is not improbable that the defense government was
secretly pleased to be rid of this ferocious intransigent, and disappointed
when the German blockade compelled him to abandon his project; his
effort, anyway, would have been as fruitless as that of Thiers in whom the
liberal republicans placed greater faith.

Locked up in Paris, Blanc became more and more patriotic à la 1792.
Dreaming of a *levée en masse,* he and Charles joined the National Guard,
and in spite of his sixty-nine years Louis tried to drill with the troops.
He and Hugo, who wore a *képi* cocked over his ear, became symbols of
the republican old guard, the irreconcilables. Before long, Blanc suspected that the war effort was flagging. On October 13 he went to see
General Trochu, charged with the defense of Paris, and announced that it
was time to launch a mass attack. His fervor was soon dampened as the
old general referred to the defense of Paris as a *folie.* Trochu would
make a show of resistance for the sake of honor—more the honor of the
army than that of France—and would then surrender in the traditional
fashion. Blanc angrily went out, the word *traitor* in his heart if not on his
lips. He approached Hugo with the suggestion that they call upon the
military governor either to save Paris or to resign, but when the poet refused, the plan fell through.[14] Blanc had as little sympathy for the other
members of the government, finding them far too complacent toward
the enemies of republicanism. Their grievous error lay in their excessive
desire to placate conservatives, even Bonapartists, with the result that
they refused the services of ardent republicans. Certainly unity was necessary, but the excessive emphasis on moderation in politics and war
revealed their weakness. On October 24, Blanc expressed his fears to Edmond Adam, a member of the government, and urged on him three immediate measures: abolition of the stamp tax, of *caution,* and of the
prefecture of police.[15]

Critical as he was, Blanc was really not prepared to favor the violent
overthrow of the men in power. Although he desired an elected municipal council to replace the arbitrarily chosen Government of National
Defense, he explained that the Government must favor such an election.
"What is essential in the present circumstances," he wrote, "is to stimu-

late the defense government without upsetting it, and to avoid every chance of a collision in the presence of the enemy." [16] That Blanc became fixed in this view explains his opposition to every insurrectionary movement threatening constituted power while Prussians remained on French soil. On October 31, extremists led an insurrection to set up a commune like that of 1792. Lists of names were drawn up which included Blanc, Ledru-Rollin, Hugo, Raspail, Delescluze, Blanqui, and Pyat. Blanc was certainly not an instigator and in spite of supplications from many quarters, he refused to go to the City Hall in order to put himself at the head of the movement. An insurrection of this sort, although carried out to the cries of *La guerre à outrance,* was, he insisted, the work of obscure men like Flourens and widely feared men like Blanqui; it would destroy the unity of defense and open the gates for the Germans.[17] Already Blanc was suspicious of the men who would, five months later, set up the Commune.

On the other hand, it does not seem that he was entirely happy with the official plebiscite of November 3, which overwhelmingly endorsed the Government of National Defense, and which was, therefore, a vote of approval for the *assermentés*. His resentment of them vented itself against Ferry who, relating the events of the October 31 uprising, lashed out at its instigators. Impatient, the old proscript replied: "What! You have been full of goodness, full of patience, full of forgetfulness for our mortal enemies, the Bonapartists, and, as soon as it is a question of republicans, at the slightest struggle you become angry and spiteful? Who are you then, you, the *assermentés* of the Empire? Whom do you dare call the rebels?" [18] However much he disapproved the abortive uprising, he realized by November that it had had the essential merit of preventing an armistice. But it did not stir the men in power to make reforms equalizing the burdens of the siege.

Among the lower classes, the siege came to mean food shortages, and as winter came, cold rooms and sickness. They demanded rationing but the bourgeois politicians preferred "rationing by dearness," and rejecting a maximum law, they fixed prices on only several types of foods, without, however, controlling the supply. Until it was too late, they indifferently allowed the worst types of speculation and profiteering by unscrupulous merchants.[19] And yet, it was the lower classes who were the most determined to fight, and Louis Blanc, spared some if not all of their physical hardships, stimulated their hardy spirit. It was to them that he appealed in the cold of November when he spent many nights in the outposts. There, he tried to explain away the suspected timidity of Trochu, but at the same time pressed the guardsmen to demand action.[20]

By January the situation was worsening, and rumors of impending surrender undermined morale. Blanc, in a moment of desperation, wrote a public letter to Hugo, reaffirming his belief in ultimate victory. What was significant in the letter was his new thesis that if Paris fell, France would

fight on to avenge this surrender. He practically called for guerrilla warfare waged by the people.[21] For republicans like Blanc, victory was necessary, for it would stabilize the republic already proclaimed in their hearts
and, they insisted, in the country; whereas defeat would make possible,
perhaps inevitable, its downfall. Therefore, where Favre undertook negotiations for an armistice in late January, Blanc feared that all was lost.
His bitterness was profound. After twenty-two years of exile he had returned full of hope and courage, but somehow everything had gone
wrong. Feeling himself again on the threshold of proscription, he poured
out his hatred for the army and for the *réactionnaires capitulards*. In similar circumstances during August, 1848, his youth had suffered frustration,
but his indomitable will had cushioned the shock of failure. In January,
1871, however, he was an old man who, learning of the surrender, could
only moan, "I wish I were dead!" [22]

III

Still, the pessimism of old age, the despondency of defeat could not
quite shatter Blanc's basic urge to accomplish his lifelong democratic purpose, and if he needed a stimulant, it was furnished by the preparations
for the new elections provided for in the armistice terms. Bismarck, man
of authority, demanded a legal authority in France to accept his peace
terms. Blanc and the bellicose left accepted the election essentially on
these terms. On January 30, Blanc stressed that the assembly, chosen as it
must be under the guns of the enemy, would have but one mandate: the
continuation or the ending of the war. He apparently realized that war
was no longer possible; therefore, the assembly was to be chosen for the
sole purpose of making a humiliating surrender. Despised in public opinion by this degrading but necessary act, it would then dissolve itself,
making way for an assembly elected for drawing up a definitive constitution.[23]

As Blanc predicted, the elections did turn about the question of war or
peace. Unoccupied France, in a defeatist mood, returned monarchists
who hated the republican jingoes and who had run on a platform of
peace at almost any price. In Paris, however, there was both an unwillingness to admit defeat after months of suffering, and a strong tendency
to vote according to political considerations. Without repudiating the
republican *assermentés*, Paris turned to the older men, the *gloires* of '48.
Blanc, Ledru-Rollin, Hugo, Pyat, Delescluze, Quinet were on practically
all the electoral lists, and Blanc, with 216,000 votes, stood first among the
forty-three successful candidates, the enviable position of Lamartine in
1848. Could any event have more firmly supported his contention that
refusal to acknowledge the Empire had been a "political act"? Yet he
must have recognized that most of the voters who chose him had done so
in recognition of his sacrifices before 1870 and his republican patriotism

during that year. His had been a clarion voice of opposition to the ineffectual defense government, not the voice of '48 singing the sweet promise of social paradise. Public opinion did not reveal any serious concern for social issues. Certainly Blanc was not unaware of the utter defeat of the lists put forward by social revolutionaries, or unmindful of the fact that only on these lists did his name not appear.[24] Of the younger socialists, only a few, such as Cluseret, looked upon him as a chief and hailed his victory as one for the cause. Small wonder that he became increasingly suspicious of the extremists, the men who would soon take part in the Commune. To his right were the republican and neo-Jacobin *assermentés*, whom he disliked; to his left was a type of intransigent whom he feared, especially after he took his seat in the National Assembly at Bordeaux. With its preponderant majority of royalists, he quickly realized that even a moderate republican would have to walk lightly amidst this *"débris"* of royalty; one shock, and the unsteady framework of the Republic, erected since September 4, would be broken up by hostile hands.

On February 16 an ominous note was sounded in a report which, although it offered Thiers the title, Chief of the Executive Power of the French Republic, clearly pointed out that the Republic was accepted only provisionally. Debate was held on the next day. Blanc favored the choice of the aging Orleanist, but insisted that France was a republic, and that not even denial by universal suffrage could legitimately change this fact. He repeated the thesis he had defended in the Provisional Government during the evening of February 24, 1848. Annoyed, a royalist accused him of proposing a "divine right republic," and his voice was ironic, reflecting the views of the unconverted majority which voted for the report.[25]

Blanc's intransigent republicanism was soon matched by his uncompromising national spirit which compelled him to oppose the idea of accepting the German demand for Alsace and Lorraine. Debate on the peace terms was heated from the beginning. On March 1, Thiers, in chorus with the royalists, defended the cession with the argument that France had no other choice. Soon the assembly became noisy, at times almost violent. The deposition of Napoleon III, willingly made the scapegoat by almost all the delegates, was wildly applauded; the victims of the "crimes of December" were avenged. And when Blanc mounted the rostrum, dressed in black, his mouth hard-set, his eyes animated, his little body rigid, he had the appearance of the avenger. In cadenced, classic oratory, he denounced the Bonapartes, and called upon Europe in this last moment to redress the balance of power by resisting Pan-Germanism. The question before France, he explained, is not a simple one of war or peace. An appeal to arms for defense being legitimate, the "choice to make is between war for the preservation of right and peace with the violation of right." The republicans, he continued, do not preach fighting for its own sake; they do not favor permanent armies which make for despotism; they know that the absurd love of glory is too often a trap set for liberty.

They comprehend, rather, that the proposed peace will bring ruin and shame to the homeland. Therefore, if the Germans insist, let the French resist; let there appear stalwart patriots filled with faith in France to harass the enemy until he bleeds from a myriad of small wounds. France has her people, her vast stretches of land, her forests, her mountains, her ocean, her sea in which the enemy will lose himself. France must renew her faith in herself; but surrender her land and her people, never, never, never! [26]

Many members of the Bordeaux assembly applauded with enthusiasm, but most preferred to crow three times rather than repeat his triple "never." An inner force was lacking, both in the conservative majority whose coolheaded acceptance of peace stemmed from their identification of total war with Jacobinism, and in the fire-eating orators of the Left, men of '48, who could not rekindle the old enthusiasm which had lost most of its heat during exile. The vote was overwhelmingly in favor of the preliminary treaty, 546 to 107. In protest, some members of the Left resigned, an action which had the unfortunate result of weakening the republican group in parliament, and of strengthening Paris' distrust of the predominantly rural majority at Bordeaux. Already an enraged republican had shouted from the galleries, "You're a bunch of hicks!"

Louis Blanc decided this time against quitting the real source of power, a wise decision, for the Commune, which was already looming, would become as ineffectual as the Luxembourg Commission of '48, and more baneful to the social republican movement. Returning from exile, Blanc had forgotten nothing, but learned much, particularly the force of patience, with the result that he became a far better politician. He also became a far more sympathetic human being. To be sure, his earlier jingoism, restrained by the doubts and pessimism of exile, had surged forth forth anew during the war, and he, Quinet, Hugo, and others had signed an address to the people of the lost provinces, which ended with the solemn promise that the Republic would eternally lay claim to them. For a short while he added his voice to the clamor of the *revanchistes*. And he continued to believe in the legitimacy of "defensive" wars, without taking into consideration that practically all states explain away their aggressions as defensive measures. However, he soon banished the desire for a war to recover Alsace-Lorraine, his first step toward a sincerely pacifist attitude. He favored the League for Peace, and joined the Workers' Association of the Friends of Peace, a short-lived, ineffectual group. He himself had no concrete proposal, save a vague suggestion for a world court that would bring peace to the new generation. Nonetheless, he was entirely sincere in his hope for peace, and the depth of his feeling was revealed in his simple statement: "The slaughter of several thousands of men, the despair of their mothers and wives, the distress of their children, the depopulation of the countryside, the abandonment of agriculture, the paralyzing of industry and commerce, the undue growth of taxes, all this is the balance, not only of defeat, but of victory. To the ignoble cry 'Woe to the vanquished!' history makes this avenging reply: 'Woe to the victors!' " [27]

IV

Blanc had spoken out against civil war long before he took his firm stand against international war; however, his increasing pacifism made him a more determined man of peace than he had been before. He became as apprehensive of revolutionaries as he was of generals. Consequently, by early March he was a troubled man. He realized that an insurrection might easily result from the distrust of Paris for the provincials, and from the provocation, planned or not, of the Bordeaux assembly which expressed its firm desire not to place the seat of government in the great metropolis.

A thorough Parisian, Blanc was most disagreeably aroused by the latter proposal, and only the extreme seriousness of the national situation inclined him to moderate his feelings by an appeal to the reason of his fellow deputies. He therefore urged them, during the debate on March 10, to remove as quickly as possible to Paris. The city, he affirmed, was calm, and the assembly need have no fear of its violation. But would the city remain calm if the proposal to decamp to Fontainebleau or to Versailles was carried out? With a balanced voice Blanc declared that it would not, and he warned: "To despoil Paris of its role as capital would unify all Paris, the rich, the poor, the young and old, in a feeling of rage and of formidable rage perhaps. . . . It would impel Paris to set up its own government against which the Assembly either could do nothing, or could do something but at the price of cruel violence. It would complete by French hands, this mutilation of our beloved France that enemy hands have begun, and from the disasters of a foreign war bring on a civil war, even more horrible." [28] Once, during his speech, a royalist interrupted him with a laconic and rhetorical question, "And May 15, 1848?" which summed up all the suspicion of the provincial conservative for the traditional center of insurrection. Blanc's eloquence had no more effect on March 10 than it had had ten days earlier. It was Thiers who finally persuaded the majority to abandon Fontainebleau in favor of Versailles as the new seat of government. Thiers, however, remained in Paris until the eve of the civil war.

When Thiers and his administration deserted the City Hall the Central Committee of the National Guard moved in. On the next day it announced that elections would be held on March 22 for an autonomous municipal council of the Commune of Paris, and for the officers of the National Guard. The mayors of the *arrondissements*, the only legal authorities remaining in the city, were delegated to negotiate with the rebels in order to forestall a civil war. Acting with them were the republican deputies of Paris, among whom was Blanc; he had just returned in all haste from London where he had gone, presumably, to reassure his wife. In the evening of March 19 he and his colleagues met with several delegates from the Central Committee. He was hardly in a conciliatory mood and, when the committee's delegates insisted upon early elections and recognition, he snapped that they were insurgents, and worse, insurgents against the most freely elected government France had ever had. Tragically perhaps, it was Blanc who now assumed the awkward role of defending a conservative assembly against the demands of revolutionary Paris; he found himself, when he exclaimed that Paris was not all of France, resorting to the same argument that he had rejected in 1848. He ended by refusing to recognize the *de facto* authority of the Central Committee.[29] He favored the holding of municipal elections, but not under its auspices. In agreement with the deputies and mayors of Paris, he drew up a proclamation announcing their intention of proposing that the National Assembly adopt measures to arrange for the election of municipal councilors and officers of the National Guard.[30] The next day, however, the Central Committee rejected the concessions of its delegates, refused to surrender the City Hall, and purposely asserted that the deputies had agreed to elections for March 22. This assertion was contrary to Blanc's proclamation which had referred the issue to the assembly.

The action of that body depended on the initiative of Thiers. He listened with apparent sympathy to the Paris deputies, but insisted that time was needed, the city constituting a special problem. He gave no definite answer and, with equivocation, spoke first of opening his arms to Paris, then declared that only firmness would cause Paris to save herself. He seemed far more favorable to a proposal, defended by Trochu, to place the capital in a state of siege. This Blanc resolutely opposed, positing that such a measure would provoke civil war, not prevent it.[31] Although Blanc reproved the disorders that had broken out, he was finally shouted down by the Right, which followed Trochu's counsel. Blanc's active role as a mediator now came to an end; he no longer returned to Paris. Soon fighting occurred between conservatives and communards.

The republican mayors, frightened by a rumor that the Orleanist pretender was to be restored and by the occupation of their offices by communards, decided to favor elections for the twenty-sixth. Blanc refused to join them in this step, but he approved of their proclamation and on the eve of the elections he urged the assembly to decree that they had acted as good citizens. Therefore, while he would not accept the elections as legal, he was patently seeking the assembly's support of the mayors in order to strengthen them during the next day's campaign. His proposal was buried in committee and finally rejected without debate.[32]

During the municipal elections Blanc received a few thousand votes, though he naturally did not stand for office.[33] On the contrary, he repudiated the Commune that was chosen and when the civil war began, refused to resign from the assembly. This decision was forced on him by circumstance and ideology. His Jacobin-socialist ideas ran counter to those of the communards. Many members of the revolutionary Paris government, such as Delescluze, were almost pure Jacobins.[34] By 1871 Blanc's Jacobinism had become fairly moderate; moreover, he had been opposed to the federal ideas of the orthodox Jacobins since the beginning of his exile. He had also had a violent polemical debate with Proudhon and the admixture of anarchism in the Commune was in part derived from Proudhon. Blanc still defended communal autonomy or administrative decentralization, but firmly championed political centralization, the republic one and indivisible, with its center of national power and control in Paris. Independent municipalities appeared to him as the fragmentation of authority, as a form of political individualism which, emphasizing localism, would make for disharmony among urban centers, dissolve national patriotism, weaken France in Europe, and render impossible the co-ordination of industry at the national level.[35] He also repudiated the Blanquist tendency toward violence, another element in the Paris movement.[36] Blanc had concluded in the 1840's that violent insurrection was practically useless, and after long years of exile he was convinced that it was completely useless; worse than useless, it was baneful to the cause of republicanism. In his speech of March 10 he had referred to the false revolutionary spirit in Paris.[37] He meant that of Blanqui. In his heart he condemned the Commune before he did so in public on April 26. By this time he could no longer discern anything but madness among its leaders. His beloved city was in flames, and in the destruction and killing, he recognized the action of a new evil. For whatever nobility of aim existed at the start, it had ebbed with the chances of victory. Loyal and sincere men had been replaced by irresponsible fanatics who both usurped power and violated the course of history by recreating a committee of public safety. Blanc's own indignation, swelled by the dreadful carnage of the Bloody Week and by the jibes of the conservative journals gloating over his dilemma, provoked his angry reply: in the *Figaro* on June 8, he denounced the abominations—incendiarism, pillage, murder—of which Paris was the theater and the victim.[38]

Had he cried out as forcefully against the brutalities of the regular troops and the provincial guardsmen, he might have saved some of his reputation among left-wing elements. He was silent. Yet he certainly did not condone the tortures inflicted upon helpless prisoners; he was, in this time of troubles, trapped by the mandate of his lifelong mission: the founding of a republic. Without hesitation, but with great mental anguish, he submitted to the circumstances imposing upon him the decision to support Thiers, seeing in him now the bulwark of the Republic set up on September 4. His acceptance of the chief executive's leadership resulted from two official speeches made by Thiers on March 10 and 25, both of which granted *de facto* recognition to the Republic. However dim had been Blanc's hope, he had refused to follow his indignant colleagues of the Left when they decided to quit the assembly, since to do so, he reasoned, would have left the royalists in complete control and so weakened the position of Thiers. The folly of the Commune had only served the cause of monarchy by frightening the middle classes and the peasants. Thiers now served to counterbalance the communards when, by adhering to the republican form, he made it seem indispensable. Blanc, while rigid in his denial that the Republic could be destroyed even by popular vote, recognized that earnest defenders of the new government were few in number. These few, he argued, must avoid all provocation by practicing that most republican of virtues: prudence.[39] Here is the key to his activity during the 1870's.

CHAPTER SEVENTEEN

The Intransigent

I

℘ LOUIS BLANC'S REPUBLICAN IMPERATIVE was not an easy burden to carry during the 1870's. The responsibilities it involved, the self-effacement it imposed, called for a man of formidable conscience. Convinced of the validity of his mission, he fortified himself against the violence done to his feelings. And with greater tolerance than in 1848, with greater stoicism than in exile, he entered upon a second heroic period, with a heroism different from that of the barricades, being without fanfare, without demagogy, without, at last, the stridency of immature Jacobinism and frustrated socialism. Moved by his humanitarian and reformist goal, he avoided both revolutionary bombast and radical opportunism.

During the reaction following the Commune, republicans of all shades felt the need for moderation lest they play into the hands of the monarchists seeking as usual to link republicanism and terrorism. Moderation paid off and the parliamentary Left was markedly strengthened in the summer by-elections of 1871. The radicals then formed their own organization, the Republican Union, which was rather solidly unified during the fall and winter. It alone, with a few exceptions, favored an amnesty for the communards, and Brisson, supported by Blanc and forty-seven republicans, proposed one during September in the face of a violently hostile majority of royalists and moderate republicans. The radical Left was even more strongly drawn together in its opposition to the assembly's wish to assume constituent powers as proposed by the Rivet-Vitet bill. Although supporting Thiers, Blanc spoke against the bill, for it cast doubt on the undeniable existence of the Republic, and granted new powers to a body which had been elected purely and simply on the issue of war and peace. With Gambetta, Quinet, and Alfred Naquet, he called for dissolution and new elections, on the understanding, of course, that the new elections were not to involve the present form of government, but only to bring forth a new personnel to organize it.[1] The extreme Left was as uncompromising as the extreme Right which also voted against the Rivet-Vitet bill merely because it contained the word "republic."

There was undoubtedly a connection between Blanc's demand for dissolution and his parliamentary speech of September 7 in which he urged the assembly to take up its residence in Paris. He contended that if Paris was not made the capital again, she would continue in her surly mood, and either resort to a new commune or give herself to the Bonapartists. He hoped, too, that an assembly in Paris would become more amenable to the republican spirit of the city. He did not intend that the mob should threaten the deputies, and in his speech he deplored such episodes as the May 15, 1848, invasion. The Right and Center interrupted him frequently and finally rejected his proposal. The monarchist majority remained in Versailles, refused to use its self-arrogated constitutional powers to draw up a definitive government for France, and, awaiting the decision of the legitimist pretender Chambord, only temporarily organized the public powers. Blanc and the Republican Union abstained from these labors to which the right and left Centers and the Right so assiduously applied themselves. It was rather in their press—Gambetta in his *République française* and Blanc in the *Rappel*—that the radicals attacked the plans for a monarchist restoration. Gambetta, closely tied to Thiers, emphasized that a republic would be, above all, practical rather than Utopian. Blanc, on the other hand, was more abstract in his arguments, which consisted largely of the ideas he had first put forward in the *Revue du progrès* in 1840.[2]

The summer by-elections of 1872 were another success for the republicans, and again proved that moderation was attractive to the voters—which made it all the more attractive to the politicians. The monarchists, however, grew fearful. The man most widely recognized as their head, Duke Albert de Broglie, returned from England to assume leadership and to compel Thiers to stand either with him or against him. The chief executive, however, refused to combat the Left, a decision that committed him to a republic, but a republic that would be, as he put it, profoundly conservative. At this the Left rejoiced. The extreme Left, however, had relatively little cause for rejoicing; Thiers was openly against nearly every principle it stood for. On July 16, 1872, an amnesty bill was the subject of a committee report, and when Blanc urged debate on the issue his speech was greeted with noisy threats of cloture and his motion was voted down.[3] Then, during the parliamentary vacations from August to November, 1872, he and Gambetta decided upon a speaking tour of the provinces to spread republican ideas and win popular support for their demand of dissolution. Although Gambetta not only urged moderation but converted it into a cult, the Thiers government did everything in its power to prevent him from addressing large audiences.[4] Blanc had to cancel temporarily his plans because of the grave illness of his wife.[5] Then, when he prepared to lecture at Marseilles and La Rochelle, the police forbade him to do so. Consequently he published his ideas in a brochure entitled *Le parti qu'on appelle radical, sa doctrine, sa conduite.*[6] This little work was important not only for its content but also for its place in the political development of French radicalism. It was the clearest expression yet of the extreme Left's program for both political and social reform. On the latter issue, Blanc and Gambetta were already at variance, but in order to safeguard republican unity, Blanc did not now bring it up for extensive discussion. Echoing his comrade-in-arms, he emphasized the need for alert moderation and explained why Thiers, even though he was a persecutor, had to be given the support of the extreme Left. Radical in its goal the party was sober in its means, full of tolerance and willing to bend to the needs of circumstance, aware as it was that its goals could not be achieved in one leap. But on one point it would not bend: parliamentary dissolution.[7]

When the assembly reconvened in November, 1872, Blanc was unanimously elected president of the Republican Union. Thiers had openly disapproved of his brochure and of Gambetta's speeches, and now appealing to the Centers, he recognized the constituent power of the assembly. On November 29, a committee of thirty was established to prepare a constitution. Its first act was to formulate a proposal limiting the chief executive's power. Meanwhile the radicals, calling upon their electors, managed to have a large number of petitions for dissolution inundate the assembly when debates began on December 14. Gambetta spoke first. After him came Blanc with the accusation that the majority, by refusing to end the life of the assembly, was harming France. The cabinet's instability, its swinging from Right to Left and back again, resulted from the uncertainty of the assembly, unable, because of its present composition, to restore a monarchy or to organize the Republic. In consequence, the country suffered: the economy was stagnant, work was lacking, and martial law oppressed the people.[8]

When the left Center rejected his proposals, Blanc and the radicals decided that Thiers and his intimate followers had sold out to the monarchists. Angrily the radicals concluded that their sacrifices, their self-effacement, had been offered to no avail. Indeed, Thiers seemed bent on provoking them, and his ministry was no more lenient toward them now than during the previous year. In early March, 1873, he suspended the radicalist *Corsaire,* an aggression that angered the journalist in Blanc, all the more so since he dared not enter the lists against his unchivalrous opponent who was negotiating with the even more unchivalrous Germans for the evacuation of French soil. Blanc and some other radicals reached Thiers privately and obtained the lifting of the suspension.[9] But this concession did not fully compensate for the suppression or suspension of other republican journals or, worse, for Thiers' opposition to dissolution. Therefore, Blanc contended, the Republican Union would do well henceforth to support Thiers only if Thiers reciprocated.

The hero of France, the liberator of the sacred soil, probably did not even notice his diminutive opponent. In the complementary elections of April he openly patronized the neo-royalist candidate, Rémusat, who had also the backing of most moderate republicans of the Left and left

Center. The Republican Union, however, threw its weight—decisive in Paris—behind Barodet, an old-line democratic radical. Too ill to take an active part in the campaign, Blanc wrote a letter which Martin Nadaud read before public meetings and in which Blanc insisted that it was time for Thiers to show some gratitude toward the extreme Left for its support and patience. The chief executive had scorned and refused to consider its proposals to end martial law, grant an amnesty, dissolve the present assembly, and preserve the autonomy of Lyons.[10] On April 27, in a pouring rain, the electors went to the polls, 135,028 for Rémusat, chiefly in the west end, and 180,045 for Barodet, chiefly in the east end where the Commune had been strongest and the reaction most brutal. "Long live the republic" had been the rallying cry. And there was an increased response in the provinces where republican victories mounted.

Without doubt, the Paris victory influenced Blanc and others in the Republican Union; it was a mandate reviving their old faith and determination, and caused them to move gradually but knowingly toward a position of intransigent opposition. The new orientation, however, was not a sudden one, for the turn of events after the elections made unwise a precipitate shift in policy. The fall of Thiers, brought about by the royalists under de Broglie's leadership and excused by Barodet's success, had a marked influence on the radicals' plans. Marshal MacMahon, who replaced Thiers, chose de Broglie for his chief minister, with the result that the administration was now definitely monarchist and prepared to clamp down on the opponents of a restoration. Blanc and his associates realized the gravity of the situation and published a proclamation urging the people of Paris to remain calm; France and the Republic were at stake, they warned, since disorder would strengthen the Right.[11] Yet the old socialist, recently recovered from a protracted illness, was not entirely displeased by the turn of events. To be sure, he had voted for Thiers on May 24, but he could not regret Thiers' now complete rupture with the monarchists. Having severed that bond and become head of the left Center, Thiers made impossible a fusion of the Centers, and so greatly strengthened the entire Left.

This new force occurred at a most opportune moment. The monarchists were feverishly preparing for a restoration in the summer and fall of 1873. It was during this period that Blanc sought to reassure his colleagues and followers. On August 10 he wrote, "Not only is the Republic not in peril, but never, according to me, has its intrinsic force been affirmed in a more singular and significant fashion." [12] The design to fuse the two Bourbon branches would prove chimerical. "One must, in effect, close one's mind voluntarily to the teachings of history in order to consider monarchic heredity as a realizable thing in our country." [13] The strange forces of destiny, whose general movement Blanc had described in his histories, were ineluctable. He had written a year earlier that republicans had been persecuted by Bourbons, Orleanists and Bonapartists, and yet, France was now a Republic.[14] If, for the present, the Republic was almost without republicans, its establishment and the steady increase of its advocates would eventually dispel all threats to its future. As though part of a divine plan, the very menace of the royalists served to strengthen it. Unable to unite behind an acceptable pretender, they found unity only in their opposition to the Left. Should the Republic crumble, the competition of the dynasties would be unleashed and anarchy result. France must therefore choose between the Republic and chaos.[15] The Republic not only divided France least, it also offered her the stability and repose she sought.

As yet concerned mainly with safeguarding the Republic, Blanc again accepted the leadership of Thiers. He also placed himself behind the lengthening shadow of Gambetta, who became the mediator between the moderate and the extreme Left. With the Right divided yet menacing, the unity of all the Left was the prime necessity; therefore Blanc cheered with the entire Left when Thiers returned to the assembly as a simple representative of the Seine, and signed the proclamation of his fellow deputies of that department to the effect that Thiers represented the feelings of all France. This, the Paris Manifesto of October 17, also revealed the determination of the radicals to oppose, with force if need be, the plan of the royalists. Going beyond Thiers, they affirmed their decision to preserve not only the republican form of government, but also "civil, political, and religious liberties conquered by our fathers and . . . inseparable from the maintenance of the Republic." [16] By October 24, defense preparations were complete. The entire Left formed an alliance and its determination to prevent a restoration rallied even the fence-sitters of the Center when it made clear that a *coup* would produce a revolution. To the old men, France seemed to have returned almost to July, 1830, save that Thiers now pushed for a conservative republic and Gambetta seemed a sobered Godfrey Cavaignac. Perhaps the most significant innovation was the role played by Louis Blanc, who, without an 1830 precedent, carved out a definite and eventually respectable place on the far Left for his movement, Jacobin-socialism.

The unity and determination of the republicans, coupled with the inability of the legitimists and Orleanists to work out a program acceptable to Chambord, destroyed the possibility of his return. By November, the royalist threat had passed. All deputies, Right and Left, now agreed that France must come out of her provisional state. Blanc argued, "There is no other remedy for the situation save dissolution and an appeal to the sovereign country." [17]

II

The constitutional issue brought significant change in the tactics and in the organization of the extreme Left. During the winter of 1873–74 the

Republican Union remained united in its desire for dissolution and in the defense of its own constitutional ideas as opposed to those of liberal republicans and monarchists. Disagreement was not expressed openly, however, for once more the union decided to efface itself during the debates on the bill defining the president's powers. Blanc explained this silence as a political necessity. The radicals, had they openly opposed the bill, would have made its victory all the easier. The left Center, fearful of the extreme Left, would have shifted toward the right, and probably voted for the ten-year term desired by de Broglie rather than for the seven-year term which it originally favored. Blanc and his comrades certainly disliked the idea of prolonging MacMahon's term, especially since his powers and the limitations on them had not yet been defined. After the bill became law, Blanc expatiated on its essential faults: it placed the executive above the legislation already existing, thereby creating an interim of absolutism, and imposed him, by a seven-year term, on the next legislature, which would not have chosen him. It was clear in Blanc's mind that the monarchists, unable to effect a restoration, were bent upon setting up their creature as a *"monarque transitoire."* They therefore had solved nothing; they merely dragged on the provisional.[18]

Irritated beyond endurance, Blanc finally, in January, 1874, ended his parliamentary silence and entered the debate dealing with the role and powers of communal mayors. De Broglie favored their appointment by the central government, now in the control of the royalists. Blanc clearly perceived and denounced his motive: the use of the mayors and their adjuncts as monarchist electoral agents, reinforcing and extending to the tiniest hamlet the power of the departmental prefects and therefore of the central state. As of old, Blanc came to the defense of municipal self-government, arguing that each commune has a reality and unity of its own, and is important to local citizens who are involved in its rule and who are thereby schooled in the duties of citizenship. Autonomy would not make for disunity, he pursued, for local interests, when freely expressed and respected, would become enlarged, eventually merging with national interests. There would be balance between them, rather than brutal uniformity.[19] Blanc, while he had been opposed to the Paris Commune, was a champion of local self-government. On July 31, 1871, before the smoke of the civil war had cleared, he had stated before a markedly hostile assembly that the department was an artificial creation, lifeless, useful only for oppression by the central state whenever the central state was oppressive. It is not clear from this speech whether or not he desired the abolition of departments. It is improbable that he did, since he never called for an end to the prefects. Rather, Blanc envisioned a considerable reduction of their powers so that in the future, when France would enjoy the beneficent rule of the radicalized Republic, they would serve as intermediaries between the central and the local assemblies, whose bonds would be strengthened by the disappearance of all other bodies. For the same reason that he opposed an upper house in parliament, he criticized the departmental councils. These, he claimed, were the strongholds of privileged groups, and would have no reason for being in a Republic without privileged groups.[20] In January, 1874, Blanc was not alone in the defense of local autonomy, but de Broglie still controlled a majority, and his bill became law by a vote of 359 to 318.

The Cissey-Fourtou cabinet went even further in its conservatism, seeking to reduce the number of voters by raising the voting age from twenty-one to twenty-five and by instituting more stringent requirements for eligibility, such as three years' residence in the same commune. The old men of '48 at once discerned the intentions of the Right. It sought, as in 1850, to disfranchise the lower classes, many of whom were migrant workers. Ledru-Rollin, the "father of universal suffrage" in France, was the first to denounce the measure. Then, on June 4, Louis Blanc made what was probably the most effective speech of the last phase of his career. In this discussion, he dropped the scheme of proportional representation he had favored in exile, the Hare system, and returned to the ideas he had elaborated prior to 1848, ideas that lent themselves to the exalted oratory he employed as a means of persuading the Centers. Probably the part of his address most convincing to the practical men of the left Center was his emphasis on the need to preserve universal suffrage lest the Bonapartists restore their influence by championing it. Closing the suffrage would be opening the way to a *coup d'état*.[21] Apart from this pragmatic consideration, his speech was chiefly the defense of a principle, and a principle, he concluded, making for progress and order. Gambetta's attack upon the cabinet's project was exclusively practical, an emphasis which revealed his consistent tendency. Indeed, it revealed more, for everyone soon realized that in the course of his rollicking oratory he was granting recognition to the constituent power of the assembly.[22]

It might have seemed that Blanc too, having taken part in the debate, had acquiesced in the assembly's pretentions. He soon made clear that he intended nothing of the sort. He opposed a bill whose success, he feared, would aid the revival of Bonapartism, and its failure reassured him as did the continued electoral success of republicans. But the slight reawakening of the imperialists had thrown the Gambettists into consternation. They could be induced now to accept a republic made by the Right in order to lift France out of the provisional condition that favored the schemes of adventurers.

By mid-June the radicals split into two groups and the Casimir-Périer bill made the schism definite. The bill called for a strong president and two chambers, that is, a form of government distrusted by the radical. Prior to the session in which the bill was to be debated, the Republican Union held a meeting of its members. Here Gambetta laid down the essentials of a political attitude later called "opportunism" when he argued that the prescription of practicality demanded concessions to the moderates in order to obtain the desired objective: the legal establishment of the Republic. Blanc, on the other hand, insisted that the Republic already existed and that discussion of the bill, therefore, would put its existence in doubt. He was not, at this particular moment, prepared to bow to policies contrary to his principles. But his opposition to Gambetta's methods was mild compared to the bitterness he felt later when many of his fellow radicals dropped their accepted political ideals.[23]

As yet, Blanc was not prepared to defy openly the Gambettists although they voted with the left Center, which was under the orders of Thiers and favored the Casimin-Périer bill. Rather, he, Quinet, and Alphonse Peyrat abstained. They were of the opinion that Gambetta, in seeking to curry the good favor of the left Center, had lost his independence of decision and sacrificed the essentials of radicalism in return for the word "Republic," which was contained in the bill only as a decoy for the Left. But not even the word was accorded: on July 23 the bill was rejected by the royalist majority. Gambetta, in a rage, wrote the next day that the only policy left was dissolution. By now, however, the republican camp was in confusion, the turnabout having won both praise and reprobation. At any rate, Gambetta had returned to the fold of radical ideas, or so it seemed, and during the winter of 1874–75 the Republican Union was again tenuously united. It remained so, however, only because many members of the left Center, disappointed by the negative vote of the right Center in July, came to demand new general elections. Unity of the radical Left, consequently, depended upon disunity between the Centers. Gambetta, having discarded his principles once, was not to be held by them permanently. Aware of this precarious balance, Blanc continued to deny that the present assembly had constituent powers and pressed for its demise.

By late January of 1875 the committee of thirty had prepared its report on the constitutional laws, and once more the assembly became charged with excitement. There were angry murmurs after the reading of the Ventavon bill for it would enlarge the executive's powers to those of a constitutional monarch. The Republican Union took no part in the debate, having once more chosen silence under the watchful eyes of Gambetta and of Blanc, "buttoned up in his hostile reserve." The union finally voted against the bill which not only failed to mention the word "republic" but which left the definitive form of government to be settled only at the end of MacMahon's term. Edouard Laboulaye, a *rallié* of the left Center, then offered an amendment containing the precious word: "The government of the Republic is composed of two Chambers and a President." The Gambettists were again ready to swallow this pill, made more palatable by Laboulaye's brilliant oratory; he was widely applauded and saluted by all republicans save the intransigents. There were shouts for the vote; the parliamentary day was nearing its end. The Republic, Gambetta felt, deformed as it might be, was in the pocket. But then

Blanc, in a firm voice, demanded to speak, and mounted the tribune.
Many members of the Left cried out against him, yet he stood waiting for
silence, cold-faced, arms folded. Supported chiefly by the Right, he denounced the project of a second chamber.[24] Angry shouts filled the place;
the president's bell jingled uselessly; few heard the orator, but every
one knew what he was saying. The vote was postponed.

The next day, January 29, Blanc was greeted by a scathing attack in
Gambetta's *République française*. At about three in the afternoon, voting
began on the Laboulaye amendment. Determined to abstain, Blanc went
to the library where, away from the noise, he prepared his reply to Gambetta. He drew up a list of the young radical's earlier ideas, and revealed
how they had almost all been repudiated by him.[25] Suddenly Peyrat burst
in shouting that only five votes were needed for the amendment to pass.
His meaning was clear. Only five members of the union, Blanc, Quinet,
Madier de Montjau, Jacques Marcou and Peyrat himself had refused
to cast their ballots. Taking Blanc by the arm, he hustled him into the
huge assembly room. The agitation was at its peak. The "Five," cajoled,
exhorted by the Left, solemnly mounted the tribune where they dropped
their white slips into the glistening urn. Blanc was bitter in heart, struggling with his conscience, and yet he could not resist the entreaties of his
colleagues. Their resounding applause "entered his heart like arrows." [26]
But, in the end, the royalists defeated the measure by twenty-three votes.
There had been an error in calculation and the mental sacrifice was in
vain. The Five were again applauded at a meeting of the Republican
Union held the following day, the day when Blanc once more gave way
and voted for the Wallon amendment, which was substantially the same
as that of Laboulaye, and which passed by one vote. This was his last
compromise, however, on the constitutional issue.

Intransigent again, he refused to vote for the entire body of legislation
that would compose the Constitution of 1875. He examined article after
article and asked, Where is the Republic? It is not in the presidency
which is monarchical and controls all administrative appointments; it is
not in the choice of a capital since Paris, heart of democracy, is replaced
by Versailles, center of monarchy; it is not in the chamber subject to dissolution by the president and senate, and powerless to defend the Rights
of Man which do not exist in the Constitution; nor is it in the senate,
favored by conservatives to check the will of the people, especially the will
of urban France, by denaturing universal suffrage. By means of the upper
house the smallest, most backward communes might swamp by their
numerical strength the enlightened influence of the large communes.
Blanc favored municipal autonomy because he hoped to protect the communes from excessive control by the state; he opposed the senate in order
to protect the chamber from the excessive control of the communes. There
is in the Constitution, he caustically replied to his critics, the word but not
the thing. The "neo-republicans" of the Left have betrayed the republi-

can movement by submitting to the "neo-monarchists" of the left Center.[27]

On February 25 the constitutional project won a resounding majority, 425 to 252. De Broglie voted for it while Blanc and thirteen republicans abstained. Again it was the conjunction of the Centers that split the Republican Union, and Blanc, distrustful of them, explained why the Orleanists had chosen to support the project and why the liberal republicans were dupes. "Ah," he said, "if ever the monarchists see the occasion to call back the king, they will have only one word to erase in the constitution, only one word, and they will be able to shout to their master: 'Come! everything has been organized in advance; the monarchy is not to be made, it is made!' " [28] On June 21, speaking before the assembly, Blanc prophesied by implication a black future for the republicans. Drawing lessons from history, he pointed out with remarkable precision that in all the past regimes in which the executive dominated or attempted to dominate over the legislature, revolution or tyranny resulted. Suddenly many radicals shouted for him to desist, which he would not, and turning frankly toward Gambetta, he asserted that he would not sacrifice the permanent and supreme interest of public peace in the future for the sake of transient expedients.[29] Descending from the tribune Blanc was greeted with applause by the extreme Right and with cold silence by most of the Left. In the press he was made the subject of abuse and caricature, being treated as an out-dated old man, a ghost of the past, an ambitious publicity seeker, a stupid intransigent. Only the two journals of the extreme Left, the *Rappel* and the *Evénement,* expressed thanks to him for saying aloud what French democracy was saying in whispers. Individuals too, known and unknown to him, sent letters of encouragement which, he affirmed, "compensated for the attacks of the neo-republicans who began and finished their republican education in the antechambers of the Empire." [30]

His analysis, at least for the immediate future, was remarkably accurate. After the vote on the Constitution, power fell into the hands of Louis Buffet, who ordered the police to place the republicans under constant surveillance, and who practically accused Blanc and Gambetta of being the chiefs of the revolutionary movement. Finally on November 12, Armand Dufaure, the attorney-general and a leader of the left Center, put forward his proposal for a new press law, generally restrictive of liberty for it would establish high *caution* and deprive journalists of trial by jury for certain types of violations. The entire radical Left could readily oppose such a bill; however, Dufaure had included in it provisions for ending martial law in the pro-radical departments of the Seine, Seine-et-Oise, Rhône, and Bouches-du-Rhône, as well as in Algiers. Blanc spotted the bait at once and demanded a separate bill for ending the state of siege, this "regime of the sabre." He insisted that all the great centers of France, Paris, Lyons, Marseilles, were tranquil, that there was no longer any need for martial law, that the government had used it to attack republican journals. Now, he pointed out ironically, the cabinet would abolish it in some localities, but preserve by means of a new law a muzzle for the press, for opinion, for the organs of enlightenment throughout France.[31]

Despite Blanc's energetic oratory, only the extreme Left voted against the bill. The Gambettists, primarily concerned with lifting the state of siege, voted with the huge majority, wanting as they did greater freedom of action during the coming elections. On December 31, 1875, the National Assembly came to an end and the candidates found themselves face to face with their electors. The dissolution which Louis Blanc had called for since 1871, had at last arrived.

III

Although Blanc and Gambetta had been separated by several issues, the menace of the royalist Buffet government prompted them, as leaders of the two most important radical groups, to join hands. The Republican Union, now under Gambetta's control, did not serve as the rallying organization. It was, rather, within the Masonic Order that some of the old bonds were forged again. Both men were members of the Grand Orient, Blanc having been initiated into the lodge called Les Libres Pen.eurs de Pecq. During the 1870's and even later, the order served as a converging point for almost all shades of republican opinion.[32]

At once Blanc put forward his electoral ideas, urging all republicans to vote for the candidates of their choice on the first ballot and then to rally around the most popular republicans for the run-off.[33] He also suggested that left-wing candidates go before the electorate with a platform calling for constitutional revision. Gambetta's press "greeted with great pleasure and gratitude the excellent counsel of Louis Blanc." However, in his public declarations the young radical did not mention revision, and in his electoral speech at Lyons he even intimated that if the President chose him to form a cabinet, he would offer every consideration to the executive's views and rights.[34] Small wonder then, that Blanc's extreme Left opposed him on the first ballot. The extreme Left, however, followed some curious policies of its own. For all his opposition to the upper chamber, Louis Blanc posed his candidacy in the Seine for a seat in that body. Naturally he was defeated. With the moderate republicans refusing to co-opt for him, he received only 87 out of 222 votes and his group won only seven seats.[35]

The radicals of Paris were enraged by his defeat and for elections to the lower house offered to pose his candidacy in the twenty districts of the capital. Blanc advised against this extravagance, and chose to stand in the fifth district, "quarter of study and youth" where he presented himself as a republican man of letters, and in the thirteenth, where he presented himself to the poverty-stricken as a friend of the working class. He also ran in the district of Saint-Denis. Too ill to speak before the voters, he published his program, which consisted of the most advanced radical ideas.[36] However, choosing to put aside once more his dedication to principle, he said nothing about revision which, consequently, did not become a major issue. Probably it was the pressure of political expediency, to whose demands his ears were not entirely closed, that caused him to demand merely the subordination of the executive to the legislature.

His candidacy was successful in all three districts, with 9809, 6988, and 8386 votes respectively, overwhelming majorities which placed his name at the head of the lists.[37] His very name had again become a symbol; his printed words were potent social magic for the poor and the young. His success did not depend upon his sick and aged person, but upon the people's faith in his mission. His immense popularity in the city, especially the east end, the quarters where in the depths of poverty his moderate socialism was still vivid, was revealed not only by his great political victory but also by the reaction to the untimely death of his wife, which occurred on April 26, 1876. No one had announced it and the sick, mourning husband certainly did not intend to make a political event of her funeral. Yet, as the conservative *Figaro* admitted, an immense crowd of workers and political leaders gathered, voluntarily and spontaneously, before his apartment in the Rue de Rivoli where they shared his sadness.[38] Their presence and their fraternal gesture were clear indications that Louis Blanc was still regarded as one of the chiefs of the social movement in Paris.

CHAPTER EIGHTEEN

A Little Thunder on the Left

I

℧ WHEN THE NEW ASSEMBLY convened, Louis Blanc could not deny that the doctrinal pliability of opportunism had proven successful at the polls. The voters had returned a republican majority and in many instances had fixed their choice on moderate radicals. Gambetta's lieutenant, Charles Lepère, was now chosen president of the Republican Union, and in his first discourse before it he asserted that it had "attained its goal and found sanction for its policy." [1] Blanc was not among those who applauded. He looked upon the electoral victory as even less than pyrrhic; success had come only after the sacrifice of principles. His sense of honor, firmer than his sense of party discipline, drove him at once to quit the Republican Union.

On June 30 he called together at his home the radical deputies sharing his views, and addressing them, condemned the policies of the Gambettists, the continuators of the *assermentés* of the Empire. "Never forget," he went on, "that when you speak to the assembly, the country listens; give precedence, not to certain parliamentary maneuvers, but to the necessity of keeping public opinion awakened, and of enlightening it; do not cede to the exigencies of tactics until after having loudly proclaimed and sought to implement principles; do not vote for the *least* until after having demanded and sought to obtain the *most;* safeguard for the initiative and independence of each of us a support against the exaggeration of what one calls *discipline*." He closed by emphasizing that the new organization must be frankly and firmly revisionist. [2]

Those assembled were in general accord with Blanc and constituted themselves a parliamentary group. This reunion, for all its seeming numerical insignificance, was of considerable historic importance, for it caused in France the emergence of a new extreme Left, as well as the revival of the social awareness of radicalism. The Belleville Manifesto, which had been popularized by Gambetta in 1869, and which had served as the springboard for the extreme Left of the early 1870's, was quite weak and vague in regard to the reform of society. In consequence of this new schism, however, the extreme Left's program now incorporated plans for improving the conditions of the working class, plans calling even for the encouragement of co-operatives and the nationalization of certain key industries.

By July 4, 1876, Blanc's little troop was as fully formed as it ever would be and on August 14 it issued a manifesto calling for a new constitution and denouncing clericalism. The signatories were: Blanc, Barodet, Jules Bouquet, F. Jean Cantagrel, Georges Clemenceau, Emile Crozet-Fourneyron, Augustin Daumas, Gaston Douville-Maillefeu, Armand Duportal, Pierre Durand, Charles Floquet, Jean Girault, Edouard Lockroy, Madier de Montjau, Jacques Marcou, Martin Nadaud, Alfred Naquet, Francisque Ordinaire, V. F. Raspail (father), Benjamin Raspail, Jean Turigny, and Emile Vernhes.[3] Most of these represented the Paris and Rhône regions. In order to put forward their ideas, they founded their own journal, which they called *Homme libre*. Blanc, appointed its editor-in-chief, explained that the title was chosen to indicate the ultimate goal of the group, the political liberation of man as a member of the Republic, the social liberation of man as a member of society. The Republic would grant him the Rights of Man, society would offer him the power to enjoy these rights. Political liberty and social solidarity, then, were the complementary watchwords of the new paper.[4] To his electors Blanc later explained: "If . . . someone asked me: are you a radical? Are you a socialist? I should reply: I am one and the other." [5] This position had the effect of embittering his relations with his radical rival.

The tenuous bond which held Blanc and Gambetta in the same party was the desire to consolidate the Republic. Thus they could form alliances for elections and during the Seize Mai crisis. However, by the mid-1870's the social question emerged from its obscurity. The problem of the reform of society not only divided the two men but also provoked important changes in their political philosophies.

Gambetta, as he became a national figure, embraced an image of France in which her people, he believed, were not proletarians, but peasants and petty bourgeois, the "new social classes" as he called them, living largely in rural villages and small towns. That this was the real France of the radicals cannot be doubted, and that some other extreme Left leaders, such as Clemenceau, began as radical-socialists and ended in the camp of the orthodox, reveals to what extent the self-mindedness and the independent life of the peasant and petty bourgeois were attractive. The radicals came to represent everything that was little, or, as they would have put it, everything that was individual. Therefore, Gambetta came to favor a bicameral legislature, perceiving in the Senate a body well fitted to represent these individualistic, local, almost personal interests. With consummate accuracy, he referred to it as the "grand council of the communes of France." As he intended, it became the stronghold of orthodoxy, both liberalist and radicalist, and as the leader of those classes least amenable to social change, he never felt behind him sufficient pressure to take up the cause of reform for the growing proletariat.[6]

Louis Blanc, on the other hand, was subjected to the pressures of opinion that manifested themselves in the cities, especially in Paris. He therefore came to oppose Gambetta, chiefly because of the younger radical's acceptance of the Senate. Blanc was not blind to the conservative character of that body; he might almost have predicted that the men of the upper house would bring down the only two ministries in the history of the Third Republic which made social reform the essence of their existence: the Bourgeois cabinet of the 1890's and that of Blum in the 1930's. Since 1848, Blanc had looked upon the peasants of France with distrust, and while recognizing them as an honest, laborious, essential part of the national population, he expected little in the way of progressive views from them. Unlike Gambetta, who modeled to a certain extent his thinking upon theirs, Louis Blanc concluded that they must be stimulated, educated, pushed along gently in the direction of Jacobin-socialism. This stimulus, he convinced himself, would come from the cities, from the enlightened middle classes and the workers—hence his desire to reconcile these two classes, the most dynamic of the population. At the same time, he realized that the deep chasm between city and countryside must be closed. The most suitable agency for accomplishing this union would be a republic representative of both areas.[7]

In spite of this difference in attitude, Blanc and Gambetta still joined forces in the mid-1870's to express one other common passion, their anticlericalism. In unison they raised on many occasions their battle cry: "Clericalism, there is the enemy!" Singling out the widely decried *Syllabus of Errors,* Blanc referred to it as the "most frightful war cry that anyone has raised against the regime of justice given birth by the French Revolution; it denies progress, flouts reason, and challenges the liberty of conscience." [8] Blanc himself never became an atheist, but he was far more rabidly anticlerical now than before 1848 when he had hoped for an alliance with the legitimists and the church against the Voltairian July Monarchy. He now held the extreme Right in abhorrence, frowned on Gambetta's dealings with them—his own policy in the 1840's—and attacked the clerics who, it must be remembered, had completely repudiated the republican sympathies they had manifested in the 1840's.

The religious problem inevitably involved that of education, and both became tense political issues in December, 1874, when Bishop Dupanloup introduced a bill to grant complete freedom of teaching to Catholic schools. Appealing for liberal support, the determined churchman demanded freedom "not as a Catholic but as a citizen." At once the radicals were in a furor, and condemned the bishop's distinction. Blanc angrily argued in the press that a clergyman was not in a position to appreciate the real meaning of liberty, for the claim of infallibility precluded the toleration of dissent. As though to expose a cunning plot, he asked rhetorically, who would profit from such liberty? The church, of course, for it had the money, the patronage, and the personnel to set up at once a large number of schools. The state, on the other hand, was not as yet prepared to establish a public educational system. The requested freedom of teaching therefore would benefit the clericalist enemies of the Republic.[9] That the religious teaching congregations were the Republic's enemies was, of course, never doubted by Blanc. Permitted to teach, they would inculcate antiscientific, antirepublican and antisecular ideals in the youth of France with the result that the next generation would not be mentally prepared for life in the Republic. Indeed, the Republic, if it abdicated in the field of education, would eventually cease to exist.

Blanc made clear that he was not opposed to all private schools. On the contrary, he considered them a desirable supplement to the state schools which would necessarily be somewhat standardized. Private schools would offer variety of subject matter to a people whose excessive uniformity already tended to stifle individualism. Curricula would be broadened enough to allow for a wide variety of aptitudes and tastes.[10] Blanc was undoubtedly thinking of the independent schools set up in the larger cities by men of republican leanings. These centers of learning, however, were generally small, lacking adequate funds, and unable to compete with the church schools. Here was the rub. The really independent schools were not financed by the state, whereas the church schools received economic aid from a subsidized church. The competition between them was hardly fair to the independent schools, and could not be so until state and church were separated. Only when the church ceased to receive the taxpayers' money, Blanc asserted, would he and the radicals favor complete freedom of education. But to the consternation of the left, Dupanloup won the essentials of his bill in July, 1875, in a chamber still predominantly monarchist. The church schools won greater freedom and continued to receive state financial support.

Clericalism and its opposite became two dominant extremes during the 1870's and after, and while the church had brought upon itself much of the animosity of the radicals, certain manifestations of this animosity were far from laudable. Certainly such organizations as the Democratic Union of Anticlerical Propaganda, patronized by Blanc, Hugo and Victor Schoelcher, were innocent enough, and even praiseworthy in their defense of the Republic against the excesses of clericalism. However, in the heat of battle, high-minded men like Louis Blanc sometimes stooped to the particularly vile kind of demagogy which characterized their weekly magazine, the *Semaine anticléricale*. To his credit, Blanc wrote no more than a brief introduction to the first number, yet he and Hugo were its chief patrons and must bear the burden of its scurrility.

What Blanc failed to realize was that the anticlericalist campaign with all its noise, particularly that of the orthodox radicals, was used largely to divert left-wing public attention from his constant demand for political revision and social reform.

II

Louis Blanc's position as a champion of social reform was much affected by his opposition to the revolutionary radicalism of the communards. His hostility to the Commune had resulted in large measure from his distrust of the men who captured control of it and who were, in his eyes, "agents" of the International, "exclusively preoccupied with cosmopolitan interests and concerned very little with Parisian or French interests." He also convinced himself that behind the disorders were Bonapartist and Prussian influences.[11] When the Central Committee voted an order condemning him to death, he could no longer harbor any doubts that the Commune had fallen into antirepublican hands.

After the tragic suppression of the insurrection, Blanc's position in Paris was most delicate, especially in the workers' quarters of the east end where the Versailles army had crushed the last of the insurrection with a barbaric ruthlessness that made the massacre of the Rue Transnonain seem like child's play. Having remained at Versailles, Blanc was, in the popular mind, associated with Thiers "the butcher." On June 29, he even attended a huge reception given by the Chief of the Executive at Versailles.[12] Such acts, however valid they were as a part of Blanc's policy to safeguard the Republic, had the effect of giving substance to rumors hostile to him. It was rather widely bruited that he both execrated the revolution and voted thanks to the army which so cruelly crushed it. This accusation he denied, asserting that neither he nor the extreme Left would vote for or even associate themselves with a victory of Frenchmen over Frenchmen in a civil war.[13]

He found himself now, much to his discomfort, in a position remarkably like the one he occupied after the June Days of 1848. To the conservatives he was little better than a communard; to the revolutionaries he was something worse than a Versailles reactionary. The latter belief grew into a legend that his leftwing enemies went to great lengths to cultivate. The communard Prosper Lissagaray in his *Histoire de la Commune de 1871,* published in Brussels in 1876, was the first well known author to picture Blanc as a cowardly turncoat. Francis Jourde, in his *Souvenirs,* followed this trend. Louis Fiaux, in his biography of Blanc, was somewhat less vindictive but not less clear in his portrayal of him as an acolyte of the hated Thiers. The anarchist Elie Reclus in his *Commune au jour le jour,* the Marxian Louis Dubreuilh in Volume XI of Jaurès' *Histoire socialiste,* and more recently Frank Jellinek in his *Paris Commune,* have condemned him. It is interesting to note that Karl Marx, who also denounced the insurrection until he found it inexpedient to do so, has been spared such abuse. He, of course, had the sagacity to publish a brochure hailing the Commune as a great proletarian event—which it was not.

Louis Blanc deplored the outbreak as a revolutionary aberration at a moment when moderation and republican unity were needed. Yet, for all his rage against the destroyers of Paris, whose blackened and smoking ruins seemed to be a symbol of the fate of the Republic, he was not prepared to run with the reaction. There lay deep in his mind a knowledge explaining why so many Parisians, the rank and file, had taken up weapons; and however grave their error, they were now to be pitied and assisted, not trod upon. Above all, the distress of their families awakened Blanc's sympathy and it was for humanitarian, not political reasons, as Lissagaray insisted, that he formed part of the Committee of Succor for the families of the prisoners.[14] The desire to foster social reconciliation, to heal the wounds created as much by mental as by physical violence, induced him in September, 1871, to favor the mild Brisson bill proposing an amnesty for political prisoners. It was buried in committee. An even more limited bill put forward by Edmond de Pressensé was reported before the assembly, and on July 16, 1872, Blanc urged the deputies to debate it before adjournment. He was greeted by angry shouts for the cloture and his motion was defeated.[15] With an angry pen he wrote to the *Temps:* "I am for everything that tends to aid the triumph, in our troubled situation, of a policy of appeasement, for all that tends to raise above party, the great cause of humanity." During the Barodet elections of 1873 he again brought up the amnesty issue when he asserted that clemency would be an act of political strength not of weakness, since it would restore peace and order to the country.[16]

But the communards were as scornful as the Right. "The deputies of the extreme Left," snarled Lissagaray, "having had the impudence to demand an amnesty, were left with their thirty pieces of silver like Judas." [17] The extremists never paused to ask how Blanc could be considered a traitor to a movement with which he had absolutely nothing to do. If Lissagaray implied that he was a traitor to social democracy, his charge was totally lacking in substance. It was rather Blanc who had the right to claim that the Commune had set the socialist movement back by several decades, for it had the effect of deepening the animosity between urban and rural France, of wasting the forces of progress in Paris and thereby of strengthening the forces of conservatism which, having captured the government, modeled it practically unopposed in the image of their own ideals. Blanc might have said, but did not, that the revolutionaries had not learned from his own mistakes in 1848.

The revolutionaries failed also to discern that his support of an amnesty was a definite step toward a policy of appeasement, not of the conservatives, but of the very far left, a policy which recognized no enemies to the left. Undoubtedly his ultimate objective was to become the mediator between the champions of revolution and the defenders of republican order. He could then serve in the radical movement as a counterweight to Gambetta and the *assermentés* who, he concluded by 1873–74, were leaning too far toward the left Center. However, many labor leaders, by the time they again became active, had been prejudiced against Blanc through the unrelenting attacks upon him of leading communards.

III

During the year 1872 there were several indications that the labor movement was beginning to reawaken. A few workingmen's circles were founded, and quickly dissolved by the police; a few brochures were published by cautious men inside France and by communards in exile. By no means was Louis Blanc unaware of this very modest beginning; indeed, he acted to encourage and guide it by his speeches and his publications. It may even have induced him to challenge Gambetta's exclusive emphasis on political issues, for in 1872 he insisted that there was a social question, and published his brochure, *Le parti qu'on appelle radical,* in which he outlined a program of mild social reform, and overcoming his dislike of the International, spoke against Armand Dufaure's bill to outlaw it.

The awakening labor movement combined in its aspirations both pure trade unionism and socialist co-operation. The two tendencies were not entirely incompatible, and Louis Blanc, seeking to revive interest in his own social ideas, embraced both. He became an active contributor to an important radical daily, the *Rappel,* and it was in its columns that he spread his influence, which, in the early 1870's, was significant.[18]

Blanc's politically oriented socialism did not go unchallenged. There remained a strong current of Proudhonist distrust of government intervention, and the syndicalist *mystique* that labor must go it alone was deeply entrenched in the minds of labor leaders such as Charles Chabert and democratic journalists such as Joseph Barberet. Barberet referred to the socio-political reformers as the "Pharisees of socialism" and unequivocally charged them with seeking to use the labor movement for their own political ambitions.[19]

Since Blanc had never abandoned his belief that the state must foster co-operatives, he was particularly anxious to combat this theory of isolation, later known as *ouvriérisme.* However, he recognized that outright opposition to it was neither wise nor entirely justified. Not in the history of France could he point out a government really sympathetic to the aspirations of labor, and among the least favorable were those of the 1870's. Consequently, parliamentary dissolution before 1875 and constitutional revision thereafter were important parts of his plan to win the workers to republicanism. In this, his political objective, he soon found a sympathizer in Barberet who supported him in the *Rappel.* Later, in the *Homme libre,* Blanc praised Barberet's short-lived Cercle de l'Union Syndicale Ouvrière.[20] It was not that political frustration had driven him into the camp of apolitical syndicalism. On the contrary, he perceived shortly after his return from exile that trade unionism had grown considerably during his long absence. His earlier opposition to it was no longer feasible, particularly since there was a definite bond between it and the co-operative movement.

It will be recalled that organization along professional lines, moribund before 1848, had been resuscitated by the Luxembourg Commission. In the 1870's Blanc and other associationists came to look upon the *syndicat professionnel* as a desirable complement to co-operative organization, the trade union serving as a means of grouping more easily all the members of a profession into large producers' associations. The plans for large co-operatives of professional workers had first been put forward by Blanc in 1840, and put into effect on a limited scale by him in 1848. Naturally, then, during the 1870's, he became an ardent protagonist of corporative syndicalism, as distinct from multi-professional industrial unionism, as a means of bringing together workers with common interests and of instilling in them the fraternal sentiments necessary to co-operative success.

The first national labor congress, held in Paris during October, 1876, definitely encouraged and influenced his thinking. The resolutions, although sometimes vague, announced in general terms the union of syndicalism, co-operatism and socialism, and stated without ambiguity that the instruments of production must become the "impersonal, indivisible, and inalienable property of the mass of workers, . . ." [21] This objective was to be attained by the establishment of large, profession-wide associations, the type envisioned by Blanc, not the small, restricted ones dear to Buchez. A clearly collectivist ideal, therefore, was adopted in the first national congress, a fact overlooked by all of the Marxian historians and first emphasized by Maxwell Kelso. However, unlike the later congresses, the one of 1876 repudiated violence, whether in the form of revolution or strikes, as a means of obtaining collectivist control of the instruments of production.

Blanc sought to urge the labor leaders to continue in this collectivist direction. During October, November and December of 1876, he wrote extensively in the *Homme libre,* in a special column, "Le mouvement social." Above all, he stressed the need for solidarity, and urged his readers to organize their professional groups. He affirmed that he and his colleagues in parliament were struggling to pass a bill legalizing all associations. But there was no need to await its passage. The government at least tolerated national and local labor organizations, and to counterbalance the *syndicats* of employers, the workers must form their own.[22] Blanc did not intend that the workers wage industrial warfare against their employers by resorting to strikes. On the contrary, he stressed, as of old, the uselessness of strikes, and repudiated all acts of violence. He did not conceive of unions as agencies for forcing economic concessions from employers, but as organizations to facilitate the founding of producers' associations. He emphasized that solidarity must extend beyond each profession. Co-operatives, he urged, must not struggle among themselves or seek to enfranchize a limited number of workers, an élite which would soon become an "aristocracy of labor." They must bring about the full liberation of all workers, and co-operate among themselves by creating bonds of fraternal amity and economic exchange.[23]

Shortly after the Commune, Blanc had been somewhat mockingly asked if he were really a socialist. He had answered in the affirmative, and his writings now proved that he was still the man of '48. In fact, during the 1870's, he exerted much energy and time to rehabilitate himself through a defense of his role during the Second Republic. He had, shortly before he returned to France, published his *Histoire de la Révolution de 1848*, two stout little volumes in which he appeared as a hero of democracy and of socialism, and as a friend of the workingman. Blanc consciously strove to establish an intimate relationship between the social movement of 1848 and that of the 1870's. Thus, when he was called upon to speak before two newly created associations, those of the tailors and of the lithographers, he reiterated the basic concepts of his *Organisation du travail,* which he hoped would become the bible of the revived co-operative movement; he pointed to his Luxembourg Commission as the precursor of the annual labor congress, and, with greater accuracy, looked upon the tailors' and lithographers' associations as the continuators of those he had patronized over a quarter of a century ago. True to the spirit of '48, he even defended the old term, *association,* against the new one, *coopération,* which had largely replaced the first after being imported from England. Lest the events of February 24, 1848, fade into obscurity, he also helped to organize banquets for celebrating the anniversaries of the February Revolution, and never failed to remind his constituents and his various audiences of the greatness of that event.[24]

Certainly there was one phenomenon common to the social movements of 1848 and the 1870's: the failure of the co-operatives patronized by Blanc. And as in 1848, they failed chiefly from their lack of funds. The eternal dilemma of the co-operators lay in the fact that adequate credit could be derived chiefly from one source, the state, but the Jacobin-socialists were not more than a handful in the midst of the socially conservative politicians. It was not surprising that the workers remained highly distrustful of the government and expected more animosity than beneficence from monarchists and republican liberals. They recognized that the entirely fraternal society to which they aspired would not result from political action; consequently, Blanc's electoral campaign in the early part of 1876, emphasizing as it did the need for state aid, did not register among the new labor leaders, hardened as they were by governmental repression. It was inevitable that they would become steeped in the apolitical *mystique* of Proudhon and Chabert. In the mid-1870's there was even a keen distrust of all intellectuals, and great care was taken by the organizers of the first congress to safeguard its purely labor character by excluding non-workers and politicians.[25] The nascent *ouvrié-risme* of the French section of the International survived much longer than the International itself.

To counteract this tendency, Blanc sought to interest the workers in politics, to revive the spirit which had led those of the old Luxembourg Commission to draw up an electoral list in 1848. He soon found himself at odds with a deeply enrooted tradition. Even the delegates of that commission had revealed a marked distrust of bourgeois politicians and had composed at first a list consisting almost exclusively of worker candidates. It had been largely Blanc's intervention which had induced them to add some intellectuals. The defeat of that list in Paris had undoubtedly helped to alienate labor from politics, an alienation reinforced by Proudhon as well as by the overwhelming defeat of the few worker candidates in the 1863 elections. Now, in the 1870's, Blanc sought to dispel this hostility and urged the workers to put forward and elect their own candidates.[26]

Well aware that the liberals were hostile to governmental aid for the workers, and more than hostile to any scheme smacking of socialism, he still hoped to arouse the workman's interest in politics by demanding practical projects of reform. Thus, as early as November, 1872, Blanc came forward to defend a bill for abolishing child labor. However, it was not until June, 1874, that a law in this field was finally passed. Once again, Blanc defended it, but also insisted that it was quite inadequate, and for this reason he entered the debate only during the first reading, not the third.[27] That the law was a considerable improvement over the one of 1842 was significant, but in no way an indication that the parliament was becoming more interested in social problems. A parliamentary committee was established to investigate labor conditions in general: as in 1848–49, the politicians preferred to investigate rather than to act. Disgusted, Blanc did not bring up the issue of social reform again until March, 1881, when he denounced the excessively long hours of labor in factories. His humanitarian fervor did not stir the parliament, and his proposal was not acted on.[28] In fact, only a year earlier the chamber had abolished an old law forbidding work on Sundays.

Although Blanc continued to agitate for social reform and to expose in the press, in public lectures, and in political campaigns the wretched conditions of the urban laborers, he was not blind to his failure to make a forceful impression on public opinion. The growing popularity of the Gambettists revealed that not only the petty bourgeois and the republican peasants, but also many workers voted orthodox radical rather than Jacobin-socialist. The shibboleths of the moderates—republican defense, anticlericalism, limited social improvement—seemed to be atrophying the people's desire for those lofty principles that would make for greater social equality. Moderation, which for Blanc was never more than a means, was, he feared, becoming an end. He did not reject it and become a revolutionary. Rather, he continued to stress that immediate practical reform was desirable, and that the "promised land" of socialism could not be reached "in one leap." However, he warned that timid reform, made at random, could be more dangerous than beneficial. "Let us beware," he said, "of partial reforms which are not connected to a combination of well-defined doctrines. Often a palliative is really a deception. To displace the evil is not to cure it." [29] This was the message he brought to many parts of France in 1879.

The year 1879 was a triumphant one for all republicans. Jules Grévy replaced MacMahon in the executive, which was now further weakened; a slight republican majority appeared in the Senate, Gambetta became president of the chamber, and the *Marseillaise* was decreed the national anthem. With the intention of spurring this swing to the left, Louis Blanc made an extensive speaking tour of Eastern and Southern France. His strategy consisted of rallying all leftwing elements to his banner. Thus, at Troyes, he sought to connect the magic of his own reformism with that of Blanqui's revolutionary *mystique,* when he said: "The Republic declares that it is not afraid of its enemies; must one say that it is menaced by its friends, by men such as Rochefort and Blanqui who have combatted and suffered for it?" [30] He brought up Rochefort because he was a friend, and Blanqui because the old rebel had been chosen as a deputy in the April by-elections at Bordeaux. When the deputies had decided to invalidate Blanqui's election, only the extreme Left, led by the old men of '48, Blanc, François Cantagrel, Nadaud, and the young men of '70, Clemenceau, Barodet, Jean Girault, Georges Périn and Edouard Lockroy, had opposed the majority.

Moving on to the Midi, Blanc arrived at Marseilles on September 21, where he was greeted by a crowd almost delirious in its acclaim. It unhitched the horses from his coach and pulled him along the boulevards, much to the indignation of his conservative opponents. Soon he went on to Cette, then to Montpellier, Nîmes, and Toulon, where, widely applauded, he repeated his apostolic message. Important was his stay at Port-Vendres, for at this moment arrived the ship *Calvados* bearing one of the first cargoes of amnestied communards. As they stood gathered around a tricolor, Blanc officially welcomed them back. If there were any among them who had forgotten his refusal to join them in 1871, they were reminded of it by his enemies. Yet, for all the cynical remarks his reception of them occasioned, Blanc was not without claim to their gratitude. In 1875 he had favored the Naquet amnesty bill and the next year that of the elder Raspail.[31] When these had been defeated, the latter by an overwhelming majority, he gave public lectures whose proceeds were devoted to relieving the distress of communard families. Finally on February 21, 1879, months before he left on his tour, Blanc had again mounted the parliamentary tribune, this time to plead for a full amnesty, an important revision of the earlier bills, which all, except Naquet's, had excluded those guilty of so-called "common law" crimes. On this occasion Blanc also went beyond his usual appeal to his fellow deputies by a vivid description of the sufferings of the prisoners' families, and became practically an apologist of the Commune, at least of its causes, which he limited to disappointed patriotism and fervent republicanism. Cognizant that feelings had been awakened against the military since 1877, he took special pains to point out that the prisoners were the victims of unjust military tribunals, whose judges had, only moments before the hearings, laid down the arms they had used to combat the prisoners who were to be judged. A full amnesty, he argued, was necessary to redress injustice, and to foster peace, order and social unity.[32]

Clemenceau, Nadaud and Lockroy had strongly supported Blanc, but the majority would not go beyond a partial amnesty liberating nearly 3500 communards, not all of whom regained their civil and political rights. This measure left imprisoned 1198 men, of whom 554 were still in New Caledonia. These were accused of common law crimes that the ministry and the military claimed to distinguish from political crimes. Feeling that the ministry's division was not valid, Blanc decided to take the issue of full amnesty before the country, and his tour of 1879 combined that cause with his program for social reform. When he quit Port-Vendres he went to Perpignon where he devoted his entire discourse to the plenary amnesty.

After visiting Narbonne and Cavaillon, Blanc made his way back to Paris. Before entering the city, however, he held a public meeting on October 26 at Belleville, Gambetta's bailiwick. Here, summing up his earlier speeches, he laid down the essentials of his group's social program: "Society owes to each of its members both education, without which the human spirit canot expand, and the instruments of labor, without which human activity cannot forge ahead; therefore, encouragement by state laws to workers' associations, [state] purchase of the railroads, the transformation of the Bank of France into a national bank, implementation of the rights of assembly and association; centralization and development of insurance." To the old program of 1848 he now added the demand for a single tax, that is, a progressive income tax to replace all others, separation of church and state, military service limited to three years, and complete abolition of the death penalty. These proposals, complementing his political program, called for the reorganization not only of work but of much of French society.[33]

Very few were the politicians advocating extensive social reform during the first two decades of the Republic. Louis Blanc declared in 1876 that he was both a radical and a socialist, and soon the parliamentary extreme Left began referring to itself as radical-socialist.[34] However, Clemenceau, Lockroy, Naquet, Floquet, and Peyrat, leaders of the extreme Left, were never complete socialists in the sense that they wished to abolish all private property. Even Blanc seemed more radical than socialist. Seeking unity with the extreme Left in the early 1870's, he did not inject a full measure of collectivism into his public pronouncements. To many he did not appear to be appreciably in advance of his more individualistic colleagues. He leaves the impression that he, like them, favored a mixed economy with co-operative as well as private property. It is for this reason that the political historians Edouard Renard[35] and Albert Milhaud[36] consider him the founder of radical-socialism.

Now there is some reason for considering Blanc a contributing force to the growing social consciousness of the extreme Left in the chamber. He identified himself with this group rather than with the out-and-out collectivists. In the 1876 general election he ran against a socialist in the fifth *arrondissement*.[37] Five years later, when he moved farther to the left, he publicly supported a leftwing radical who defeated a collectivist candidate in Paris.[38] Albert Milhaud defends his thesis by pointing out that Blanc repudiated the Commune, refused to quit the Versailles assembly, quoted Thiers in asserting that property is a fundamental right inherent in human nature, and stressed moderation in politics. In this light Blanc stands out as a vital contributor to the rise of radical-socialism in the 1880's, the group which later formed the leftwing of the Radical and Radical-Socialist party in 1901.

But in answer to Milhaud's point of view, one might say, first of all, that Blanc embodied the social consciousness of radicalism in the 1870's and helped to make political democrats aware of social issues by his constant insistence that the radical republic, when founded, must serve as the instrument for improving society. That is, he revived the social, as distinct from the socialist, Jacobinism of the 1840's. He then based upon it his opposition to the socially moderate ideals of Jules Simon and Gambetta, who had become the spokesmen of the extreme left in the 1860's. His was therefore an important role in the social orientation of the democratic tradition. However, it cannot be concluded from this role that Blanc was *the* founder of radical-socialism. No one person founded the movement, and he must share the distinction with others.[39]

Curiously, there often creeps into the writings of leftwing democrats a certain distrust of Blanc. He was one of them and yet he was never really at one with them. For there is another aspect of Blanc which Renard and Milhaud overlooked: he remained a socialist at heart, and in the later 1870's he tended more to follow his heart. Now often leftwing radicals claimed that they were socialists.[40] And they were in their demand for the nationalization of certain big industries and utilities. However, they clearly distinguished between their ideal of a mixed economy and a collectivised one. To a man, they defended petty property, seeing in it the basis of individual freedom.[41] On the other hand, Louis Blanc, although he continued to collaborate with radicals, abandoned their limited position and moved steadily to the socialistic left after 1876.

He was undoubtedly encouraged by the first workers' congress in 1876, a congress which called for socialistic co-operatives. In the *Homme libre* he encouraged their creation, and, as in the 1840's, he called for large co-operatives utilizing heavy machinery and modern techniques. Unlike the leftwing radicals, he did not defend petty enterprise or the backward methods of individualistic craftsmen and peasants. He became an ardent proponent of universal expositions and urged the workers to send delegates to the exposition at Philadelphia in 1876 to observe how mechanization had benefited labor there. To help defray their costs, he and Hugo contributed the revenue from a public lecture they gave together in April, 1876.[42] Blanc spoke again two years later at the Workers' Exposition in Paris where once more he lauded machines. At the same time he warned that unless these "slaves with steel muscles" were possessed collectively by the workers, they would continue to augment the power of capital and decrease that of labor.[43]

In the hope of reviving support of his Jacobin-socialism, Blanc published in five volumes between 1879 and 1882 his collected doctrinal works, under the title, *Questions d'aujourd'hui et de demain*. Included was the ninth edition of *Organisation du travail*, the most far-reaching of all his writings. In it he called for the complete abolition not only of industrial private property but also of peasant holdings. The entire economy of France was to be based on a vast system of interconnected co-operatives. Blanc placed on his agenda both for the present and the future the triumph of Jacobin-socialism.

It is more clearly as a socialist than as a radical that the influence of Blanc can be documented. He was one of the major nineteenth-century theorists who prepared the way for the democratic socialism of the turn of the century and after. The first editor of the *Revue socialiste,* Benoît Malon, argued that Pecqueur, Blanc and Vidal "created practical collectivism." He was of the opinion that Blanc's ideas were still valuable in the 1890's, and recommended them to socialist representatives in parliament.[44] Jean Jaurès, who like Blanc passed through a stage of orthodox radicalism, also came to champion a philosophy of democratic socialism. He was clearly in the Jacobin-socialist tradition when he announced in the 1890's to the voters at Carmaux, "It is necessary to annex to the economic program of the socialists the political program of the radicals." [45] He also defended the socialism of Blanc against the attacks of Jules Guesde.[46] However, Jaurès felt that Blanc was too authoritarian, too Jacobin. He therefore sought to combine his ideas with the anarchism of Proudhon.[47]

To a great extent it was Louis Blanc who stressed the non-revolutionary bias of French democratic socialism. He had always opposed violent upheaval; in the 1870's, however, he became a champion of authentic gradualism. Prior to 1848 he had not been a real gradualist, believing as he did that great changes would come about rapidly after a period of indoctrination. Now he called for a step-by-step advance within the framework of republican legality. To the end of his life he preached as his motto, "The Republic: the means; social regeneration: the objective." [48] Only in a republic, he was convinced, would all citizens enjoy liberty defined as the right to think, speak, and assemble freely, and as the power to improve physical as well as mental capacities.

The Third Republic had not granted either form of liberty. The liberals and some of the radicals, although they had clamored for the Rights of Man during the Second Empire, did not hasten to sanctify them after assuming power. Most objectionable to these ultra-individualists was the right of association as demanded chiefly by the extreme Left. Blanc had proposed it as early as 1872. Four years later his colleague Lockroy offered a bill to legalize professional associations; it was defeated. When in March, 1878, the ministry made use of the Dufaure law to suppress the international labor conference organized by Jules Guesde, Blanc returned to the attack by putting forward in June a bill providing for freedom of assembly and of association. [49] Such a law, he believed, was a necessary complement to the practice of universal suffrage, which alone could not bring about proletarian emancipation. Political power tends to follow wealth, he argued, with the result that the rich acquire control over much of the press, many of the voters, and most of the politicians. What, then, can unorganized labor do to oppose those employers, the mine operators in particular, who act to suppress democratic ideas and to prevent their employees from forming even innocuous consumers' associations? A large majority of deputies, not at all embarrassed by such questions, rejected his proposal.

Moderation, then, as preached by Blanc, seemed not a successful way of obtaining results from the government, and growing distrust of it brought about a swing of socialist opinion away from the temperate resolutions of the Paris labor congress of 1876. That reformist co-operation was losing its predominance was apparent as early as the Lyons congress of 1878. Both the social indifference of the politicians and the failure of the associations sponsored by Blanc contributed to the disenchantment of many workers with democracy. The methods of extremism received new encouragement. Blanc's position as a socialist leader was being undermined even while he was making his triumphal tour in 1879. [50]

In Marseilles, where Blanc had been so joyously acclaimed, the third national labor congress opened shortly after his visit there. The majority of the labor delegates proclaimed a series of resolutions which rejected pure trade unionism as well as reformist co-operation. They demanded a more extensive collectivism, that is, public ownership of all industrial and agricultural implements, property and produce. The influence of Marx's ideas, spreading in France through the action of Jules Guesde, Paul Lafargue and others, was clearly visible, all the more so in the renewed demand for revolutionary action as part of the class struggle, itself now praised as the means to achieve the end. [51]

As a portent of things to come, a Paris delegate, Eugène Fournière, went to the speaker's stand on October 26, the day of Blanc's Belleville speech, and denounced the "man whom France still considers the leader of socialism," for his attitude during the Commune. He read the letter which Blanc had sent to the *Figaro* in June, 1871, and in which Blanc had disassociated himself from the outrages of the more fanatical communards. Fournière's outburst created a tumult that held up the session for fifteen minutes. Blanc had many defenders. In fact, he had helped to defray the expenses of the Paris labor delegation, and it now rose to his defense.[52] To settle the affair, a vote was held on whether or not Fournière might continue his speech. He won by 76 to 34, a vote which the young Léon Blum considered tantamount to a vote of confidence lost by Blanc. Undoubtedly Blum, as yet a young and ardent reformer, oversimplified the issue. Had the old socialist been there, he would probably have voted with the majority, for the issue was freedom of speech. Yet it cannot be denied that his strong emphasis on moderation made him many enemies, or that on his left a new revolutionary movement was rapidly taking shape which rejected his Jacobin-socialist philosophy as outdated. His repudiation of violence alienated the impatient trade unionists, and his defense of parliamentary democracy brought the scorn of both the Blanquists and the Marxists.[53]

The opposition to Blanc was by no means united. The next year the syndicalists broke from the socialists who, in turn, split among themselves. This schismatic propensity did not diminish the thunder on the left but it prevented the revolutionary rains from coming. A steady drizzle of reform might have descended had Blanc succeeded in convincing most of the working class that something could be done with the Republic. This he failed to do. Undoubtedly the blame was partly his, for he made in the 1870's the same error he had made in 1848. His excessive belief in ideas and in the force of individual action, a kind of artisan technique in politics—such as his tour in 1879—caused him to neglect disciplined political organization. It was in part his fault that the Jacobin-socialist philosophy he propagated never became the nucleus for a genuine Jacobin-socialist party with its own leadership, its own organization, and its own program. However, the Commune left an unpreventable scar which disfigured both the labor and socialist movements in France. There appeared by 1880 a cult in which the Commune was endowed with a class basis and idealized as the architype of proletarian revolution.[54] Blanc's opposition to it alienated him from the self-appointed high priests of this cult, the revolutionaries. This group would probably have excluded him even without the excuse of the Paris insurrection. But unfortunately his stand in 1871 also alienated him from the communards who became reformists: Fournière, who continued to distrust him in later years; [55] Jules Joffrin, Paul Brousse and Jean Allemane, who founded socialist *possibilisme,* a hybrid between Gambetta's opportunism and Blanc's gradualism. And theirs was only one of the secessions from the socialist party founded in 1879. The insurrectionary *mystique* proved to be the heaviest burden borne by the French labor movement. Its fanaticism had the effect of creating both myths and schisms which confused and wasted the energy of the working class attempting to take the fortress of social conservatism. It was a mysticism beyond the understanding of the average worker and, in the end, repudiated by many who had, as Denis Brogan put it, more to lose than their chains. It also created an extravagant verbiage which, surviving the spirit, had the effect of frightening the peasants and the middle classes who connected reform, almost any kind of social change, with cataclysmic upheaval. It made impossible Blanc's lifelong mission, the separation of socialism from the bloody image of the Terror.

CHAPTER NINETEEN

In Opposition Until the End

I

❧ BY THE CLOSE OF 1879 Blanc was not in a position to resurrect his somewhat dwindling popularity. The tremendous ovations given him on his speaking tour, which shocked and angered both orthodox liberals and revolutionary socialists, left him overwhelmed with pleasure, for while he loved the abstract concept of humanity, he was always particularly pleased by its concrete applause. However, the inconvenience and exertion of the long trip and the many speeches left him gravely fatigued. He was often now too ill to attend the sessions of the chamber, and when he did put in an appearance his physical degeneration was striking. During most of his life he had kept his almost boyish mien, so that when he finally aged he looked strange. His little body had already become bent, his flesh pale and rather flabby and dark shadows gathered under the eyes that Carlyle had once admired for their brightness. But his mouth retained its firm elegance, his hair was still abundant and mostly black, and his mind was still very much alive.[1]

It was his sense of mission, perhaps his Corsican will, that brought Blanc to his seat beside Clemenceau in the chamber on January 22, 1880, when he proposed another bill for full amnesty. His speech, which was lucid and clear, involved a complete repudiation of his letter to the *Figaro* in 1871. He now looked upon all the communards as innocent of crimes against common law, and he sarcastically distinguished between the indulgence shown the monarchist conspirators of the May 16 affair and the severity extended to the vanquished of the Commune.[2] The ministry, however, refused to concede, and a complete amnesty was not granted until July when Gambetta, now the prima donna of the assembly, belatedly rallied to it as a cause safe enough to be championed. Blanc also made another and now last attempt to push through a bill granting full liberty of association and assembly. Although he failed to convince the majority, many of the workers of Paris were grateful to him, for during the spring several of their public assemblies had been broken up by the police. They took the occasion on July 14, decreed a national holiday the year before, to gather at Blanc's apartment, in a crowd of some 2000 men who represented the chief crafts of Paris. This was good medicine for the old man who, although gravely ill, came down to welcome them and to extend to them the hand that had written the *Organisation du travail.*[3]

During the elections of 1881 Blanc was too ill to campaign in person, and once more his program was read to the public by his friends. With the extreme Left he called for the *mandat impératif,* a system by which the deputy would become no more than the agent of his constituents, bound to obey strictly the program he presented them before his election. He also called for penal reform, the abolition of capital punishment, the elections of judges and of administrators, a citizens' army in place of a professional one, and an educational system which, offering technological and scientific training, would emphasize republicanism, patriotism and secularism. Although it was clear that he probably would not sit again in the parliament, his electors in the fifth district gave him 6837 out of 8540 ballots cast. This was a vote of recognition for his long service, a vote singling him out, not only as a great democrat, but also as one of the immortals of the Left. With considerable pain Blanc quit his bed to speak at a banquet on September 21. This date in his calendar was also immortal, being the birthdate of the movement he had championed during most of his life.[4]

II

His last days were lonely ones. His wife had died in 1876 and although ill himself, he had walked behind her body to the cemetery of Père Lachaise. At the grave Victor Hugo intoned majestically, "There you are alone, oh Louis Blanc! Oh dear refugee, it is now that your exile begins!" And indeed, the statement was true. Old friends died, François-Victor Hugo, son of the poet, Ledru-Rollin, George Sand, Quinet; and new ones were not easily made at Blanc's age. The young generation of radical-socialists, while they accepted his leadership and admired him, tended to find him overbearing, cold and proud. However vigorous his position he was for them the man of '48, set in his ways, rather dull, academic, too much like a "bourgeois idling along on his dividends."[5]

As always, his real companion was his brother. Charles too, had become an "immortal," in a more literal sense, for he had been elected to the Académie Française and taught esthetics at the Collège de France. For a while he had been director of fine arts in the government but was dismissed by the royalists. The brothers in their last years were constantly together and were often to be seen strolling arm in arm along the boulevards.[6] Then, in January, 1882, Charles died, a blow from which Louis never recovered. On February 12 he wrote to a friend, "Here am I now given entirely over to my suffering and my black thoughts. If one could have the desire to persevere in a life full of agitation and bitterness, I should have lost it in losing the two beings I loved the most. I try in vain to react against the state of dejection in which I am, I tell myself in vain that if one does not have the force to wish to live, it is necessary at least to have enough to die standing up, [but] this lasts briefly and I fall again as though crushed beneath my unhappiness."[7] In September he wrote to Mme Ernst, "I have only the strength to send you a shake of the hand, so much do I suffer."[8]

He finally gave way to the entreaties of his friends and went to Cannes at the end of October, 1882, before the rigorous winter of Paris set in. After his arrival there he went one morning to visit a friend just outside the city. On the way he was caught in a downpour, during which the harness of his horses was broken, and unable to continue on foot, he remained exposed for over an hour to the bitter winds and rain. He was taken with a chill that he could not throw off after his return. Finally, on December 6, the man and his pen ceased to function. They had been painfully active until the end and there lay on his table the manuscript of an unfinished work against capital punishment, and beside that, the proofs of his *Histoire de la Constitution du 25 février 1875*, his last thrust at the orthodox radicals.[9]

The next day the chamber and the Senate, with several exceptions, proclaimed that Blanc should have an official funeral, and the general council of the Seine as well as the municipal council of Paris voted to attend it. Moreover, both councils agreed to rename the street in which he had once lived, the Rue Louis Blanc. Only one voice was raised in objection, that of the socialist Jules Joffrin who asserted that Blanc was in part responsible for the massacres of 1871.

Blanc's body arrived at Paris on December 10, covered with floral crowns laid upon it by the municipal councils of Toulon and Marseilles. The funeral, purely civil, took place two days later. An immense crowd, estimated at some 150,000 persons, turned out. Every labor corporation sent delegates bearing flowers to honor the veteran of social democracy. The streets to Père Lachaise were lined with men and women in their work clothes, and at the cemetery the president of the Association Ouvrière de l'Imprimerie Nouvelle, spoke in their name: "Louis Blanc, receive our supreme homage. You have died too early. The Revolution is not over." More prophetic, Victor Hugo, too ill to attend, wrote for the occasion: "The death of a man like Louis Blanc is a disappearance (*disparition*). It is a light which goes out. One is seized by a sadness that is like a prostration. But the prostration lasts briefly; believing men are strong; to live is to hope. A light does not go out. Men like Louis Blanc are necessary; they reappear when needed; their work cannot be discontinued; it is part of the very life of humanity."[10]

Notes

CHAPTER I

1. Blanc, *Histoire de la Révolution fran-çaise* (Paris, 1847–62), I, "Préface."
2. Georges Weill, *Histoire de l'éduca-tion secondaire en France, 1802–1920* (Paris, 1921), p. 38; B. Lunet, *Histoire du Collège de Rodez* (Rodez, 1881), pp. 237–38.
3. See list of awards in the archives of the Collège de Rodez, now called Lycée Ferdinand Foch.
4. No one seems to know the exact re-lation between Mme Blanc, née Pozzo di Borgo, and the count whose family has denied any connection. Blanc, however, once asserted that his mother belonged to the same family. See Blanc to Richard Griffin, Oct. 19, 1859, in *Miscellaneous Papers*, 28509, fols. 165–66, British Museum.
5. *Voltaire*, Sept. 25, 1882; Edouard Pailleron, *Discours de réception à l'Académie Française, le 17 janvier 1884* (n.p., n.d.), pp. 5–6, 8–9.
6. E. de Goncourt, *Journal des Goncourt* (Paris, 1887–96), V, 218.
7. Louis Fiaux, *Portraits politiques con-temporains*, Vol. III: *Charles Blanc* (Paris, 1883), p. 9.
8. Blanc, *Révélations historiques* (Brus-sels, 1859), I, 149–50.
9. Paul Tierney, *Alexis Hallette, un bienfaiteur de la ville d'Arras* (Arras, 1931), pp. 3–18; *Progrès du Pas-de-Calais*, July 8, 1846.
10. *Revue du progrès*, I (Jan. 15, 1839), 15, note 1; see below, Chap. IV, sec-tion x. Hereafter cited as *Rev. prog.*
11. Pailleron, pp. 9–10; see Blanc, *Révo-lution de février au Luxembourg* (Paris, 1849), p. 146.
12. Henri Sée, *La vie économique de la France sous la Monarchie censitaire* (Paris, 1927), p. 91.
13. Otto Warschauer, *Geschichte des Sozialismus und neueren Kommu-nismus*, Vol. III: *Louis Blanc* (Leipzig, 1896), pp. 4–5.
14. Edouard Renard, *Louis Blanc, sa vie, son oeuvre* (Paris, n.d.), pp. 43–44.
15. Gustave de Hauteclocque, "Seconde Restauration dans le Pas-de-Calais, 1815–30," *Mémoires de l'Académie d'Arras*, XLI (1910), 39 ff.
16. G. Weill, *Histoire du parti républi-cain en France, 1814–70* (2d ed.: Paris, 1928), pp. 1–7.
17. For Degeorge see Hauteclocque, pp. 116–17; Weill, *Hist. parti répub.*, p. 80.
18. L. Fiaux, *Port. polit. contemp.*, Vol. II: *Louis Blanc* (Paris, 1882), p. 17; Eugène Courmeaux, *Louis Blanc* (Châlons-sur-Marne, 1884), p. 4.
19. For the influence of Degeorge on Blanc see Blanc to Guillemot, May 2, 1873, *Fonds Couderc*, in Bibliothèque Municipale de Versailles.
20. *Propagateur du Pas-de-Calais*, July 22, 1833.
21. Blanc, *Histoire de la Révolution de février 1848* (Paris, 1870), II, 74.
22. Sébastien Charléty, *Monarchie de juil-let* (Paris, 1921), pp. 42–53. Roger Picard, *Le romantisme sociale* (New York, [1944]), pp. 59–70, 407–9, Max-ime Leroy], *Histoire des idées sociales en France* (Paris, 1946–54), II, 374–75, III, 173. Pierre Martino, *L'époque romantique en France* (Paris, 1944), p. 17; see the novels of Stendhal, *Le rouge et le noir*, and of Honoré Balzac, *Histoire de la grandeur et de la décadence de César Birotteau*.
23. Charléty, pp. 11–12, 100–5; Charles Pouthas, "Les ministères de Louis Philippe," *Revue d'histoire moderne et contemporaine*, I (1954), 108–24;

Sherman Kent, *Electoral Procedures under Louis Philippe* (New Haven, Conn., 1937), pp. 70–73, 85–86, 114, 195–97, chap. x; Daniel Stern (pseudonym of Marie d'Agoult), *La Révolution de 1848* (1st ed.: Paris, 1850), I, 7. Henceforth notes refer to this edition unless otherwise stated.

24. See Louis Cauchois-Lemaire's description in *Autographes du XIXe siècle,* n.a.f. 22889, ff. 95–99, in Bibliothèque Nationale.

25. Gabriel Perreux, *Aux temps des sociétés secrètes; la propagande républicaine au début de la Monarchie de juillet* (Paris, 1930), pp. 219–21.

26. Blanc, *Histoire de dix ans, 1830–40* (11th ed.: Paris, n.d.) I, 133. Hereafter cited as *Dix ans.*

27. See Blanc's speech at funeral of Rodde in *National,* Jan. 2, 1836; *Dix ans,* IV, 96–97; Fiaux, *Louis Blanc,* 27–28.

28. Irene Collins, "The Press in France during the Reign of Louis Philippe," *English Historical Review,* LXIX (1954), 268–74.

29. Blanc, *Questions d'aujourd'hui et de demain* (Paris, 1879–82), I, 43. Hereafter cited as *Questions.*

30. *Dix ans,* I, "Introduction."

31. *Ibid.,* V, 54.

32. *Bon Sens,* Oct. 25, 1834.

33. *Revue républicaine,* II (Aug., 1834), 188.

34. *Dix ans,* V, 388.

35. *Ibid.,* III, 4.

36. *Ibid.,* V, 256.

37. *Ibid.,* V, 301–7.

CHAPTER II

1. Herman Pechan, *Louis Blanc als Wegbereiter des modernen Sozialismus* (Jena, 1929), pp. 106–28.

2. Leroy, *Hist. idées sociales,* II, 455; Elie Halévy, *Histoire du socialisme européen* (Paris, 1948), pp. 63–64.

3. G. D. H. Cole, *A History of Socialist Thought,* Vol. I: *The Forerunners* (London, 1953), p. 169.

4. See Arthur Rosenberg, *Demokratie und Sozialismus* (Amsterdam, 1938), pp. 9–15 ff.

5. Marcel Prélot, *L'évolution politique du socialisme français, 1789–1934* (Paris, 1939).

6. André Lichtenberger, *Le socialisme français au XVIIIe siècle* (Paris, 1895), p. 157.

7. Abbé B. de Mably, *Oeuvres complètes* (Lyons, 1792), VI, 525; Alfred Cobban, *Rousseau and the Modern State* (London, 1934), chap. vii.

8. Henri Sée, *Les idées politiques en France au XVIIIe siècle* (Paris, 1920), pp. 180–90.

9. Albert Mathiez, *La Révolution française* (Paris, 1951), II, 66–67; Ralph Korngold, *Robespierre and the Fourth Estate* (New York, 1941), pp. 87–88.

10. *Hist. Révol. franç.,* X, 249–50; *Dix ans,* IV, 105–9.

11. See Maurice Dommanget, ed., *Pages choisies de Babeuf* (Paris, 1935), p. 145; Rosenberg, *Demokratie und Sozialismus,* p. 9.

12. See article XII of "Acte d'insurrection" in Paul Louis, *Histoire du socialisme en France* (5th ed.: Paris, 1950), p. 53. Also Victor Advielle, *Histoire de Gracchus Babeuf* (Paris, 1884), I, 197–217.

13. Weill, *Hist. parti répub.,* pp. 35–36.

14. *Dix ans,* IV, 182.

15. *Procès des quinze* (Paris, 1832), pp. 45–55.

16. Godfrey Cavaignac, *Procès du droit d'association* (Paris, 1832).

17. Perreux, *Aux temps des sociétés secrètes,* p. 24.

18. David Thomson, *The Babeuf Plot* (London, 1947), p. 64.

19. Quoted in Pierre Angrand, "Les tendances égalitaires et socialistes dans les sociétés secrètes françaises, 1830–34," *1848 et les révolutions du XIXe siècle,* XXXIX (1948), 26.

20. Marc-René-Marie de Voyer d'Argenson, *Discours et opinions* (Paris, 1845), II, 280–81.

21. For Fourier see H. Bourgin, *Charles Fourier* (Paris, 1905); and for Owen see G. D. H. Cole, *Life of Robert Owen* (Rev. ed.: London, 1930).

22. See Frank Manuel, *The New World of Henri Saint-Simon* (Cambridge, Mass., 1956).

23. I. Tchernoff, *Le parti républicain sous la Monarchie de juillet* (Paris, 1901), p. 75.

24. Armand Cuvillier, *P.-J.-B. Buchez et*

les origines du socialisme chrétien (Paris, 1948), p. 33.

25. *L'espérance*, 1856–57, p. 172.
26. *Revue encyclopédique*, 1832, p. 305.
27. Quoted in Tchernoff, p. 107

CHAPTER III

1. *Rev. prog.*, I (Jan. 1, 1839), 1.
2. *Hist. Révol. franç.*, I, 362.
3. *Ibid.*, I, 117.
4. *Dix ans*, V, 225, 453–54.
5. *Ibid.*, IV, 208.
6. *Ibid.*, III, 314; Blanc, *Organisation du travail* (5th ed.: Paris, 1847), p. 20. Hereafter cited as *Organ. trav.*
7. Prélot, *Evol. polit.*, p. 45; Paul Keller, *Louis Blanc und die Revolution von 1848* (Zurich, 1926), p. 49.
8. *Dix ans*, IV, 117.
9. *Organ. trav.*, p. 19.
10. *Rev. prog.*, II (Dec. 15, 1839), 492.
11. Blanc, *Histoire de la Révolution de 1848* (Paris, 1870), II, 235.
12. *Questions*, I, 279; see also Vol. III, 233.
13. *Ibid.*, I, 285–91, 304; *Bon Sens*, March 6, 1836.
14. *Organ. trav.*, pp. 15–16, 149–50, 161–65.
15. *Questions*, I, 172–74.
16. *Rev. prog.*, II (Nov. 1, 1839), 344; *Dix ans*, V, 304; *Questions*, III, 226, V, 231.
17. *Rev. prog.*, II (Oct. 15, 1839), 306.
18. *Ibid.*, p. 209.
19. *Ibid.*, I (Jan. 15, 1839), 14.
20. *Ibid.*, II (Oct. 15, 1839), 296.
21. *Questions*, I, 38.
22. *Rev. prog.*, II (Oct. 15, 1839), 302–4.
23. *Ibid.*, I (Feb. 1, 1839), 102; I (March 1, 1839), 213–14; I (May 1, 1839), 463.
24. *Dix ans*, II, 283, V, 457.
25. *Rev. prog.*, I (April 1, 1839), 312; II (July 15, 1839), 47; IV (June 1, 1840), 477.
26. *Ibid.*, II (Oct. 15, 1839), 290.
27. *Rev. répub.*, V (April, 1835), 146.

CHAPTER IV

1. Engels to Marx, in A. Bebel and E. Bernstein, eds., *Der Briefwechsel zwischen Friedrich Engels und Karl Marx, 1844 bis 1883* (Stuttgart, 1913), I, 74.
2. Archives Nationales, BB 18 1386, dr. 957.

3. *Organ. trav.*, pp. 76–77; see especially chap. iii.
4. *Organ. trav.*, p. 25.
5. *Dix ans*, II, 287.
6. *Nouveau monde*, I (Jan. 1, 1850), 311.
7. *Rev. prog.*, IV (July 1, 1840), 590 ff.
8. *Dix ans*, I, 135–36.
9. *Organ. trav.*, pp. 1–2.
10. *Dix ans*, V, 461.
11. *Hist. Révol. franç.*, I, 262–70 ff.
12. *Rev. prog.*, IV (May 1, 1840), 383.
13. *Organ. trav.*, p. 102.
14. *Ibid.*, pp. 104, 156–57, 170–71, 270 ff.
15. *Rev. prog.*, II (Dec. 1, 1839), 440, 446.
16. *Questions*, III, 227; *Hist. Révol. franç.* (Paris, 1878), II, 161, X, 246. See also A. Menger, *Le droit au produit intégral du travail*, translated from the second German edition (Paris, 1900), p. 35.
17. L. A. Garnier-Pagès, *Histoire de la Révolution de 1848* (Paris, 1861–72), IV, 88–89.
18. Stern, *Hist. Révol. 1848* (2d ed.: Paris, 1862), II, 571.
19. *Organ. trav.*, pp. 103–6, 160.
20. *Ibid.*, p. 113.
21. The assertion that Blanc was a disguised Saint-Simonian was made by S. Charléty, *Histoire du saint-simonisme* (Paris, 1931), p. 280.
22. *Organ. trav.*, p. 165; *Dix ans*, III, 101.
23. *Organ. trav.*, p. 81.
24. See his *Hist. Révol. franç.* (Paris, 1878), II, 198, VII, 280.
25. *Questions*, V, 196.
26. *Rev. répub.*, I (May, 1834), 277.
27. *Almanach populaire* (n.p., n.d.), p. 91.
28. I (Jan. 15, 1839), 3, for first quote, and p. 13, for second.
29. *Rev. prog.*, I (June 1, 1839), 539–41.
30. *Organ. trav.*, p. 109.
31. *Ibid.*, p. 103.
32. *Ibid.* (Paris, 1840), pp. 108–9.
33. *Ibid.* (Paris, 1841), p. 74.
34. *Dix ans*, II, 253.
35. *Rev. prog.*, IV (Aug. 1, 1840), 30; *Organ. trav.* (Paris, 1840), pp. 108–9; (Paris, 1845), pp. 116–17; (Paris, 1847), pp. 157–58.
36. *Ibid.* (Paris, 1850), p. 92. See also *Pages d'histoire de la Révolution de février 1848* (Paris, 1850), p. 296.
37. *Moniteur universel*, April 3, 1848.
38. *Questions*, IV, 145.

39. *Ibid.*, IV, 94.
40. *Dix ans,* IV, 87.
41. *Organ. trav.,* pp. 116–17.
42. Blanc to unknown addressee, June 25, 1877, card no. 49412 at Chavaray and Co. in Paris.
43. *Organ. trav.,* p. 180.
44. *Hist. Révol. franç.* (Paris, 1878), X, 247.
45. *Rev. prog.,* VI (Sept. 1, 1841), 75, note 1.
46. *Dix ans,* II, 265, note 1. III, 89.
47. *Rev. répub.,* I (May, 1834), 275.
48. *Dix ans,* IV, 447.
49. *Organ. trav.,* p. 221.
50. *Ibid.,* p. 257.
51. *Rev. prog.,* II (Dec. 15, 1839), 491.
52. *Ibid.,* I (Jan. 15, 1839), 15, note 1; *Organ. trav.,* pp. 112, 195; *Pages d'hist.,* p. 287; *Dix ans,* I, 134–35.
53. *Organ. trav.,* p. 164; *Hist. Révol. franç.,* I, 235.
54. *Rev. prog.,* II (Jan. 1, 1840), 542.
55. *Ibid.,* II (Aug. 1, 1839), 61; *Organ. trav.,* p. 115.

CHAPTER V

1. Edmund Silberner, *The Problem of War in Nineteenth Century Economic Thought* (Princeton, 1946), pp. 216, 233–34, 244–47.
2. *Rev. répub.,* II (Aug., 1834), 194.
3. *Nouvelle minerve,* II (Aug., 1835), 458.
4. *Rev. prog.,* IV (Oct. 1, 1840), 165.
5. *Ibid.,* II (Jan. 1, 1840), 534.
6. *Ibid.,* p. 546.
7. *Dix ans,* II, 89, 91. Also see "Introduction" of Vol. I.
8. *Rev. prog.,* IV (Oct. 1, 1840), 168.
9. *Questions,* I, 279, III, 233.
10. *Ibid.,* I, 39.
11. *Dix ans,* II, 403.
12. *Organ. trav.,* pp. 97–101. Blanc's review was active in spreading this thesis before the Marxists took it up. See especially the article by Alexander Rey, "De la situation," V (Feb. 1, 1841), 21–40.
13. *Organ. trav.,* pp. 27, 86–89; *Rev. prog.,* IV (Aug. 1, 1840), 76. The following quotations are from pp. 78–79.
14. *Hist. Révol. franç.,* VII, 316.
15. *Dix ans,* II, 405.
16. *Rev. prog.,* II (Aug. 1, 1839), 58.

17. *Ibid.,* II (Dec. 15, 1839), 528; *Dix ans,* V, 138.
18. *Dix ans,* IV, 137.

CHAPTER VI

1. For Cavaignac's defense of state credit see *Journal du peuple,* Jan. 17, 1842.
2. G. Marcy, *Constantin Pecqueur, fondateur du collectivisme d'état* (Paris, 1934).
3. *Dix ans,* II, 335–37.
4. See *Réforme,* July, 29, 1843.
5. Alvin Calman, *Ledru-Rollin and the Second French Republic* (New York, 1922), chap. i.
6. Quoted in Stanislas Mitard, *Les origines du radicalisme démocratique: L'affaire Ledru-Rollin* (Paris, 1952), p. 73.
7. Robert Schnerb, *Ledru-Rollin* (Paris, 1948), p. 59.
8. *Réforme,* Sept. 11, 18, Oct. 18, 22, 27, 28, 30, Nov. 1, 5, 1843; April 1, 10, 15, 23, 29, 1844.
9. Hilde Rigaudeau-Weiss, *Les enquêtes ouvrières en France entre 1830 et 1848* (Paris, 1936), pp. 171–78.
10. Henri Avenel, *Histoire de la presse française depuis 1789* (Paris, 1900), pp. 370–71; Marcel Dessal, *Un révolutionnaire Jacobin, Charles Delescluze* (Paris, 1952), pp. 43–44.
11. *Rev. prog.,* II (Aug. 15, 1839), 112.
12. *Voltaire,* Sept. 25, 1882.
13. Blanc, *Hist. Révol. 1848,* II, 215–18; F. Briffault, *The Prisoner of Ham* (London, 1846), pp. 376–78; J. Blanchard, *Life of Napoleon III* (Paris, 1874–82), II, 297.
14. *Nouveau monde,* I (Aug. 15, 1849), 3–6.
15. Elias Regnault, *Histoire de huit ans* (3d ed.: Paris, 1871), I, 319.
16. F. Arthur Simpson, *The Rise of Louis Napoleon* (London, 1925), p. 347.
17. Wladimir Karénine, *George Sand* (Paris, 1899–1926), III, 393: Sand, *Correspondance, 1812–76* (Paris, 1882–84), II, 324.
18. Quoted in Frances Winwar, *Life of the Heart, George Sand and Her Times* (New York, 1945), p. 201.
19. Karénine, III, 537.
20. Blanc, *Révélations historiques,* II, 216–17.

21. *Dix ans*, IV, 209.
22. Arnold Ruge, *Sammtliche Werke* (2d ed.: Mannheim, 1848) , V, 149–52.
23. Martin Nadaud, *Mémoires de Léonard* (Bourganeuf, 1895) , pp. 282–84.

CHAPTER VII

1. Leo Gershoy, "Three French Historians and the Revolution of 1848," *Journal of the History of Ideas*, XII (1951) , 131–46.
2. See David Thomson, *Democracy in France* (2d ed.: London, 1952) , p. 22.
3. See the testimony of the revolutionaries in *Journal des tribunaux*, April–May, 1849.
4. For the banquets see John Boughman, "The Political Banquet Campaign in France, 1847–48," (Unpublished Ph.D. dissertation, University of Michigan, 1953) .
5. Stern, *Hist. Révol. 1848*, I, 28.
6. Blanc, *Discours politiques* (Paris, 1882) , pp. 9–10.
7. Garnier-Pagès, *Hist. Révol. 1848*, IV, 211.
8. Albert Crémieux, *La Révolution de février 1848* (Paris, 1912) , pp. 65, 88–89. Much of the information that follows comes from this source.
9. Lucien de La Hodde, *Histoire des sociétés secrètes et du parti républicain de 1830 à 1848* (Paris, 1850) , p. 419.
10. Bebel and Bernstein, eds., *Briefwechsel zwischen Engels und Marx*, I, 74.
11. *Dix ans*, I, 453.
12. Stern, I, 285–87.
13. *Pages d'histoire*, p. 11.
14. J.-B. Sarrans, *Histoire de la Révolution de février 1848* (Paris, 1851) , I, 46.
15. *Pages d'histoire*, p. 17.
16. Crémieux, *Révol. fév. 1848*, pp. 421–22; Blanc, *Hist. Révol. 1848*, I, 68, has several errors of fact.
17. This is Blanc's version in *Hist. Révol. 1848*, I, 72, and although exaggerated by his desire to present himself as the darling of the people, he was certainly widely applauded.
18. Stern, I, 249; Blanc, *Hist. Révol. 1848*, I, 76.
19. Adolphe Crémieux, *En 1848, discours et lettres* (Paris, 1883) , pp. 318–19; *Pages d'histoire*, pp. 20–21.
20. The disposition of the moderates, who were of the *National* coterie, will be made clear during this and the next few chapters. Illuminating are the strategems they used to obviate serious social measures: the Luxembourg Commission, the National Workshops, and the organization of provincial regiments in the event of a renewal of insurrection in Paris. See Alphonse de Lamartine's *Histoire des Girondins*, A. Crémieux, *En 1848*, and Garnier-Pagès for their adherence to the Girondin tradition. The thesis of "two revolutions" is effectively explained in Crémieux, *Révol. fév. 1848*, pp. 467–71.
21. *Hist. Révol. 1848*, I, 83–84.
22. Charles de Lavarenne, *Le Gouvernement provisoire et l'Hôtel de Ville dévoilés* (2d ed.: Paris, 1850) , p. 24.
23. *Hist. Révol. 1848*, I, 84.
24. *Ibid.*, I, 85.

CHAPTER VIII

1. *Hist. Révol. 1848*, I, 126 ff.
2. Stern, II, 39–40; *Pages d'histoire*, p. 31; Garnier-Pagès, VI, 56.
3. *Moniteur*, Feb. 26, 1848.
4. Garnier-Pagès, VI, 67.
5. *Histoire de la Révolution de 1848* (Paris, 1849) , II, 56.
6. G. Perreux, "Le drapeau rouge," *Revue d'histoire économique et sociale*, X (1932) , 181–94.
7. Stern, II, 33.
8. Lamartine, I, 425.
9. See his letter in Jacques Vier, *Daniel Stern* (Paris, 1951) , p. 79. In his *Hist. Révol. 1848*, I, 116, he simply wrote, "des objections s'élevèrent."
10. Stern (2d ed.: Paris, 1862) , I, 373.
11. Stern, II, 149.
12. Elias Regnault, *Histoire du Gouvernement provisoire* (Paris, 1850) , p. 119.
13. Stern, II, 36 ff.
14. *Pages d'histoire*, p. 33.
15. Garnier-Pagès, VI, 189. See also the position of François Arago in, France. Assemblée Nationale Constituante, *Rapport . . . de la Commission d'enquête . . . sur l'insurrection qui a éclaté dans la journée du 23 juin et sur*

les événements du 15 mai (n.p., 1848) , p. 224. Hereafter cited as *Rapport*.

16. *Dix ans*, V, 541.

17. *Ibid.*, IV, 422.

18. *Ibid.*, I, 313.

19. *Questions*, IV, 317–18.

20. *Moniteur*, March 1, 1848.

21. See his letter to Stern in Vier, p. 59.

22. Stern, II, 47.

23. *Hist. Révol. 1848*, I, 141.

24. *Moniteur*, March 3, 1848.

25. *Ibid.*. March 11, 1848.

26. *Ibid.*, March 16, 1848.

27. Edouard Renard, *Louis Blanc*, p. 118, claimed they were ended but I found no decrees to this effect in the *Moniteur*.

28. *Moniteur*, March 5, 1848.

29. *Ibid.*, April 7, 1848.

30. *Ibid.*, March 6, 1848.

31. *Ibid.*, March 11, 1848. See *Illustration*, March 18, 1848.

32. G. Cohen, "Louis Blanc et la Commission du Luxembourg," *Annales de l'Ecole Libre des Sciences Politiques*, XII (1897) , 194.

33. April 27, May 2, 3, 6, 1848.

34. See B. Malon, *Histoire du socialisme* (Paris, 1882–83) , II, 192, and especially *Le socialisme intégral* (Paris, 1892) , I, 156–57, II, 170, 202–3 ff. Georges Renard, *La République de 1848*, p. 272; and *Le régime socialiste* (Paris, 1898) , p. 23.

35. Blanc, *Hist. Révol. 1848*, I, 177.

36. Donald McKay, *The National Workshops* (Cambridge, Mass., 1933) , pp. 31–33, 39–41.

37. Blanc, *Hist. Révol. 1848*, I, 183; Garnier-Pagès, VI, 327–28.

38. Paul Hubert-Valleroux, *Les associations coopératives en France et à l'étranger* (Paris, 1884) , p. 31.

39. *Nouveau monde*, I (Jan. 15, 1850) , 270–80.

40. Emile Heftler, *Les associations coopératives de production sous la deuxième République* (Paris, 1899) , pp. 43–48.

41. *Moniteur*, May 1, 1848.

42. P. Chalmin, "Une institution militaire de la seconde République: la Garde Nationale Mobile," *Etudes d'histoire moderne et contemporaine* (Paris, 1948) , II, 46.

43. March 26, 1848.

44. Jean Gaumont, *Histoire générale de la coopération en France* (Paris, 1923–24) , I, 370.

CHAPTER IX

1. Charles Rappoport, *Jean Jaurès* (Paris, 1915) , p. 373.

2. Aaron Noland, *The Founding of the French Socialist Party* (Cambridge, Mass., 1956) , p. 108.

3. Stern (2d ed.: Paris, 1862) , I, 509.

4. Garnier-Pagès, VI, 180–81.

5. A. Antony, *La politique financière du Gouvernement provisoire* (Paris, 1910) , pp. 30 ff.; Stern (2d ed., 1862) , I, 455.

6. Garnier-Pagès, VII, 40.

7. *Ibid.*, VIII, 330.

8. *Moniteur*, March 8, 1848.

9. See J. J. Baude, "Les ouvriers," *Revue des deux mondes*, XXII (1848) 440–52. Proudhon, Lamennais, Buchez in particular denounced both Blanc's experiments and their costs. However, after Albert and Flocon, Blanc was the least expensive member of the government. He did not use the treasury's money for his experiments and he limited the costs of the Luxembourg Commission to 37,024 francs. See *Moniteur*, April 26, 1849. Neither did he draw a salary from the government. For the persistence of these false and pernicious rumors see Count Victor Castellane, *Journal* (Paris, 1896–[1930]) , IV, 47–48; Lucien de La Hodde, *Parti républicain*, pp. 504–5; Eugène de Mirecourt, *Les contemporains: Louis Blanc* (Paris, 1857) ; Victor Bouton, *Profils révolutionnaires* (Paris, 1849) .

10. Garnier-Pagès, VI, 390.

11. S. Wassermann, *Les clubs de Barbès et de Blanqui en 1848* (Paris, 1913) , p. 69.

12. *Rev. prog.*, IV (June 15, 1840) , 520; *Organ. trav.* (5th ed., 1847) , p. 14. Blanc often referred to the government as *"le pouvoir."*

13. Comité National du Centenaire de 1848, *Procès-verbaux du Gouvernement provisoire et de la Commission du pouvoir exécutif* (Paris, 1950) , p. ix.

14. *Hist. Révol. 1848,* II, 9.
15. McKay, *National Workshops,* chaps. iii–iv.
16. *Rapport,* p. 118. His statement was made on March 28, but it was not recorded in the *Moniteur.*
17. This assertion will be explained in the following pages. On Blanc's ambitions see Stern, II, 194 ff.
18. *Révélations historiques,* II, 6–8.
19. Stern, II, 219, note 1.
20. Wassermann, pp. 62 ff. See Alan Spitzer, *The Revolutionary Theories of Louis Auguste Blanqui* (New York, 1957), chap. vii.
21. A. Calman, *Ledru-Rollin and the Second Republic* (New York, 1922), p. 122.
22. A. Crémieux and G. Génique, "La question électorale en mars 1848," *Révolution de 1848,* III (1906–7), 252.
23. Garnier-Pagès, VI, 423; Blanc, *Hist. Révol. 1848,* II, 217–18.
24. See above, Chap. III, section iii, Chap. VII, section iv.
25. Garnier-Pagès, VI, 420–23. For the opposition of the moderates see VI, 221.
26. It is reproduced in *Les affiches rouges* (Paris, n.d.), p. 70.
27. Blanc, *Hist. Révol. 1848,* I, 309.
28. *Garnier-Pagès,* VI, 430.
29. Blanc, *Hist. Révol. 1848,* I, 311.
30. *Moniteur,* March 18, 1848.
31. Blanc, *Hist. Révol. 1848,* I, 313.
32. *Moniteur,* March 20, 1848.
33. *Ibid.,* March 26, 1848.
34. For the agents of Ledru-Rollin see P. Haury, "Les commissaires de Ledru-Rollin en 1848," *Révolution française,* 57 (1909), 438–75.
35. *Moniteur,* March 17, 1848.
36. Calman, pp. 132 ff. Blanc, *Hist. Révol. franç.,* I, 284.
37. A. de Lamartine, *Histoire de la Révolution de 1848* (Paris, 1849), II, 230, 297.
38. For purpose of the Garde Mobile see McKay, pp. 45–46; for their antipathy to the Clichy tailors see above, Chap. VIII, sect. iv.
39. McKay, pp. 39 ff.
40. See their placard in *Les affiches rouges,* p. 134.
41. Renard, *Louis Blanc,* p. 142.

42. In the Bibliothèque Thiers, Paris, there is a collection of pamphlets generally hostile to Blanc's socialism. They are listed under Masson 800.
43. See the latter of Genevay, governor of the Luxembourg Palace, in Blanc, *Hist. Révol. 1848,* II, 39.
44. Renard, p. 143. For Blanc's refutation of this calumny see the *Globe,* Oct. 20, 1848; also Garnier-Pagès, VIII, 188.
45. See J. A. Langlois, ed., *Correspondance de P. J. Proudhon* (Paris, 1875), II, 317; Proudhon, *Confessions d'un révolutionnaire* (Brussels, 1849), pp. 19–20; *Voix du peuple,* Dec. 3, 27, 1849.
46. Wassermann, pp. 102–4.
47. Blanc to Altaroche, card no. 47180 at Chavaray and Co., Paris.
48. See Maurice Dommanget, *Un drame politique en 1848* (Paris, 1948), pp. 46–53, 120. In 1840 Blanc revealed a certain sympathy for Blanqui, and his collaborator, Dupont (of Bussac) had offered to defend the conspirator in court. See *Rev. prog.,* IV (Feb. 15, 1840), 97–99. Barbès felt Blanc had been too easy on him in *Histoire de dix ans.* Barbès to David (of Angers), *Nouvelle revue,* Sept. 15, 1897, pp. 195–96.
49. Stern (2d ed., 1862), II, 156.
50. Blanc, *Hist. Révol. 1848,* II, 12–13; Garnier-Pagès, VII, 337–38.
51. *Rapport,* p. 12.
52. Stern (2d ed., 1862), II, 173–74; see also Wassermann, pp. 124–25.
53. Calman, p. 145.
54. *Rapport,* p. 280.
55. Lamartine, II, 307.
56. *Ibid.,* I, 345.
57. Emile Thomas, *Histoire des Ateliers nationaux,* Vol. II in J. A. R. Marriott, ed., *The French Revolution of 1848 in Its Economic Aspect* (Oxford, 1913), pp. 200–1.
58. KcKay, pp. 49–51.
59. Stern, II, 176; Calman, p. 155.
60. Quoted in Dautry, p. 142.
61. Lamartine, II, 332.
62. Lamartine's egoism, his view of himself as a savior, literally exudes from his history of 1848. See also H. Guillemin, *Lamartine en 1848* (Paris, 1948), pp. 50–51.
63. Louis Ménard, *Prologue d'une révolu-*

tion, in *Cahiers de la quinzaine* (June, 1904) , p. 80. See also Garnier-Pagès, VII, 406.

64. *Moniteur,* April 18, 1848.
65. Garnier-Pagès, VII, 360.
66. *Ibid.,* VIII, 45.
67. Wassermann, p. 131, note 4.

CHAPTER X

1. G. Cahen, p. 372. This amount was given to Ledru-Rollin, probably not to Blanc.
2. Garnier-Pagès, VI, 245.
3. He admitted deleting the compromising passages before publishing his speeches in the *Moniteur.* See *Moniteur,* Aug. 26, 1848. However, they were brought to light when the stenographer present at these meetings reproduced them for the parliamentary investigating committee. Blanc never denied the accuracy of the stenographer but only the accusation that he took part in the final choosing of the Luxembourg's candidates. See his *Hist. Révol. 1848,* II, 202.
4. *Rapport,* This and the following quotations are from pp. 117–20.
5. See, for example, *Assemblée nationale,* April 16, 1848.
6. See their proclamation in *Les affiches rouges,* p. 143.
7. See the proclamation of a vice-president of the commission in *Les journaux rouges* (Paris, n.d.) , p. 13; see also *Les affiches rouges,* p. 134.
8. McKay, p. 101.
9. *Les affiches rouges,* pp. 140–41.
10. Emile Thomas, pp. 216–17.
11. McKay, pp. 57–58.
12. Stern (2d ed., 1862) , II, 205.
13. Georges Duveau, *La vie ouvrière en France sous le second Empire* (Paris, 1946) , p. 208.
14. Thomas, pp. 211–13.
15. See the excellent descriptions in A. de Tocqueville, *Recollections,* edited by J. P. Mayer (New York, 1949) , pp. 93–94, 102. Also George Sand, *Journal d'un voyageur* (3rd ed.: Paris, 1871) , pp. 22–23. Writing in the late 1860's Mme Sand pointed up the peasant's submission to authority, a characteristic Blanc had emphasized in the 1840's. See his *Dix ans,* II, 283, V, 457.

16. See his realistic novel, *Education sentimentale* (Paris, 1923) , p. 425. See also the views of a typical petty bourgeois, Jules Simon, *Premières années* (Paris, [1901]) , p. 406, and *Figures et croquis* (Paris, 1909) , pp. 227–48.
17. *Moniteur,* May 18, 1848.
18. *Rapport,* pp. 12–13.
19. *Moniteur,* May 3, 1848.
20. Peter Campbell, *French Electoral Systems and Elections* (London, 1958) , p. 65; Garnier-Pagès, VIII, 288 ff.
21. *Moniteur,* May 7, 1848.
22. *Ibid.,* May 10, 1848.
23. *Prologue d'une révolution,* chap. xiv.
24. Jean Gaumont, *Histoire générale de la coopération en France* (Paris, 1924) , I, 252.
25. Caussidière, *Mémoires* (Paris, 1849) , II, 106–11.
26. See *Journaux rouges* (Paris, n.d.) , p. 13.
27. *Journal des débats,* March 8, 1849.
28. See Gioia-Macchioro Benedetto, "Louis Blanc e la Rivoluzione di febbraio," *Nuova rivista storica,* XXXV (1951) , 265.
29. *Rapport,* p. 230. See below, chap. xi.
30. *Ibid.,* p. 276; *Moniteur,* Aug. 26, 1848.
31. *Rapport,* p. 355.
32. Thomas, p. 323; *Rapport,* pp. 242, 352.
33. This letter is in the appendix of *Pages d'hist.*
34. Quoted in Stern, II, 219, note 1.
35. Blanc, *Hist. Révol. franç.* (Paris, 1898) , II, 143.
36. *Rapport,* p. 104; for activities of Huber, see pp. 227–28. It has been asserted that Huber was in the pay of Marrast. See H. Guillemin, *Lamartine en 1848* (Paris, 1948) , p. 61, and Blanc, *Hist. Révol. 1848,* II, 78.
37. *Ibid.,* pp. 73, 75, 104–6.
38. *Ibid.,* p. 73.
39. *Ibid.,* p. 30–31.
40. Blanc, *Hist. Révol. 1848,* II, 85.
41. *Rapport,* p. 76.
42. *Moniteur,* May 17, 1848. Four representatives, Lacaze, Bidard, Baze, and Roux-Lavergne, insisted that he said to the mob, "Vous venez de conquérir (ou de reconquérir) le droit de pétition." See *Rapport,* pp. 76–77. However, B. Pons, in a letter he sent to the investigating committee, affirmed that

he was standing next to the official stenographer and saw him write exactly what was reported in the *Moniteur*. See *Rapport*, p. 111. Representative Demontry supported Blanc. See *Rapport*, p. 77.

43. Deposition of Dautriche, *Rapport*, p. 79. If Blanc had made this statement it is doubtful if he would have acted as he did shortly afterward in the assembly.

44. *Ibid.*, pp. 78–80, 315.

45. *Ibid.*, p. 104.

46. *Ibid.*, p. 113.

47. *Ibid.*, p. 111.

48. *Ibid.*, p. 105. Again the witnesses are not in accord. Those clearly hostile to Blanc and to socialism, Dautriche, Artigue, Mallaude and Paillet, insist that he warned the people against another betrayal and said, "Une démonstration comme celle d'aujourd'hui n'est pas de celles qui ébranlent seulement, mais qui renversent!" *Rapport*, pp. 68, 83–86. Mallaude claimed to have written down these words on the spot and handed the committee the card he had used. Paillet asserted that he too, had written the words but had no card to offer. Pons, editor of the *Haro*, of Caen, an artist friend of Charles Blanc, Brown-Sequart (or Lequart), a doctor, and Dienne, a proprietor, supported Blanc. *Rapport*, pp. 86–111, 113. It is possible that Blanc's adverse witnesses failed to hear the first part of his statement and drew their conclusion from the second part, "une révolution de ce genre n'est pas de celles qui ébranlent les trônes, mais qui les renversent." Hearing "de ce genre," they may have concluded that he was referring to the May 15 affair. On the other hand it is possible that certain of his pronouncements were of an inflamatory nature. Before the committee Blanc said that he dared not abruptly tell the people to go home. He tried, he said, to enter into their generous sentiments with appropriate expressions and thus win their confidence, after which he could more easily send them away. This was probably his real intention. However, on another occasion he admitted that

he had modified the published versions of his speeches in the Luxembourg because in the heat of extemporaneous oratory he had made certain statements which seemed a bit too fiery. See *Moniteur*, Aug. 26, 1848. It is therefore possible that the completely improvised harangues of May 15 contained several traces of an enthusiasm rather easily stirred to life by its environment.

49. *Rapport*, p. 111. For the following information see pp. 87–116.

50. *Moniteur*, Aug. 26, 1848.

51. *Rapport*, pp. 34, 102.

52. *Moniteur*, Aug. 26, 1848.

53. *Moniteur*, May 16, 1848.

CHAPTER XI

1. Blanc, *Hist. Révol. 1848*, II, 114. For the vote see *Moniteur*, May 27, 1848.

2. *Moniteur*, June 14, 1848.

3. Calman, p. 189.

4. *Moniteur*, June 1, 1848.

5. *Ibid.*

6. *Ibid.*, June 3, 1848.

7. *Jules Favre* (Paris, 1912), p. 115.

8. *Moniteur*, June 4, 1848.

9. A. Crémieux, *En 1848, discours et lettres* (Paris, 1883), pp. 267–68.

10. Paul Bastid, *Doctrines et institutions politiques de la seconde République* (Paris, 1945), I, 225.

11. *Ibid.*, I, 80–83; Georges Weill, *Hist. parti répub.*, pp. 138–43.

12. McKay, pp. 106 ff.

13. Thomas, pp. 141–42.

14. See Marriott, ed., I, pp. xciv–xcv; Benedetto, p. 257.

15. Thomas, pp. 214 ff.

16. Guillemin, *Lamartine*, p. 71.

17. McKay, p. 167.

18. Dautry, p. 224.

19. Charles Schmidt, *Les Ateliers nationaux aux barricades de juin* (Paris, 1948), p. 27; McKay, p. 71, estimates that only 14,000 assembled at the Place de la Bastille.

20. *Vrai république*, May 26, 1848 and *passim*.

21. *Rapport*, pp. 246–48.

22. McKay, pp. 101 ff.

23. *Les journaux rouges*, pp. 92–93.

24. *Moniteur*, June 16, 1848 and *passim*.

25. Cahen, p. 475.

26. *Rapport,* p. 115.
27. Blanc, *Hist. Révol. 1848,* II, 146.
28. Blanc was typical in his distrust of the rural population. In April, 1848 it was openly affirmed by the left-wing that if the peasants voted conservative, Paris would have to renew the revolution. This Blanc emphasized in secret meetings of the Luxembourg. The feeling of the superiority of Paris was rampant in the clubs and motivated their demand for postponement of the elections so that they might "educate" the countryside.
29. S. Mitard, *Les origines du radicalisme démocratique,* pp. 35 ff., 53. *National,* May 21, June 29, 1840.
30. See *Les affiches rouges,* p. 260; Dautry, p. 210.
31. Blanc, *Hist. Révol. 1848,* II, 166–67.
32. *Moniteur,* July 29, 1849.
33. *Ibid.,* Aug. 8, 1848.
34. *Ibid.,* June 25, 1848.
35. See his *Etudes et souvenirs sur la deuxième République et le second Empire* (Paris, 1901), I, 78–90.
36. *Moniteur,* Aug. 26, 1848.
37. Blanc, *Hist. Révol. 1848,* II, 203.
38. *Rapport,* pp. 67, 236.
39. *Presse,* July 25, 1849.
40. Blanc, *Hist. Révol. 1848,* II, 204.
41. *Ibid.,* II, 206.
42. Details on Blanc in Belgium may be found in Luc Sommerhausen, "Louis Blanc en Belgique," *Flambeau,* II (1932), 411–32.

CHAPTER XII

1. *Pages d'histoire,* p. 42.
2. A. Barbou, *Louis Blanc* (Paris, 1880), p. 87.
3. See these letters in *Collection Lovenjouel de Sperlberch,* E912, fols. 215–16, D665, fols. 82–83, at the Bibliothèque de Chantilly, France; also the letters from d'Orsay in the Bibliothèque de Nantes, and those from Delhasse in *Papiers de Thoré,* 7916, in the Bibliothèque de l'Arsénal, Paris. Yet, Blanc was bitter and disillusioned, as he wrote to Mme Montmahon on several occasions. See his letters to her in the Blanc collection at the University of Wisconsin library.
4. Blanc to d'Orsay, April 26, 1849, copy of an autographed letter at Chavaray and Co.
5. April 23, 1849, in Léo Lucas, ed., *Correspondance d'H. Lucas* (n.p., 1914), p. 74. This is a typewritten work in the Bibliothèque Nationale.
6. *Nouveau monde,* I (July 15, 1849), 3–4.
7. *Ibid.,* I (Jan. 15, 1850), 299–301. The Falloux Law weakened the monopoly of the Université and entrenched the Catholics in state schools.
8. Archives Nationales, BB 18 1449.
9. *Nouveau monde,* II (Aug.–Oct., 1850), 89.
10. *République une et indivisible* (Paris, 1851), "Préface."
11. Blanc to Delhasse, Feb. 1850, *Papiers de Thoré,* 7916.
12. J. Prudhommeaux, "L'opposition socialiste sous la présidence de Louis Napoléon," *Révolution de 1848,* VI (1909), 68–81.
13. *Populaire,* Sept. 6, 1851.
14. Henri Peyre, *Louis Ménard* (New Haven, Conn., 1932), p. 77, note 20.
15. Vier, p. 64.
16. J. Rouquette, *Louis Blanc* (Paris, 1877), p. 6.
17. *Union socialiste,* May 10, 1852.
18. Gustave Lefrançais, *Souvenirs d'un révolutionnaire* (Brussels, 1902) pp. 192 ff. See letter of April 4, 1851 in Blanc collection at the University of Wisconsin library.
19. Alvin Calman, *Ledru-Rollin après 1848 et les proscrits français en Angleterre* (Paris, 1921), pp. 35–37, 140 and *passim.*
20. *Home Office Papers,* O. S. 4816, Public Records Office, London.
21. Edmond Plauchut, *Autour de Nohant; lettres de Barbès à George Sand* (Paris, 1897), p. 239.
22. *Proscrit,* July 5, 1850, p. 5.
23. Letter dated Sept. 3, 1850, J. Jeanjean, "Louis Blanc et Ledru-Rollin, lettres inédites," *Révolution de 1848, VII* (1910–11), 111–12.
24. Letter dated Oct. 15, 1850, Sand, *Correspondance,* III, 208–9.
25. Jeanjean, p. 112. For the committee see Calman, chap. VI, and René Gossez, "La proscription et les origines de l'Internationale," *1848, revue des révo-*

lutions contemporaines, No. 189 (1951) , 97–115.

26. *Voix du proscrit,* Dec. 19, 1850, p. 124.

27. Ledru-Rollin in *ibid.,* Jan. 13, 1851, p. 233.

28. *La législation directe par le peuple* (Paris, 1851) .

29. *La solution ou le gouvernement direct par le peuple* (Paris, 1851) .

30. *Plus de Girondins,* p. 77.

31. *Questions,* I, 68–69.

32. *Ibid.,* I, 124–25.

33. *Plus de Girondins,* pp. 86–87.

34. *Moniteur,* Aug. 8, 1848.

35. *Rev. prog.,* II (Oct. 15, 1839) , 290.

36. *Hist. Révol. franç.,* I, 117.

37. *Dix ans,* I, 142.

38. *Plus de Girondins,* p. 33.

39. *Questions,* I, 119.

40. *Ibid.,* I, 170, for first quote, I, 120 for second.

41. *Nouveau monde,* I (April 15, 1850) , 443.

42. *Ibid.,* I (May 15, 1850) , 496.

43. *Questions,* I, 37.

44. *Ibid.,* I, 341.

45. *Nouveau monde,* I (July 15, 1849) , 22–32; I (April 15, 1850) , 442.

46. *Ibid.,* I (April 15, 1850) , 443–45.

47. Blanc, *Lettres sur l'Angleterre* (Paris, 1865) , II, 327; *Questions,* I, 239–50.

48. *République une et indivisible,* p. 28.

49. *Plus de Girondins,* p. 52.

50. *Ibid.,* pp. 89–90.

51. Vidil to Blanqui, July 15, 1850, *Manuscrits de Blanqui,* n.a.f. 9583, fol. 143, at Bibliothèque Nationale. Blanc to Mme Montmahon, 1849, in the Blanc collection at the University of Wisconsin.

52. Lefrançais, pp. 194–96; Nadaud, p. 370; Sébastien Commissaire, *Mémoires et souvenirs* (Lyons, 1888) , II, 77–78.

53. Maurice Dommanget, *Blanqui à Belle Ile* (Paris, 1935) , p. 73.

54. *Times* (London) , March 5, 1851. Although Blanc never really became reconciled with Blanqui he protested when the Empire prepared to send Blanqui to Cayenne. See *Times,* April 20, 1859. He also exposed the intolerable conditions there. *Times,* Aug. 25, Oct. 7, 1851.

55. *Banquet des égaux* (Paris, [1851]) , pp. 1–28.

56. Bebel and Bernstein, eds., *Briefwechsel,* I, 311.

57. Lefrançais, pp. 206–7; *Révolution de 1848,* VII (1912) , 444.

58. *Le parti républicain et l'amnistie* (Brussels, [1859]) , pp. 12, 40–50.

59. *Nouveau monde,* II (Jan. 15, 1851) , 155.

60. Blanc to Mme Montmahon, 1849, Univ. of Wisconsin collection.

CHAPTER XIII

1. Garnier-Pagès, VII, 143–44.

2. Lefrançais, p. 203.

3. See his articles in the *Peuple,* Feb. 19, 1849, and in the *Voix du peuple,* Dec. 3, 27, 1849, and especially his *Confessions d'un révolutionnaire* (Brussels, 1849) .

4. Hubert-Valleroux, p. 138, and A. Vermorel, *Les hommes de 1848* (Paris, 1869) , pp. 145–46, and *Courrier français,* Oct. 7, 14, 1866.

5. *Louis Blanc* (Paris, 1851) , pp. 131 and *passim.*

6. J. Langlois, ed., *Correspondance de P.-J. Proudhon* (Paris, 1875) , II, 307.

7. Emile Heftler, pp. 165–88, 206–39.

8. Hubert-Valleroux, pp. 32–33.

9. Gaumont, I, 270–71, 435–36.

10. Quoted in E. Renard, *Louis Blanc* (Toulouse, 1922) , p. 75.

11. *Nouveau monde,* I (Sept. 15, 1849) , 15; I (Oct. 15, 1849) , 38 ff.

12. E. Dolléans, *Histoire du mouvement ouvrier* (Paris, 1948) , I, 247.

13. *Nouveau monde,* I (Dec. 15, 1849) , 33 ff.

14. Blanc, *Hist. Révol. 1848,* II, 211–12.

15. Rosenberg, p. 160; S. Molinier, *Blanqui* (Paris, 1948) , pp. 57 ff.; Dolléans, I, 277. Lassalle was influenced by Blanc, and state socialism, under the direction of Lassalle, found the roots in Germany which it could not find in France during the Second Empire. See Paul Keller, *Louis Blanc und die Revolution von 1848* (Zurich, 1926) , p. 288; Otto Warschauer, *Louis Blanc* (Leipzig, 1896) , p. 161; E. Dennis, *L'Allemagne, 1810–52* (Paris, [1898]) , p. 234.

16. See Charles Andler's preface to A. Thomas, *Histoire du second Empire,*

in J. Jaurès, ed., *Histoire socialiste* (Paris, [1907]) , p. ii.

17. H. Tolain, *Quelques vérités sur les élections de Paris* (Paris, 1863) .

18. *Temps,* Oct. 5, 1866.

19. Gaumont, I, 465.

20. Benoît Malon, *L'Internationale* (n.p., 1872) , p. 45; Jules Puech, *Proudhonisme dans l'Association Internationale des Travailleurs* (Paris, 1907) , pp. 7, 84, 102.

21. Bebel and Bernstein, III, 205–6.

22. A. de Molinari, *Le mouvement socialiste et les réunions publiques avant la Révolution du 4 septembre 1870* (Paris, 1872) , p. 9.

23. Paul Nerrlich, ed., *Arnold Ruges Briefwechsel* (Berlin, 1886) , II, 253–54.

CHAPTER XIV

1. *Dix ans,* "Préface."

2. Blanc to editor of *Indépendance belge,* 1844, in *Collection de Lovenjouel de Sperlberch,* D665, fol. 72.

3. *Questions,* III, 333.

4. One of his basic weaknesses was that he did not have access to important primary sources. A notable exception was his use of the manuscripts in the British Museum which had to do with the Vendée revolt.

5. *Hist. Révol. franç.,* IX, 162–67, 459–63, note 1; X, 10–11.

6. A. Aulard, "Michelet, historien de la Révolution française," *Révolution française,* LXXXI (1928) , 145.

7. *Hist. Révol. franç.,* I, 9.

8. *Ibid.,* I, 10. Blanc identified individualism with bicameral parliamentary government.

9. *Ibid.,* II, book iii, chaps. i–iii.

10. *Questions,* III, 419.

11. *Hist. Révol. franç.,* I, 10. Blanc identified fraternity with Jacobin-socialism.

12. *Ibid.,* I, book iii, chap. iii; II, book i, chap. vi. See also *ibid.* (Paris, 1878) , I, 212–13, 285.

13. Sidney Hook, *From Hegel to Marx* (New York, [1936]) , p. 61.

14. *Hist. Révol. franç.,* I, 11, 335.

15. To unknown addressee, Nov. 2, 1857, letter in possession of author.

16. *Hist. Révol. franç.,* XII, 587 ff, X,

1–3, book ii, chap. v; XI, 455; XII, 155 ff.

17. *Rev. prog.,* II (Aug. 15, 1839) , 99.

18. Warschauer, pp. 130, 161; Keller, pp. 56, 209–10.

19. Nerrlich, I, 313.

20. B. Nicolaievsky and O. Maenchen-Helfen, *Karl Marx* (London, 1936) , p. 81.

21. Katë Stark insists that Blanc's dialectic may be traced back to his *Dix ans;* but she makes no effort to support this statement. She seems to confuse Blanc's belief in progress with the dialectic. See her "Louis Blanc als Historiker der fransösischen Revolution" (Unpublished doctoral dissertation, University of Hamburg, 1935) .

22. *Questions,* III, 31.

23. *Hist. Révol. franç.* I, 430.

24. *Rev. prog.,* II (Aug. 15, 1839) , 98.

25. *Questions,* I, 3.

26. *Hist. Révol. franç.,* I, p. xxxi.

27. *Ibid.,* I, p. xiv.

28. *Ibid.,* I, 172.

CHAPTER XV

1. *Reasoner,* V (Sept., 1848) , 239; Holyoake, *Sixty Years of an Agitator's Life* (London, 1902) , II, 260–61.

2. Quoted in James Froude, *Thomas Carlyle* (London, 1884) , I, 452.

3. Nadaud, p. 373; Bebel and Bernstein, II, 8. See Blanc's laudatory address made on the occasion of the death of Ernest Jones, in *Dix ans de l'histoire d'Angleterre* (Paris, 1879–81) , IX, 34. Hereafter cited as *Hist. d'Angle.*

4. Blanc, *Lettres sur l'Angleterre* (Paris, 1865) , I, 97.

5. *Hist. d'Angle.,* VIII, 261.

6. *Révélations historiques,* I, "Préface."

7. Letter dated Dec. 7, 1866, in *Archives particulières de Mme Jules Ferry,* Fondation Jules Ferry at the Sorbonne.

8. *Hist. d'Angle.,* I, pp. iv–v: X, 28, 46.

9. Mill to Max Kullman, Feb. 15, 1865, in H. Elliot, ed., *Letters of John Stuart Mill* (London, 1910) , II, 18.

10. *Morning Advertiser,* April 26, 1860.

11. Vier, p. 100.

12. These letters make up his *Hist. d'Angle.,* 10 vols.

13. See especially the *Athenaeum,* July,

1867; *Spectator,* July 27, 1867; *Daily News,* July 26, 1867.

14. Vier, p. 87.

15. *Ibid.,* p. 100.

16. J. Salmson, *Entre deux coups de ciseau* (Paris, 1892), p. 175.

17. Fiaux, *Charles Blanc,* pp. 35–36.

18. Letter dated July 28, 1858, *Correspondance de Louis Blanc,* n. a. f., 11398, fol. 83, in Bibliothèque Nationale.

19. M. Meysenbug, *Mémoires d'une idéaliste* (Paris, 1900), II, 17–18.

20. *Voltaire,* Sept. 20 1882; Blanc to Louis Ulbach, Oct. 6, 1869, 38510E, fol. 66, in British Museum.

21. D. A. Wilson, *Carlyle* (London, 1929), V, 463. See also IV, 87.

22. Blanc to Lucas, May 7, 1866, *Corresp. Lucas,* p. 76; Louis Ulbach, *Nos contemporains: Louis Blanc* (Paris, 1869), pp. 59 ff.; *Blind Papers,* 40124, fols. 18, 340, in British Museum.

23. *Nouveau monde,* II (Jan. 15, 1851), 155; Blanc, *Les prochaines élections en France* (n. p., [1857]), pp. 1–2.

24. J. Adam, *Nos sentiments et nos idées avant 1870* (Paris, 1905), p. 44.

25. *Eclaireur de Saint-Etienne,* April 9, 1869.

26. *Rappel,* June 6, 1869.

27. Renard, *Blanc* (Toulouse, 1922), p. 122.

28. Rochefort to Blanc, June 21, 1869, *Corresp. Blanc,* fols. 257–58.

29. *Démocratie,* Sept. 26, Nov. 21, 1869.

30. *Rappel,* Oct. 24, 1869.

31. *Siècle,* Oct. 25, 1869.

32. Renard, *op. cit.,* p. 125.

33. *Questions,* II, 259–63.

CHAPTER XVI

1. See above, Chap. V.

2. See above, Chap. VI, sect. iii.

3. *Hist. d'Angle.,* I, 1.

4. *Révélations historiques,* I, "Préface."

5. *Hist. d'Angle.,* IV, 120, VI, 186–91.

6. Blanc to Arthur Ranc, Jan. 9, 1870, in A. Ranc, *Souvenirs, correspondance, 1831–1908* (Paris, 1913), p. 143.

7. E. H. Carr, "The League of Peace and Freedom," *International Affairs,* XIV (1935), 837–44.

8. *Hist. d'Angle.,* VIII, 15–20.

9. *Ibid.,* X, 175.

10. *Ibid.,* X, 182.

11. *Rappel,* Dec. 1, 1870; see *Questions,* II, 307–11, 313–19.

12. *Questions,* II, 332.

13. *Journal officiel de la République française,* Sept. 16, 1870.

14. Renard, *Blanc,* pp. 229–30; *Questions,* V, 363 ff.

15. *Questions,* V. 366.

16. *Rappel,* Oct. 13, 1870.

17. E. de Goncourt, *Journal,* IV, 106.

18. J. Adam, *Siège de Paris, journal d'une parisienne* (Paris, 1873), p. 207.

19. Melvin Kranzberg, *The Siege of Paris, 1870–71* (Ithaca, N. Y., 1950), pp. 62 ff.

20. Adam, *Siège de Paris,* p. 241.

21. *Rappel,* Jan. 2, 1871.

22. Adam, *Siège,* p. 343.

23. *Questions,* II, 349–58.

24. P.-O. Lissagaray, *Histoire de la Commune de 1871* (New ed.: Paris, 1947), p. 55.

25. *Journal officiel,* Feb. 17, 1871.

26. *Discours politiques,* pp. 78–85.

27. Quoted in Silberner, p. 233.

28. *Discours,* p. 88.

29. Lissagaray, pp. 96–97; Edmond Lepelletier, *Histoire de la Commune de 1871* (Paris, 1911–13), II, 91 ff.

30. Jules Clarétie, *Histoire de la Révolution de 1870–71* (Paris, 1875), IV, 163.

31. *Journal officiel,* March 21, 1871.

32. Lepelletier, II, 382–99, 452; *Enquête parlementaire sur l'insurrection du 18 mars* (Paris, 1872), p. 24.

33. Lissagaray, p. 117.

34. Dessal, *Delescluze,* Chap. XII.

35. See above, Chap. XII, sect. iv.

36. Alan Spitzer, *Revolutionary Theories of Louis Auguste Blanqui,* pp. 14–15.

37. *Discours,* p. 89.

38. See *Figaro,* June 8, 1871; see also *Journal officiel,* Aug. 19, 1871 for his repudiation of Commune.

39. Blanc, *Le parti qu'on appelle radical* (Paris, 1872), pp. 19–23.

CHAPTER XVII

1. Blanc, *Histoire de la Constitution du 25 Février 1875* (Paris, 1882), pp. 8–9.

2. *Questions,* II, 372 and *passim.*

3. Jean Joughin, *The Paris Commune in French Politics* (Baltimore, 1955), I, 70–71.

4. Gabriel Hanotaux, *Histoire de la France contemporaine* (Paris, 1907–8), I, 478.
5. *Blind Papers*, 40125, fols. 99–100, 127.
6. (Paris, 1872). See pp. 5–6 for his difficulties with the local administration.
7. See also *Questions*, II, 386–87, 406–12.
8. *Discours*, pp. 139–51.
9. *Avenir national*, March 19, 1873.
10. *Questions*, II, 439–49.
11. Hanotaux, II, 4.
12. *Questions*, II, 463.
13. *Rappel*, Sept. 30, 1873.
14. *Questions*, II, 363.
15. *Rappel*, Aug. 23, 1873.
16. Hanotaux, II, 204.
17. *Opinion nationale*, Nov. 25, 1873.
18. *Questions*, III, 289–93.
19. *Discours*, pp. 162–72.
20. *Ibid.*, pp. 90–97.
21. *Ibid.*, pp. 174–85.
22. Harold Stannard, *Gambetta and the Founding of the Third Republic* (London, 1921), p. 159.
23. *Hist. Consti. 1875*, pp. 15, 34–39.
24. *Ibid.*, pp. 82–84.
25. See *République française*, Feb. 29–30, 1875.
26. *Hist. Consti. 1875*, pp. 99–101.
27. *Ibid.*, pp. 150 and *passim*.
28. *Questions*, III, 467.
29. *Discours*, pp. 90 ff.
30. Quoted in Renard, *Blanc*, p. 275.
31. *Discours*, pp. 215–23.
32. Margaret Headings, *French Freemasonry under the Third Republic* (Baltimore, 1949), pp. 39–40.
33. *Rappel*, Oct. 12, 1875; *Questions*, III, 500.
34. Stannard, p. 179.
35. *Rappel*, Feb. 8, 1876.
36. Renard, *Blanc*, pp. 280–81.
37. Bourloton, *Dictionnaire des parlementaires français*, I, 338.
38. Oct. 15, 1879. This statement may be doubted; however, it is important to remember that the workers' congress of 1876 still emphasized co-operation, as will be shown in chap. xviii. The votes he won in the February, 1876 election are indicative of his popularity. In the 13th arrondissement he obtained 6,938 as against 1,355 for his opponent. In the 5th he gained 9,809 out of 15,693 votes cast. In 1877 he won 12,333 in the 5th.

CHAPTER XVIII

1. Quoted in Renard, p. 283.
2. *Questions*, V, 385–89.
3. *Rappel*, Aug. 14, 1876.
4. *Homme libre*, Oct. 27, 1876.
5. Quoted in Renard, p. 309.
6. Frank Brabant, *Beginning of the Third Republic in France* (London, 1940), p. 378; Stannard, *Gambetta*, p. 166.
7. *Rappel*, April 28, 1871.
8. *Homme libre*, Nov. 14, 1876; see also *Questions*, II, 452–62.
9. *Questions*, III, 395–99.
10. *Ibid.*, V, 419–20.
11. See Lissagaray, pp. 409–10.
12. Frank Jellinek, *The Paris Commune of 1871* (London, 1937), p. 373.
13. Bourloton, *Dictionnaire des parlementaires français*, I, 337. *Citoyen de Paris*, July 7, 8, 1881.
14. Lissagaray, p. 386.
15. Assemblée Nationale, *Annales*, XIII, 176–78. Blanc had made a public speech at Nantes in February, 1872 in favor of an amnesty. See *Phare de la Loire*, Feb. 13, 14, 15, 1872. For the amnesty issue consult the excellent study by Mrs. Jean Joughin, *The Paris Commune in French Politics* (Baltimore, 1955), 2 vols.
16. *Questions*, II, 431–38.
17. *Commune*, p. 371.
18. Gaumont, *Hist. . . . coopération*, II, 22.
19. See his *Mouvement ouvrier à Paris de 1870 à 1874* (Paris, 1874), pp. 99–100.
20. Nov. 3, 1876.
21. Translated in M. Kelso, "The Inception of the Modern French Labor Movement," *Journal of Modern History*, VIII (1936), 179.
22. *Homme libre*, Nov. 2–3, 1876.
23. *Ibid.*, Nov. 10, Dec. 6, 30, 1876; Jan. 21, 1877.
24. *Questions*, V, 305–10; *Discours*, pp. 231–42.
25. Léon Blum, *Les congrès ouvriers socialistes français* (Paris, 1901), I, 7.
26. *Homme libre*, Nov. 25, 1876.
27. *Discours*, p. 132.

28. *Ibid.,* pp. 420 ff.
29. *Ibid.,* p. 373.
30. Quoted in Renard, p. 298.
31. *Homme libre,* Oct. 27, 28, 1876. See also Jan. 4, 1877.
32. Joughin, I, 212.
33. *Discours,* pp. 382–91.
34. *Justice,* Aug. 20–22, 1881.
35. *Blanc,* pp. 309–10.
36. *Histoire du radicalisme* (Paris, 1951), pp. 70–76.
37. *Droits de l'homme,* Feb. 11, 1876; *Rappel,* Feb. 2, 1876.
38. *Justice,* Aug. 21, 1881.
39. This is the conclusion of Jacques Kayser whose history of radicalism will appear sometime in the future.
40. These assertions are to be found frequently in Clemenceau's *La Justice;* see, for example, the electoral speech of Alphonse Humbert in the Aug. 20, 1881 issue. They also appeared frequently in party congresses after 1901. See Armand Charpentier, *Le parti radical et radical-socialiste à travers ses congrès, 1901–11* (Paris, 1913), pp. 427–28 and *passim.*
41. *Ibid.,* pp. 444–45. See also Pierre Avril, "Radicalisme et socialisme," *Cahiers de la République,* I (1956), 14–15.
42. *Rappel,* April 16, 1876.
43. *Discours,* p. 331.
44. *Socialisme intégral* (Paris, 1892), I, 25, 52, 156–57, II, 202–4.
45. Quoted in Jammy Schmidt, *Les grandes thèses radicales* (Paris, 1932), p. 325.

46. Rappoport, *Jaurès,* pp. 357–58.
47. *Revue socialiste,* XXII (1895), 138.
48. *Questions,* V, 455.
49. Hanotaux, *France contemporaine,* IV, 283.
50. See the May, 1877 numbers of *Le travailleur; Egalité,* May 27, 1878. Both journals attacked him for his moderation and his opposition to the Commune.
51. Blum, I, 33–47.
52. *Journal des économistes,* Dec. 1879, pp. 405–6.
53. *Prolétaire,* Jan. 29, 1879; *Citoyen de Paris,* July 8, 1881.
54. Joughin, II, 376.
55. See his book, *Les théories socialistes au XIXe siècle* (Paris, 1904), pp. 118 ff.

CHAPTER XVIX

1. Fiaux, *Louis Blanc,* p. 191.
2. *Discours,* p. 403. See also Joughin, II, 325–46.
3. Fiaux, p. 171.
4. *Discours,* p. 446.
5. Fiaux, pp. 180–81; Edouard Lockroy, *Au hasard de la vie* (Paris, 1913), p. 243.
6. Salmson, *Entre deux coups de ciseau,* p. 176.
7. *Rappel,* Dec. 10, 1882.
8. *Voltaire,* Sept. 20, 1882.
9. Renard, *Blanc,* p. 312.
10. *République française,* Dec. 14, 1882.

Bibliography

Pertinent Bibliographies:

The best bibliographies of social history are those of Georges Bourgin, *Notes bibliographiques sur l'histoire sociale de la France* (Leiden: E. J. Brill, 1937); and Edouard Dolléans and Michel Crozier, eds., *Mouvement ouvrier et socialiste, chronologie et bibliographie* (Paris: Les Editions Ouvrière, 1950). The most useful work is that of Edouard Renard, *Bibliographie relative à Louis Blanc* (Toulouse: Imprimerie Régionale, 1922). Since little has been written on Blanc since 1922 Renard's work is not out of date. The bibliographical sections of the *International Review of Social History* are indispensable.

Publications of Louis Blanc:

Appel aux honnêtes gens; quelques pages d'histoire contemporaine (Paris: Au Bureau Central, 1849). *Catéchisme des socialistes* (Paris: Bureau du *Nouveau monde*, 1849). *Discours de M. Louis Blanc contre le projet concernant les affiliés à l'Association Internationale des Travailleurs* (Paris: Chevalier, 1872). *Discours politiques, 1847–1881* (Paris: Germer-Baillière, 1882). *Dix ans de l'histoire d'Angleterre* (Paris: C. Levy, 1879–81), 10 vols. *Histoire de la Révolution de 1848* (Paris: Lacroix, Verboeckhoven, 1870), 2 vols. *Histoire de la Révolution française* (Paris: Langlois and Leclercq, 1847–62), 12 vols. *Lettre à Louis Blanc; question de l'amnistie*, by Félix Pyat (n.p., n.d.). Contains letters of Blanc on amnesty of 1859. *Lettre de Louis Blanc à Garibaldi, suivie de la réponse de Garibaldi* (London: W. Allen, 1864). *Lettres sur l'Angleterre* (Paris: Librairie Internationale, 1865–67), 4 vols. *Observations sur une récente brochure de Kossuth, Ledru-Rollin et Mazzini* (London: Holyoake, [1854]). *Organisation du travail* (Paris, 1840), many editions. The last and most complete is the ninth, published in 1850. *Pages d'histoire de la Révolution de février 1848* (Paris: Bureau du *Nouveau monde*, 1850). An expansion of *Appel aux honnêtes gens* and *Révolution de février au Luxembourg. Parti républicain et l'amnistie* (Brussels: Rozez, 1859). *Plus de Girondins* (Paris: C. Joubert, 1851). *Prochaines élections en France* (n.p., 1857). *Questions d'aujourd'hui et de demain* (Paris: E. Dentu, 1879–82), 5 vols. Contains many of his publications listed here. *République une et indivisible* (Paris: A. Naud, 1851). *Révélations historiques* (Brussels: Méline, Cans et Cie., 1859). The English edition is entitled, *1848: Historical Revelations, Inscribed to Lord Normanby* (London: Chapman and Hall, 1858). *Révolution de février au Luxembourg* (Paris: Lévy, 1849). *Histoire de la Constitution du 25 février 1875* (Paris: Charpentier, 1882). *Le parti qu'un appelle radical, sa doctrine, sa conduite* (Paris: Leroux, 1872). He edited *Revue du progrès, Nouveau monde, Homme libre.*

Archival Materials:

I was able to find only a few archival documents bearing on Louis Blanc. There are some police records, dealing chiefly with his publications, in the Archives Na-

247

tionales, Paris, BB 18 1449–50, BB 18 1628, BB 30 394. F 17 80.311 is his scholarship to Rodez. In the archives of the Lycée Ferdinand Foch, formerly Collège Royal de Rodez, are his student records.

Unpublished letters are to be found in the Blanc collection at the library of the University of Wisconsin. There are 44 letters, most written during exile, which will eventually be published by Professor Henry Bertram Hill. This collection is one of the most important. The "Archives particulières de Mme la Marquise Arconati-Visconti," in *Papiers Peyrat,* vol. XXXVIII, in the Bibliothèque Victor Cousin at the Sorbonne. Five letters. In the private archives of MM. Gaston Bosquet of Versailles and Mérat of Auxerre, one and three letters respectively. The private archives of Mme Jules Ferry, in *Fondation Jules Ferry* at the Sorbonne. Five letters. In the following municipal libraries: Carpentras, one letter; Grenoble, two letters; Nantes, one letter; Reims, two letters; Rouen, three letters; Troyes, one letter; Versailles, *Fonds Couderc,* ten letters. *Blind Papers,* 40124–26, British Museum. Nearly 100 letters from 1856 to 1877. There are three unclassified letters in the B. M. *Collection Lovenjoul de Sperlberch,* Bibliothèque de Chantilly. Seventeen letters. *Correspondance d'Edgar Quinet,* n. a. f., 20782, Bibliothèque Nationale. Four letters. *Correspondance de Louis Blanc,* n. a. f., 11398, Bibliothèque Nationale. The title is deceptive; only one letter in this collection was witten by Blanc. The rest, over 100, were addressed to him by friends, but have very little biographical value. Some of these were published in part by G. Vautier, "La Correspondance de Louis Blanc," *Révolution de 1848,* XXI (1924), 193–212. *Papiers de Thoré,* 7916 and 7922, Bibliothèque de l'Arsénal, Paris. 7916 contains what seems to be the bulk of the Blanc-Delhasse correspondance from 1850 to 1854. 7922 has numerous clippings relative to Blanc. I possess eight letters.

Unfortunately, only a few of the above letters have any importance for the biography of Blanc. They are oftentimes merely invitations to dine, or thank-you notes. The useful ones have been cited in the text and the footnotes.

Published Correspondance:

In the *Amateur d'autographes* and the *Revue d'autographes,* of Chavaray et Cie. of Paris, there are excerpts from some Blanc letters. In Jacques Arnna, ed., *Rachel et son temps, cataloque de lettres autographes* (Reims: Imprimeries de Nord-Est, 1939), p. 59, there is one letter. Leo Lucas, ed., *Les correspondants de Hippolyte Lucas, lettres d'écrivains* (n.p., 1914). In the Bibliothèque Nationale, four letters. *Nouvelle revue,* CVIII (1897), 209, 385–402, 577–90, letters to Noël Parfait and Barbès. J. Prudhommeaux, "L'opposition socialiste sous la présidence de Louis Napoléon," *Révolution de 1848,* VI (1909), 68–89, Blanc to Cabet *et al.* In the *Révolution de 1848,* II (1905), 430; IV (1906–7), 329; V (1908), 262; VII (1910–11), 109–14; VIII (1911), 198–99, 439–47, there are several letters. Jacques Vier, ed., *Lettres républicaines du Second Empire, documents inédits* (Paris: Editions du Cèdre, 1951), contains letters from Blanc to Mme d'Agoult.

Biographies of Blanc:

Alfred Barbou, *Les amis du peuple: Louis Blanc, sa vie, ses oeuvres* (Paris: Roy, 1880) is eulogistic of Blanc the man but adversely critical of the thinker and his ideas. Typical orthodox radical interpretation; mediocre, many errors. Louis Fiaux, *Portraits politiques contemporains,* Vol. II: *Louis Blanc;* Vol. III: *Charles Blanc* (Paris: Marpon and Flammarion, 1882–83) always feels that Blanc is a fine radical who unfortunately has socialist leanings. Interesting for relations of Blanc brothers. M. Golliet, *Louis Blanc, sa doctrine, son action* (Paris: Pedone, 1903) and Emile Laurens, *Louis Blanc, le régime social du travail* (Paris: Rousseau, 1908), are doctoral dissertations and deal more with Blanc's ideas than his life. Much more important was the dissertation of Edouard Renard, *Louis Blanc, sa vie, son oeuvre* (Toulouse: Imprimerie Régionale, 1922). It was the first full-life biography of Blanc, and while later editions of it have been published by Hachette, this is the only one with the footnotes which are so helpful. It is purely descriptive and is therefore limited in its significance. The earliest biography of Blanc was that of Charles Robin, *Louis Blanc, sa vie, ses oeuvres* (Paris: Naud, 1851). Robin was acquainted with Blanc, and his work is indispensable for the pre-1848 period of Blanc's career. The very brief studies of I. Tchernoff, *Louis Blanc* (Paris: Société Nouvelle de Librairie, 1904), and Jean Vidalenc, *Louis Blanc* (Paris: P. U. F., 1948), are useful chiefly for Blanc's ideas, the former especially for his ideas on credit, the latter for an excellent, succinct statement of Blanc's socialism. Otto Warschauer, *Geschichte des Sozialismus und neueren Kommunismus*, Vol. III: *Louis Blanc* (Leipzig: Fock, 1896) is also chiefly useful for Blanc's ideas rather than his life. Warschauer was among the first to give some attention to Blanc's historiography, without, however, fully understanding it.

Biographical Sketches of Blanc:

Jules-Amédée Barbey-d'Aurevilly, *Polémiques d'hier* (Paris: Savine, 1889), is mediocre. Henri Baudrillart, *Publicistes modernes* (Paris: Didier, 1863), is filled with errors. Karl Blind, "Personal Recollections of Louis Blanc," *Century Magazine*, XII (1885), 75–81, was a personal friend who gives here a short portrait of no great importance. Victor Bouton, *Profils révolutionnaires* (Paris, 1849), is useless. Maurice de Casanove, *Portraits d'hier* (Paris: Fabre, 1912), adds nothing new. Hippolyte Castille, *Portraits politiques au 19éme siècle, Louis Blanc* (Paris: Sartorius, 1856), kindly advises Blanc on what he should have done in 1848. C. Chojecki, *Louis Blanc* (Paris, 1882), is brief and exceedingly sympathetic. Eugène Courmeaux, *Louis Blanc* (Chalons-sur-Marne: Le Roy, 1884), is Radical in sympathy and friendly to Blanc. Too short to be of any value. His friends rarely give any information about his private life. This is true of Frédéric Frossard, "Un souvenir de Louis Blanc," *Bibliothèque universelle et revue suisse,* s. 3, XVIII (1883), 66–71, and Benjamin Gastineau, *Les génies de la liberté* (Paris: Librairie Internationale, 1865). More important although quite brief is Edouard Pailleron, *Discours prononcé le jour de sa réception à l'Académie Française, le 17 janvier 1884* (Paris, C. Lévy, 1884). Pailleron took Charles Blanc's seat and dug up pertinent details on the life of the Blanc brothers during their early years in Paris. For details on Blanc's life in England see Louis Ulbach (pseudonym, Ferragus), *Nos contemporains, Louis Blanc* (Paris: Chevalier, 1869). Proudhonian criticisms of Blanc are the substance of A. Vermorel, *Les hommes de 1848* (Paris: Décembre-Alonnier, 1869), which sought to discredit him during the 1869 elections. Seeking to enhance his popularity was Charles Hugo, *Les hommes de l'exil* (Paris: Lemerre, 1875). Overly eulogistic was Charles Edmond, *Louis Blanc* (Paris: Quantin, 1882).

Monographs on Blanc:

Georges Cahen, *Louis Blanc et la Commission du Luxembourg* (Paris: Alcan, 1897), is still the basic monograph on this subject. Pierre Loustau, *Louis Blanc à*

la Commission du Luxembourg (Paris: Bonvolet-Jouve, 1908), has nothing new
to add and confined himself to describing Blanc's socialist speeches in the commission. Paul Chanson, L'organisation du travail selon Louis Blanc (Paris: In-
stitut d'Etudes Corporatives et Sociales, 1943), is a Vichyite disciple of La Tour
du Pin, sees the germs of a corporative society in the social workshops. Herman
Pechan, Louis Blanc als Wegbereiter des modernen Sozialismus (Jena: Fischer,
1929), sees in Blanc the link between Utopian and scientific socialism. He seems
to imagine that only the socialisms of Marx and Lassalle are modern or scientific.
Several studies have appeared on Louis Blanc in 1848. Paul Keller, Louis Blanc
und die Revolution von 1848 (Zurich: Girsberger, 1926), is excellent as far as it
goes, but oftentimes loses sight of Blanc who, like the proverbial forest, cannot be
seen for the mass of material on economic conditions. More informative is Gioia-
Macchioro Benedetto, "Louis Blanc e la Rivoluzione di febbraio," Nuova rivista
storica, XXXIV (1950), 438–82, XXXV (1951), 244–87. Benedetto takes the view
that Blanc was morally responsible for the National Workshops. So does J. A. R.
Marriott in his introduction to The French Revolution of 1848 in Its Economic
Aspect (Oxford: Clarendon Press, 1913), 2 vols. This assertion, I feel, is basically
unsound. Written largely from limited sources is Richard Gustafson, "Louis Blanc
and the Revolution of 1848." Unpublished Ph.D. dissertation, University of Wisconsin, 1945. On Blanc in Belgium there is Luc Somerhausen, "Louis Blanc en
Belgique," Flambeau, revue belge . . . , II (1932), 411–32. It is based on Blanc's
police dossier in Belgium. The only full-scale study of Blanc's history is that of
Kate Stark, "Louis Blanc als Historiker der französischen Revolution." Unpublished doctoral dissertation, University of Hamburg, 1935. Chiefly a comparison of
Blanc with Michelet and Quinet. Some comments on Blanc's writing of history can
be found in A. Aulard, "Michelet, historien de la Révolution française," Révolu-
tion française, LXXXI (1928), 136–50, 193–213; Paul Farmer, France Reviews Its
Revolutionary Origins (New York: Columbia University Press, 1944); and Rob-
ert Flint, Historical Philosophy in France and French Belgium and Switzerland
(New York: Scriber, 1894). It is doubtful if Flint read all of Blanc's history. V.
Totomiantz, "Louis Blanc comme coopérateur," Revue des études coopératives,
VII (1928), 159–62, is really a condensation of Paul Keller's work. G. Wyrouboff,
Louis Blanc et Gambetta (Versailles, 1883), is a positivist who finds these two
radicals quite unscientific.

Memoirs Containing Some Information on Blanc:

Juliette Adam, Mes sentiments et nos idées avant 1870 (Paris: Lemerre, 1905),
and Mes premières armes littéraires et politiques (Paris: Lemerre, 1904). Important for the opinions of republicans in the 1860's and the emergence of Gam-
betta. Sébastien Commissaire, Mémoires et souvenirs (Lyons: Meton, 1888), 2
vols. A few details on Blanc and the French exiles after 1848. Alexander Herzen,
Erinnerungen (Berlin: Wiegandt and Grieben, 1907), 2 vols. George J. Holyoake,
Sixty Years of an Agitator's Life (London: Fisher, Unwin, 1902), 2 vols. Gustave
Lefrançais, Souvenirs d'un révolutionnaire (Brussels: Temps nouveau, 1902).
Pierre Leroux, Grève de Samarez (Paris: Dentu, 1863), 2 vols. Edouard Lockroy,
Au hasard de la vie (Paris: Grasset, 1913). Malivida Meysenbug, Mémoires d'une
idéaliste (Paris: Fischbacker, 1900), 2 vols. Martin Nadaud, Mémoires de Léon-
ard (Bourganeuf: Duboneix, 1895). Arthur Ranc, Souvenirs, correspondance
(Paris: Cornely, 1913). J. Salmson, Entre deux coups de ciseau (Paris: Lemerre,

1892). A Scheurer-Kestner, *Souvenirs de jeunesse* (Paris: Charpentier, 1905). All of the above contain some details on Blanc's life although not much. They are generally more helpful in studying opinion of him.

The Social Movement:

Charles Bouglé, *Socialismes français: Du socialisme utopique à la démocratie intellectuelle* (Paris: Colin, 1932), points up the complexity of French socialist movements. Armand Cuvillier, *Un journal d'ouvriers, "l'Atelier,"* (Paris: Alcan, 1914), excellent for the disciples of Buchez, but not always fair to Blanc. Edouard Dolléans, *Histoire du mouvement ouvrier* (Paris: Colin, 1948), 2 vols., indispensable, but written too much from the Proudhonian point of view. E. E. Fribourg, *L'Association internationale des travailleurs* (Paris: Chevalier, 1871), and James Guillaume, *L'Internationale* (Paris: Société Nouvelle de Librairie, 1905–10), 4 vols., were written from the anarchist point of view. Roger Garaudy, *Les sources françaises du socialisme scientifique* (Paris: Hier et Aujourd'hui, 1949), is the work of a communist. Jean Gaumont, *Historie générale de la coopération en France* (Paris: Fédération Nationale des Coopérateurs de Consommation, 1924), 2 vols. Definitive. Emile Heftler, *Les associations coopératives de production sous la deuxième République* (Paris: Rousseau, 1899). Old but still useful. The same is true of Paul Hubert-Valleroux, *Les associations coopératives en France et à l'étranger* (Paris: Guillaumin, 1884). Lucien de La Hodde, *Histoire des sociétés secrètes et du parti républicain de 1830 à 1848* (Paris: Julien, Lanier, 1850), the memoirs of a police spy and written purposely to contribute to the reaction after 1848. Maxime Leroy, *Histoire des idées sociales en France* (Paris: Gallimard, 1946–54), 3 vols., gives less attention than he merits to Blanc. Karl Marx, *Les luttes de classes en France, 1848–50* (Paris: Editions Sociales, 1946), is quite hard on Blanc. An important study is that of Jules-L. Puech, *Proudhonisme dans l'Association internationale des travailleurs* (Paris: Alcan, 1907). Excellent studies on the 1870's are those of M. Kelso, "The Inception of the Modern French Labor Movement," *Journal of Modern History*, VIII (1936), 173–93, and Jean Joughin, *The Paris Commune in French Politics, 1871–80* (Baltimore: Johns-Hopkins Press, 1955), 2 vols. Important works in the field of Radicalism are Stanislas Mitard, *Les origines du radicalisme démocratique; l'affaire Ledru-Rollin* (Paris: M. Rivière, 1952), and Albert Milhaud, *Histoire du radicalisme* (Paris: Société d'Editions Françaises et Internationales, 1951). Milhaud's work has some doubtful, if not to say oversimplified, conclusions. Georges Weill, *Histoire du parti républicain en France, 1814–70* (Paris: Alcan, 1928). This work corrects but does not replace I. Tchernoff, *Le parti républicain sous la Monarchie de juillet* (Paris: Pedone, 1901). An excellent study is that of John Boughman, "The French Banquet Campaign of 1847–48," *Journal of Modern History*, XXXI (1959), 1–15. Very informative is Armand Cuvillier, *Hommes et idéologies de 1840* (Paris: Rivière, 1956). J. Gouault, *Comment la France est devenue républicaine* (Paris: Armand Colin, 1954) is excellent.

Biographies:

Some information of Louis Blanc's relations with Louis Napoleon can be found in F. Briffault, *The Prisoner of Ham* (London: Newly, 1846), and André Lebay, *Louis Napoléon et la Révolution de 1848* (Paris: Juven, 1907–9), 2 vols. Both are decidedly pro-Napoleon. Studies of the orthodox Jacobins are Alvin Calman,

Ledru-Rollins après 1848 et les proscrits français en Angleterre (Paris: Rieder, 1921) , and *Ledru-Rollin and the Second French Republic* (New York: Columbia University Press, 1922) , Robert Schnerb, *Ledru-Rollin* (Paris: P. U. F., 1948) , S. Mitard, *Origines de radicalisme démocratique: L'affaire Ledru-Rollin* (Paris: M. Rivière, 1952) , Marcel Dessal, *Un révolutionnaire jacobin, Charles Delescluze, 1809–71* (Paris: M. Riviére, 1952) . The only study of any worth on Barbès is J.-F. Jeanjean, *Armand Barbès, sa vie, son action politique* (Paris: Cornely, 1909) . Decidedly pro-Barbès and weakened by this lack of objectivity. The best biography of Leroux is that of P. Thomas, *Leroux* (Paris: Alcan, 1904) . The more recent study, David Owen Evans, *Le socialisme romantique, Pierre Leroux et ses contemporains* (Paris: M. Rivière, 1948) , is quite good, chiefly for Leroux's relations with Sand and Hugo. The most complete biography of Sand is Wladimir Karenine, *George Sand* (Paris: Ollendorfe, 1899) , vols. I–II; Paris: Plon, 1912– 26) , vols. III–IV. It is definitive. There does not exist a definitive or even a first-rate biography of Proudhon. A. Desjardins, *Proudhon* (Paris: Perrin, 1896) , 4 vols. is decidedly hostile, while Edouard Dolléans, *Proudhon* (Paris: Gallimard, 1948) , is too sympathetic. For the Blanc-Blanqui feud the following are useful: Maurice Dommanget, *Auguste Blanqui à Belle-Ile, 1850–57* (Paris: Librairie du Travail, 1935) , and Alan Spitzer, *The Revolutionary Theories of Louis Auguste Blanqui* (New York: Columbia University Press, 1957) . The most complete study of Cabet is Jules Prudhommeaux, *Icarie et son fondateur, Etienne Cabet* (Paris: Cornely, 1907) . On the founder of "Opportunism" there are two good studies: Joseph Reinach, *Leon Gambetta* (Paris: Alcan, 1884) and H. Stannard, *Gambetta* (London: Methuen, 1921) . Neither work has been superseded by the popularly written study of Raymond Cartier, *Léon Gambetta* (Paris: Gutenberg, 1943) .

Index